DAILY LIFE IN

18TH-
CENTURY
ENGLAND

DAILY LIFE IN

18TH- CENTURY ENGLAND

KIRSTIN OLSEN

The Greenwood Press "Daily Life Through History" Series

GREENWOOD PRESS
Westport, Connecticut • London

Library of Congress Cataloging-in-Publication Data

Olsen, Kirstin.
    Daily life in 18th-century England / Kirstin Olsen.
       p. cm.—(The Greenwood Press "Daily life through history"
  series, ISSN 1080–4749)
    Includes bibliographical references and index.
    ISBN 0–313–29933–1 (alk. paper)
    1. England—Social life and customs—18th century. I. Title.
  II. Series.
  DA485.O47 1999
  942.07—dc21   98–44593

British Library Cataloguing in Publication Data is available.

Library of Congress Catalog Card Number: 98–44593
ISBN: 0–313–29933–1
ISSN: 1080–4749

First published in 1999

Greenwood Press, 88 Post Road West, Westport, CT 06881
An imprint of Greenwood Publishing Group, Inc.
www.greenwood.com

Printed in the United States of America

The paper used in this book complies with the
Permanent Paper Standard issued by the National
Information Standards Organization (Z39.48–1984).

10 9 8 7 6 5 4 3 2 1

For my son Devon

Contents

Acknowledgments

Anyone who has tried to write a book with toddlers in the house knows that it doesn't get done without help. I had plenty. Thanks and more thanks to my husband, Eric Voelkel, my sister Erica, and my parents and in-laws for all the help with the kids, the house, and the manuscript. Thanks to Naomi Andrews for help in the early stages, and for introducing me to people as "a historian." Thanks, too, to Gillian for terming me "an independent scholar" rather than a dilettante. When one is trying to sustain a career from home while raising kids, it's delightful to be mistaken for a grown-up.

I owe my first interest in the eighteenth century to Margaret Doody, and I remain grateful to her. I am deeply appreciative of the patience and professionalism of everyone at Greenwood.

Finally, I could not have obtained the illustrations for this book without the assistance of Richard Williams and Joan Sussler of Yale's Lewis Walpole Library. They were gracious, helpful, and staggeringly knowledgeable.

All of the illustrations in this book come from the Lewis Walpole Library, Yale University.

Introduction

Imagine a country both moved by and sick of the plight of its poor. The high infant mortality rates of the poor are a national scandal, and it has become embarrassingly obvious that a family can work hard and still not make a living wage. Many complain, however, that the problem is not low wages, but laziness and a willingness to abuse the system. The country, seeking answers, turns the problem of the poor over to local agencies and experiments with making the poor work for their handouts.

Imagine a country where crime is expanding at a frightening rate. A newly mobile society makes criminals hard to track and catch, and the criminals are often better armed than the people trying to subdue them. Capital punishment is praised as a deterrent, and the number of capital crimes is increased, but executions seem unable to reduce the crime rate.

Imagine a country in which the nature of the family and of marriage is changing. Traditional values are being eroded, some claim, by the popular media. Parents are more interested than ever in the business of parenting, but their influence over their children seems to be diminishing.

Imagine a country with a widespread but often faltering educational system. Its citizens worry about the quality of education as traditional curricula are replaced by new studies.

Imagine a country with changing work conditions. The old organizations that used to protect the rights of workers are out of fashion, and machines are doing tasks more quickly and more efficiently than humans.

Imagine a country of flourishing commerce, where manufacturers strive to market their products in every conceivable manner. Advertisements imply that the owner of this or that new item will be popular, sophisticated, envied, and up to date. Image, states one major manufacturer, is far more important than the merit of the product. Companies strive not only to fill demand but to create it.

Imagine thoroughfares choked with traffic, streets full of noise and dirt, casual acceptance of violence, slums, exciting but rather frightening increases in the speed of communications and transportation, fortunes won and lost in the stock market, rapid scientific and technical advancement, the feeling that the old-style family farm is an endangered species, the exploitation of cheap overseas labor and materials, a love-hate relationship between the country and its military, riots in the streets spawned chiefly by bigotry, a questioning of the relationship between religion and the state, and, through it all, a conviction that the country in question is the greatest ever to exist in the whole of human history.

It is not modern America.

It is, of course, 18th-century England.

He was describing France, not England, but Charles Dickens perhaps said it best, in the famous opening lines of *A Tale of Two Cities*, when he pointed out that the 18th century was a time of contrasts. It sometimes seems to be "the best of times," populated by fat, boisterous, patriotic squires and tall-haired, witty society matrons; symbolized by foxhunts, roast beef, quaint peasant pastimes, "God Save the King," and Bonnie Prince Charlie; decorated with Chippendale furniture, neoclassical architecture, boxy hooped skirts, and dueling pistols; and ruled by stout kings named George, well-mannered aristocrats, and Parliament. This is the idea most people have, rather fuzzily, of the 18th century, an idea nurtured by such contemporary novels as *Tom Jones* and by later fictions like *Kidnapped* and *The Scarlet Pimpernel*. It is an image that, like most compelling images, is not entirely false.

However, it is not entirely true. The 18th century was also "the worst of times": there were high taxes, riots, wars, regional rivalries, technological changes, brutal public executions, widespread poverty, transportation and branding of criminals, anxieties over gender roles, and unsettling changes in trade, communications, transportation, and agriculture. The century also saw two major democratic revolutions—one in France and one in the American colonies—that shook the complacency of Britain just as it was beginning to feel imperial.

Each view is true, to some extent, and the muddled area between them is where the real truth lies. There were good times and bad, stability both comforting and frustrating, changes both pleasing and frightening. There were fat, happy, vulgar landlords like Fielding's Squire Western, but there were also a great many people whom the vague popular notion of 18th-century Britain ignores: engineers, female silk manufacturers, tin miners, toymakers, and provincial journalists. This book will attempt to describe the lives of the squires and peers without relegating the working people, who made up the vast majority of the population, to the decorative background. Similarly, there were revolutions and riots—this was the century in which the phrase "reading the Riot Act" was coined—but these, while significant, did not occupy the average 18th-century mind as much as the daily business of life. Whatever the news, people must still eat, sleep, dress, drink, marry, give birth, work, swear, play, worship, sicken, and die. Nothing that happened in the 18th century was cataclysmic enough to eradicate those basic imperatives.

Of course, change occurred, and sometimes with far-reaching consequences, as when machine-filled textile mills began to replace hand spinning and weaving done in the home. In this case especially, observers and historians have tended to see change as the "best" or "worst" outcome. Eighteenth-century English men and women lauded the new factories for their productivity and mighty machinery; later reformers and polemicists would view industrialization as an unmitigated evil. Between unbridled optimism and gloomy hindsight, however, lay the average laborer, who adapted little by little, not necessarily knowing where change would lead, moving to a parish with more jobs, or buying cheaper manufactured goods, or sending his daughter to work in a factory to earn more than she could as a servant. In making each choice, he gained a little and lost a little, learned new skills and forgot old ones, and changed the nation's direction one small decision at a time. The new world that resulted was still recognizable, but it was not quite the same as the old.

In every aspect of British life—the family, health care, transportation, communication, leisure, work, and etiquette—there were changes and constants, shaping the bread people ate and the clothes they wore, the way they paid their bills and the way they danced, just as the human body changes one cell at a time, becoming a new version of the same organism. In describing the organism known as the 18th century, it is all too easy to slip into convenient generalizations, to overemphasize the forces of change or of stability, to make unwarranted comparisons to modern experience and thought, or, conversely, to treat the inhabitants of that time and place as if they were merely quaint and alien, forgetting their humanity.

And as different as the 18th century is from our own in outward forms, the essentials of both are the same. People wonder whom to marry, whether and how to feed the poor, how much government should interfere in the lives of the governed, how crime can be controlled, what to do about widespread addiction, and how to accommodate religious differences. The problems were similar (though not identical); the people who faced them were like us (but not wholly so). They made choices in largely the way we do today, not always seeing exactly where we are going, not always thinking very far in advance, small daily decisions forming a collective urge toward something comfortable but new.

I expected to find 18th-century England very different from my own time and place, and indeed it was. For one thing, I myself would have been an exhibit in a London freak show: a college-educated Latin-reading woman author who kept her own name after marriage. The Latin-reading woman author part would have consigned me to the small circle of bluestockings, but in 18th-century England, no woman went to a university.

Actually, I probably would not even have been permitted to learn any Latin at all. I probably would have been born poor and sent to a local charity school for a few years if I were lucky. There I would have learned the rudiments of reading and perhaps writing, along with useful skills such as needlework. If unlucky, I might follow the harlot's progress immortalized by William Hogarth. If lucky, I might marry a man of my own social class or a little above, keep out of the workhouse, become pregnant seven or eight times, see a couple of those babies to adulthood, be unable to vote or own property or secure a divorce, and die late—perhaps even in my fifties or sixties—of an unspecified "fever."

My life would be vastly dissimilar from the one I've really led. Yet it would bear enough similarities to be recognizable. My fears would be debt, disease, dangers to self and family. My sources of joy would include family celebrations, local fairs, popular entertainment, the marvelous wonders of science and exploration, the growth and marriages of my children, and the companionship to be found within marriage.

It is the details that change: Will I most likely die of cholera or cancer? Do I ride in a car or a carriage? Do I earn my living as a seamstress or a writer? Do I influence the government through a vote or participation in a riot? Do I read the news or hear it called aloud to me by a peddler of up-to-the-minute gossipy songs? Am I learning to use a computer or a spinning jenny?

We are born, live, love, hate, work, play, die.

This book is about the details.

1

"A Nation of Prime Ministers": Politics

There is not another government in Europe who could long with-
stand the attacks to which this is continually exposed. The things
published here would set on fire any other hearts in the world.
—Louis Simond, early 19th century, speaking of Great Britain

The 18th century is sometimes considered a placid, peaceful time. It
hardly seemed so then. It brought a major change in the borders of the
nation, the birth of an empire, the loss of major colonies, a new dynasty,
two invasions, frequent riots, and the fear of revolution. For nearly half
the century Britain was at war. That the system of government remained
largely unchanged throughout the century is little short of miraculous.

In 1700 the king was William III, widowed husband of Mary II. He
was succeeded in 1702 by Anne Stuart, who had no surviving children.
Her nearest Stuart relative, her brother James, was barred from the
throne because of his Catholicism, but he was regarded by many as the
rightful ruler of Britain. Jacobites (after "Jacobus," the Latin version of
"James") supported James (the Old Pretender) and his son Charles (the
Young Pretender, known to Jacobites as "Bonnie Prince Charlie").

WHIGS AND TORIES

There were two political parties in England, the Whigs and the Tories,
each of whom had their own newspapers, parades and celebrations, and

favorite theaters (Tories preferred Drury Lane, Whigs the Haymarket) and coffeehouses (Whigs met at the Kit-Kat Club, Tories at the Cocoa Tree, and, from the 1760s, at Wildman's). Tories, associated with the church and the rural gentry, tended to be religiously orthodox, with little sympathy for Dissenters. They controlled much of the church hierarchy, most of Oxford University, and the London Common Council.[1] They also tended to support the Jacobite cause. Whigs, on the other hand, were more sympathetic to religious minorities, often belonging to Dissenting sects themselves. They were often businessmen, financiers, civil servants, naval officers, and urbanites. They predominated at Cambridge University from about the late 1720s and among London's aldermen.[2]

The Whigs, a minority party in the opening years of the century, saw the failure of the Stuart dynasty as their chance for power. They urged Parliament to pass over the Catholic James Stuart and to choose a new ruling house, distantly related to the old one, that currently ruled the German electorate of Hanover. The idea was not universally popular and led to demonstrations, sometimes violent, between opposing factions. But the idea of a Catholic monarch in largely Protestant England was so abhorrent to most that, in 1714, upon the death of Queen Anne, George I, a dour German who spoke almost no English, was proclaimed king. The Stuart response was to launch an invasion, headed by James, in 1715. It failed but provoked nationwide outrage against Jacobites.

George I rewarded his supporters by becoming a devout Whig, and his son George II followed his example. During their reigns, Tories were replaced by Whigs as magistrates and army officers. Clerical posts went to Cambridge, rather than Oxford, graduates. The Tories spent huge sums trying to regain control of Parliament (£40,000 in the 1754 Oxfordshire election alone[3]) but gained seats in only one general election between 1713 and 1760.[4] Between 1715 and 1760, England was run by Whigs.

George III, who succeeded his grandfather George II in 1760, relaxed this policy somewhat. By then the Hanoverian succession was secure; a second Jacobite invasion, in 1745, had been so soundly crushed that the Stuarts were no longer a threat. Slowly, Tories began to reclaim some positions as magistrates, members of Parliament (MPs), and ministers. Though the parties continued to squabble, they were by century's end united in their desire to keep power in the hands of the gentry. Nothing terrified both parties so much as the idea of a French-style revolution in England, or the possibility of an invasion by the French themselves.

THE CROWN AND PARLIAMENT

Parliament's role in the succession underscored a basic principle of 18th-century politics: Britain's monarchs were becoming less important just as Britain was becoming more important. At the beginning of the century, monarchs theoretically had quite a lot of power, though not as much as their Continental counterparts. They headed the executive and judicial branches of the government as well as the Church of England. They could veto legislation, declare war, make peace treaties, pardon criminals, prorogue (dissolve) Parliament, reward loyal supporters with cushy government jobs, and use troops to quell rebellion and riot. They could appoint cabinet ministers and military officers. They nominated judges, ambassadors, and bishops. They awarded all titles, including peerages and knighthoods. They could charter new corporations or colonies. And they had a personal staff of about 1,500 courtiers and servants.[5]

In practice, however, these powers were limited. The Crown was heavily dependent on Parliament, which approved the royal budget, known as the Civil List. In the reigns of the first two Georges, this amounted to from £700,000 to £800,000, out of which the king had to pay all his staff and appointees, maintain his houses, and keep his own family in regal style. Monarchs were perpetually in need of funds for wars, building projects, and patronage, and therefore had to take the demands of Parliament quite seriously. Moreover, the Hanoverians in particular were on the throne by virtue of legislative intervention; the removal of Queen Anne's father, the dictatorial James II, demonstrated what happened to kings who defied Parliament.

Even in what was theoretically the monarch's sphere, Parliament had a role. The Privy Council, a body of dozens of advisers to the ruler, included officials of the royal household and the archbishop of Canterbury but was formed chiefly of past and present Parliamentarians. The Cabinet, a subset of the Privy Council, was a more powerful advisory body. It always included the prime minister and the secretaries of state, who were members of Parliament as well. These men served as advisers to the Crown, but they answered indirectly to Parliament, which could impeach them or (more commonly) demonstrate that it would no longer support their plans. Once such a failure of confidence in the ministry occurred, the prime minister usually resigned, and a new government would be formed.

Little by little, royal power receded. Anne was the last British monarch to veto legislation. George I was the last to attend Cabinet meetings on a regular basis. George III lost the power to dismiss judges and to name the members of his own household staff. What remained was ceremonial function and influence: pressuring government employees to vote for a particular Parliamentary candidate, or killing a bill in the House of Lords by threatening to withdraw royal favor from those who voted for it.

However, the less powerful rulers became, the more popular they seemed to grow. This was partly a result of less fear of tyranny and partly an accident of personality and foreign events. George I was a forbidding sort of man who clearly preferred Hanover to England. No more congenial to his family than to his subjects, he imprisoned his wife, Sophia Dorotea, for thirty-two years for suspected adultery.[6] George II, though somewhat more accustomed to England, still displayed an almost humorous lack of rapport with the common people; for example, a 1749 Royal Fireworks show featured banners with patriotic mottoes—in Latin.[7] Perhaps the best criticism of him came from the eccentric duchess of Queensberry, who had been banished from court. Her response was a piece of effrontery that would never have been tolerated by a Continental monarch:

> The Duchess of Queensberry is surprised and well pleased that the King hath given her so agreeable a command as to stay from court, where she never came for diversion, but to bestow a great civility on the King and Queen; she hopes that by such an unprecedented order as this is, the King will see as few as he wishes at his Court, particularly such as dare to think or speak truth.[8]

George III, by contrast, decidedly considered himself an Englishman. A simple man who lived frugally (and was thus affectionately satirized as "Farmer George"), he reigned long, always mysteriously attractive in itself, and earned some sympathy when he went mad for a time late in the century. He also benefited from the surge in anxious patriotism that accompanied the French Revolution.

Just as an unpopular king could be reviled while the institution of monarchy was respected, people revered Parliament while firmly believing all politicians to be scoundrels. John Gay's *Beggar's Opera* satirized Prime Minister Robert Walpole as "*Robin of Bagshot*, alias *Gorgon*, alias *Bluff Bob*, alias *Carbuncle*, alias *Bob Booty*"[9] (and it was for patronizing Gay that the duchess of Queensberry was exiled from court). Gay wrote to a friend in 1723, "I cannot wonder that the Talents requisite for a great Statesman are so scarce in the world since so many of those who possess them are every month cut off in the prime of their Age at the Old-Baily,"[10] meaning that those who had the "natural" criminality for public life, and had not the good fortune to be born rich, were hanged as thieves instead of elected members of Parliament. There was an assumption that everyone, from poor law overseers to excise officers to magistrates to the prime minister himself, was skimming a little off the top for himself, and in many cases, popular perception was correct. Walpole, for example, used an Admiralty barge to smuggle wine past customs.[11]

Parliament, this "gang of notorious robbers,"[12] had two divisions, the House of Commons and the House of Lords. The 558 members of the Commons were usually wealthy landowners and were elected to their posts. The House of Lords was composed of the 180 or so English and Welsh peers, 16 elected Scottish peers (after the Act of Union which joined Scotland and England in 1707), and the 26 Anglican bishops. The peers were referred to as Lords Temporal, and the bishops as Lords Spiritual. All members of Parliament, in both houses, were Protestant; it was illegal for Catholics to hold office or to vote.

Parliament was the most powerful legislature in Europe, but by modern standards it was an unrepresentative and often unprofessional body. It met in Westminster, sometimes observed by a gallery of spectators, in a room that was too small and poorly designed. There was no official transcript of the debates, and an earnest effort was made in the first half of the century to keep the press from making a record as well. Sometimes the bills passed were printed and published, sometimes not.[13] Moreover, Parliament did very little, especially early in the century. It approved the budget and levied taxes, directed foreign policy, and exercised some control over executive and judicial appointments. Bills had to pass three "readings" and votes in each house, then went to the king or queen for royal assent or veto (a formality after the reign of Queen Anne).

Parliament also passed private acts sponsored by individuals or private organizations, usually to get divorces, enclose land, gain citizenship, or build improvements such as lighting, turnpikes, and canals. It could take as long as eight years to get a private act through Parliament. Even including private bills, Parliament passed only about fifty acts a year in the early decades of the century, and about two hundred a year in the 1780s. Absenteeism was high in the second half of the century, with more than half the members in attendance only rarely. Education, welfare, health care, law enforcement, and a host of other important issues were left largely to local government or private enterprise.

LOCAL GOVERNMENT

Numerous local officials included sheriffs, who administered elections for each county and for the city of London; churchwardens, laymen who helped to administer parish church property; parish poor law overseers; town mayors; aldermen; city councilors and members of town corporations; burgesses, twelve of whom governed the city of Westminster; constables; and magistrates, or justices of the peace (JPs), who served as local lawmakers, administrators, and judges. Most of these could not be Dissenters or Catholics, though there were some regional exceptions, and a Dissenter could be elected to local office if he were willing to conform temporarily to the established church. Dissenters often chose instead to serve on private or quasi-private organizations that were founded for a specific purpose—for example, to install street lights or to maintain the roads.

ELECTIONS

The electorate for both local and national office was extremely small. Women and Catholics were barred from voting. In 1782 excise and customs officials were also denied the vote. Of those adult male Protestants who remained, only a minority could vote, even for local office. For example, London's aldermen and councilors were elected by a scant 12,000 men,[14] and that was an unusually representative contest. Estimates of the total parliamentary electorate range from about 300,000 in the first two decades of the century to Thomas Jefferson's much later figure of 160,000.[15] The number of eligible voters actually dropped during the course of the century, to about 3 percent of the total population and about 7 percent of the adult male population.[16] The percentage of adult males who could vote was both absolutely and proportionately larger in England than it was in Scotland, where fewer than 3,000 men had the franchise.[17]

There were two types of seats in the Commons: county and borough, the latter meaning that the constituency was a particular town. Typically, the right to vote was earned, for county constituencies, by owning land valued at forty shillings (£2) per year. In "freeman boroughs," one could vote by being a "freeman," in other words by being granted the town's "freedom"—the right to carry on one's trade within its walls. Not all boroughs, however, were freemen boroughs; in some, only the members of the town corporation (or council) might hold the franchise. In 1761, 201 boroughs had fewer than 500 eligible voters.[18] The town of Bath had just thirty-two.[19] Yet there was little outrage. Agitation to expand the electorate, a major political issue in the 19th century, was barely uttered in the 18th except as a small radical yelp during the 1790s. In fact, legislation was passed in the middle of the century to shrink the pool of qualified voters.

Representation in Parliament was not only limited but also haphazard. The population distribution shifted dramatically over the course of the century, but no effort was made to redistribute seats accordingly. As a result, the county of Cornwall, with about a hundred thousand inhabitants, had twenty-one boroughs and a comparable number of county seats.[20] Industrial Lancashire, on the other hand, with a booming population in the second half of the century, had only six boroughs, and Middlesex, west of London, and with a population of one million, had only eight seats total in the Commons. Since the MP for a particular county or borough did not have to reside there, the rationalization was that areas like Lancashire were "virtually represented" by Lancashire landowners standing for seats elsewhere. It was certainly true that many of Cornwall's seats were held by outsiders and that those men would be likely to listen as much to their actual neighbors as to the residents of the county they supposedly represented.

According to the terms of the Septennial Act (1716), it was necessary to hold a general election at least every seven years (although the monarch could prorogue a particular Parliament earlier and thus call for an early election). In an election year, some seats would not be contested at all, as in "pocket boroughs" or "rotten boroughs." "Pocket boroughs" were so called because their voters were all, or almost all, dependent in some way upon a wealthy individual or family and would vote as directed. They were thus "in the pocket" of someone, and could be granted to a younger son, a political ally, or someone else who had earned the family's favor. "Rotten boroughs" were towns whose voting population had diminished to the point of near disappearance. Other seats would not be contested because Whigs and Tories, or powerful landowners, colluded to eliminate competition. As a result, twelve counties did not hold their elections from 1754 to 1790. County seats went uncontested in Shropshire from 1722 on and in Wiltshire (with one exception) from 1713 on.[21] Of the seats that were contested, some would be held in freeman boroughs, and whatever party was currently in power would rush to create new freemen, who often did not even live in the town. Gloucester, for example, created 469 freemen in 1727 for this purpose.[22] In county elections, party leaders would grant forty-shilling annuities to loyal followers.

When family control, creation of new voters, or party collusion failed, there would be an actual contest, and the bribery, intimidation, and finagling began. Candidates wooed local voters with cash, trinkets, public entertainments, speeches, flattery, and open houses. The earl of Cork loathed the last tactic, but endured it anyway:

> [O]ur doors are open to every dirty fellow in the county that is worth forty shillings a year; all my best floors are spoiled by the hobnails of farmers stamping about them; every room is a pig-stye, and the Chinese paper in the drawing room stinks so abominably of punch and tobacco that it would strike you down to come into it.[23]

Voters who could not be won by proximity to greatness could be bullied by sermons in the local churches or even by the threat of mob violence. Further control was exerted through the office of the sheriff, who dictated the place, time, and procedures of the election itself. One way or another, Commons was owned by the rich and well connected. Peers' sons accounted for more than 10 percent of the Commons, and perhaps another 10 to 20 percent were elected due to the influence of peers. Men

1.1 An election procession, 1781, with music, drink, banners with slogans, and symbolic cockades. The verse below the original picture read: These stanch friends to freedom you here do behold,/Will be bribed with good eating tho' they spurn at yr gold/For offer them money it's such a disgrace,/'Tis a thousand to one they don't spit in your face:/But give them pudding & beef with compliments civil,/To serve you they'll go 'ay e'en to the devil. Courtesy of the Print Collection, Lewis Walpole Library, Yale University.

in trade did sometimes make it into Parliament, but they were vastly outnumbered by the landed gentry, and they owed even this slight representation to sheer wealth.

POPULAR POLITICS

Despite the effective monopoly of national politics by the rich, the disenfranchised were fascinated by Parliamentary activity. Royal and legislative doings were recorded, discussed, and satirized in political magazines and newspapers, cheap pamphlets, ballads, riddles, handbills, graffiti, and scatological cartoons. The plays of Henry Fielding and John Gay, Alexander Pope's *Dunciad*, and Jonathan Swift's *Gulliver's Travels* all depended on audiences that knew the political institutions and individuals being lampooned. Organized political clubs and impromptu gatherings met at coffeehouses and pubs, and crowds gathered outside the Houses of Parliament on days of important debate. On February 2, 1778, the crowds were so numerous and enthusiastic that they actually broke down the doors of Parliament, swarmed the galleries, and had to be forcibly ejected.[24] Footmen held mock parliaments; a Surrey town held mock mayoral elections at which voters had to have "enjoyed a woman in the open air in the district."[25] As early as the 1720s, the British liked to call themselves a "nation of politicians" or a "nation of Prime Ministers."[26] Even carters and shoe-blacks were surprisingly well informed and opinionated. One foreign traveler remarked, "In general nothing is more difficult than to make an Englishman speak, he answers to everything by *yes* or *no*; address him, however, on some political subject and he is suddenly animated; he opens his mouth and becomes eloquent."[27]

Some women, too, took an interest in public affairs, though for genteel women it was an extremely delicate business. Advocacy of a particular candidate was acceptable only if he were a husband, relative, or close family friend. Georgiana, the duchess of Devonshire, discovered this when she supported Charles James Fox for the Westminster seat in 1784. She was savaged by the press and the caricaturists, who implied that she was unnatural and that Fox was her lover. Prints showed her suckling a fox, carrying foxtails, and leaving the duke to change his child's diaper at home while he mutters, "This Work does not suit my Fancy. Ah William every one must be cursed that like thee, takes a Politic Mad Wife."[28] To emphasize the masculine nature of the political arena, the galleries of Parliament were forbidden to women in 1778.[29] Lower-class women, who had more freedom of action, often participated in bread riots and street demonstrations.

The authorities, far from congratulating themselves on the widespread interest in politics, found it a little unsettling. Censorship was imposed on the theater, and offensively satirical plays were banned. Time and again, both Houses tried to suppress accounts of Parliamentary debates, but they succeeded only in delaying reports, or in forcing editors to disguise the accounts as conversations in a gentleman's club, or the activities of the senate of Lilliput. Such reports, which had to rely on memory since note taking was forbidden in the gallery, were often much abbreviated and sometimes inaccurate. The last serious attempt to suppress the publication of Parliamentary debates occurred in 1771, but the tension between privacy and publicity continued until the end of the century.[30]

Meanwhile, the common people had other ways of making their political voices heard. They could petition Parliament or the court. The repeal of an unpopular tax on retail shops, for example, was achieved largely through an aggressive petition drive.[31] Those who could not write, or who felt petitions inadequate to the task, used other tactics. They staged public processions full of symbolism: loaves of bread draped in black or stained with blood meant hunger; the scales cried for justice; a boot stood for George III's minister, the earl of Bute; a turnip was George I. Images of death were used as not-so-subtle threats, as when effigies of unpopular figures were burnt or hanged, or when supporters of John Wilkes ostentatiously drove a hearse to St. James's Palace to intimidate the king.[32] Crowds would wait for the emergence of the MPs, cheering those who were popular and assaulting the carriages of those who were not. Anonymous death threats were left at the house of various JPs. When all else failed, there was a riot. Benjamin Franklin, visiting Britain in 1769, commented,

> I have seen, within a year, riots in the country, about corn; riots about elections; riots about workhouses; riots of colliers, riots of weavers, riots of coal-heavers; riots of sawyers; riots of Wilkesites; riots of government chairmen; riots of smugglers, in which custom house officers and excisemen have been murdered, the King's armed vessels and troops fired at.[33]

He might have added, had he been in the country longer, riots over turnpikes, the Irish, brothels, and the availability of gin.

For much of the century, there was a certain willingness to tolerate mob action. That tolerance evaporated after the Gordon Riots of 1780 and the French Revolution of 1789. At first, the revolution was greeted with some sympathy. The Reign of Terror, however, especially the executions of Louis XVI and Marie Antoinette, reduced support for the revolution to radical groups. Anything that hinted at rebellion at home was promptly suppressed. Legislation of the 1790s suspended habeas corpus, limited public gatherings, and rewarded informers. Trials for sedition, though often resulting in acquittals, attempted to squelch dissent. Author Hannah More expressed the sentiments of a weary, anxious nation when she wrote, near the end of a far-from-placid century, "From liberty, equality and the rights of man, Good Lord deliver *us*."[34]

TIMELINE

1701	The Act of Settlement bars Catholics from the English throne.
	James II, the deposed and exiled king, dies. His son James Edward Stuart, the Old Pretender, is recognized as King James III of England by France.
1702	William III dies and is succeeded by his sister-in-law, Queen Anne, the last Stuart monarch. She will be pregnant seventeen times, but only five of her children will be born alive, and none will survive to adulthood.
	England enters the War of the Spanish Succession.

1707	The Act of Union formalizes the political union of Scotland and England, with Scotland gaining representation in Parliament.
	Queen Anne is the last monarch to use the power of the veto.
1708	The Old Pretender attempts an abortive invasion of Britain at the Firth of Forth.
1713	The Treaty of Utrecht ends the War of the Spanish Succession; its terms give Britain control of Gibraltar and Minorca.
1714	Queen Anne dies on August 1 and is succeeded by George I of Hanover.
1715	A major uprising of Jacobites erupts in Scotland. The Old Pretender lands in Scotland, but the rebellion, known as "the Fifteen," fails.
1716	The Old Pretender returns to France.
	The Septennial Act dictates that Parliamentary elections be called at least every seven years. The previous term was three years.
1727	George I dies and is succeeded by his son George II.
1734	Election violence results in troops being sent to the Welsh marches.
1740	The War of the Austrian Succession begins.
1745	Charles Edward Stuart, the Young Pretender, lands in the Hebrides, takes Edinburgh, wins the Battle of Prestonpans, and reaches Derby with an army of 5,000. This invasion is known as "the Forty-Five."
1746	In April, the Battle of Culloden effectively ends the Jacobite threat. The Young Pretender escapes to France.
1748	The Treaty of Aix-la-Chapelle ends the War of the Austrian Succession.
1751	Frederick, Prince of Wales and son of George II, dies.
1756	The Seven Years' War begins.

1760	George II dies and is succeeded by his grandson George III.
1763	The Peace of Paris ends the Seven Years' War with significant territorial gains for Britain.
	Parliamentary acts limit the voting power of nonresident freemen and the granting of forty-shilling annuities.
1764	John Wilkes is expelled from the House of Commons.
	Britain begins several years of taxing its American colonies to pay for their defense in the Seven Years' War; resistance to these taxes will later lead to the American Revolution.
1768	Wilkes is returned to the Commons from Middlesex in a controversial election.
1776	America issues its Declaration of Independence.
	Thomas Paine publishes *Common Sense*.
1780	The Gordon Riots erupt in London.
1782	Customs and excise officers lose the franchise.
	On March 20, Lord North resigns.
1783	The Peace of Versailles ends the American Revolution.
1784	George III dissolves Parliament three years early and calls a general election.
1788	Charles Edward Stuart, the Young Pretender, dies.
1789	The French Revolution begins.
1791	Thomas Paine publishes his *Rights of Man*.
1793	On February 1, France declares war on Britain.
1801	Irish peers become eligible for Britain's House of Lords.
1834	The Houses of Parliament burn down.

2

"Not Created Equal": Class and Race

We hold, they say, these truths to be self-evident: That all men are created equal. In what are they equal? Is it in size, strength, understanding, figure, moral or civil accomplishments, or situation of life? Every plough-man knows that they are not created equal in any of these.

—The *Gentleman's Magazine*, 1776,
in response to the American Declaration of Independence

For 18th-century men and women, class determined almost everything—diet, dress, times of waking and sleeping, occupation, education, even, sometimes, cause of death and means of burial. They knew their places in the local hierarchy, deferred (at least outwardly) to those above them, pitied those below them, and perhaps tried against tremendous odds to rise a notch or two higher. The attempt to rise, if successful, would probably take their whole adult lives.

Several contemporary writers made guesses about the population and its division into classes. These guesses, while not wholly reliable, give a general picture of the populace. One such estimate was compiled in 1759 by Joseph Massie.

Table 2.1
Massie's Population Estimates

Annual Family Income (£)	Occupations	Number of Families
800 or more	aristocracy and squires	2,070
400–799	gentlemen, merchants, and tradesmen	10,300
200–399	gentlemen, merchants, tradesmen, and manufacturers	28,700
80–199	clergy, lawyers, military officers, freeholders, tenant farmers, tradesmen, innkeepers, and manufacturers	84,000
50–79	clergy, liberal arts (e.g. writers), bureaucrats, freeholders, tenant farmers, tradesmen, innkeepers, and manufacturers	156,000
40–49	farmers, cottagers, tradesmen, and manufacturers	327,500
25–39	freeholders and manufacturers	148,000
15–24	husbandmen, ale sellers, seamen, London laborers, and manufacturers	500,000
14 or less	country laborers and soldiers	218,000
		1,474,570[1]

Massie lumps squires and aristocrats together, but the number of actual title holders was extremely small. They made up less than 0.02 percent of the population at the end of the eighteenth century.[2] The number of peerages remained remarkably constant, numbering 178 in 1720, 181 in 1750, and 185 in 1783.[3] From 1784 on peerages were created at a faster rate, but even in 1800 aristocrats were a very small group, marrying and socializing mostly among themselves. For such a small group, peers owned a great deal, controlling about 20 percent of England's land value.[4] At a time when the median income was well below £100, Horace Walpole could call the fourth earl of Cholmondeley's £2,500 a year "a small fortune for an earl."[5]

In addition to those with titles, there were those whose wealth alone raised them to the upper class. The great magnates were, like peers, very rare, belonging to perhaps a hundred families.[6] However, there were thousands of other families with fewer holdings whose land rents still enabled them to live lives of leisure.[7] These were the gentry, whose ranks most middle-class Britons yearned to join. The gentry were composed chiefly of those who owned land but did not till it themselves. Some gentry also owned land in and around London and augmented their fortunes by developing upscale housing projects. Others invested in stocks, turnpikes, mining ventures, and trading companies.

Younger sons of upper-class families also entered the genteel professions: the military, politics, and the clergy. By 1800, 38 percent of navy officers (and even more army officers) came from the aristocracy and gentry. As early as 1720, one in four peers held a political post of some kind. Hundreds of members of Parliament were scions or protégés of wealthy landed families. The gentry also controlled a number of religious appointments and increasingly named family members to fill these positions.[8]

Below the gentry—great magnates, petty squires, military officers, bishops, parsons, and MPs—stretched the vast, ill-defined territory of the "middling sort." This group included merchants and shopkeepers, bankers, prosperous small farmers, clerks, attorneys, apothecaries, schoolmasters, industrialists, innkeepers, architects, curates, and engineers. These were the people, usually, who had education, business acumen, or a special craft skill to recommend them. Defined by income, that middle class stretched from an annual income of about £300 or £400 down to £40 or £50, though even wealthy businessmen might be considered middle rather than upper class because of their dependence on trade rather than land. Depending on where the line is drawn, the "middling sort" may have included anywhere from about 16 to 42 percent of all families.

Those who had little but their bodies to offer, or whose crafts paid poorly, formed the lower class. These were the wage laborers in field and factory, miners, peddlers, seamstresses, prostitutes, canal bargemen, domestic servants, knife-grinders, ostlers, cattle drivers, fishmongers, paupers, and common soldiers and sailors. There were a great many of them—more than 600,000 domestic servants alone.[9] The poor certainly made up over half the population. The minimum income for survival was about £20 a year, and there were a good many people making well below that sum. More than 20 percent of all families required charitable assistance.[10]

SOCIAL MOBILITY

It is uncertain how much social mobility actually existed. There were many successful tradesmen and manufacturers who had humble origins, though usually men who rose far and fast had had a boost from good fortune—marriage to an heiress, an inheritance, or the influence of "friends" (not one's intimate companions but people in a position to help one's career). A woman could enhance her social status usually only by marrying. Women were often accused of undue social ambition, as were prosperous tenant farmers and anyone else who threatened, in the words

2.1 "Following the Fashion" (Gillray 1794) attacks social climbers: "St. JAMES's giving the TON, a Soul without a Body. CHEAPSIDE aping the MODE, a Body without a Soul." "Ton" meant high fashion; Cheapside was a district in London that housed tradesmen and their families, while St. James's Square was an ultra-chic area for gentry and aristocrats. Courtesy of the Print Collection, Lewis Walpole Library, Yale University.

of one observer, "to mingle every man with the class that is superior to him, and . . . to support a gay and splendid appearance utterly inconsistent with their station and circumstances."[11] The upper classes liked to ridicule or pity the poor for their lack of social graces, but heaven help the man or woman who made an attempt to learn those graces. The reason for the hostility was simple: the appearance of gentility was often most of the substance of gentility. One foreign commentator judged that "the title of gentleman is given in England to all that distinguish themselves from the common sort of people by a good garb, genteel air or good education, wealth or learning."[12]

However, if the appearance of gentility was available to all, true rank and its privileges remained closely guarded. It was extremely rare for a man still active in trade, however successful, to rise to membership in Parliament or to win a bride from a prominent landed family.[13] It was more common for his daughter to marry a gentleman, winning status for the rest of her family with a trade-fattened dowry. A man might invest his mercantile profits in land, thus moving into the gentry, but this was not easy. Huge country estates rarely became available for purchase.[14] Entry into the peerage on one's own merits was nearly impossible. Though a number of peerages were created during the century, most were promotions of lesser peers or replacements of lines that had died out. In the last two decades of the century, a few dozen men rose to the House of Lords by virtue of outstanding achievement in politics, law, diplomacy, or the military, but a surgeon was not granted even a knighthood until 1778, and no engineer would be knighted until the 1840s.[15]

CLASS AND THE LAW

English law, though much celebrated, showed more favor to the duke with a hundred thousand acres than to the vagrant passing through his lands. Lawsuits required money for court and attorneys' fees and for bribing, transporting, or locating witnesses; increasingly, the poor simply could not afford it.[16] There was no public prosecutor's office, either; if you wanted someone prosecuted, you had to bring (and pay for) the prosecution yourself. Another type of legal recourse, the private act of Parliament, was sought by some individuals to secure divorces or to enclose land. Logistically tricky and staggeringly expensive, private acts required both cash and influence. Their benefits were therefore reserved for the upper class. Stringent penalties for petty theft, incarceration for debt, and the restrictions of the Poor Law weighed more heavily on the poor. Peers had additional privileges. They were entitled to be tried by their *own* peers—in other words, by the House of Lords. They could offer testimony on their personal honor, rather than on oath. According to the law, men were *not* created equal.

Not all laws, however, favored the gentry. Many taxes were designed specifically to penalize the rich. By Continental standards, English nobles were positively oppressed; even an earl, passing through a turnpike gate, had to pay the toll. In some cases, being rich made life more complicated. Divorce for the very rich was difficult, expensive, and protracted. (For the middle class it was virtually impossible.) But for the poor, who had little property, dissolving a marriage was much easier, because one could simply ignore the law. All that was required was the community's approval, the consent of all parties, and a change of households. It was one of the few instances in which being truly poor was a distinct advantage.[17]

CLASS AND LIVING CONDITIONS

The middle and upper classes took pride in the sheer quantity—particularly of meat and liquor—they could consume; poor families were seldom able to gorge themselves. Though actual starvation was rare, hunger was common. In hard times, bread might constitute almost all of one's diet. Low wages, especially toward the end of the century, meant that one setback could be the difference between subsistence and destitution. A wage earner's loss of employment, illness, injury, desertion, or imprisonment could mean that his or her family would be "thrown onto the parish" for assistance, unable to feed and clothe themselves.

Housing for the very poor was also dismal. In the cities, they crowded into cellars and flimsy shacks, or huddled together in "rookeries," so called because they resembled the crowded nesting areas of birds called rooks.[18] In the country, shelters were often built of nothing more than turf or wattle (poles interwoven with sticks or reeds), and they often had to house animals as well as people. Often, the local forests were controlled by great landowners who reserved the timber for themselves, leaving the poor without firewood for heating and cooking. The marquis of Bath's steward summed up the misery of the rural home, "Humanity shudders at the idea of the industrious laborer, with a wife and five or six children, being obliged to live or rather to exist, in a wretched, damp, gloomy room, of 10 or 12 ft square, and that room without a floor."[19] Even these inadequate dwellings were sometimes torn down by the local authorities: without a residence, a poor family had no more claim to the parish's institutionalized charity.

CLASS AND HEALTH CARE

Class also influenced how one sickened and died. Though the poor seldom died from starvation alone, their sparse and unvaried diet, poor housing, crowded conditions, and inadequate hygiene certainly made them susceptible to certain diseases, including smallpox and what the records of the time, lacking a more specific term, refer to as "fevers." During the course of the century, hospitals were founded to care for the indigent sick, partly for their own sake and partly to keep them from infecting their employers, but how much hospitals helped to cure disease (or spread it) is a matter of some dispute. The upper and middle classes, nursed at home, and benefiting from better hygiene, had better health and lower mortality rates. Reformer Jonas Hanway, comparing twenty-two impoverished London parishes with the wealthier area of Westminster, found the death rate was more than three times higher in the former.[20] The rich lived not only better, but also longer.

TITLES

The rich were also recognized by public deference and the use of honorific titles. Titles were not limited to the aristocracy. By mid-century, any well-dressed gentleman expected to be referred to as "Sir" or "your Honor," and his wife would expect to be called "Madam." During the second half of the century, "Mr." and "Mrs." came into wide use for people of the middle class.[21] These titles might also be used for any superior, or for anyone to whom one wished to show respect. For example, a housekeeper might call the gardener Robert, but expect in return to be called Mrs. Perkins.

CLASS ROLES

The classes were vastly unequal, yet there was no revolution, as there was in France late in the century. Most people, even the poor, believed in the system *in its ideal form*. The upper class had the most to lose from a massive revision of the hierarchy, and naturally they wanted nothing of the kind. The middle class had enough upward mobility to keep it reasonably content. The lower class believed in a kind of feudal responsibility of rich to poor; even when they resented the gentry, they expected it to fulfill its obligations to the needy.[22] Even the privileged agreed in theory with this ideal. Spiritual leaders, such as Bishop Butler, encouraged the rich to think of the poor as their special burden; Butler claimed that "God has distributed men into these different ranks, and has formally put the poor under the superintendency & patronage of the rich."[23]

If excessive ambition was the fault most commonly attributed to the middle class, failure to provide a suitable example and to care properly for their subordinates were the most common complaints against the rich. The aristocracy was widely seen as preoccupied with duels, London, adultery, foreign fashions, fox hunts, and gambling. The Reverend Sydney Smith attacked it for suppressing the favorite entertainments of the poor, while engaging in cruel sports itself. He noted, "A man of £10,000 a year may worry a fox as much as he pleases, encourage the breed of a mischievous animal on purpose to worry it: & a poor labourer is carried before a magistrate for paying sixpence to see an exhibition of courage between a dog and a bear."[24]

The poor, in turn, were taken to task for insubordination, drunkenness, criminality, ignorance, improvidence, self-indulgence, and laziness. Rural laborers were called "perverse, stupid and illiterate," urban workers "debauched, ill-mannered," and all "swinish."[25] The popular and rarely challenged assumption of the upper and middle classes was that a decent

Table 2.2
Titles and Modes of Address

Rank	Addressed or Referred to as	Wife	Son	Daughter
Duke*	His Grace, the Duke of X** / in conversation, Your Grace or Sir.	Her Grace, the Duchess of X** / in conversation, Your Grace or Ma'am.	Eldest: next-highest family title (e.g. Marquess). Younger: Lord John Y / in conversation, Lord John. His wife is Lady John Y / Lady John.	Lady Anne Y / in conversation, Lady Anne.
Marquess	The (Most Honourable the) Marquess of X / Lord X.	The (Most Honourable the) Marchioness of X / Lady X.	See dukes' son.	See dukes' daughters.
Earl	The (Right Honourable the) Earl of X / Lord X.	The (Right Honourable the) Countess of X / Lady X.	Eldest: next-highest family title. Younger: The Honourable John Y / Mr. John Y. His wife is The Honourable Mrs. John Y / Mrs. Y.	See dukes' daughters.
Viscount	The (Right Honourable the) Viscount Y / Lord Y.	The (Right Honourable the) Viscountess Y / Lady Y.	All: The Honourable John Y / Mr. Y. Wives: The Honourable Mrs. John Y / Mrs. Y.	The Honourable Anne Y / Miss Y.
Baron	The (Right Honourable the) Lord Y / Lord Y. Never Baron Y. Baron and Baroness are the lowest ranks of the peerage.	The (Right Honourable the) Lady Y / Lady Y, if she holds the title by marriage to a Baron. If she holds the title in her own right, she is The (Right Honourable the) Lady Y or Baroness Y.	Honourable—see above.	Honourable—see above.
Baronet***	Sir John Y, Bart. or Sir John Y, Bt.	Lady Y	no title	no title
Knight***	Sir John Y	Lady Y	no title	no title

Notes: *Non-royal. Royal dukes and duchesses have different forms of address; **X in this chart indicates the name of the title—Northumberland, Queensberry, Bute—and Y indicates a family name, such as Beaumont, Gordon, or Banks; ***A person of this rank is not a member of the peerage.

Military and official titles precede titles of rank, e.g., Admiral the Honourable George Clinton. So do first names, e.g., The Right Honourable Charles Lord Halifax. The daughter of a Duke, Marquis, or Earl who marries a commoner retains her rank: i.e., Mr. George and Lady Anne Smith. A commoner who obtains her title by marriage, is widowed, and then marries a commoner goes from Miss Elizabeth Jones to Lady Silverspoon to Mrs. George Smith.

standard of living—not luxury, but freedom from want at least—was within the grasp of most, if they worked hard. Philanthropist Frederick Morton Eden dismissed the entire idea of poverty as arising completely from "improvidence and unthriftiness."[26]

The poor were subjected to countless lectures and sermons on good work habits, meek religiosity, and the virtue of starving quietly. Hannah More put her advice into rhyme, speaking through a suitably resigned protagonist:

> And though I've no money, and tho' I've no lands
> I've a head on my shoulders and pair of good hands.
> So I'll work the whole day, and on Sundays I'll seek
> At Church how to bear all the wants of the week.[27]

Frederick Eden, likewise an admirer of workers who shut up about their troubles, lauded Surrey farm laborer James Strudwick, who worked until the age of eighty at the rate of a shilling a day without once seeking a raise in pay or charitable assistance.[28] Throughout all of this material runs the assumption that the poor were a problem to be solved by the rich since the poor were obviously too lazy or stupid to "fix" themselves.

Rules for the Poor

1. Keep steadily to your work, and never change masters, if you can help it.
2. Go to no gin-shops, or alehouse: but lay out all your earnings in food, and clothes, for yourself, and your family, and try to lay up a little for rent and rainy days.
3. Avoid bad company.
4. Keep no dogs: for they rob your children, and your neighbours.
5. Go constantly to church, and carry your wives, and children with you, and God will bless you.
6. Be civil to your superiors, and they will be kind to you.
7. Learn to make broth, milk pottage, rice-pudding, etc. One pound of meat, in broth, will go further than two pounds boiled or roasted.
8. Be quiet, and contented, and never steal, or swear, or you will never thrive.

Rules for the Rich

1. Abolish gravy soups, and second courses.
2. Buy no starch when wheat is dear.
3. Destroy all useless dogs.

4. Give no dog, or other animal, the smallest bit of bread or meat.

5. Save all your skim-milk carefully, and give it all to the poor, or sell it at a cheap rate.

6. Make broth, rice-puddings, etc., for the poor, and teach them to make such things.

7. Go to church yourselves, and take care your servants go constantly.

8. Look into the management of your own families, and visit your poor neighbours.

9. Prefer those poor who keep steadily to their work, and go constantly to church, and give nothing to those who are idle, are riotous, or keep useless dogs.

10. Buy no weighing meat, or gravy beef: if the rich would buy only the prime pieces, the poor could get the others cheap.[29]

A few disagreed with this majority view of the poor. John Wesley, for example, wrote of one miserable slum in 1753,

> I found some in their cells, others in their garrets, half starved with cold and hunger, added to weakness and pain. But I found not one of them unemployed who was able to crawl about the room. So wickedly, so devilishly false, is that common objection, "They are poor because they are idle."[30]

There was no shortage of ideas about how to deal with the poor. Some wanted them to have fewer children. Some believed that the only solution was to keep wages low, forcing workers to labor constantly to survive, and giving them no time to indulge their ostensibly natural vices. Some argued against charity entirely, believing that it encouraged idleness. Joseph Townsend wrote, "Hunger will tame the fiercest animals, it will teach decency and civility, obedience and subjection to the most perverse. . . . In general, it is only hunger which can spur and goad the poor on to labour; yet our laws have said they shall never hunger."[31] Most people, however, felt that some system of charity, public or private, was warranted.

CHARITY

Public charity, like most government programs, was extremely limited. Parliament did occasionally pass legislation concerning the distribution of charity or the arrest of vagrants, but it left administration to local town or parish government. Poor Law "settlements"—the right to receive parish charity—were usually obtained through birth, residence, or employment within the parish. Enforcement of the Poor Law ultimately resided with the JP, who granted certificates for new settlements, appointed overseers (who disbursed funds to the poor), set the poor rate (the tax on substantial citizens for the care of the poor), dictated the removal of paupers without proper settlement, and sentenced vagrants to whipping, imprisonment, or transportation.[32]

The poor rates were a source of constant irritation to those who paid them. They varied widely from place to place and from year to year depending on employment levels, food prices, epidemics, and war. And, despite the good intentions and numerous plans of reformers, poor rates continued to rise, due at least in part to inflation and increased population. In 1700 the national poor-relief bill probably totaled about £600,000 or £700,000; by 1803, it was £4,200,000.[33] The village of Wigston Magna (in Leicestershire) paid £95 toward poor relief in 1754 and £1,776 in 1802.[34] Mushrooming costs left the gentry and the more prosperous merchants anxious to do anything to reduce the number of poor dependent on their own parish.

Thus the poor were harried with the intention of forcing them to pay their own keep or driving them away to become a burden on another parish. Overseers of the poor might interfere in a marriage between paupers, fearful that the marriage would result in burdensome children. They prosecuted men who refused to support their wives or children.[35] They drove away the elderly and the sick. They sometimes forced publicly supported paupers to wear the letter ''P'' on their clothing. They spent vast sums, as much as eighty pounds in the single case of a one-legged man with a blind wife, to settle handicapped paupers in other parishes. They sent poor infants to venal caretakers, who often kept the maintenance money and allowed the children to die. The spectre of illegitimate children being born inside the parish bounds, and thus gaining a settlement, kept many an overseer alert to pregnancies in the district. A pregnant, unmarried woman would be bullied into naming the father; if the father could not be found, or could not be made to support his child, the mother could be forced to marry a man from another parish, or hurried while in labor to another parish to ensure that the baby became some other overseer's problem.[36]

Some adjustments to the Poor Law system were clearly needed. The plight of children practically condemned to death by the indifference of overseers was ameliorated somewhat by reformer Jonas Hanway, whose efforts resulted, in 1767, in Parliamentary action. The new act provided funds to send urban orphans to country wet nurses and offered financial incentives for the children's survival. In 1795 the ''topping-up'' of workers' wages to subsistence level was linked to inflation, allowing cost-of-living increases in relief for the laboring poor.[37] But the classic 18th-century proposal for ending poverty and idleness, the one that early

2.2   Plate 4 of William Hogarth's "The Harlot's Progress" (1732) shows the pounding of hemp in the Bridewell workhouse. Courtesy of the Print Collection, Lewis Walpole Library, Yale University.

reformers endorsed enthusiastically and later skeptics attacked cynically, the one that nearly every part of the country adopted sooner or later, the one that even today embodies the futile dehumanization of the poor, was the workhouse.

Ideally, a workhouse sheltered the poor and gave them employment to offset the cost of their maintenance. Its conditions were intended to be favorable enough to sustain life, but uncomfortable enough to deter able-bodied indigents from seeking charity: "a mill," as Jeremy Bentham put it, "to grind rogues honest, and idle men industrious." With this lofty goal in mind, the first workhouses were commissioned in the late seventeenth century. In the early 1720s, parishes were given the power to commit any pauper who sought relief to a workhouse. By 1776 there were about 2,000 of these "mills," warehousing approximately 90,000 men, women, and children.[38]

In reality, workhouses could not make much of a profit; they existed, after all, because there was simply not enough well-paid work to go around. They also tended to be the last resort of those least able to work:

the sick, the old, the handicapped, the mentally retarded, and the very young. Moreover, the administrators considered themselves businessmen rather than social workers. Often paid a fee for each pauper housed, they were free to spend the money as they chose and were expected to pay themselves out of the surplus.

Infants consigned to workhouses, prior to Hanway's intervention, were virtually sentenced to death. He found that a one-to-three-year-old's life expectancy in a London workhouse was about a month, that the infant mortality rate in one workhouse was 100 percent, and that the overall rate between 1750 and 1755 was just under 93 percent.[39] Hanway was certain that parish officers actually intended that poor children should die, and he condemned the practice in passionate terms, calling one London workhouse "the greatest sink of mortality in these kingdoms, if not on the face of the whole earth."[40] Other observers, though they lacked Hanway's fierce conviction, echoed his conclusions. Parson Woodforde wrote of a Norfolk workhouse, "About 380 Poor in it now, but they don't look either healthy or cheerful a great Number die there, 27 have died since Christmas last."[41]

Despite the fact that the numbers of the poor continued to grow, despite the fact that mortality in the workhouses was high, despite the fact that these enterprises consistently failed to pay for themselves, almost no one was willing to consider an alternative. Workhouses, after all, had their advantages. Their cost could seem comparable to that of subsidizing paupers scattered in individual hovels around the parish. They also served aesthetics and conscience by keeping the most miserable members of society well out of sight. Authorities thus clung doggedly to the idea of workhouses. Perhaps, they concluded, it was a problem of scale. Therefore, in 1782, Parliament authorized cooperation by groups of parishes to build larger, centralized workhouses. Some areas took advantage of this opportunity, but those that did found that it offered no long-term savings.

Many concluded that public assistance was inadequate and founded private organizations. These philanthropists were usually members of the middle class, whose businesses were directly dependent on the diligence and good health of the poor. One advocate of charitable endeavors stressed "consideration of interest":

> For neglect this poor man's numerous family, leave them to follow their own imagination and to make what wretched shift they can, and experience the sad consequence. They will soon grow up to public nuisances, infect your families with their idle disorderly behaviour, fill your streets with vice and violence ... take the same persons under your patronage, teach them what is right and hear

how you will be repaid. They will be serviceable to you in many ways. . . . Your city will be stocked with honest laborious ingenious artisans, some of the most useful members of a community; wealth will increase.[42]

Certainly those who received assistance were happier fed than hungry, but the acknowledged goal was not to make people happy, but to make them useful. The great charities of the age—the Foundling Hospital, the Marine Society, and the Magdalen House—were dedicated to breeding and raising more and better laborers, servants, sailors, and soldiers.

The Foundling Hospital's goal was to take in orphaned and abandoned children, send the babies and toddlers to the country for nursing, and clothe, house, and educate them until they were old enough to work. At that point, the girls became domestic servants, and the boys became sailors or farm laborers. Eighteenth-century England's most fashionable charity, it was supported by aristocratic ladies at Court, the composer George Frideric Handel (whose *Messiah* was performed at concerts to benefit it), and the artist William Hogarth (who served on the board of governors and arranged public art shows at the hospital to draw potential donors).[43]

Jonas Hanway's Marine Society took in poor men and boys, issued them each a new set of clothes, and sent them into the Navy. The organization kept a special ship that housed a hundred boys, a schoolmaster, and officer-instructors. In just over three years, it raised almost £25,000; in seven years, it equipped 10,000 recruits with help from more than 1,500 donors.[44]

The Magdalen House, which tried to reform prostitutes, took in fewer than a hundred women a year on average, with the intention of either restoring them to their families or sending them out as servants. Evidence from 1761 suggests that the success rate was low. It is also possible that some of the "reformed" prostitutes returned later to their former profession. There were also considerable pressures placed on female servants to provide sexual favors to their male employers, so that becoming a maidservant was not necessarily a path to virtue. In fact, it was often simply a less profitable whoredom.

Other privately funded charities included hospitals, dispensaries, and infirmaries, both in London and the provinces. There were charities to support the impoverished insane, to offer inoculation, to provide midwives to poor married women, to aid those imprisoned for debt, to provide trusses to injured laborers, to collect supplies for soldiers serving abroad, to award prizes for commercial achievements and useful inventions, to teach the making of cheap soups, and to distribute religious tracts.[45] However, private charity, like public charity, worked haphaz-

2.3 Frontispiece to Jonas Hanway's *Three Letters on the Subject of the Marine Society*, J. B. Cipriani, 1758. **Pauper boys being outfitted for the sea by the Marine Society. Courtesy of the Print Collection, Lewis Walpole Library, Yale University.**

ardly at best. Low funds, poor organization, greed, misunderstanding of the causes of poverty, and corruption doomed many attempts to make the poor less miserable, or at least less visible.

BLACK BRITONS

To the three classes of society—upper, middle, and lower—could be added one more, for much of the 18th century at least. Black slaves made up a small percentage of the population, but they did exist, and they formed a fourth class whose existence made white Britons increasingly uncomfortable. On the one hand, abolishing slavery was problematic. The slave trade made possible, in large part, the booming economies of Liverpool and Bristol. Half a million slaves came through the port of Bristol between 1698 and 1807, and even more were transported from Liverpool.[46] Slave labor made commodities like sugar, rum, and cotton cheaply available. Slave boys—the darker the better—made a decorative contrast to the whiteness of fashionable ladies' skins.[47] And if slavery were ended in Great Britain, where slaves were few, what would happen in the colonies, where their numbers were huge? Pro-slavers argued that an end to slavery would mean increased black immigration, lower employment for whites, and an end to a system that they claimed suited slaves as well as masters. (Many of the traits they ascribed to blacks— laziness, stupidity, immorality—were the same ones being used to describe working-class whites.)

On the other hand, it became increasingly apparent that slavery was simply wrong. Public figures, including John Wesley, Samuel Johnson, Adam Smith, and William Cowper, declared themselves against it. Activist groups, notably the Society for the Abolition of the Slave Trade (founded in 1787 and also known as the Abolition Committee) and the all-black Sons of Africa, worked to raise public awareness. Poems, plays, novels, and autobiographies broadcast the suffering of boys (most slaves in Britain were male) kidnapped from Africa, kept as liveried ornaments with silver padlocked collars, then sold into plantation slavery in the West Indies as soon as they reached adulthood. Even more sympathetic to the white public were stories of black men who had married in England and were separated from their wives by slavers, or African princes betrayed into slavery by unscrupulous traders. The most popular abolitionist work of art was a medallion designed by Josiah Wedgwood portraying a chained black man on his knees crying, "Am I not a man and a brother?" The design soon spread to snuffboxes, bracelets, and hairpins.[48]

Nevertheless, the trade and its outrages continued. Newspapers advertised slaves for sale, and although abolitionists sometimes succeeded in using writs of habeas corpus to demand the release of kidnapped slaves, these writs were also used by the opposition to require the return of runaways.[49] One of the worst incidents occurred in 1781 aboard the slave ship *Zong*. Its captain, Luke Collingwood, knowing supplies to be low, and knowing that the ship's insurance carrier would reimburse the owners for slaves lost at sea but not through illness, ordered 133 sick slaves hurled overboard. On the third and last day of these executions, a group of thirty-six slaves resisted and were ordered shackled before being thrown over the side.[50]

With such dramatic examples of cruelty at hand, abolitionists slowly gained ground. Boycotts of slave-produced sugar and rum were organized. Petition drives in 1788 and 1792 amassed thousands of signatures from hundreds of towns. William Wilberforce introduced the topic into the House of Commons in 1789, proclaiming, "We are all guilty."[51] He and his supporters made annual attempts to abolish the slave trade until they were finally successful, in 1807. In the meantime, there was a widespread belief after 1772 that slavery was illegal in Britain itself, due to Lord Mansfield's ruling on the freedom of one James Somerset. Actually, Mansfield was highly reluctant to rule on the legality of slavery and so made his decision as narrow as possible, but most people took it as a precedent-setting decison against slavery in the British Isles. Though the Somerset ruling acted as de facto abolition in Britain, ownership of slaves was still perfectly legal elsewhere in the British Empire until 1833.

Estimates of the total black population of Britain vary widely, but it seems likely that there were from 15,000 to 20,000 black residents of London, with others scattered in port towns and the occasional rural household. Of these, fewer than half were slaves.[52] The others, whether they had ever been enslaved or not, met with a limited tolerance. They belonged mostly to the lower class, and the vast majority were servants (see Illustration 8.1), but some rose higher, and their lives were very much like those of whites of similar income. They became boxers, musicians, authors, sailors, and entrepreneurs. They held all-black social events and formed their own clubs, pubs, and churches. Many married whites, and this appears to have caused little alarm as long as no class boundaries were crossed. A few were quite well-off, like Soubise, the protegé of the duchess of Queensberry, or Dido (Elizabeth) Lindsay, great-niece of Lord Mansfield.[53]

Nonetheless, it was an uneasy tolerance, and black Britons were always aware of color. Shopkeeper Ignatius Sancho wrote of an outing to Vauxhall with three of his daughters in 1777 that they had a good time, especially the girls, though they "were gazed at—followed, &c. &c.— but not much abused."[54] Abuse was forthcoming from other directions. In 1731 "blacks were forbidden by the Lord Mayor's proclamation to learn trades."[55] Plays attacking slavery were undercut by other works that satirized or attacked black servants. Black loyalists who came to Britain after the Revolutionary War were less likely to receive compensation for their efforts than whites.[56] An attempt was even made to send London's black poor to a colony in Sierra Leone, but the effort was plagued by corruption, bad weather, disease, and hostile locals.[57] There was a widespread attitude that, while slavery was wrong, blacks were, in philosopher David Hume's words, "naturally inferior to the whites." Thus, their degradation, like the right of peers to be judged by the House of Lords, could be justified as part of the natural inequality of man.

TIMELINE

1662	The Poor Law governing parish settlements is passed.
1711	A Qualification Act sets land ownership requirements for members of Parliament.
1723	The Knatchbull Act authorizes parishes to refuse charity to those who will not enter workhouses.

1739	The Foundling Hospital is chartered.
1756	The Marine Society is founded.
1758	The Magdalen House is founded.
1760	A new Qualification Act strengthens the stipulations of the 1711 act.
1762	Parliament passes an act requiring that pauper children be registered, in the hope that evidence of their existence will make them easier to track, and make workhouse masters less likely to allow them to die.
1767	The Hanway Act provides for pauper children to be sent into the country, with funds for their maintenance.
1772	On June 22, Lord Mansfield rules that Charles Stewart may not kidnap and sell his former servant James Somerset. The ruling is widely (though falsely) believed to end slavery in Britain.
1782	The Gilbert Act allows parishes to consolidate charity efforts to form larger, centralized workhouses.
1783	Quakers organize the first antislavery petition.
1789	On May 12, William Wilberforce gives the first antislavery speech in the House of Commons.
1791	Wilberforce's first bill against the slave trade fails.
1807	On March 16, the antislave trade bill receives its third reading in the Commons. It passes the Lords on March 23 and is approved by the king on March 25.
1833	Slavery is abolished throughout the British Empire.

3

"Twenty Pounds Will Marry Me": The Family

This day . . . to my irreparable Loss, and very just and great affliction, my most dear and honoured wife, Elizabeth Yorke, departed this life.

There was a wonderful sweetness in her manners, in her Countenance, and Disposition, which engaged, & that very soon, all persons of all ranks. . . . This much I have chosen to note here (not without many tears) of this most excellent Woman, and in so doing I have weakened, rather than extended her merits; But my sense of her worth, will be best spoken by what I suffer in her death.

—Philip Yorke, 1779

If we could travel in time to the 18th century and enter a house, who might we expect to be living inside? Those who guess a large extended family, with the grandparents by the fireside, would almost certainly be wrong. Eighteenth-century households typically contained nuclear families, with children often leaving in their teens for apprenticeships, domestic service, or other work. Marriage usually took place only when the courting couple could afford to set up house on their own, so the average age of marriage was relatively late, about twenty-five to twenty-seven. Some people never succeeded at all; 10 to 20 percent of the population never married.[1] Even among the wealthy, there was an early dispersal of children, with boys (and sometimes girls) being sent to boarding schools. The boys then went to a university, perhaps, or to travel abroad, while the girls were married off as soon as possible.

For all the gray and white powdered wigs being worn in the streets, England was a nation of children. Over 45 percent of its people were under age twenty, and 25 percent were under age ten.[2] Mortality in general was very high. It was common for one parent to die before all the children had grown up, and for the surviving spouse to remarry, sometimes several times. Some women were better off after a husband died; 18th-century marriage could be more like a jail sentence than a loving companionship, and rich women were often allowed a sum of money, called a jointure, in widowhood. Widows also enjoyed more legal freedom than married women. But for most women, who earned far less than men for the same work, widowhood meant instant poverty.

Infant mortality was very high but was offset by a prodigious birthrate. Cookbook author Hannah Glasse had eight children, while her competitor Elizabeth Raffald had thirteen daughters.[3] Elizabeth Yorke, a Welsh squire's wife, died at twenty-nine in 1779, after bearing seven children in nine years.[4] Lady Bristol, married in 1695, had twenty children, most of whom died young.[5] George III and Queen Charlotte were more fortunate; all but two of their fifteen children lived beyond infancy.[6]

ANIMALS

The typical English home contained an animal of some kind. The 18th century was an age of casual cruelty to animals, of brutal overwork for beasts of burden, and of open contempt for a new breed of reformer, the animal-rights activist. (The Middleton curate Richard Dean was threatened with prosecution for suggesting that animals might have souls.[7]) Yet it was also an era of widespread animal ownership, in the country and the city alike. The wealthy kept horses, hunting dogs, lapdogs, and sometimes monkeys, parrots, goldfish, bullfinches, or squirrels in rolling cages. Lord North had a tiger, though it was hardly tame enough to be called a pet.[8]

Middle-class families had pets as well, including dogs, cats, and birds. Some families kept a guard dog, such as a mastiff. Pets were popular enough that there were special sellers of "cats' and dogs' meat"—butchers' leavings sold as pet food.

Even the poor kept animals. Some—cows, pigs, and geese—provided food. Some, including horses, oxen, herd dogs, and seeing-eye dogs, were beasts of labor. Performing animals, such as dancing dogs, acrobatic monkeys, or fighting cocks, might earn the family money. Food was expensive enough that few animals were kept purely as pets, and middle- and upper-class critics considered the poor's dogs a waste of food and a possible aid to poaching. Every shaggy mutt being dipped in a river for fleas was an offensive luxury, but, in the 1790s, the law recognized the right to own a dog by making one dog per family tax free.[9]

MALE AND FEMALE ROLES

Men tended to earn most of the income and women to do most or all of the housework, but plenty of women earned money and did tasks similar to men's. On farms, men did the hardest physical tasks—clearing, plowing, sowing seed, harvesting, and threshing—with the help of sons or hired laborers, while women, helped by daughters or domestic servants, cooked, brewed ale, knitted, washed, taught young children, gardened, made butter and cheese, sewed, and kept chickens for eating and egg production. Women might bring their chickens, eggs, butter, fruit, or vegetables to market to sell, keep a small shop, or do some spinning or carding of wool. Women might help in the fields at harvest time or do factory work, though their wages for these jobs tended to be about half to two-thirds of men's. On occasion, when the woman's labor was better paid than the farm work, roles might be reversed. One late-century Welsh family made it through a hard winter by relying on the wife's knitting skills and turning over the churning, washing, bed making, cleaning, and animal care to her husband, who added them to his farm chores.[10]

The Division of Labor

In shopkeeping families, women and men alike helped out in the store. In artisanal families, the wife was principally responsible for the housekeeping, but she might also oversee the workers while her husband was away, help out with the work (especially if her father had been in the same trade), and even inherit the business when her husband died.

The crushing economic realities of the 18th century made it imperative for many women to work at something. Most hoped to work in youth, save enough money to marry, and then settle into a life of housework only. But many, from ambition or necessity, worked all their lives. There were huge numbers of women in domestic service and prostitution and small numbers of female coffeehouse proprietors, butchers, artists, weavers, tollgate collectors, coal dealers, preachers (chiefly among the Quakers but to a lesser extent among the Methodists), boxers, patent-medicine makers, and mill owners.[11] More commonly, women were hawkers of food and ballads, washerwomen, lace makers, milliners, needleworkers, midwives, spinners, and stocking knitters. They did auxiliary work at coal mines, taught in small schools, and were quite often the keepers of jails. Between 1688 and 1775, more than a quarter of jailkeepers were widows, who usually inherited their positions from their late husbands.[12]

However, one of the trends noted by contemporaries was the gradual disappearance of respectable work for middle-class women. Anxious to imitate the rich, more and more middle-class wives hired servants to do the housework. At the same time, men were providing competition, sometimes overwhelming competition, in traditionally female fields, including midwifery, mantua making, stay making, embroidering, hairdressing, and peruke making.[13] Few occupations opened to compensate for these losses. Women were still forbidden entry to Parliament, the bar, institutionalized medicine, the Anglican clergy, and the magistracy. That left them not with occupations but with hobbies: music, drawing, needlework, and artistic or social patronage.

Perhaps the only significant field newly open to women was that of the arts. Women became actresses, playwrights, and novelists. Some, including Mary Manley, Anne Dodd, Lady Mary Wortley Montagu, Eliza Haywood, and Charlotte Lennox, founded and edited newspapers.[14] Because writing was still not considered entirely respectable, some women wrote anonymously, or they wrote effusive apologies for their sex as prefaces to their work. By the 1770s, however, English society was celebrating the "Nine Living Muses": historian Catherine Macaulay, poet and translator Elizabeth Carter, poet Anna Letitia Barbauld, popular novelist Charlotte Lennox, playwright Elizabeth Griffin, singer Elizabeth Linley, painter Angelica Kauffmann (an immigrant to England in 1766), Bluestocking Elizabeth Montagu, and poet and dramatist Hannah More, who wrote cheap repository tracts for the poor in the 1790s and died in 1833 with a fortune of £30,000.[15] There were swarms of female novelists, most of whom wrote ephemeral fiction, but a few of whom became quite famous. Ann Radcliffe mastered the Gothic, and Frances Burney the novel of manners.

Attitudes Despite the partnership of wives and husbands on farms, and the activity of women in commerce and craft, there was a very definite idea of a private sphere, inhabited and tended by women. Women were consequently not able to vote, hold property while married, go to a university, earn equal wages for equal work, enter the professions, or be protected by law from marital beatings and rape. There were demands that women not tax themselves with too much unfeminine study and urgent counsels to keep what learning one had "a profound secret, especially from the men." Women as well as men made such arguments. Lady Mary Wortley Montagu thought a woman's learning ought to be hidden "with as much solicitude as she would hide crookedness or lameness." Elizabeth Montagu connected wit in a woman to lack of chastity.[16] Hannah More, in *Essays Addressed to Young Ladies* (1777), declared, "Girls should be taught to give up their opinions betimes, and not pertinaciously to carry on a dispute, even if they would know themselves to be in the right." More, later in the century, found the entire concept of women's rights ridiculous, snorting, "It follows that the world will next have—grave descants on the rights of youth—the rights of children—the rights of babies!"[17] Women who were too argumentative or opinionated could be subjected to formal and informal penalties, including a ducking in the local pond, a sentence to wear a humiliating headdress called a scold's bridle, or a public parade in front of her house shaming her (and the husband who failed to control her).[18]

A few people, mostly women, argued in favor of a wider sphere for women. "My own sex, I hope, will excuse me," Mary Wollstonecraft wrote in *A Vindication of the Rights of Woman*,

> if I treat them like rational creatures, instead of flattering their *fascinating* graces, and viewing them as if they were in a state of perpetual childhood, unable to stand alone. . . . I wish to persuade women to endeavour to acquire strength, both of mind and body, and to convince them that the soft phrases, susceptibility of heart, delicacy of sentiment, and refinement of taste, are almost synonymous with epithets of weakness.[19]

Even Wollstonecraft, however, was quick to point out that she only wanted women to imitate manly virtues, not manly activities. Hester Chapone, whose *Letters on the Improvement of the Mind* were more sensible and equitable than most guides to female education and conduct, still recommended meekness and patience. Of Wollstonecraft's work, Chapone could only say (and this was a more generous review than most) that it contained "some strong sense, amidst many absurdities, improprieties, and odious indelicacies."[20]

COURTSHIP

Early in the century, people of property were married by arrangement. It was common for families to decide on a union, haggle over the financial ramifications of the marriage, and then present it to the prospective bride and groom, who were given an opportuinity to meet and (usually) to veto the match if they found it too distasteful. Lady Mary Wortley Montagu, who was in such a position as a young woman, wrote, "People in my way are sold like slaves, and I cannot tell what price my masters will put on me."[21] Actually, it was the other way around: it was the young men who were purchased. Fathers offered, along with their daughters, a sum of money called a dowry to help the couple get started in life. This might be quite a small nest egg in the case of a servant who had saved her own dowry, or a staggering quantity of money or land. Elizabeth, countess of Sutherland, brought her husband an 800,000-acre dowry in 1785.[22]

By 1800 the tide had turned. The dowry was still of critical importance, and parents still threatened to withdraw financial support for a son or daughter who married against their wishes; however, now the young people met at assemblies, balls, and spas; chose their own spouses; (usually) presented the choice to their parents for approval or veto; and then began a round of haggling over the financial settlements. Thus Thomas Blundell wrote of his daughter Molly,

> I have long since told her that I would not compel her to marry, much less to marry one she could not love and so to make her miserable as long as she lives, so to leave her entirely to please herself. . . . All I require is that he be a gentleman of a competent estate, one of good character and a catholic.[23]

James Boswell and Samuel Johnson, like many of their contemporaries, thought parents should offer advice only.[24] A father approached by a suitor seeking permission to court his daughter often put out feelers, sometimes through the mother, to see if the suit was acceptable before granting the suitor's request, or made permission contingent on the daughter's approval. When a parent put his foot down, results varied. Edward Gibbon bowed to filial duty: "I sighed as a lover; I obeyed as a son."[25] Lady Mary Wortley Montagu rejected her father's choice and eloped with the man she preferred.

Below the middle class, most of the control over courtship remained, as it had always been, in the hands of the courting couple. There were no great estates to dispose of, no huge dowries to foster parental influence, and, for the most part, less chaperonage, since both parties were likely to be out of the house and working by age fifteen or sixteen. Couples met at fairs, in the workplace as fellow servants, or at church. Often, they were longtime acquaintances; most villagers married people from within ten miles of home.[26] A man might give his sweetheart ribbons, fans, food, gloves, and other small tokens of affection, all of which had to be returned if the woman broke off the courtship for any reason.[27]

PREMARITAL SEX

In many cases, courtship was a prolonged affair. Even in prosperous families, it might last from four months to two years, and among poorer folk, where saving up for a house, a shop, or children was extremely difficult, it might last much longer. That meant several years, between puberty and marriage, of either celibacy or illicit sexual activity. Some resorted to masturbation, or, as a mid-century medical textbook called it, "mastupratio." The consensus of medical opinion, however, was that this was an intensely dangerous activity. Dr. James Graham claimed that masturbation could cause "debility of body and of mind,—infecundity,— epilepsy,—loss of memory,—sight, and hearing,—distortions of the eyes, mouth and face,—feeble, harsh and squeaking voice,—pale, sallow and blueish black complexion,—wasting and tottering of the limbs,—idiotism,—horrors,—innumerable complaints—extreme wretchedness—and even death itself."[28] Such dire predictions, combined with a belief that men would suffer injury from too much sexual restraint, made a little discreet fornication a perceived necessity—for men.

There were rules regarding the pursuit of premarital sex. It was considered permissible to seduce housemaids and even to use a limited amount of force or threat in addition to cajolery. But in order to be sporting, one had to give one's conquests presents or money and to pay for the maintenance of any illegitimate children that might result. In practice, many men were unwilling to acknowledge responsibility for their bastards, and the inconveniently impregnated maids were often dismissed and driven away from the parish without a good reference. In many areas, a woman who bore a child out of wedlock also had to appear in a white sheet on the church porch as penance for her sin.[29]

There was a rise in illegitimate births that cannot be entirely imputed to lecherous masters and hapless maids. The rate of illegitimacy rose from 1.8 percent of all births in 1700 to 5 percent in 1790, and from 6 to 20 percent of first births between 1690 and 1790. One-third of all brides were pregnant at their weddings.[30] The higher illegitimacy rates may be due to better nutrition, which led perhaps to increased fertility and more conceptions; more planned marriages falling through due to accidents of war or the economy; or more uncertainty about what constituted a marriage. English law was moving away from the recognition of contract marriages, in which the ceremony was a simple promise made in front of witnesses or even when the couple were alone. Thus a couple, relying on old forms and traditions, might think themselves married when they were not, or a man might make a promise to marry in the future which his lover interpreted as a contract marriage in the present. Many people thought, mistakenly, that the gift of a ring or a broken coin constituted a wedding, only to find out later that it did not.[31]

If one party backed out of such an arrangement, the only recourse was a breach of promise suit or a seduction suit, in which a father could sue his daughter's seducer for the loss of her household work during pregnancy. Of course, the daughter had to get pregnant for this to be an effective tactic. One could not sue for loss of virginity. Furthermore, it was inapplicable to servant girls, who had already left home and deprived the family of their housework (and who were, of course, the most sexually vulnerable group in the kingdom).[32]

Another factor in premarital pregnancy was that a couple with serious intentions, though not necessarily a full-fledged engagement, might court by "bundling." This meant staying together all night in the woman's home, with or without her female relatives in the room, with or without explicit or tacit parental consent, and with varying degrees of sexual contact. Actual intercourse was discouraged but probably took place in some cases.[33] Also, after an engagement, many families found it quite all right for the couple to become sexually active.

CHOOSING A SPOUSE

As the burden of choosing a spouse moved from parents to children, parents rushed to offer advice. The earl of Mar told his son to balance fortune, beauty, and love in choosing a wife but concluded, "Do not marry where you cannot love."[34] *A Letter of Genteel and Moral Advice to a Young Lady* (1740) advocated a more specific collection of traits: "The chief things to be regarded in the choice of a husband, are a virtuous disposition, a good understanding, an even temper, an easy fortune, and an agreeable person."[35] Most authors agreed that looks were desirable and tempting, but often misleading. The result was a confusing series of pronouncements to women about how to dress well, walk well, and look pretty without seeming artificial, coquettish, provocative, or unduly concerned with fashion.

Age was an issue to some extent. A husband ten or fifteen years older than his bride would arouse little comment, but significantly larger differences in age, or differences of several years when the woman was the elder, might attract ridicule. In the late 1770s, there was shock and revulsion when historian Catherine Macaulay, age fifty-seven, married a man of twenty-one.

There is ample evidence, however, that money continued to be a prime criterion in the choice of a spouse, rivaling sexual attraction for preeminence. In an era when a fair complexion was equated with beauty, a children's rhyme went,

> What care I how black I be?
> Twenty pounds will marry me;
> If twenty won't, forty shall,
> For I'm my mother's bouncing girl.[36]

Shopping for the best income or dowry continued well after the rise of the companionate, love-centered marriage, and it remained an important factor in parental consent. Often the dowry was the cash infusion that could start or rescue a man's career, for example by buying him a military commission, allowing him to set up his own workshop, or getting him out of debt. For an ambitious mercantile family, a huge dowry might attract a peer's son, allowing the bride's family to move up in the world. For a struggling family, a son's bride's dowry might provide dowries in turn for his sisters.[37]

Pragmatism flourished. Matthew Boulton advised, "Don't marry for money, but marry where money is."[38] Plenty of bitter verses from rejected suitors attest to the existence of women who spurned impoverished merit in favor of fancy plate, a carriage, and a big London house. In *The Clandestine Marriage*, there are several rounds of bargaining. Mr. Sterling, father of the heroine, Fanny, tells a suitor, "Add one little round o to the sum total of your fortune, and that will be the finest thing you can say to me." In the following scene, Fanny's sister chides her for her "romantick" notions, snorting, "Love and a cottage!—Eh, Fanny!—Ah, give me indifference and a coach and six!"[39] Money made some marriages and prevented others, and it continued to be important in the choice of a spouse.

MARRIAGE

The ideal wedding began with securing the community's permission to wed, in the form of obtaining a license or pub-   **Weddings** lishing the banns, in which an announcement of the wedding was read aloud on three successive Sundays at church. Publishing the banns was cheaper than getting a license, but it was more public and therefore, to some people, more embarrassing. The couple then went to church between the hours of 8 A.M. and 12 P.M. and were married before the communion table by a clergyman.[40] In theory, the groom could be as young as fourteen and the bride as young as twelve, but usually they were about twice this age.[41] People seldom married during Lent, as it was believed to be unlucky.[42]

The bride and groom recited their vows, and the groom gave the bride a ring. Grains of wheat were scattered for fertility, and pieces of the wedding cake were passed through the bride's ring and fed to the unmarried, that they might be married soon.[43] Then there was as much festivity as the bride's family could afford. The guests kissed the bride, played practical jokes, sang obscene songs, danced, and ate. Edward Chicken's "The Collier's Wedding" gives a long and vivid description of a working-class wedding feast, with "smoking beef," gravy, geese, chickens, and veal being eaten while the groom brings drinks "With napkin round his body girt, / To keep his clothes from grease and dirt." The bride's mother anxiously keeps track of her dishes and of dishes borrowed from friends for the occasion. The feasting over, the table is pushed to one side, and pipers play. The bridegroom

> . . . dances all the maidens o'er;
> Then rubs his face, and makes a bow,
> So marches off, what can he do?

> He must not tire himself outright,
> The bride expects a dance at night.

At last even the bride's mother is pulled into the dance. She directs the musicians:

> Play me *The Joyful Days are coming;*
> I'll dance for joy, upon my life,
> For now my daughter's made a wife.[44]

The gentry's wedding festivities, if they could not outdo the collier's in sheer joy, were certainly grand. One in Northumberland in 1725 was marked by bonfires, bell ringing, gun salutes, an illumination of the crags at Wellington, and "a large punchbowl cut in the rock, and filled with liquor, &c."[45] Often, the guests received wedding favors of some kind, like gloves, scarves, garters, or ribbons.[46] In various areas, there were additional ceremonies. In some places, goods or money were collected to be given to the new couple. In others, the groom was ridden on a pole to a pub to treat his friends to a drink.[47]

After the ceremony and the feast, the bride and groom were escorted to their home. There the groomsmen took off the bride's garters and tied them to their hats. The bridesmaids took the bride away and undressed her, while the groomsmen helped the groom disrobe. Then the groom, according to Henri Misson,

> comes in his Night-gown, as soon as possible to his Spouse who is
> surrounded by Mother, Aunt, Sister and Friends, and without further
> ceremony gets into Bed. The Bride-men take the Bride's stockings, and
> the Bride-maids the Bridegroom's. Both sit down at the Bed's Feet,
> and fling the Stockings over their Heads, endeavouring to direct them
> so as they may fall upon the marry'd Couple. If the Man's stockings
> thrown by the Maids fall upon the Bridegroom's Head, it is a sign she
> will quickly be marry'd herself; and the same Prognostick holds good
> for the Woman's stockings thrown by the Man.[48]

Afterward, bride and groom were left alone in the room to consummate the marriage, while outside the revelers sang dirty songs and shouted insinuations about what was going on in the bedroom.

Irregular Marriages In practice, not every wedding proceeded as described above. The church recognized a verbal contract or "spousals"—witnessed, consummated consent, even without a public wedding—as forming a binding marriage, though property law did not.[49] A contract marriage could help those wanting to circumvent parental objections, to avoid the embarrassments of banns or being bedded by drunken guests, to complete the ceremony quickly without having to wait for banns, or to spare the expense of an official license and certificate. Sometimes women, particularly widows, wanted to avoid a more official union, since a common-law marriage allowed them to retain control of their own property.

For those who needed a more official ceremony, there was the clandestine marriage, considered binding by both church and state, and allowing children and the widow to inherit according to common law. This was the standard service, read by a clergyman, but usually not performed in church, and certainly not in the couple's own parish church. No banns were proclaimed and usually no license was issued. Clandestine marriage offered speed, economy, and secrecy. The last was crucial when one of the parties was a servant afraid of dismissal, an heir or heiress afraid of being disinherited, a bigamist in danger of being found out, or a widow in danger of losing a portion of her previous husband's estate.[50]

The capital of the clandestine marriage business was the district around London's Fleet Prison, where clergymen imprisoned for debt married anyone willing to pay. Between 1700 and 1710, about fifty to sixty weddings a week took place in the prison itself; later, the trade moved into the inns and houses nearby, where prisoners granted "the Liberty of the Fleet" were permitted to live. In theory, a clergyman who performed such a service was liable to pay a £100 fine, but since these men were already in jail for debt, there seemed little point in trying to impose such fines. Fleet marriages employed not only the parsons, but their runners (who pestered passersby with questions like, "Sir will you be pleased to walk in and be married?"), women and men who kept the registers, and publicans who profited from the feasts held afterward. Some publicans, in fact, kept parsons on retainer. By the 1740s, perhaps as many as 15 to 20 percent of marriages were conducted clandestinely.[51]

In 1753 Lord Chancellor Hardwicke pushed a marriage act through Parliament that banned contract and clandes- **Hardwicke's** tine marriages once and for all. A legal marriage had to **Marriage Act** be performed in church during the daytime by a regular clergyman, with banns or a license and parental consent for any party under the age of twenty-one. Stiff penalties were imposed for clergymen who defied the law. Since the bride's and groom's ages were central to the legislation, errors or falsifications of age in the banns or license could nullify the marriage.

The act contained several loopholes. Jews and Quakers (but not Dissenters or Catholics) were exempted from its regulations; peers were permitted to obtain special licenses from archbishops allowing them to marry when and as they liked; and Scotland, whose marriage and inheritance customs differed from England's, was exempted entirely from the act. One clause made a false statement of place of residence (unlike a false statement of age) legal on a marriage license. Couples could

A FLEET WEDDING.

3.1 "A Fleet Wedding." J. June, 1747. A sailor and his landlady's daughter shop for a parson to perform a clandestine wedding. A vendor to the left of the picture, with a basket on his head, is selling rue (a symbol of the regret a hastily married couple might feel) for a farthing a bunch. Courtesy of the Print Collection, Lewis Walpole Library, Yale University.

therefore go somewhere where they were not known, lie about being residents of the parish, and be married quietly far from home. Couples too poor to afford a license could go to a crowded city parish where the banns could be published by clerks who were too busy to check or to care about accurate statements of residence.[52] The most colorful loophole, as it turned out, was the Scottish one. A man and woman desperate to be married, regardless of parental vetos, could sneak away to Scotland where Hardwicke's Act did not apply. Usually they went to Gretna Green, just inside the border, where almost anyone could witness their exchange of rings. It was a convenient tactic for the poor of northern England and the fashionable and daring of the entire nation, although the ceremony was of questionable validity once the couple returned.[53]

Once married, a woman became a ghost or shadow— present yet not present—in the eyes of the courts. Accord- **Legal Rights** ing to Sir William Blackstone, it was simple: "[I]n marriage **of Wives** husband and wife are one person, and that person is the husband" with "the very being, or legal existence, of the woman . . . suspended during marriage."[54] All her property and debts at marriage became her husband's, as well as any wages she earned or property she acquired thereafter. Nothing in her husband's home, not even her own undergarments, technically belonged to her, nor could she give anything away or bequeath anything in a will without his consent. Her children were his to dispose of as he pleased; she had no legal right over their education, housing, or marriages. If her husband accused her of adultery and sued her lover for damages, she was barred from testifying or from calling witnesses in her own behalf. There was no such thing as marital rape under the law; a man was entitled to have sex with his wife whenever he chose. He could send her to a private madhouse. He could confine her to her home against her will. He could beat her as long as he used a stick no bigger in circumference than his thumb, hence the phrase "rule of thumb." Women could "pray the peace" against their husbands for repeated and particularly vicious attacks, putting them on a kind of probation, though this recourse was seldom used. Women could also ask for a separation on the grounds of cruelty, though the suit could be denied if they had offered any provocation, disobedience, or bad temper at any time in the marriage, and even if granted, a separation would have condemned most women to abject poverty.[55]

As always, there was a gap between theory and practice. Certainly there were men who used every legal inequity at their disposal, but not every husband did so. Cautious and wealthy women could have property settled on them before marriage by placing it in a trust. Others knew the value of their wage labor to family survival and exploited that advantage.[56] Neighbors intervened when men beat their wives, shaming the abusers with public processions and chants, or simply stopping a beating, as a saddler did in 1703. "God damn you what makes you here?" the abusive husband, Mr. Austin, demanded. "Because you shall not beat your wife," replied the saddler.[57] Sometimes, men simply loved their wives and treated them kindly. One has only to look at the epigraph to this chapter to see that the worst-case scenario is not the only scenario.

Opinions of Marriage   The most typical attitude toward marriage evinced in 18th-century literature and visual art is a sly, collegial misery. Shrewish wives and oafish husbands are a dime a dozen.

One author compares jail favorably to marriage, noting that while he was in the Bridewell he was untroubled by the demands of his "freakish wife" and "lawless brats."[58] A similarly bitter tone can be found in the works of female authors, such as Hetty Wright, who calls wedlock

> Thou source of discord, pain and care,
> Thou sure forerunner of despair,
> Thou scorpion with a double face,
> Thou lawful plague of human race,
> Thou bane of freedom, ease and mirth.

The "wretch," she wrote, "if such a wretch there be,/Who hopes for happiness from thee,/May search successfully as well/For truth in whores and ease in hell."[59] Typical of the period's satirical attitude toward marriage is Matthew Prior's "A Reasonable Affliction," in which the dying Lubin and his wife both weep for different reasons: "Poor Lubin fears that he will die, His wife, that he may live."[60]

Nevertheless, there were plenty of happy marriages. One town held an annual competition in which the happiest couple was awarded a flitch of bacon. And shopkeeper Ignatius Sancho, writing to a friend, called his wife Anne "the treasure of my soul" and added, "I am not ashamed to own that I love my wife—I hope to see you married, and as foolish."[61]

DIVORCE AND SEPARATION

Happy couples had no need of an escape, but unhappy ones felt keenly the permanence of an English marriage. Divorce was possible by private act of Parliament, but getting such an act passed could be difficult, time consuming, and expensive; this method was therefore reserved for the very rich and very determined. Only thirteen such divorces were granted between 1700 and 1749. Although the numbers rose in the second half of the century, successful petitions never exceeded ten per year. Women could not sue for divorce themselves, nor was a husband's adultery grounds for divorce. In fact, as procedures evolved, a husband's adultery could scuttle the divorce by seeming to provide a cause for the wife's own adultery, and only an unprovoked, marriage-ruining, inheritance-

3.2 "Courtship and Marriage," c. 1745. This print, which can be read right-side-up or upside-down, illustrates the satirical view of marriage found throughout the century. Courtesy of the Print Collection, Lewis Walpole Library, Yale University.

threatening act of betrayal by the wife was grounds for divorce.[62] Often, the divorce act was preceded by supporting maneuvers, like a legal separation or a civil suit for damages against the wife's lover, known as a "criminal conversation" or "crim. con." suit. Once a divorce was granted, both parties were free to remarry.[63] In fact, it was not unknown for husbands and wives to collude in the wife's adultery, either to collect a large crim. con. settlement or to secure a divorce.[64] A few couples in the second half of the century took advantage of the nullification provisions of Hardwicke's marriage act. They simply called attention to mistakes or lies about age in their marriage licenses, which automatically voided their marriages, no matter how much time had passed.[65]

Either as a prelude to a divorce petition or as an end in itself, some couples sought a judicial separation from an ecclesiastical court or

3.3 "The Pleasures of Matrimony," Thomas Colley, 1773. A positive, some-what sentimentalized view of family life shows the mother playing with an infant while the father reads to his son. The intimate touches in the picture—the baby reaching into her mother's bosom, the boy resting casually against his father's leg—suggest a close, companionate family, and the badminton equipment on the floor implies that the children are well supplied with toys. Courtesy of the Print Collection, Lewis Walpole Library, Yale University.

drafted a private separation agreement themselves (with a trustee acting for the wife, since, as a married woman, she was legally incapable of entering into a contract). A separation did not allow partners to remarry, but it did get them into separate houses. A judicially separated wife was entitled to alimony but was still subject to all the legal penalties of married women and could not borrow money, buy property, or sign contracts on her own. Moreover, it was not a quick process. An undefended judicial separation took from four to nine months to resolve, and a contested one took much longer.[66] The incentive for husbands was that children conceived after a judicial separation were deemed illegitimate and unable to inherit the husband's estate, whereas children conceived after a private separation were deemed legitimate.[67]

A private agreement could be concluded more quickly and discreetly and often contained clauses protecting the wife from certain kinds of harassment by the husband. It could also be negotiated for any reason, whereas a judicial separation was granted only on the grounds of adultery or cruelty. Private agreements generally granted the wife alimony and released the husband from responsibility for her debts, granting her some limited control over her own property. Each party had to pledge a bond of some kind to be forfeited if the agreement were broken. After the establishment of separate homes, the wife had to continue to be on her best behavior, lest her husband take custody of her children and cease paying her maintenance allowance. The husband, however, could continue to commit adultery without any penalty.[68]

For those who could not afford lengthy legal proceedings, there were few options, and no respectable ones. Divorce would not become a legal alternative for the majority until 1857. In the meantime, the working classes found their own ways around the law. Some, often with the community's tacit consent, moved apart and took up with new partners. If community approval was not forthcoming, some simply abandoned their old families and contracted bigamous marriages in other towns. Bigamy was, until the 1790s, a hanging offense, but convicted offenders could claim benefit of clergy, which mitigated the sentence to branding on the thumb, and frequently the branding iron was never even heated. In the last decade of the century, the punishment was changed to seven years' transportation without benefit of clergy, and enforcement became more vigorous.[69]

One way of gaining the community's acknowledgement and support for a marital breakup was to conduct a symbolic sale of the wife. Such sales were rare—only ninety-one were recorded between 1730 and 1799[70]—and not a legal means of divorce, but in working-class society they served as de facto divorces, allowing the spouses to set up new households with the permission of their peers. The husband brought his wife to a marketplace in a rope halter and paid a toll for her, as one would pay for a beast brought to market. The husband or another individual served as auctioneer, elaborating on the wife's virtues to potential buyers, or detailing her faults as a means of humiliating her. When someone (often the wife's lover) bought her, the halter was transferred to the new "owner" to symbolize that he was now the woman's husband and responsible for her debts and maintenance. Then the parties and their friends might go to a tavern together to celebrate, and the "former" husband might even give his "former" wife a present to start her in her new life.[71]

SEX AFTER MARRIAGE

There was a great deal of frankness about sexual desire. Married women made sly jokes, read sex manuals like *Aristotle's Masterpiece*, and held impotent husbands in high contempt. Men read pornographic journals like *Rangers Magazine*, and both sexes perused the scandal columns of *Town & Country Magazine*, which detailed the adulteries of hundreds of famous men. Crowds of women gathered at a popular swimming spot to watch the men cavort in the nude.[72] Nevertheless, the later years of the century saw a growing interest in modesty. Nude bathing was denounced, togas were put on statues, and etiquette books called for more reticence about sex, especially from women. After the novel *Tristram Shandy* linked winding the household clock with conjugal pleasures, a clockmaker protested, "The directions I had for making several clocks for the country are countermanded; because no modest lady now dares to mention a word about winding-up a clock, without exposing herself to the sly leers and jokes of the family."[73]

When sex within the marriage grew wearisome or impossible, some people engaged in adultery. A woman in such a position could expect little sympathy in a society that considered her body the property of her husband. Dr. Johnson, even in the case of a woman who turned to a lover after the repeated and continual cruelty of her husband, concluded, "the woman's a whore, and there's an end on't."[74] In 1768 Johnson elaborated on his views:

> Confusion of progeny constitutes the essence of the crime; and therefore a woman who breaks her marriage vows is much more criminal than a man who does it. A man, to be sure, is criminal in the sight of GOD; but he does not do his wife a very material injury, if he does not insult her; if, for instance, from mere wantonness of appetite, he steals privately to her chambermaid. Sir, a wife ought not greatly to resent this. I would not receive home a daughter who had run away from her husband on that account. A wife should study to reclaim her husband by more attention to please him.[75]

The woman is at fault if she commits adultery, if her husband commits adultery, or if she leaves him because he committed adultery. This was the reaction of the majority, not merely Johnson. Plenty of prominent men openly kept mistresses and supported whole families of illegitimate children. Some wives were mortally offended but kept silent, others no doubt objected in some way, while still others greeted the adultery with relief because it freed them from the sexual demands of an unloved husband and the possibility of getting pregnant.

Later in the century, fidelity became more fashionable, due in part to the example of George III. Unlike his predecessors, he was faithful, loving, and happily domestic. Threat of punishment deterred other would-be adulterers. In the working class, adulterers who carried on shamelessly might find themselves the target of a "skimmerton" or "skimmington," a noisy shaming parade that called attention to their transgression and warned them to stop. The skimmerton participants might carry a petticoat to symbolize a woman or horns to symbolize cuckoldry.[76] In the middle class, a cuckold might formulate his own revenge, as a Banbury man did when he found his wife in flagrante delicto in 1751. He

> got assistance and took them out of bed, and tying their arms together set them before a large fire, and had tea, coffee and punch

provided; then he went to invite his neighbours, to whom he exposed his wife and her gallant for some hours to their extraordinary mortification, while the husband appeared perfectly contented.[77]

Among the wealthy, there was the "crim. con." suit, in which the husband sued the seducer for violating the husband's "property." There were fewer than twenty such cases per decade until the 1760s, when the numbers rose to a peak of seventy-three cases in the 1790s, partly because a lawsuit was an attractive alternative to a duel, partly because it could support a petition for a Parliamentary divorce, and partly because damage awards rose into the thousands of pounds.[78] Adultery was also technically a misdemeanor, and prosecutions continued in Scotland throughout the century, but in England no one was punished under this law after 1746.[79]

PROSTITUTION

Many men chose to get their sexual gratification from prostitutes, who were denounced by doctors, besieged to reform by religious activists, and defended by some as being the safety valve that protected respectable women's virtue. There were more than 10,000 prostitutes in London, most of them in their teens. Sometimes, women who were temporarily unemployed took to prostitution to tide them over.[80] In novelist and magistrate Henry Fielding's view, poverty was the only reason they took to the streets. "Who can say these poor children had been prostitutes through viciousness?" he asked. "No. They are young, unprotected and of the female sex, therefore they become the prey of the bawd and the debauchee."[81]

Prostitutes plied their trade throughout the city, but they were especially numerous near Covent Garden, Drury Lane, Charing Cross, the Strand, and Fleet Street. Displaying themselves in windows and doors, or wandering in groups of five or six, they accosted passersby, saying, "Come, my lord, come along, let us drink a glass together," or "I'll go with you if you please," or, after the publication of *Tristram Shandy*, "Sir, will you have your clock wound up?"[82] Prices ranged from about sixpence to six guineas, and the variety staggered one foreign traveler, who said you could have women

> got up in any way you like, dressed, bound up, hitched up, tight-laced, loose, painted, done up or raw, scented, in silk or wool, with or without sugar, in short, what a man cannot obtain here, if he have money, upon my word, let him not look for it anywhere in this world of ours.[83]

Some offered their services in rooms or brothels; others worked in alleys, coaches, or wherever the customer wanted. Boswell "picked up a strong,

3.4 "The Country-Man in London," John Collet, A. Bannerman, 1771. A bumpkin is being fleeced by two prostitutes. One offers him punch while the other steals his purse. Pictures on walls in eighteenth-century engravings often make a symbolic comment on the main action; this one shows a sheep being shorn. Behind the pickpocket is a bawd with one finger to her eye, a gesture of shrewdness and lewdness that also appears often in such engravings. Courtesy of the Print Collection, Lewis Walpole Library, Yale University.

jolly young damsel" and had sex with her on the newly opened Westminster Bridge: "The whim of doing it there with the Thames rolling below us amused me very much."[84] For those with very particular tastes, there were specialty brothels and guides to London's prostitutes.

CONTRACEPTION

It was mostly to avert sexually transmitted disease that prostitutes and their clients adopted a new form of contraception, condoms, known to Boswell as "armour" and to Casanova as "English overcoats." Made of sheep's intestines, they were washed, dried, softened by being rubbed with bran and almond oil, and tied at one end with ribbon.[85] Although they were of dubious effectiveness, they were no worse than most of the other methods available—coitus interruptus (a notoriously unreliable approach), abstinence (effective but hard to sustain), and lactation (somewhat effective, but of no use to the many women who did not nurse

their own babies). Some women, who were unmarried or simply unwilling to risk the very real dangers of childbirth, resorted to chemicals
and plant extracts, like wormwood, saffron, hyssop, ergot, pennyroyal,
and savin, in hopes of aborting a fetus. Some believed that drinking
heavily or being bled in the feet would do the trick.

If these remedies failed, one might wait until the baby was born and
then kill it, or find a local woman willing to induce an abortion surgi-
cally. Grace Belfort, in 1732, paid Eleanor Beare 30s. for an abortion. The
two got drunk on "Cyder and Brandy." Then Beare put a skewer-like
instrument into Belfort's body "a great Way." There was pain, blood,
and the next day a miscarriage; later Belfort testified against Beare, and
Beare was twice pilloried and pelted by the crowd with so much food
and garbage that blood was drawn.[86]

HOMOSEXUALITY

The same vicious antipathy shown to abortionists was also offered to
homosexuals. When suspected, they were exposed to hostility and ridicule in skimmertons. When found out, their careers and reputations were
ruined; actor Samuel Foote and playwright Isaac Bickerstaffe were both
punished this way. When convicted, they were attacked in the pillory
and sometimes even killed there.[87] On at least one occasion, a wife whose
husband had been found guilty of attempted sodomy was granted a
separation on the grounds of cruelty.[88]

Despite these obstacles, there was a definite gay presence in 18th-
century England. Special brothels and clubs served gay men, who called
themselves "mollies" and "queens" (both terms for female prostitutes),
gave themselves female pseudonyms like "Princess Seraphina" and
"Garter Mary," called each other "Madam" and "Your Ladyship," held
mock weddings and lyings-in, and addressed each other as women, saying "Where have you been, you saucy Queen?" or "If I catch you stroll-
ing and caterwauling I'll beat the milk out of your breasts, I will so."[89]
There were also lesbians, who attracted attention primarily when they
tried to marry other women. The actress Charlotte Charke traveled with
another actress whom she called her wife. Another lesbian, Ann Marrow,
was pilloried in 1777 for dressing as a man and marrying three women;
the pelting was so furious that she was blinded in both eyes.[90]

CHILDREN

A woman's lying-in, or labor, was a busy affair. The mother-
to-be had perhaps prepared for the occasion by sewing a slice **Infancy**
of witch-elm into her petticoat, or by securing an "eagle-
stone,"a hollow rock with rattling fragments inside, both believed to be
good luck in labor.[91] Anesthetized only by liberal quantities of alcohol,

she was attended by relatives and by a midwife or doctor, who might or might not have washed their hands before reaching into the birth canal. Once the baby was born, it was often fed liquor, or a "comforter" of butter and sugar.[92] When mother and child were well enough, the former returned to society by being churched, and the latter was introduced to society by being christened.

The baby's nourishment might come from several sources. In well-off families, particularly in the first half of the century, it was likely to be turned over to a wet nurse, a servant whose one qualification was an abundant supply of milk. In richer families, the wet nurse lived in the baby's family home; in middle-class families, the baby lived with the wet nurse until weaned. Samuel Johnson was sent out in this way as a baby, and his mother made frequent, regular visits to see him.[93] A wet nurse might also be used by a working mother who could not bring her baby to work with her.[94] From the middle of the century, however, there was an increasing tendency for even middle- and upper-class women to nurse their own babies, and late-century dresses for such women had vertical slits to allow easy access to the nipple.[95] Mother's milk was inefficiently supplemented with pap (bread or flour soaked in milk, water, or beer) and possets (moistened flour and sugar, sometimes flavored with extracts of almonds or violets). Babies were fed with pewter or wooden pap bowls and spoons, or a pewter or ceramic cone called a "bubby-pot" with a linen-covered sponge at the end to serve as a nipple or

> a small polished cow's horn which will hold about a gill and a half. The small end of it is perforated and has a notch round it to which are fastened two small bits of parchment shaped like the tip of the finger of a glove and sewed together in such a manner as that the food poured into the horn can be sucked between the stitches.

The cow's-horn device required food to be diluted so much that children simply became bloated without being adequately nourished.[96]

Attitudes Toward Children Prior to the 18th century, children were viewed as small, unruly adults. This perception was reflected in their "literature" (Bible stories and tales of witches and demons designed to frighten them into docility), the ferocious chastisements to which they were subjected, and their clothes, which were almost exactly like those of adults. During the 18th century, however, there was an increasing tendency to view childhood as a special state of innocence, during which children could be molded and shaped by love and education. During the second half of the century, there were ample signs that things were changing. The increase in maternal breast-feeding was one example of a more hands-on approach to parenting. Fathers and mothers proudly played with their children and commissioned more

3.5 "Mr. Deputy Dumpling and Family Enjoying a Summer Afternoon," Bowles and Carver, 1781. The mercantile vulgarity of the Dumplings is being satirized, but the affection of the parents for their children is evident nonetheless. The father carries the youngest, while the elder two play with a wagon and doll. Courtesy of the Print Collection, Lewis Walpole Library, Yale University.

portraits of them, and children began addressing their parents by informal, affectionate names like "mama" and "papa." Children, especially younger children, were given nicknames like Sukey and Jackee, and were dressed in looser, less formal clothes. Discipline in many families became less harsh, even lax.[97]

Still, it is possible to overemphasize the revolution in attitudes. Even early in the century, fondness for one's children was considered natural. Joseph Addison wrote in 1711 that "Of all Hardnesses of Heart, there is none so inexcusable as that of Parents toward their Children. An obstinate, inflexible, unforgiving Temper, is odious upon all Occasions, but here it is unnatural."[98] Hetty Wright wrote a poem, "To an Infant Expiring the Second Day of Its Birth," in 1728, in which she murmurs,

> Ere the long-enduring swoon
> Weighs thy precious eyelids down;
> Oh! regard a mother's moan,
> Anguish deeper than thy own!

Later in the poem, she begs, "Let me be/Partner in thy destiny!"[99] Some historians have emphasized parental detachment from their children in the early part of the century, but Wright's agony sounds like anything but detachment.

Also, whether early or late in the century, some families were simply dreadful. Parents had near-total control over their children and took full advantage of it. The actress Fanny Kemble was imprisoned in a shed for a week as punishment for misbehavior, and Francis Place was beaten until the stick broke. Susanna Wesley, mother of Methodist preachers Charles and John, bragged that her children "when turned a year old (and sons before) . . . were taught to fear the rod, and to cry softly." Many parents still expected silence and unquestioning obedience, and many children still regarded their parents with respect or fear rather than warmth.[100] In poorer families, children were put to work by age four or five. They helped with laundry, farm chores, textile work (like spinning and carding wool) done at home, factory work, and shopkeeping. London's urchins worked as crossing sweepers or chimney sweeps. Some children had teeth sold to make dentures for the rich. Some were abandoned or orphaned and turned to prostitution and thievery. The revolution in attitudes toward childhood was a slow and gradual one indeed, for it was accompanied by an acceptance, even an enthusiasm, for child labor. Jonas Hanway, a reformer who took up the causes of workhouse infants and chimney sweeps, was revolted by families who sought charity when they had children from ages eight to fourteen who were earning no wages.[101] Dan Tucker, in 1758, wrote that Birmingham button factories, by hiring children, saved "80 or even 100 *per cent*" while training "Children to an Habit of Industry, almost as soon as they can speak."[102]

Childish Things   There were special activities and products for children. Oral tales of fairies, Will o'the Wisp, and other folk creatures were supplemented by children's books, a whole new genre created by publisher John Newbery. Children's songs and rhymes included variations of rhymes still familiar today, like "Hush-a-bye baby, on the tree top," "Lulliby Baby Bunting," "Jack and Gill" (an early illustration shows both these characters as boys), "Bah, bah, black sheep," "Old King Cowl was a jolly old soul," "High diddle,

diddle, The Cat and the Fiddle," "London Bridge," and "Hickere, Dickere Dock."[103] Some bore familiar names but had more sinister lyrics, like this rhyme from about 1744:

> Sing a Song of Sixpence,
> A bag full of Rye,
> Four and twenty
> Naughty boys
> Bak'd in a Pye.[104]

Others are less familiar today, like "Wide-Mouth Waddling Frog."[105] The purposes of these songs, however, were the same as today—to entertain and to calm children. The latter purpose is evident in a direction that follows a version of "Baby Bunting": "*Encore 'till the Child's asleep.*"[106]

Parents also bought toys for their children, including rattles, small tops called tetotums, dolls, wagons, and sports equipment. Children also made up their own amusements. They played hoops, trap-ball, and barley-break. Bad little girls called names and pulled off visitors' wigs; good little girls practiced milking the cow or "dressed Babies [dolls], acted Visitings, learned to Dance and make Curtsies."[107] Bad little boys threw snowballs at coachmen; good little boys played football or cricket.[108] Play, in short, was one part mischief, one part organized game, and one part pretending to be an adult—in preparation for courtship, the marriage market, and founding a family of one's own.

TIMELINE

1712	Marriages within the Fleet Prison are banned by Parliament, which makes the jailer subject to a £100 fine for each infraction. The trade in clandestine marriage accordingly moves outside the prison to the buildings nearby.
1748	William Cadogan publishes *An Essay upon Nursing*, an influential work encouraging women to breast-feed their own babies.
1753	Hardwicke's marriage act passes Parliament.
1765	James Fordyce publishes *Sermons to Young Women*. It chides women who attempt strenuous exercise, abstract thought, public service, or business, granting them instead the qualities of "complacence, yieldingness, and sweetness" and the "empire" of love "secured by meekness and modesty."

1778	The House of Commons bans women spectators from its debates.
1792	Mary Wollstonecraft publishes *A Vindication of the Rights of Woman.*
1857	Divorce is legalized in England.[109]

4

"The Supreme City": London

I have often amused myself with thinking how different a place London is to different people. . . . A politician thinks of it merely as the seat of government in its different departments; a grazier, as a vast market for cattle; a mercantile man, as a place where a prodigious deal of business is done upon 'Change; a dramatick enthusiast, as the grand scene of theatrical entertainments; a man of pleasure, as an assemblage of taverns, and the great emporium for ladies of easy virtue. But the intellectual man is struck with it, as comprehending the whole of human life in all its variety, the contemplation of which is inexhaustible.

—James Boswell, *Life of Johnson*, 1791

What the Revd. Thomas Gisborne called "the supreme city" was, by today's standards, a middling metropolis, home to about half a million people in 1700, to 900,000 in 1801, and to a bit more than 10 percent of England's population as a whole. By 18th-century standards, however, it was a giant—a magnificent Colossus or a ravening monster, depending on one's biases—vastly larger than any other town in the nation. Its closest competitor in 1801 was Liverpool, with only 78,000 residents.[1] Daniel Defoe thought it surpassed any human settlement in history, "except old Rome in Trajan's time."[2] Josiah Tucker thought it "no better than a wen"—a huge wart on the face of England.[3] For better or worse,

London remained the center of England's political, financial, commercial, cultural, and intellectual life.

London dazzled the visitor with its sheer size and variety. There were glass-fronted shops crammed with merchandise, bustling docks forested with towering ships' masts, ferries, brothels, heavy and perilous shop signs, hospitals, hundreds of coffee houses,[4] hundreds of taverns, thousands of alehouses and brandy shops,[5] three synagogues, and 300 churches with their spires rising high above the other structures.[6] There were houses whose upper stories jutted out over the streets (at times nearly meeting the upper stories of the homes across the way). There were dozens of markets, including Billingsgate for fish and coals, Covent Garden and the Stocks for vegetables, Leadenhall for meat and leather, Smithfield for livestock, Bear Key and Queenhithe for grain and meal, and a host of others for hay, cherries, apples, and cloth.[7] There were also fairs, circulating libraries, and above all the great cathedral of St. Paul's whose huge dome dominated the London skyline.

Then there were the people: servants running errands, sedan chairmen carrying wealthy passengers, pickpockets, footpads, prostitutes, beggars, ballad sellers, rioters, country squires in town on business, lawyers, craftsmen, doctors, booksellers, printers, and footmen clinging to rattling carriages. There were milkwomen, town criers, knife grinders, boys gambling at dice, and street vendors crying their wares—fish, oysters, apples, oranges, nuts. Tinkers wandered through the streets calling for pots to mend. Carters drove through the streets cursing pedestrians who got in their way, bouncing on rutted streets past communities of Welsh, Cornish, Irish, black, Huguenot, German, Swiss, and Jewish Londoners.

London had an abundance of everything, from traffic to culture to filth. It had newspapers, art exhibitions, freak shows, streets full of sewage and horse dung and butchers' offal, hundreds of hackney coaches for hire, 15,000 street lamps,[8] cattle and sheep being driven to market, and skies almost perpetually full of rain or coal smoke. Sunny days were rare enough in the metropolis to create a holiday spirit. At times the skies were night-dark as early as 10 A.M.; soot fell in the rain, and the stench of the city could carry, with the right wind, for miles.[9] The city was noisy, dirty, smelly, crowded, and deadly. Diseases, particularly the ubiquitous "fevers," spread rapidly, and for much of the century deaths exceeded births,[10] though immigration from the countryside continued to raise the population.

STREET CONDITIONS

The streets were atrocious in the first half of the century, full of dust in dry weather and mud in wet, with puddles and small streams collecting in the centers. These streams were augmented by dirtied water tossed by maids from the upper stories, by gutters that ran directly onto the streets and pavements,[11] and by rainstorms, which carried into them "Sweepings from butchers' stalls, dung, guts, and blood, / Drowned puppies, stinking sprats, all drenched in mud, / Dead cats and turnip tops."[12] The streets were dirtied not only by horse manure but also by human waste, particularly from beggars and children who urinated and "cacked" next to buildings.

In the 1760s the streets improved from atrocious to merely bad. A series of acts of Parliament shifted the responsibility for paving from individual householders to regional commissions, which replaced the pebbles found in most streets with paving stones, raised the centers of streets and built gutters to improve drainage, removed hazards and traffic obstructions, and arranged for regular street cleaning. Dangerous shop signs were abolished, and houses were eventually numbered.

Contributing to the disarray of the streets was, ironically, the earnest effort being made to improve the delivery of water. Water was pumped from the Thames through wood (later iron) pipes about six inches in diameter that were joined with iron unions and which led to public pumps or to the lead plumbing of private houses. Houses with this service paid 12s. a year at mid-century for water, which ran only three times a week. Even this was enough to reduce George Keate to breathless raptures about "the astounding supply of water . . . even to profusion!—the superflux of which clears all the drains and sewers, and assists greatly in preserving good air,—health,—and comfort!" The wooden mains, however, lasted only a few years and leaked vigorously under the best conditions, so they created mud, required frequent repairs, and had to be replaced every four years.[13]

If visitors to London were impressed by its indoor plumbing, they were dazzled by its street lights, which helped to prevent accidents and robberies. London, while not brilliantly illuminated—in 1765 its lights made the sidewalks visible but "convey[ed] to the middle of the street only a glimmering"—was better-lit than most European cities. Initially houses were required to provide lantern light on moonless winter nights; these horn candle-lanterns were eventually replaced by oil lamps and reflectors and maintained by a company under contract to provide light till about midnight. In 1736 the period of lighting was extended to sunrise. Those who felt the need of additional light would hire torch-bearing link boys to see them home.[14]

THE THAMES

Through all the filth, smoke, noise, excitement, crime, and growth wound the Thames, London's great waterway, running from the western countryside all the way to the sea in the east. Trout, shad, lampreys, eels, flounder, salmon, and even a few sturgeon swam in its waters, which were wider and shallower than today.[15] When it froze, as it did occasionally in the 18th century (and never afterward due to man-made adjustments to the water's flow), "frost fairs" were held on the ice, with booths, streets, games, and roasted meat, to celebrate the spectacle of the Thames "in icy fetters bound."[16]

When not held prisoner by ice, the Thames was the greatest roadway of the town, alive with ships bearing ivory, oil, wine, tobacco, rice, indigo, cotton, grain, furs, hemp, tallow, coal, iron, and lumber. There were slave ships, small boats carrying fish to the Billingsgate market, passenger ships, and cargo ships. Swiss visitor César de Saussure claimed that "the Thames below the bridge is almost hidden by merchant vessels from every country."[17] Because the river grew shallower to the west, bigger ships docked in the east, at Woolwich, Blackwell, and Deptford, and transferred their cargo to smaller boats to be carried farther upstream. These small craft, along with large ships capable of navigating farther, traveled west through Wapping, past Execution Dock (where pirates were hanged and chained in place till three tides had covered them),[18] and past the vast yards of shipbuilders, mast makers, rope makers, and sail makers, to the Lower Pool, by Wapping New Stairs. Middle-sized ships could continue to the Middle Pool, between Wapping New Stairs and Union Hole, and the smallest ships could dock in the Upper Pool, between Union Hole and London Bridge, an area designed to hold 500 ships but often harboring as many as 1,800.[19] On the north side of the river, between the Tower and London Bridge, lay the Custom House and the legal quays through which all goods entering the city had to pass. Here were customs officers, porters, watchmen, and thieves, all plying their trades among the warehouses, stairs, docks, and barges.

For the first half of the century, London Bridge was the only bridge across the river. Crowned with shops and houses, and adorned below with a huge waterwheel and piers that posed a serious hazard to watermen, it was low enough to the water to prevent high-masted ships from proceeding upriver. In addition to being the principal connection between the City and Southwark, it was one of London's most fascinating sights, 915 feet long, 45 feet wide, with a 31-foot central roadway for carriages and pedestrian walkways on either side.[20] It was insufficient to handle the growth of the metropolis, however, and those who chose not to take the bridge were forced to take the horse ferry between Westminster and Lambeth (which moved horses, coaches, and people alike) or to hire one of the nearly 40,000 watermen who rowed passengers up, down, and across the river. A passenger would descend one of the many sets of stairs to the Thames, perhaps clutching a rate map showing charges to each destination. He was then beset by competing watermen "calling out lustily, 'Oars, oars!' or 'Sculler, sculler!' " When one boat was chosen,

4.1 "The South West Prospect of London. From Somerset Gardens to the Tower," drawn by T. Bowles and T. Melish, engraved by Bowles. The Tower, London Bridge, and the Monument are all visible, but it is St. Paul's that dominates the skyline. Courtesy of the Print Collection, Lewis Walpole Library, Yale University.

the other watermen "at once unite[d] in abusive language at the offending boatman." The passenger would then be rowed to another set of stairs somewhere along the river. The boats, usually red or green, were equipped with awnings for summer and heavy tents for rain, and capable of seating six.[21]

The system as it stood could not last. Boats were so numerous that at times they jostled each other in the water. London Bridge was picturesque but also hopelessly impractical. Change came when Westminster Bridge, begun in 1739, opened for traffic in 1750 and put the old horse ferry out of business. It became a popular site for pleasure strolls, though its pedestrian alcoves, designed as rain shelters, proved too hospitable for footpads and were later demolished.[22] The structures atop London Bridge were removed, and in 1769 Blackfriars Bridge opened just west of the City, about midway between the other two bridges.

THE CITY

Central London—the City—was divided into twenty-five wards. Each ward was divided into parishes and governed by an alderman, who served for life, and a Common Council, annually elected from members of the ancient City livery companies. The twenty-five aldermen, together with the Lord Mayor, made up London's Court of Aldermen; the 234 councillors made up the Court of Common Council. The aldermen, generally wealthy merchants and bankers, could veto acts of the lower house, and there was considerable friction between the two groups. City government controlled ports, markets, the metropolitan coal trade, and even a private militia.[23] However, it did not govern outlying areas, such as Chelsea, Paddington, and Marylebone, and, indeed, by 1800, its resi dents were only one tenth of the total metropolitan population.[24] The suburbs, including Westminster, had their own governments.

The old City still maintained some vestiges of its walled medieval past. Seven ancient gates still stood; Lud Gate and New Gate on the western side served as prisons. They overlooked what remained of the stinking, fetid Fleet River, now called Fleet Ditch, where the poor hunted for dog carcasses to skin.[25] The Fleet was crossed near Lud Gate and New Gate by a pair of bridges, the Holborn Bridge to the north and the Fleet Bridge to the south. In 1735 this area, known as Ditchside, was paved over and a market was built atop it, leaving only a small stretch exposed. This last bit was covered, from 1760 to 1768, by a road raised on arches, the New Bridge Street, which formed the approach to Blackfriars Bridge.[26]

Near Newgate was the Old Bailey. East of Lud Gate, on Ludgate Street, was the brand-new St. Paul's Cathedral, the tallest building in London and "the beauty of all the churches in the city, and of all Protestant churches in the world."[27] Rebuilt after the Great Fire at a cost of more than £700,000, it reopened in 1697 and was finished in 1710; for a fee, known as "stairs-foot money," one could climb to the dome for a breathtaking view of the metropolis.[28] A block to the north, in Paternoster Row, book publishers like Thomas Longman set up shop.[29]

The center of the City was London's mercantile heart. Between St. Paul's in the west and London Bridge in the east were the Guildhall, where the election for Lord Mayor and drawings for the lottery took place;[30] Queenhithe Market; and one of the City's biggest tourist attractions, the Monument to the Great Fire, a pillar surmounted by an urn.[31] The chief commercial street, Cheapside, was full of dazzlingly lit shops and ran east from St. Paul's where it became Poultry Street. In the middle of Poultry, on the northern side, the street of Old Jewry (often referred to as Old Jury) held the Excise Office and the Grocers Hall, where the Bank of England had its first home. Daniel Defoe found the Bank a modern marvel: "Here business is dispatched with such exactness, and such expedition and so much of it too, that it is really prodigious. . . . No accounts in the world are more exactly kept, no place in the world has so much business done, with so much ease."[32] The bank was, indeed, so exact and expeditious that it soon outgrew its Grocers Hall quarters and moved to Threadneedle Street.

Threadneedle was the northernmost of three streets that spread like fingers, or the forks of a trident, from the east end of Poultry. On the southern side of this intersection stood a flower and vegetable market, which was cleared in 1738 to make way for the Mansion House, the residence of London's Lord Mayor. Along the three radiating roads—Threadneedle to the north, Cornhill in the center, and Lombard to the south—was the financial heart of the City. Here was the Royal Exchange between Threadneedle and Cornhill, which Joseph Addison said made "this Metropolis a kind of Emporium for the whole Earth."[33] On Lombard stood Edward Lloyd's coffeehouse, where the City's marine insurers gathered, and where *Lloyd's List and Shipping Gazette*, and the famous Lloyd's insurance company, were founded. In the 1770s Lloyd's moved to nearby Pope's Head Alley, between Cornhill and Lombard, and thence into the Royal Exchange. Also between Cornhill and Lombard lay Change Alley, where Jonathan's coffeehouse housed the newborn Stock Exchange.

In the eastern third of the old walled City, the principal east-west streets were Leadenhall, Fenchurch, Tower, and Thames. The Hall of the Ironmongers Company, one of the City livery companies, stood in Fenchurch, while Leadenhall was home to the East India Company's headquarters, which Defoe called "an old, but spacious building; very convenient, though not beautiful."[34] At the southeastern corner of the City, right on the Thames, stood the Tower of London, which housed the Crown jewels, the Mint, a menagerie that at various times included a hyena and a grizzly bear, and the occasional execution.

The Tower, open for tours to the paying public, was already militarily obsolete, as were the walls and gates it anchored. In the 1760s, with the walls crumbling, the city spreading rapidly beyond its old boundaries, and the proliferation of carriages perpetually stalled at the gates' old-fashioned portcullises, the City received Parliamentary permission to tear down the last of the medieval barricades. Newgate remained the site of a prison, but the gate itself was destroyed. Only Moorgate remained in service, after a fashion: its stones were sunk in the Thames to strengthen the supports of London Bridge.[35]

Working-class suburbs expanded north of the old Moor Gate. Thousands of watchmakers congregated in Clerkenwell.[36] In Smithfield was the market for livestock and, in summer, Bartholomew Fair. St. Giles was notoriously poor and gin soaked. Moorfields was the home of Bethlehem Hospital, a lunatic asylum known colloquially as "Bedlam," hence the origin of our word for noisy chaos. In Moorfields, too, was the Methodist preacher John Wesley's headquarters from 1739 to 1778. Preferring to preach to the working class rather than the rich, Wesley also had a chapel in Spitalfields, known particularly for its thousands of Huguenot silk weavers. All in all, the northern suburbs were unfashionable; when David Garrick referred to one of his female characters as "warm from Spital-fields," his audience knew to expect vulgarity.[37]

THE EAST AND SOUTH

Things only got worse, from a snob's perspective, as one headed east. The East End held narrow lanes, slums, shops, foreigners, and the unsightly industries that helped make London productive. Whitechapel had a noted bell foundry, the London Hospital, and most of London's 20,000 Jews. South of Whitechapel were St. Katharine's and East Smithfield, with their breweries, starch and sugar works, and descriptively named side streets: Harebrain Court, Money Bag Alley, Hog Yard, Black Dog Alley, and Butcher Row. Growth was concentrated along the riverside, in Wapping, where the smell of pitch filled the air;[38] along the Ratcliff Highway farther inland, where sailors, whores, pawnbrokers, shipbuilders, glassmakers, gunpowder manufacturers, and porters congregated; in Shadwell, where lay the ominous-sounding Cutthroat Lane; and in Bromley, Limehouse, and Poplar.[39] A 1763 commentary called the area a haven for "dissolute sailors, blackmailing watermen, rowdy fishermen, stock-fish hawkers, quarrelsome chairmen, audacious highwaymen, sneak-thieves and professional cheats . . . footpads, deserters, prisoners of war on parole, bravos, bullies and river vultures."[40] North of the waterfront and well east of the City were Bethnal Green and Mile End, where lime kilns and a bowling green could be found. Farther out still were Hackney, Old Ford, and Stratford—more respectable, certainly, than Wapping, but still worlds away from London's most fashionable districts.

Development south of the Thames was similarly concentrated around the riverbank, in Deptford, Bermondsey, and Rotherhithe, which suffered, like the East End, from an industrial reputation. They had various types of shipbuilding yards as well as oil, dye, and soap manufactories.[41] The Southwark-Lambeth area had its own fair; its own hospital, Guy's (founded in 1725); several prisons, including King's Bench and the Clink; and plenty of industry—timber yards, breweries, dyeworks, and vinegar manufactories. Farther to the southwest, Lambeth had Vauxhall Gardens, one of the premier pleasure spots of the day, which feature refreshments, music, quaintly artificial landscaping, fountains, eclectic buildings, and animated clockwork pictures: 18th-century England's answer to Disneyland.

COVENT GARDEN, THE STRAND, FLEET STREET

It was London's West End, however, that saw the most prodigious growth in the 18th century. This growth was helped by a fortunate series of partnerships between developers and aristocratic landlords, by the West End's proximity to parks and Parliament, and by the perception that the best and most fashionable people already lived there. The *World*, in 1787, reported that "No family of ton [fashion] can breathe eastward of Berkeley Square; and Turnham Green, Finchley, and Barnet are considered within the smoke of London."[42]

4.2 "A General Prospect of Vaux Hall Gardens," drawn by Wale, engraved by I. S. Muller, after 1751. An 1800 "spiritual barometer" ranked attendance at the gardens as equivalent in sinfulness to "frequent parties of pleasure; home of God forsaken; much wine, spirits, etc." Courtesy of the Print Collection, Lewis Walpole Library, Yale University.

Dividing the vulgar air of Cheapside from the glorious atmosphere of Berkeley Square was perhaps the most interesting section of 18th-century London: the area containing the Strand, Fleet Street, Covent Garden, and Holborn. It was mercantile and intellectual all at once. Here were the Inns of Court, taverns like the Devil and the Turk's Head, and the haunts of Oliver Goldsmith, Sir Joshua Reynolds, James Boswell, Joseph Addison, Sir Richard Steele, Alexander Pope, Jonathan Swift, Thomas Gray, Sir Isaac Newton, and the naturalist Sir Joseph Banks. There were printers in Fleet Street, booksellers and chic shops in the Strand, and traffic in Charing Cross. The Adam brothers' magnificent Adelphi Terrace adorned the waterfront. There were exhibitions of all kinds in Leicester Square and at Exeter Change in the Strand, and theaters in Covent Garden and Drury Lane. Furniture maker Thomas Chippendale had workshops in Long Acre, on the north side of Covent Garden, and in St. Martin's Lane, by Charing Cross.

On the western end of this area, William Hogarth showed his paintings.[43] Henry Fielding loved this part of the city, where "you may be alone and in Company at the same time," and Charles Lamb felt that "[t]he man must have a rare recipe for melancholy, who can be dull in

4.3 "A View of Covent Garden London," T. Bowles, 1751. showing the fruit and vegetable market and the arcades (pillared walkways). Much of the new construction in the West End resembled Covent Garden in structure, with a group of buildings clustered around a central square. Courtesy of the Print Collection, Lewis Walpole Library, Yale University.

Fleet Street."[44] However, the area as a whole, especially Covent Garden, grew increasingly seedy late in the century.[45]

TIIE WEST END

To escape the streetwalkers, taverns, sideshows, and shops, the fashionable fled west—to Bloomsbury's Soho, Brunswick, Tavistock, and Bedford Squares. Designed to attract the rich and titled, Bloomsbury instead appealed to the merely well off, as well as radicals, intellectuals, and artists. Carlisle House, where hostess Theresa Cornelys held fashionable musical festivities, lay in Soho Square, as did Sir Joseph Banks' home-cum-scientific salon-cum-museum, and Bloomsbury's Montagu House, formerly a private residence, opened in January 1759 as the new home of the British Museum.[46]

To the northwest, Marylebone began to follow the Bloomsbury example, and cheap houses for the middle class began to multiply north of Oxford Street. Two of the earliest projects were Portman Square and Cavendish Square; in the latter, "frightened sheep . . . with sooty faces and meagre carcasses," intended as faux-rural decorations, trembled at the approach of each carriage.[47] Also in Marylebone were Harley and Wimpole Streets, which, late in the century, became the preferred addresses for physicians. Not far away lay Baker Street, home of Pitt the Younger, actress Sarah Siddons, novelist Edward Bulwer-Lytton, and explorer Sir Richard Burton.[48] Where Dorset Square is now, the earl of Winchilsea headed the best local cricket team at the Marylebone Cricket Club. Yet Marylebone remained second class among the great West End developments.

South of Marylebone, it was another story altogether. Mayfair and St. James's, the gems of the West End, attracted those with taste, connections, and money. Splendid townhouses and wide streets fronted the squares, while stables and tradesmen's shops clustered less grandly in the back streets. In Mayfair, Hanover Square, home to a number of generals, was developed in 1714. Berkeley Square joined it in 1737; Clive of India died there, and George Frideric Handel wrote the *Messiah* nearby.[49] Also built in 1737, six-acre Grosvenor Square was the largest in London. It housed aristocrats, potter Josiah Wedgwood's state-of-the-art showroom, and at least one royal mistress. Laurence Sterne, Lord Nelson, and Lord Byron all lived at one time or another in Mayfair's Bond Street.[50]

St. James's Square had the advantage of being situated right next to a royal palace and park. Surrounded by St. James's Street in the west, Piccadilly in the north, the Haymarket in the east, and Pall Mall in the south, St. James's housed the dukes of Ormonde, Chandos, Dorset, Kent, Norfolk, Portland, and Southampton, as well as lesser nobility. Prime Ministers Sir Robert Walpole and Lord North, as well as Parliamentary demagogue Charles James Fox, lived nearby.[51] Even the businesses were high-end: gentlemen's clubs like White's, Boodle's, Brooks's, and Almack's; the Haymarket Opera House; the upscale grocers and tea dealers, Catheral and Butcher; and James Christie's auction house. South of St. James's, along the river, lay the houses of Parliament.

Still farther south lay Chelsea, home of the Chelsea Waterworks, the pleasure garden of Ranelagh with its huge rotunda, and Perrott's Luminous Amphitheatre, where one could observe a show of fountains and mirrors while consuming "as good Liquor as can be procur'd."[52] It was also the site of two of London's most famous eating places: Don Saltero's, a coffeehouse and curio museum, and the Chelsea Bun House, home of what Swift called "Rrrrrrrrrare Chelsea buns."[53]

Compared to its modern size, 18th-century London was quite small; it had not yet engulfed suburbs like Hampstead, Highgate, Kentish Town, Islington, and Camden Town. Yet the pace of its growth was sufficient to impress Horace Walpole, who wrote in 1791 that "Hercules and Atlas could not carry anybody from one end of this enormous capital to the other."[54] Poet James Bramston, in 1729, marveled at the furious expansion of the West End:

4.4   "The South East Prospect of Westminster. From Somerset House to the Westminster Bridge," engraved by Thomas Bowles, 1750. The new bridge is visible, as are the copious Thames boat traffic, Westminster Abbey, and the countryside in the distance. Courtesy of the Print Collection, Lewis Walpole Library, Yale University.

> Pease, cabbages, turnips once grew where
> Now stands New Bond Street and a newer square;
> Such piles of buildings now rise up and down,
> London itself seems going out of town.[55]

And for every cynic who could gaze at the skyline and conclude that "the gay town looks like the mouth of hell,"[56] there was an enthusiast like Charles Lamb, who reveled in

> The Lighted shops of the Strand and Fleet Street, the innumerable trades, tradesmen and customers, coaches, waggons, playhouses, all the bustle and wickedness round about Covent Garden, the very women of the Town, the Watchmen, drunken scenes, rattles,—life awake, if you awake, at all hours of the night, the impossibility of being dull in Fleet Street, the crowds, the very dirt & mud, the Sun shining upon houses and pavements, the print shops, the old book stalls, parsons cheap'ning books, coffee houses, steams of soups from kitchens, the pantomimes, London itself a pantomime and a masquerade,—all these things work themselves into my mind and feed me . . . and I often shed tears in the motley Strand from fullness of joy at so much in life.[57]

Perhaps the most balanced view came from John Bancks, who presented a mélange of sights and sins in his 1738 poem "A Description of London." After mentioning, with little elaboration, the city's houses, churches, dirty streets, mercantile wealth, shallowness, rogues, women, lords, prudes, coaches, prisons, palaces, and much more, he challenges his reader to make an independent judgment, as we, more than two hundred and fifty years later, must do also.

> Many a beau without a shilling,
> Many a widow not unwilling;
> Many a bargain if you strike it:
> This is London! How d'ye like it?[58]

TIMELINE

1697	St. Paul's Cathedral is opened for services.
1702	London gets its first daily newspaper, the *Daily Courant*.
1704	Westminster hires the Conic Lights Company to handle its street lighting.
1710	St. Paul's is completed.
1712	A well-to-do band of young ruffians, the Mohocks, terrorizes the town for several weeks, assaulting men and women after dark.
1714	Hanover Square is built.
1717	Cavendish Square is built.
1723	The Chelsea Waterworks Company is established.
1726	The East India House is built at Leadenhall and Lime Streets.
1732	10 Downing Street becomes the prime minister's residence.
1735	The Fleet River is covered between Holborn and the Fleet Bridge.
1736	Street lighting is extended until sunrise.
1737	Berkeley Square, Grosvenor Square, and the Fleet Market are built.
1739	Construction begins on the Mansion House and Westminster Bridge.

1746	The Chelsea Waterworks Company installs London's first iron water main.
1747	The Fleet Ditch is completely covered over.
1750	Two minor earthquakes cause panic and minor damage in London.
	Westminster Bridge opens.
1753	The Mansion House is completed.
1759	The British Museum opens at Montagu House in Bloomsbury in January.
1765	Josiah Wedgwood's showroom opens in Grosvenor Square; later, it will move to Greek Street and thence to St. James's Square.
1767	London houses are first numbered.
1769	Blackfriars Bridge opens.
1774	The Thames rises and floods Westminster.
1776	Bedford Square is built.
1777	Finsbury Square is begun.
1789	The Haymarket Opera House burns down.
1798	The Thames Police are established to patrol wharf areas.

5

"They Were, Once, a Kind of Barbarians": The Provinces

It is scarce half a century ago, since the inhabitants of the distant counties were regarded as a species, almost as different from those of the metropolis, as the natives of the Cape of Good Hope. Their manners, as well as dialect, were entirely provincial; and their dress no more resembling the habit of the Town, than the *Turkish* or *Chinese*. But time, which has inclosed commons, and ploughed up heaths, has likewise cultivated the minds, and improved the behaviour of the ladies and gentlemen of the country.

—George Colman, 1761

A number of factors contributed to the progressive homogeneity of British, and especially English, culture. Newspapers and novels spread ideas and mores. Mobility blurred regional differences, as landed gentry migrated between their country estates, London, and holiday spots like Bath and Brighton. Workers moved, too, to London, provincial cities, mill towns, or neighboring villages in search of jobs. Servants of the rich might travel with them, or accompany an employer's married daughter to her new household. Men (and the occasional disguised woman) joined the army, navy, or militia, and traveled around the country or the world. Others traveled to harvest crops or dig canals.

Provincial towns sprouted civilizing institutions that mimicked London's: pleasure gardens, libraries, theaters, bookstores, coffeehouses, hospitals, and scientific societies. London fashions appeared in country villages and market towns, albeit with some delay, and ladies newly arrived from the metropolis were apt to sneer at a hat or hoop a year out of date.

English daily life was slowly becoming more unified, but regional idiosyncracies remained. Weights and measures still varied from one region to another. Work conditions and wages still varied widely, with wages being generally higher in the south and east. Britain had a multitude of accents, dialects, and even languages. Cornish was still spoken in parts of the far southwest until about 1780,[1] and Welsh and Gaelic were still in common use in areas outside England. Most residents of the Isle of Man spoke their own language, Manx, as well.[2]

THE SOUTHWEST

Cornwall held tin, copper, and lead mines, china clay quarries, and pilchard and herring fisheries. It was a haven for smugglers, who made use of its isolated coastal areas.[3] Its few sizeable towns included St. Ives, the far-west town of Penzance, and Falmouth, which Defoe called "by much the richest, and best trading town in this county." Defoe also noted that the local men were renowned wrestlers, famous for "that closure, which they call the Cornish Hug," and expert at the game of "Hurlers," which he called "a rude violent play among the boors, or country people; brutish and furious, and a sort of an evidence, that they were, once, a kind of barbarians."[4]

Devonshire produced cider and salmon,[5] but it was best known for its manufacture of wool and worsted cloth. Devon's cloth manufacture suffered later in the century, however, as the West Riding of Yorkshire came to dominate the trade. Like Cornwall, Devonshire had a reputation for isolation and rurality, and Defoe admitted that it seemed, "at first sight, a wild, barren, poor country."[6] In Sheridan's *The Rivals*, the bumpkin squire Acres has his home, Clod Hall, in Devon.[7] But it was busy enough in some places. Plymouth, for example, was a significant port.

Devon was bordered on the east by two counties, Somersetshire to the north, and Dorsetshire to the south. Somerset grew gradually rather than rapidly, but it was quick to invest in important institutions. It had the first provincial hospital, built in 1735, and one of the first provincial newspapers, the *Bristol Postboy*, founded in 1702.[8] Defoe found the county's dialect laughable, citing a schoolboy's rendition of Song of Solomon 5:3 ("I have washed my coat, how shall I put it on, I have washed my feet, how shall I defile them?"): "Chava doffed my cooat, how shall I don't [don it], chav a washed my veet, how shall I moil 'em?"[9] He had respect, however, for the county's industries—the manufacture of the eponymous cheese at Cheddar, the production of cloth, and the breeding of large cart and coach horses and "[f]at oxen . . . as large, and good, as any in England."[10]

Two of Somerset's prized jewels were Bristol and Bath. Bristol, a busy port, had hundreds of shops, a 600-title subscription library,[11] almost 200 clock and watch makers,[12] and a large trade in sugar, tobacco, and wine.[13] Its near neighbor, Bath, was a town for pleasure. Its nominal attraction was its mineral spa, but it also offered concerts, assemblies, promenades, billiards, and gambling. Nurtured by the gentlemanly master of ceremonies, Richard "Beau" Nash, Bath attracted as many as 12,000 visitors a year at mid-century.[14] Bath's population sprang from fewer than 3,000 in 1700 to almost 35,000 in 1800, and the architects John Wood senior and junior rebuilt it in neoclassical style at a cost of nearly £2 million.[15] Most who braved the forty-hour ride from London found Bath's diversions pleasant enough, but many were repulsed by the dirtiness of the baths themselves, or were bored by the regimented and proper entertainments. Elizabeth Montagu expressed the boredom with morbid accuracy, "The only thing one can do one day that one did not do the day before is to die."[16]

Dorset had nothing to compare to Bristol or Bath. Primarily agricultural, it was chiefly noted for its oysters, marble, paving stone, mackerel, stockings, and sheep.[17]

THE SOUTH

Continuing east, the inland county of Wiltshire contained "that celebrated piece of antiquity, the wonderful Stone-Henge"[18] and Salisbury, whose cathedral was noted for the exceptional height of its spire. Like most important provincial towns, Salisbury acquired a hospital (1766) and a paper, the *Salisbury Journal*.[19] The Wiltshire Downs, originally dedicated to grazing sheep, were eventually converted into grainfields.[20] Other products of Wiltshire included a "soft and thin" cheese, bacon, barley for malt, mediocre steelwork, and cloth.[21] The last industry, like most of the southern textile trade, lost ground later in the century to the booming towns of the north and Midlands.[22]

South of Wiltshire, and east of Dorset, lay the coastal county of Hampshire. It held the city of Winchester and the ports of Southampton and Portsmouth, but it was mostly rural, famed for its sheep and bacon. North of Hampshire and east of Wiltshire was the small county of Berkshire, whose river workers harvested crawfish and carried malt and meal to London.[23]

East of Hampshire was another coastal county, Sussex. Its industries resembled Hampshire's: farming, tea smuggling, and logging.[24] An offshoot of its timber industry was charcoal making, which until at least the 1770s was scattered at various small sites in the forested area known as the Weald.[25] Because of its access to charcoal, the Weald was also a desirable area for iron foundries, and it was one of the last regions to make the shift from charcoal to coal in blast furnaces.[26] One of its towns was Brighton, in Defoe's day "Bright Helmstone, commonly called Bredhemston, a poor fishing-town, old built."[27] Between the Seven Years' War and the early 19th century, it became a fashionable seaside resort. At first the town's Dr. Russell advised invalids to drink seawater, but the emphasis quickly shifted to bathing in the sea. At the turn of the century, Brighton would also be the beneficiary of the prince regent's preferences, and it was he who would erect its famous Pavilion.[28]

Inland of Sussex was Surrey, its northern reaches bumping against metropolitan London itself. This proximity to the City made Surrey attractive to Londoners in search of the suburban cottages known satirically as "country boxes."[29] Summer visitors swelled the spa town of Epsom, with businessmen installing their families there for the season and joining them on the weekends. There were horse races at Epsom Downs, a large market for oats at Croydon, and another at Darking (Dorking) for poultry.[30] Surrey also had one of the country's notorious "pocket boroughs," the town of Gatton, which sent a representative to Parliament despite having only six houses and one eligible voter.[31]

Kent occupied England's southeast corner. It was a prosperous county with some manufacturing: iron works, papermaking, and the shipbuilding trades in and near Chatham. Here, with more than a thousand shipbuilders on call, the Royal Navy made, stored, and maintained its anchors, sails, cables, ammunition, weapons, and masts, the last stored "sunk in the water to preserve them."[32] What little textile manufacture existed in Kent was to falter over the course of the century,[33] but the area was famous for its produce and natural resources—apples, oysters, timber for ships' masts, white sand for glassmaking, paving stones, hops, cherries, mackerel, and huge red bullocks "with their horns crooked inward, the two points standing one directly against the other."[34] Like most coastal counties, Kent had a lively smuggling trade, landing tea, wine, brandy, pepper, coffee, tobacco, and calico cloth from Holland and France, and launching cargoes of illegally exported wool, a practice known as "owling."[35] The county had a few popular resorts, including the seaside town of Margate and the spa of Tunbridge Wells, popular for its "company and diversion," its "liberty of conversation," and its "gaming, sharping, intriguing; as also fops, fools, beaux, and the like."[36]

THE WELSH BORDER

These, then, were all the counties south of London. England's western counties, those that bordered on Wales, were Gloucestershire, Herefordshire, Shropshire, and Cheshire. Gloucestershire, the farthest south, manufactured a great deal of cloth.[37] Its other products included sheep, stockings, soft cheese, and bacon.[38] Chief among its cities were Gloucester, which had a hospital (1755), a newspaper, a population of from 5,000 to 7,000, a renovated marketplace, and a state-of-the-art jail (1792);[39] Cirencester and Tetbury, the foci of the wool trade;[40] and Cheltenham, a spa town developed late in the century. North of Gloucestershire was Herefordshire, which remained culturally almost as much a Welsh as an English county.[41] So, too, did its northern neighbor Shropshire, which had a variety of industries: grazing, farming, weaving, and iron smelting. The principal city, Shrewsbury, boasted a library, a hospital, and nearly three hundred shops.[42] The northernmost county on the Welsh border was Cheshire. Its staple products—salt, stockings, ale, and Cheshire cheese—did well enough, but its main port, Chester, gradually filled with silt. It was the textile industry that turned it from a sparsely populated county—92 people per square mile in 1700—into one almost twice as crowded.[43]

EAST ANGLIA

On the opposite side of England were Essex, Suffolk, and Norfolk along the coast, and Hertfordshire and Cambridgeshire inland. Essex had a good deal of textile manufacturing early in the century, although this industry eventually declined a good deal, leaving many villages virtually abandoned.[44] Essex harvested fish and oysters along the coast, grazed sheep in the fall to sell in London in winter, and, late in the century, developed a stocking-knitting industry.[45] Suffolk produced sailcloth, wool, and turkeys.[46] It also, near Woodbridge, produced "the best butter, and perhaps the worst cheese, in England."[47]

Norfolk, like most of the southern and eastern counties, had high wages,[48] but its chief industry, worsted spinning and weaving, suffered from the emergence of northern textile manufacture. Fortunately, it had plenty of other products: sailcloth, sheep, grain, turkeys, geese, native black cattle and imported Norfolk-fed Scottish cattle called "Scots runts," lobsters, salt, chairs, and shoes.[49] Norfolk's towns included the ancient town of Norwich. Though Arthur Young, in 1771, called its commercial activity "neither brisk nor very dull,"[50] it had the first provincial newspaper, the *Norwich Post*, a theater that could seat more than a thousand, a hospital, and fifty-three grocers and tea dealers, including one Edward Eagleton, whose stock of tea on hand totaled more than a ton. In an era when many dealers carried only a few pounds of tea at a time, he must have had quite a shop.[51] Norfolk had other busy towns, like the port of Yarmouth. Located near a dangerous stretch of coastline, Yarmouth had "no less than four light-houses kept flaming every night," though the frequent failure of such measures was revealed by the fact that nearby barns, sheds, stables, fences, hogsties, and outhouses were typically constructed from ship wreckage.[52]

Norfolk shared with its western neighbor Cambridgeshire the marshy area known as the fenland. Thinly populated and even desolate in places, Cambridgeshire was almost wholly agricultural, raising grain and ducks, and suffering heavily from enclosure.[53] It actually lost population during the century.[54]

THE MIDLANDS

Between the western counties and East Anglia were the counties known collectively as the Midlands: Oxfordshire, Buckinghamshire, Bedfordshire, Worcestershire, Warwickshire, Rutland, Northamptonshire, Huntingdonshire, Staffordshire, Derbyshire, Leicestershire, Nottinghamshire, and Lincolnshire. The area as a whole was noted for its grainfields, coal mines, and lawless forest regions. As the century passed, there was increased grazing of livestock, particularly cattle. Canal development, a supply of willing labor, and the weakness or absence of restrictive guilds and town corporations made it attractive to industry late in the century; wages and population rose.[55]

Though these trends affected the Midlands in general, each county was distinctive. Oxfordshire had a university and a hospital in Oxford, and fine steelworkers in Woodstock made top-quality scissors, buckles, and watch chains.[56] Buckinghamshire made lace, felt, and plaited straw goods; transported malt and meal, and built "country boxes" for Londoners.[57] Bedfordshire, too, had rural mini-estates; the fictional Robinson Crusoe bought a home there. It produced lace, baskets, bricks, eggs, and geese.[58] Worcestershire excelled in manufacturing gilded china.[59] Northamptonshire had a famous horse market, a vigorous shoe-making industry, a newspaper, and noteworthy production of eggs, wool, and geese.[60]

Warwickshire more than doubled its population density, from 112 to 236 people per square mile between 1700 and 1801.[61] Much of this was due to the extraordinary success of Birmingham and its outskirts. A mere village in 1700, Birmingham grew to about 37,000 in the early 1770s and became the first provincial city to exceed 50,000 around 1780.[62] Buoyed by its manufactures of toys, buttons, shoes, buckles, guns, clock parts, knives, scissors, and other metalwork, Birmingham, nicknamed the "Toy-Shop of the World," acquired a library (1779), a hospital (1766), a respected scientific club called the Lunar Society, and a lively theatrical tradition.[63]

Shoes and pottery were made in Staffordshire. Josiah Wedgwood's china works were located there. Towns included Lichfield, the childhood home of Samuel Johnson and a place "much famed for ale,"[64] and the fast-growing town of Wolverhampton, where furnaces, engines, and forges announced the advent of the machine age with "pulsations loud" and "[d]eep, sullen sounds."[65] Derbyshire made richly colored porcelain,[66] but its phenomenal growth was due more to the textile mills that grew like weeds from its riversides. Thomas Lombe built a six-story silk mill there in 1719, powered by a twenty-three-foot waterwheel and employing hundreds of workers to mind its 26,000 spindles.[67] Cotton mills came later. In the Peak District, in the northern part of the county, there were lead mines and a newborn tourist industry, as travelers came in search of romantic scenery not too far from civilized comforts.[68] Derbyshire also had its requisite spa town, Buxton, which was for most of the century difficult to reach, dirty, uncomfortable, and altogether "a *shocking* place."[69]

Leicestershire was notable among the Midland counties for its resistance to modernization. Reaction to mechanization of worsted spinning in the ancient town of Leicester led to riots, smashed machinery, and at least one death.[70] Leicester was also virtually alone among the larger towns in its refusal to lobby Parliament for an improvement act to modernize its streets, sanitation, and lighting.[71] As southern counties shifted production from livestock to grain, Leicestershire shifted from grain to livestock, raising sheep to be sent south and fattened for London consumers.[72]

Nottinghamshire proved more receptive to mechanization than Leicestershire. It had a great deal of framework knitting, as well as cotton mills, worsted spinning, and some agriculture.[73] Nottingham built a theater in 1769[74] and a hospital in 1782, but it failed to build enough new housing on the outskirts of the town, resulting in noxious slums.[75] Near Nottingham was the village of Gotham, famous as a proverbial hometown of fools. A children's rhyme, first recorded around 1765, tells a typical tale:

> Three wise men of Gotham,
> They went to sea in a bowl,
> And if the bowl had been stronger
> My song had been longer.[76]

The agricultural county of Lincolnshire derived little benefit from industrialization. In fact, unlike most of the Midlands, it lost population during the century and suffered badly during periods of enclosure. The town of Lincoln itself doubled in size over the course of the century, but in 1801 it still had only 7,000 residents. In the 1780s, a customs officer new to the town could still call it "the meanest city this day in all England."[77]

THE NORTH

Directly north of the Midlands lay Lancashire and Yorkshire. Beyond these two were Durham and Northumberland on the east coast and Westmorland and Cumberland on the west coast. The mountain range known as the Pennines ran approximately north-south through this area, crossing several county lines, and lending its slopes and swift streams to tourism and the textile industry alike.

Lancashire grew like mad when its faltering agriculture was replaced by booming cotton mills—forty of them in South Lancashire alone in 1788. Workers from nearby counties, and from Scotland and Ireland as well, thronged to the mills. Though Lancashire was known principally for its textile mills, it was also noted for its religious diversity—the largest Catholic population of any county and a large and visible Dissenting presence—and for the musical societies of its weavers.[78] It also had plenty of other industries, including china manufacture, watchmaking,[79] and the activity of its ports, especially Liverpool, which dealt heavily in human flesh. Liverpool embarked half of all England's slave ships and, in 1771 alone, launched 107 slave ships as compared to London's 58.[80] Trade across the Atlantic in general enriched Liverpool, enabling it to build new docks, a library (1768), a hospital (1745), a new lunatic asylum, and a new jail.[81] Manchester, too, grew quickly. Its paucity of water power to run mills was overcome by the advent of steam power, and in the second half of the century it acquired a Literary and Philosophical Society, a theater, and a hospital of its own (1752), making Lancashire one of the few counties in England with more than one hospital.[82] Between 1765 and 1792, Manchester also installed street lighting and established a police force.[83] A 1795 poem calls it a "Fine town, fine town—full, full of trade and riches," and a good source for leather breeches.[84]

The development of Lancashire was matched by that of Yorkshire, a large county divided into East, West, and North Ridings. Yorkshire prospered from coal, iron, a little agriculture, a fair amount of tea smuggling along the coast, and especially wool and worsted cloth. As in Lancashire, wages and population rose quickly. The standard institutions followed: libraries in Leeds (1768), Sheffield (1771), Bradford (1774), and Hull (1775);[85] newspapers like the *Leeds Mercury*; hospitals in York (1740), Leeds (1767), and Hull (1782); and specialty shops. York had 486 shops in 1785 (not counting those with rents under £5); its shopkeepers in 1797 included an optician, four china dealers, eleven wine and brandy merchants, two whip makers, three tobacconists, three jewelers, four stay makers, and seven perfumers and hairdressers.[86] Harrogate had a mineral spa but little in the way of entertainment beyond country dancing and few amenities even at the baths. Tobias Smollett's *Humphry Clinker* describes one bath as "a dark hole on the ground floor, where the tub smoaked and stunk . . . a dirty bed provided with thick blankets, in which I was to sweat after coming out of the bath."[87]

Westmorland and Cumberland were sparsely populated counties principally famed for being the home of the picturesque Lake District. Westmorland produced rugs and stockings,[88] while Cumberland was best known for its coal. Durham and Northumberland on the west coast had similar industries, and it was here that coal was shipped in huge quantities from Newcastle.

THE REST OF BRITAIN

Of Ireland, Scotland, and Wales, it was Wales that was most completely integrated with England, but even Wales was quite separate in some ways. It was extraordinarily rural, with its largest city in 1700 housing just 4,000 inhabitants, and overwhelmingly Welsh speaking: three-quarters of the nation would still be speaking Welsh as their first language in the 1880s.[89] Wales remained a region of small towns and villages throughout the century, its industries largely restricted to agriculture, tourism in "the most ravishing prospects possible to be conceived by man,"[90] and mining or smelting of copper, coal, iron, and tin. There was some infiltration of English society and politics by Welsh gentry, but not enough to frighten the English too badly, and thus prejudices against the Welsh tended to be rather milder than those against the Scots and Irish.

By contrast, prejudices against the Scottish had a vicious tone, due in part to the shorter tenure of the English-Scottish connection. A Scottish Stuart king, James I, had inherited the English throne in 1603, but the Act of Union joining Scotland to Great Britain took place only in 1707. Thereafter, Scottish troops twice attempted to invade England to replace a Stuart monarch on the throne. There were, therefore, hostile feelings on both sides of the border, especially in northern England and southern Scotland, where most of the actual fighting took place. The English answer to the second invasion was to suppress Scots culture as fiercely as possible, banning the kilt and discouraging the speaking of Gaelic.[91]

There was hostility to Scotland for other reasons as well, not least of which was that the Scots were moving to England in large numbers and daily demonstrating the superiority of their educations. Scotsmen invaded the military, government, engineering, medicine, education, and the arts, excelling in each field and worrying a good many Englishmen who saw themselves losing absolute control of power and culture alike. This fear accounts for the vitriolic nature of the attacks in prints, pamphlets, and plays: according to these sources, Scotsmen were power hungry, greedy, stingy, nepotistic, ragged and starving, tyrannical in the upper class and slavish beneath, and—a sure sign of English insecurity— sexually prodigious.[92]

Ireland was even more thoroughly despised than Scotland. It, too, sent emigrants to England to work, especially in the northern textile towns, and their presence was anathema to the English. In Ireland itself, Catholics were barred from the Parliament, absentee landlords funneled Irish rents back to England, and the continuing and significant presence of English troops made it clear that Ireland was an occupied nation.[93] The Irish were mocked for their accent and accused of drunkenness and violence.

Britain, then, was hardly a fully integrated whole but, rather, a collection of cooperating parts. Even within England alone there were strong regional differences. While London manners, fashions, accents, and entertainments were widely imitated, each area of the country helped to define what it meant to be English.

6

"Up to My Knees in Brick and Mortar": Housing

Every man now, be his fortune what it will, is to be doing something at his place, as the fashionable phrase is, and you hardly meet with anybody who, after the first compliments, does not inform you that he is in mortar and heaving of earth, the modest terms for building and gardening. One large room, a serpentine river, and a wood are become the absolute necessities of life, without which a gentleman of the smallest fortune thinks he makes no figure in his country.
—Daniel Defoe

I was bewitched to build a house!
Better in Thames my cash to souse:
Up to my knees in brick and mortar,
And work myself like any porter!
My builder charge at such a rate
Above his given estimate!
'Twas first, "Good sir, I'll never dun ye"
And now 'tis—"Zounds, I'll have my money!"
—John O'Keeffe, "I Want a Tenant: A Satire," 1791

Eighteenth-century English architecture was desperate to imitate. The only question was what to copy—the flowery embellishments of the Baroque, the pared-down Italian classicism of Andrea Palladio, a dressed-up Greek classicism with more urns and garlands and columns, the lacquer and painted porcelain and pagodas of the Chinese style, the medieval past of England itself, or the dictates of nature? Each of these philosophies had its heyday, and the styles overlapped each other to some extent.

Generally speaking, however, the Baroque was ousted in about 1715 by Palladianism, which dictated that a room be a perfect cube or, in the case of a long room, a pair of cubes, twice as long as it was high and wide. The facade of the building, door frames, chimneypieces, wall moldings, staircase balusters, and windows imitated as much as possible the proportions of a classical column or temple front. The facade, for example, had taller windows and ceilings on the lower floors, and vertical columns of windows separated by rows of brick or stucco, implying a pattern of columns and voids even when actual columns were absent. Inside, the lower moldings and dado rail on the wall imitated the pedestal of a temple front; the space above the dado rail represented the column; and the picture rail, frieze, and cornice, the temple entablature.[1]

The Palladian style was succeeded by the neoclassical, which emphasized Greek ornament, domed rotundas, top-lit staircases, ovals, curves, festoons, scrollwork, doors and fireplaces topped by triangular carved pediments, and more imitations of temple fronts.[2] Both Palladian and neoclassical architecture lent themselves beautifully to the construction of town houses. Sometimes a street would be built with a perfectly uniform row of homes, sometimes with a "palace-fronted" terrace, in which the ends, intermediate units, and grand center of the row were somewhat different but formed an aesthetic whole.[3]

Developing alongside the Palladian and neoclassical styles were two other traditions, one imported and one home grown. The import was chinoiserie, a taste for all things Chinese which asserted itself in railings, chairs, bed frames, lacquerwork, and ceramics. Near its height in the 1760s, James Cawthorn wrote,

> Of late, 'tis true, quite sick of Rome and Greece,
> We fetch our models from the wise Chinese:
> European artists are too cool and chaste,
> For Mand'rin only is the man of taste.[4]

The home-grown fad, the Gothic, became popular at about the same time, though the first fake Gothic ruin was built much earlier, in 1721.[5] Imitating, with only the faintest sense of accuracy, Europe's medieval buildings, the Gothic style featured ruins (genuine or new), vaulted ceilings, ogees (S-shaped curves), and quatrefoil (clover-shaped) or pointed windows. Most famous of all the Gothic dwellings, perhaps, was Horace Walpole's Strawberry Hill, a house he modified between 1749 and 1796 into "a little Gothic castle" with a cloister, gallery, tower, and fan-vaulted gallery.[6] (For an example of Gothic details, see the Bagnigge Wells gates in Illustration 3.5.)

OLD HOUSES in the BUTCHER ROW

The right hand corner house in this view (which stood on the east side of S.t Clements lane, near Clements Inn, and was taken down 30. March 1798) has been suggested to have been the House in which the horrid conspiracy to destroy the King and his Children and Parliament, by Gun powder, was determined upon and sworn, and that a book intituled "The Gun powder Treason" prefaced by ___ Bishop of Lincoln, (reprinted 1679) identified it as such ___ but on respect to this sugges= tion "it appears, on referring to the book, that the conspirator Thomas Winter, confised that Catesby, Percy, Wright, Guy Faux and himself met merely "behind Saint Clements" (without any farther description of the place), where they administered to each other the oath of secrecy, and after received the sacrament "in the next room". On this ground therefore, the identity of the House is still uncer= tain, and the above houses are inserted only as curious specimens of ancient modes of building in the metropolis

Pub. Aug. 10. 1791. by N. Smith, Rembrandts Head, 18 Mays Buildings, S.t Martins Lane & I.T. Smith, 40, Frith Street, Soho.

6.1 "Old Houses in the Butcher Row" (1798) shows the type of haphazard, top-heavy building that the unified Georgian squares tended to replace. Courtesy of the Print Collection, Lewis Walpole Library, Yale University.

By the end of the century, these styles were being replaced by a more organic style. Grand outdoor staircases designed to lower the occupants from the first floor (the *piano nobile* to the Palladians, the second floor to Americans) to ground level were replaced by rooms opening directly onto the lawns or gardens. Asymmetric country houses began appearing from the 1790s, and between about 1750 and 1780, yielding to the vision of landscape gardener "Capability" Brown, formal gardens thick with topiary, flat lawns, and mazes were replaced by natural-looking (but still highly cultivated) serpentine paths, ponds, trees, and rolling hills.[7]

THE COST OF HOUSING

To diarist and biographer James Boswell, "seeking a lodging was like seeking a wife. Sometimes I aimed at one or two guineas a week, like a rich lady of quality. Sometimes at one guinea, like a knight's daughter; and at last fixed on £22 a year, like the daughter of a good gentleman of moderate fortune."[8] A good two-story brick cottage could be bought for about £150; a cellar or garret could be rented for about 1s. 6d. a week in London.[9] On the upper end of the spectrum, the earl of Leicester built Holkham Hall for £90,000, and the marquis of Rockingham paid £83,000 (plus £5,000 per year in maintenance) for Wentworth Woodhouse.[10]

In London, a 1774 building act delineated between various classes of housing. It divided all residential dwellings into first-, second-, third-, and fourth-rate houses based on the size, cost, and construction of the house.

Table 6.1
House Rates

Rate	Cost	Size in Squares*
First	£850 or more	9 or more
Second	£300–£849	5 to 9
Third	£150–£299	3½ to 5
Fourth	less than £150	fewer than 3½

Note: *A "square" was 100 square feet at the main entrance level.[11]

THE MIDDLE-CLASS HOUSE

Houses of artisans, merchants, shopkeepers, and professionals varied in size, cost, and style. Some people lived in town houses—fresh new terraces with shared walls, or antique top-heavy half-timbered survivors that looked as if they intended to climb onto the roofs across the street. Others built "country boxes" and commuted to the city; such suburban residences were much ridiculed for their tiny gardens, poor views, lack of privacy, and half-hearted imitation of squires' country estates.

Still, a few generalizations can be made. First, there was a gradual change over the course of the century in the types, usage, and arrangement of rooms. This was especially true among the rich, but the middle class imitated the wealthy in having some rooms for guests—a drawing room, for example, or a parlor, or a guest ("state") bedroom—and some that were just for family and servants. In *The Clandestine Marriage*, for example, Mrs. Heidelberg expects company and has her servant Trusty "Get the great dining room in order as soon as possible. Unpaper the curtains, take the civers off the couch and the chairs, and put the china figures on the mantle-piece immediately." Clearly, this is not a room in everyday use. Similarly, Dr. Johnson recalled that his father's contemporaries "had no fire but in the kitchen; never in the parlour, except on Sunday. . . . They never began to have a fire in the parlour, but on leaving off business or some great revolution of their life."[12]

Isaac Ware described the layout of a typical town house at mid-century:

> The general custom is to make two rooms and a light closet on a floor. . . . The lower storey is sunk entirely under ground, for which reason it is damp, unwholesome, and uncomfortable. . . . The front room below in London is naturally the kitchen; the vaults run under the street with an area between, in which is to be a cistern or other vessel for holding water. . . . In common houses the fore-parlour is the best room upon the ground floor: the passage cuts off a good deal from this, and from the back parlour, this usually running straight into the opening, or garden as it is called, behind. . . . The first floor consists of the dining-room, over the hall or parlour; a bed-chamber over the back parlour, and a closet over its closet. . . . In houses something better than the common kind, the back room upon the first floor should be a drawing-room, or dressing room. . . . The two rooms on the second floor are for bed-rooms, and the closets being carried up thus far, there may be a third bed there. . . . Over these are the garrets, which may be divided into a larger number than the floor below, for the reception of beds for servants. . . . This is the common construction of a small London house, for the reception of a family of two or three people, with three or four servants.[13]

The "closets" Ware mentions were not used to store clothing. An 18th-century closet, or cabinet, was a small private office, used to store personal papers, diaries, books, memorabilia, trinkets, and collections of small objects. The kind of house that Ware describes would also have had "two staircases, one for shew and the use of company, the other for domesticks. This latter should be thrown behind, but the other is to be shewn."[14] The staircase for show, which typically ran only from the ground floor to the first floor, featured turned balusters meant, again, to imitate classical columns.

Another general truth is that, by the end of the 18th century, the standard of living for most people was higher than it had been in 1700, and this was reflected both in the materials used to build middle-class homes and in the objects that filled them. A writer in the 1770s claimed of provincial shopkeepers that they ate as well "as rich merchants . . . a hundred years ago" in "houses good and ornamented. What formerly was a downfall gable end, covered with thatch, is now brick and tile."[15] A typical middle-class home would probably have a clock of some kind, candelabra filled with wax (or cheaper tallow) candles, oil lamps filled with coal or whale oil,[16] carpets, books, a mirror (perhaps with a *papier mâché* frame made to imitate carved wood), furniture in the style of Chippendale or Hepplewhite or Sheraton, knicknacks like Mrs. Heidelberg's "china figures," screens, curtains, brass door locks, fireplace tools, and a few sentimental or satirical prints on the walls. A woman weaver in Colchester in 1744 owned a host of objects, including linens, tables, a copper saucepan, a boiler, iron pots, candlesticks, pictures, bowls, glass bottles, plates, basins, four teapots, cups and saucers, spoons, and pewter measures.[17]

The kitchen tools in the weaver's inventory are fairly typical. Cookbooks of the time mention earthen pans, stewpans, dishes, butter-plates, spoons, glasses, a "boat" for melted butter, mortars, an earthen jug to be submerged and boiled to make "jugged" hare, cups, gravy boats, pots, wooden bowls, whisks, tin pans, sieves, basins, kettles, strainers, pie plates, skewers, knives, and other tools. A typical kitchen might also boast a set of good china (Wedgwood's cream ware was popular), a teapot, a caddy to hold black and green teas, utensils of silver plate or ormolu, a punch bowl, a coffee pot, a "Toby jug" shaped like a fat man with a jug and pipe, and a novelty mug with the face of politician John Wilkes or boxer Daniel Mendoza on the side. The kitchen had a large open fireplace, fueled by coal, lit with phosphorus matches or a tinder box, and fitted with a turnspit which could accommodate skewers of various sizes—larger for huge beef roasts, smaller for fowl. The cook and her assistants, if any, tended the fire, peeled vegetables, plucked birds, preserved fruit, made cheese and butter, brewed beer, baked bread, scrubbed pots clean with sand, nibbled, talked, and granted or denied tastes of the food to other servants. Various kinds of food, like hams, bread, and onions, hung from the walls or ceiling.

The kitchen was the most important room in middle- and lower-class

Published as the Act directs 3 Jan 1785

CORPORAL TRIM's reflections on Mortality in the Kitchen, on the Death of MASTER BOBBY

"Are we not here now?' continued the Corporal, striking the end of his stick perpendicularly upon the floor, so as to give an idea of health and stability), and are we not' (dropping his hat upon the ground) 'gone in a moment'."

6.2 "Corporal Trim's reflections on Mortality in the Kitchen, on the Death of Master Bobby" (1785) shows some of the standard equipment of a good middle-class kitchen: covered saucepans, dish rack, string of onions, pot lids and candlesticks above the fire, kettle and spits in the fire, pulley and chains for turning the spits, broom, coal box, rolling pin, spoon, and bellows. The turned balusters of a staircase are just visible through the open door. Courtesy of the Print Collection, Lewis Walpole Library, Yale University.

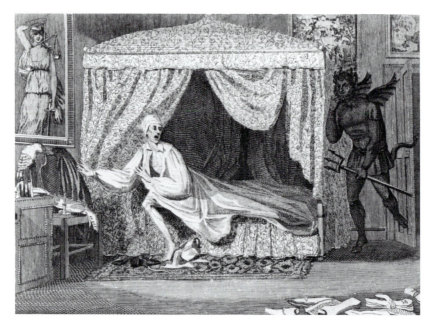

6.3 "The Devil and the Lawyer" (1785) shows an upper-middle-class bedroom. A table, cabinet, pictures, and canopied bed are visible. The startled lawyer has also overturned another ubiquitous feature of the bedroom, the chamberpot. Courtesy of the Print Collection, Lewis Walpole Library, Yale University.

households. Women, employers and servants alike, gathered there to sew by the fire. Larger houses had a separate room or building for laundering, but ordinary households probably used the kitchen for this purpose as well, since doing the laundry required access to the fire. The clothes had to be boiled first, necessitating the hauling of plenty of water. Then they were wrung in a mangle, a device with weighted rollers, the operation of which required great strength. Laundry was hung out on ropes to dry, or spread over hedges, and ironed with flat irons warmed by the fire. The irons had to be kept away from the coal, lest they dirty the linen, and they were used in sets, so that one could be warming while another was in use. Lace was washed separately and sometimes dipped in milk to stiffen it as it dried.[18]

Servants lived in out-of-the-way places: the basement and the garret in town houses, and the attic and outbuildings in the country. Increasingly, especially in the case of agricultural laborers, they lived elsewhere and simply reported to work each morning. Bellpulls were introduced in the 1760s or 1770s. These devices allowed an employer to summon a domestic servant by pulling a rope that rang a bell in the servants' quarters or kitchen.[19]

The employers slept in rooms on the first or second floor of the house. If they could afford it, they had not only a bedroom but a closet to serve as a private office and a dressing room to serve as a place to dress, primp, receive friends, and lounge. The bedroom usually had a curtained, canopied bed, drawers and wardrobes for holding clothes, and a chamberpot for relieving oneself during the night. Shortly before bedtime, a servant would light a fire in the fireplace and place a warming pan—a lidded pan filled with coals—in the bed itself, to prepare the cold room and bed for the employer's arrival. There were no bathrooms, even in the employers' suites of rooms; during the day, people used outdoor privies if they had a garden, or chamberpots emptied into a basement cesspit if they did not.

UPPER-CLASS HOUSES

The houses of the rich followed the same trends as middle-class housing—or, more accurately, *set* the trends for middle-class housing. The difference was that the elements were bigger, better, and more abundant. Public reception rooms were not limited to a front or back parlor. There might be a large circuit of such rooms, including a picture gallery, a saloon, and a ballroom, where guests talked, played cards, danced, and admired their host's taste in art. Private rooms, too, were more extensive, with more elaborate suites of apartments for the residents. The owners sometimes received business subordinates, favor seekers, or friends in their bedrooms or dressing rooms while their elaborate hairstyles and attire were being completed. As the century passed, public and private spaces became differently defined. Living rooms expanded downstairs, ousting the state bedrooms. The apartment system declined, too, and reception of guests moved from bedrooms and dressing rooms to the drawing rooms and other spaces that formerly had been used only for formal visits and parties.[20]

Furniture which had been made of oak, or of walnut veneer over another wood like beech, was now of expensive mahogany, as was the wainscotting on the walls. Gilded mirrors, hand-painted Chinese wallpaper, and collections of fine paintings hung on the walls; delicately molded plaster or stucco ornaments decorated the ceilings; and carpets from Persia or Kidderminster covered the floors. Special wings housed the servants, luxuries like water closets and bathtubs were installed, and elaborate wrought-iron gates guarded the grounds. Libraries housed thousands of volumes, and the table was set with porcelain, silver, and high-quality blown glassware. The chimney pieces and staircases might be made of marble.[21]

Erddig, an estate in Wales which was by no means the century's grandest country house, was amply supplied with conveniences. It had London-made furniture, a state bed with gilded hawk heads, tapestries, pier glasses that cost £50 in 1726, and a second-best bedroom with a bed made up in crimson damask. The entrance hall held ten black leather chairs, several tables including two specifically for backgammon and one with three sides for the three-player card game ombre, and a gilded leather screen. The saloon had gilt sconces and eight walnut chairs with gold-and-claret-colored wool velvet upholstery. The household linen inventory lists sixty-six sets of sheets, at least thirty-nine tablecloths, and at least 317 napkins of varying quality. Erddig also had whole rooms and outbuildings few mere artisans or minor tradesmen's homes could have boasted: a "New Kitchen, Brew House, Cheese Roome, Darry and Sculery, Laundry, Wash House, New Servants Hall, Old Servants hall, Powder Room, Housekeepers Room, Butlers room, Wett Larder, Small Rear Celler, Oven Parlour and Stone Parlour." The servants' rooms were not grand but were amply supplied with tables, chairs, beds, linen, rugs, and blankets. A chamber in the garret that may have been the housekeeper's contained a silk quilt, curtains with valances, a table, a mirror, and five chairs.[22]

THE GARDEN

At the beginning of the century, the ideal garden was heavy on geometry, with straight, symmetrical paths, level ground, clipped hedges, and shaped trees. Fences divided the garden from the park and fields around it to keep out cattle and deer. Such extensive reshaping of nature could not be sustained forever. In the first place, it was extremely expensive. In the second, nothing remains fashionable forever. Even by the second decade of the century, there were outcries against too much order. Alexander Pope attacked topiaries in *The Guardian* in 1713, a little over a year after Joseph Addison's *Spectator* begged people to stop molding their trees into "cones, globes and Pyramids."[23] Stephen Switzer's *Ichonographia Rustica* (1718) suggested putting in irregular walks, allowing the land to retain its natural contours, using extra soil to make hillocks planted with trees, and using water instead of fencing as an animal barrier. He wanted, he said, to "cashiere that Mathematical Stiffness in our Gardens, and imitate Nature more."[24]

Other landscape architects, like Capability Brown and Humphry Repton, agreed. Increasingly, gardens worked with nature instead of against it. Fences were replaced by a new invention designed to preserve the view while still keeping animals out of the garden. The new device was a fence sunk into the earth, with a ditch or a drop in the level of the terrain on the other side. The ditch or drop kept out animals, and also startled walkers who did not see or expect the sunken fence. Perhaps because of the surprised noises that resulted, the fence became known as a "ha-ha." The ha-ha, increasingly disguised with hills or clumps of trees, allowed longer prospects of one's land, or the illusion that one owned more than one actually did.[25]

Those with money spent it rearranging the outdoors. Formal gardens were plowed under. Avenues of perfectly aligned trees were knocked down or transplanted to irregular groves. Unsightly structures, sometimes even whole villages, were razed to improve the view. Sometimes new villages were built elsewhere to house the ousted inhabitants, sometimes not. Such decisions could be attended with second thoughts. Thomas Coke felt "melancholy" after moving the town of Holkham. "I look around," he wrote, "not a house to be seen but my own. I am Giant, of Giant's Castle, and have ate up all my neighbours."[26] Conversely, new structures were erected—grottoes, obelisks, statues, pavilions for picnics and teas, bridges, mausoleums, chapels, kennels, stables, and boathouses. Some landowners built "follies" like fake hermitages (Painshill Park in Surrey had a hired hermit),[27] fake Gothic ruins, and Roman, Greek, and Egyptian-style buildings. Social climber Sterling, in *The Clandestine Marriage*, yearns to show Lord Ogleby his garden: "my walks, and my slopes, and my clumps, and my bridge, and my flowering trees, and my bed of Dutch tulips." Later he promises, "I'll only shew his Lordship my ruins, and the cascade, and the Chinese bridge, and then we'll go to breakfast," but he can't resist pointing out one more glorious feature, a false steeple without a church "that I have built against a tree, a field or two off, to terminate the prospect. One must always have a church, or an obelisk, or something, to terminate the prospect, you know. That's a rule in taste, my Lord."[28]

Thus was born the so-called "English garden," contoured and rambling, planted with hawthorn, bay, elm, laurel, fir, box, lime, chestnut, fruit, and sycamore trees, flowering with violets, pinks, jessamines, currants, sweet peas, sweet williams, candytuft, and love-in-a-mist. Horace Walpole claimed, "We have given the true model of gardening to the world; let other countries mimic or corrupt our taste; but let it reign here on its verdant throne."[29]

Yet the English garden was no more immune to foreign influence than the English house. Foreign trees and flowers were brought into the country; the duke of Argyle brought in weeping willows and acacias, and Sir Joseph Banks introduced New Zealand's national flower, the kowhai, in 1772.[30] James Cawthorn thought it ridiculous to bring warm-weather plants to a cold, damp island, just as he thought it silly to import Mediterranean architecture, "Careless alike of climate, soil, and place." The results, he said, were

Our massy ceilings, graced with gay festoons,
The weeping marbles of our damp salons,

Lawns fringed with citrons, amaranthine bow'rs,
Expiring myrtles, and unop'ning flow'rs.[31]

Yet the wealthy continued to plant fuschias and to construct hothouses to grow pineapples.

THE HOUSES OF THE POOR

At the bottom of the socioeconomic scale, gardens were not ornamental but functional. Most large estates had a part of their gardens devoted to vegetables and fruits for the table, but for the poor this was the whole purpose of a garden. Their houses, too, were stripped to their most essential function, shelter pure and simple—slums in the city, cottages in the country. To judge by contemporary accounts, the English poor lived better than those in other countries, but they were still crowded together, often in a single room of little more than 100 square feet, sometimes in a single bed, sometimes in a simple pile of shavings or straw or matted wool on the floor. In the country, the livestock might be brought indoors at night for additional warmth. Floors were made of flagstones or packed earth (sometimes mixed with bullocks' blood). In the cities, the crowding was pitiful, with as many as ten people living in one room in Manchester. Some lived in shacks or cellars. At Bridgnorth they carved cave homes from the cliffs. At Warminster their conditions were "Mud without and wretchedness within."[32] Poets wrote of visits to cottages where wintry drafts swept "through the gaping walls," where dying men shivering in tattered flea-ridden blankets, where the smoke lingered in the small space of the one room, and where the windows were merely "a few old shattered panes."[33] (For a good, albeit simplified and exaggerated, comparison between a lower-middle-class and a lower-class interior, see the first and fourth scenes of Illustration 9.3. To compare both of these with upper-class interiors, see Illustrations 8.1, 8.2, and 10.6.)

The belongings of the poor were limited. They might have a few family heirlooms, some pots and pans, wooden platters and cups, perhaps a few pewter dishes or mugs, a roasting jack for the fire, and some cheap "ballads pasted on the wall, / Of Joan of France, and English Moll."[34] Bookseller James Lackington asserted that

even the poor country people in general, who before . . . spent their evenings in relating stories of witches, ghosts, hobgoblins etc., now shorten the winter nights by hearing their sons and daughters read tales, romances, etc., and on entering their homes you may see *Tom Jones, Roderick Random,* and other entertaining books stuck up on their bacon racks.[35]

Cottages were heated with scavenged sticks, and beds were warmed, if at all, with hot bricks wrapped in flannel. Lighting, like heating, was catch-as-catch-can. Since candles were expensive, some made their own with a rush wick and hoarded fat, or dipped rushes in fat and put them in metal holders to make rush lights.[36]

In the cottages and cellars of the humblest workers, the relative merits of the Gothic versus the neoclassical were seldom discussed. Follies and Chinese wallpaper and Palladian facades were insignificant when roof, walls, windows, floors, bedding, fire, light, and hungry children cried out alike for the bulk of the family's last nine shillings. Yet, because of the wayward and temporary nature of fashion, it is the follies, the Chinese wallpaper, and the Palladian facades that seem indelibly 18th-century, not the fragile and far more numerous homes of the poor.

TIMELINE

1696	A tax on windows is instituted; it will not be repealed until 1851.
1707	Parliament passes an act "for the better preventing mischiefs that may happen by fire," requiring party walls (short walls on the roofs perpendicular to the street) and roof parapets on terrace houses. The act also bans traditional wooden eaves, which are afterward replaced by brick or stone cornices.
1709	A Parliamentary act requires that wooden window and door frames be recessed four inches from the facade, ostensibly to hamper the spread of fires. The effect is to make London's Georgian house fronts look neater and stronger, and the effect is widely imitated outside London.
1754	Thomas Chippendale (1718–1779) publishes *The Gentleman and Cabinet-Maker's Director*, a heavily illustrated work showing the various types of rococo furniture made by his shop. His style is much imitated. Later editions of the book introduce neoclassical design elements and reflect the shift from rococo ornamentation in furniture.
1762	James Stuart and Nicholas Revett publish *Antiquities of Athens*, encouraging the shift from Palladian to neoclassical decoration and architecture.

1774   The London Building Act establishes four rates of residential houses and institutes a system of district surveyors who must be notified before building or altering any structure. This system replaces the old method of enforcing building codes with amateur informers.

1779   William Mason publishes *The English Garden.*

1783   Landscape gardener Lancelot "Capability" Brown (b. 1715) dies.

1788   The widow of George Hepplewhite, who died in 1786, publishes his *Cabinet-maker and Upholsterer's Guide.* Like Chippendale's book, Hepplewhite's is highly influential in the furniture industry.[37]

7

Cork Rumps and Cocked Hats: Clothing

[T]hese pictures were done some time ago, when beaux wore wigs, and the ladies their own hair.
—Richard Brinsley Sheridan, *School for Scandal*

WOMEN'S CLOTHING

When a woman got dressed in the 18th century, she first put on a chemise, a linen shirt or shift that hung to just below the knees. Then she tied a string around her waist, from which hung two pockets, one on either hip. Over the chemise, she wore a set of "stays"—a corset, stiffened by metal or whalebone strips (as narrow as 1/8 inch each) sewn between the layers of fabric. They were often supplemented in front by a stomacher, which was a decorative triangular piece, widest at the top, made stiff and flat by a piece of bone called a busk. Stomacher and stays were often visible through the dress and considered part of its ornament; when working women sometimes took off their bodices and worked in their stays, they were not considered indecently exposed.[1]

Undergarments

Stays grew quite short and light in the 1790s and were all but gone by the end of the century, but for most of the century, it was believed necessary for good posture to put children of both sexes into stays at an early age. This was opposed by some on the grounds of health (autopsies demonstrated that tight lacing could actually kill) and by some on the grounds of comfort. Elizabeth Ham wrote of her stays that "the first day of wearing them was very nearly purgatory, and I question if I was sufficiently aware of the advantage of a fine shape to reconcile me to the punishment."[2]

For the first decade of the century, a woman's legs were covered by a petticoat and overskirt, suspended over a "false rump," usually made of cork. But in 1709, the hoop petticoat was introduced and rapidly adopted, despite vociferous condemnation. In its early form, it was round and dome shaped, consisting of seven or eight cane or whalebone hoops strung together with fabric tapes. The whole contraption was tied around the waist with a drawstring. From 1713 to the 1740s, another style was also popular: the "fan hoop," in which additional tapes attached the front and back of the hoops, flattening them and pushing them out to the sides. In the 1740s to 1760s, the hoop became almost rectangular and very wide, and then began to disappear except at Court. For undress (casual dress), women still continued to wear small, separate side hoops, called "pocket hoops" or "false hips." In the 1770s, the "cork rump" made a reappearance, and padding shifted from the sides to the back, growing smaller and smaller with the late-century emphasis on natural, classical dress.[3] (For examples of different hoops, see Illustrations 2.2, in which the woman pounding hemp in the left foreground wears a hooped skirt, while another woman has removed hers and hung it on the wall; 3.1, in which the two women getting out of the carriage wear fan hoops; 12.2, in which the two women in the right foreground wear oblong hoops; and 10.5, in which the young woman's skirt is drawn back over a cork rump.)

Opponents of the hoop petticoat exaggerated its size and described the difficulties with which women sidled into rooms and struggled into coaches. Joseph Addison claimed a visitor had been unable to reach him because of the breadth of her undergarments. "Word was brought me," he claimed, "that she had endeavor'd Twice or Thrice to come in, but could not do it by reason of her Petticoat, which was too large for the Entrance of my House, though I had ordered both the Folding-Doors to be thrown open for its reception." He judged against the new petticoat, and ordered "it to be folded up, and sent as a Present to a Widow-Gentlewoman, who has Five Daughters, desiring she would make each of them a Petticoat out of it, and send me back the Remainder."[4] Other opponents of the hoop, objecting either to its clumsiness or appearance, called it "monstrous" and asserted that "it is a Mode very disagreeable to the Men in general."[5]

The hoop's defenders claimed that it kept men at a chaste distance, made walking easier, kept women's legs cooler, and showed off the legs and feet to advantage. Women from every social class adopted the style. Housemaids sewed penny canes into their petticoats or padded their hips with stiff, quilted petticoats to simulate hoops.[6]

Like hoops, cork rumps were the butt, so to speak, of many a joke. A 1777 poem warned, of a fashionable woman, "... never undress her—for, out of her stays,/You'll find you have lost half your wife."[7] Others satirized the fashion in prints, or in stories of women saved from drowning by their buoyant bottoms.[8] Nevertheless, women were slow to abandon their layers of undergarments.

A woman's dress consisted of three pieces—bodice, overskirt, and petticoat. Two of them, the bodice and overskirt, **Dresses** were often joined. In the front, a woman's dress could be defined as an "open robe" or a "closed robe." An open robe diverged at the waist to reveal the petticoat, which was often flowered, embroidered, or quilted. (For examples of quilted petticoats, see Illustrations 3.4 and 17.3.) For most of the century, it was a different color from the skirt. The closed robe had a closed skirt that did not reveal the petticoat. Sleeves were usually just above or below elbow-length and might have turned-up cuffs, flounces, or ruffles at the ends.[9] (In Illustration 10.6, the fashionable women playing cards have ruffled sleeves, while the maid at the left does not.)

In the back of the bodice, the two chief distinctions were between the *robe à l'anglaise* (or fourreau back) and the *robe à la française* (or sacque, or sack, back). In the *robe à l'anglaise*, the back seams were fitted to the body from neck to waist. In the *robe à la française*, the lining was fitted, but the outer fabric hung loosely in box pleats from the neck and fell in a tentlike shape (hence the name "sack") to the floor.[10]

For the first half of the century, one popular dress style was the mantua, an open robe with a trained skirt and petticoat. Appropriate for full (fancy) dress, the mantua was often worn with a buckled belt called a girdle. Middle-class women sometimes made a compromise between fashion and pragmatism and pinned up the train while working around the house.[11] The second quarter of the century brought the sacque into favor. From 1735 to the 1750s, women also wore "wrapping gowns," closed robes with tight bodices and round necklines; one side crossed over the other in front and was fastened with brooches, ribbons, or girdles.[12] The low necklines of the 1750s attracted the attention of libertines and moralists alike. Sometimes the decolletage was partly hidden by a tucker (a frilled white edging around the neckline), a modesty piece (a ruffled linen or lace covering for "the pit of the bosom"), or a large handkerchief (more like a scarf in size and usage) folded in half, laid round the neck and bosom, and tucked into the front of the bodice.[13]

The 1770s and 1780s favored open gowns with fourreau backs, tight bodices, and bosoms puffed out by starched muslin handkerchiefs called "buffons." Skirts were swept back in a three-part puff called a polonaise. Working women wore the "bedgown," a short, loose wrapover gown with an apron.[14] A riding habit, consisting of a skirt, masculine-style waistcoat, cravat, and frock coat, became popular for riding, walking, and traveling, despite a fierce outcry that it was unfeminine.

In the 1780s, a daring fashion was introduced: the chemise dress, often a simple cylinder of white muslin gathered at the neck by a drawstring and at the waist by a wide sash. In the mid-1790s, the sash grew narrower and the waist ever higher, rising to just beneath the breasts. Influenced by classical antiquity and French Revolutionary simplicity, the chemise dress featured long skirts (often with a train hitched up for dancing), little or no false rump, few underclothes, a long petticoat that matched the dress, long sleeves, and a high neckline. Tie-on pockets, which had been reached through slits in the dress and side hoops, were replaced by small handbags.[15] (The high-waisted styles of the 1790s can be seen in Illustrations 2.1 and 11.2.)

Hair and Hats   Women's hair grew tall, small, big, bigger, and small again by turns. For the first decade of the century, it was worn in a "tower" of frizzed or curled hair above the forehead, sometimes worn with a fontange (a cap with a pleated, standing front like a tall narrow fan, and two streamers called lappets hanging down or pinned to the crown of the cap). Curls hung at the temples, and the back hair was gathered into a bun.[16] Working women, and even fashionable women from 1720 to the 1750s, wore the "simple coiffure," with curls or waves around the face and a bun at the upper back of the head. From the 1730s to 1750s, some women wore the Dutch coiffure, much like the simple coiffure but with the back bun replaced by ringlets hanging to the nape of the neck.[17]

Most women wore caps, often edged with lace, both in and out of doors and under hats. The common types were the pinner (1700 to 1740s), a flattish circular cap pinned to the top of the head and sometimes featuring lappets; the round-eared cap (1730s to 1760s), shaped a little like a bonnet, with a frilled front, rounded area over the ears (hence the name), high back, and (sometimes) lappets; and the mob cap (worn throughout the century for undress, especially from the 1730s), a puffed round cap with a deep border and side pieces called "kissing strings" or "bridles."[18] For riding, women imitated men's three-cornered cocked hats.[19]

From the late 1760s to the late 1780s, peaking in about 1778, there was an era of big hair that has yet to be exceeded. These "towers of powdered hair"[20] were supported by wads of false hair, elaborately styled, greased with lard, and powdered at least once a day. To preserve the hairstyle, women wore huge nightcaps—sometimes made of silver mesh to keep out mice, though lice and other vermin still crept in. For temporary relief from the itching, fashionable women carried thin hooked scratchers so that they could reach discreetly into the hair to dislodge parasites. However, when the "head was opened," or the hairstyle dismantled and reassembled weeks or even months after the original styling, vermin were often found.[21] In the 1780s, the hair was worn wide and frizzed, *à la hérisson* (hedgehog-style). The effect was accentuated by wide, heavily decorated hats.[22] In the 1790s, some women adopted *la victime coiffeur*, with tousled hair in imitation of guillotined French aristocrats; others wore their hair close to the head, swept back from the face with a wide ribbon or gathered into a loose bun or curls.[23]

Throughout the century, the most common hat, seen on all sorts of middle- and lower-class women, was the "chip" or straw hat, usually flat-crowned, with a wide brim. The brim was sometimes flat, sometimes folded down at the sides, and often worn tilted. It was typically worn over a cap of some kind and tied onto the head.[24] (Examples of women's caps, hats, and hair can be found throughout this book. See especially Illustrations 10.6 for caps with and without lappets, 17.1 for a turban-style headdress popular in the 1780s, 10.5 for the large black hats also popular during the 1780s, 8.3 for caps worn with straw hats outdoors, and 10.4 for a modest example of the tall hairstyles of the 1770s.)

Women wore white or black stockings, sometimes with lace or colored clocks (triangular decorations widest at the ankle and narrowest at about mid-calf); some stockings were red or green, and working-class women often wore blue. **Shoes and Stockings** Most women wore worsted stockings at least part of the time, but better-off women often wore silk or cotton as well.[25] Women tied garters around the tops of the stockings. One pair, made in 1717, has "My heart is fixt, I cannot range" on one garter and "I like my choice too well to change" on the other.[26] Another, made in 1739, read, "No search."[27]

Shoes were often high-heeled, with pointed toes and straps that buckled or tied over the instep. Pumps, worn infrequently by women, were low-heeled. Slippers were backless and often quite elegant. Women, like men, wore pattens (wooden overshoes raised on tall metal rings) or clogs (a high leather undersole that strapped on over the instep) to protect their finer footwear from mud.[28]

Fashionable women wore a variety of accessories to make themselves more decorative: masks (at masquerades), jewelry, gold or silver girdle buckles, gold watches worn **Accessories** around the neck or suspended from a stay hook, nosegays of artificial flowers, tippets (short white capes), muffs, ribbon neck bands (from the 1730s), and elbow-length white or black gloves.[29] Women busy with housework all day wore working aprons with bibs and pockets; women busy with visits and whist wore ornamental aprons from the waist to the knee or hem, sometimes brocaded or trimmed with lace or embroidery.[30] (Short and long aprons can be seen in Illustrations 2.2 and 10.6. The woman in the center foreground in Illustration 8.2 wears a short apron with lace trim, a gold pocket watch hanging from her waist, two necklaces, a neck ribbon, earrings, and a knot of ribbons on her sleeve.) Many women added a "suit of knots"—a set of ribbon bows—to their hair, bosoms, sleeves, or wrists.[31]

Women also carried items with them, most of which served some useful as well as aesthetic purpose. They carried pocket-handkerchiefs (as distinct from the bosom-covering handkerchief described above), fans (as large as two feet across in the 1740s), long straight canes, parasols for the sun, umbrellas for the rain (if they were unable to afford a sedan chair or carriage), muffs to warm the hands in cold weather, and snuff-boxes.[32]

Grooming   Those who could afford to do so made liberal use of cosmetics. A rich woman's dressing table might hold wart remover, rouge, paint for whitening the face, "an excellent cosmetic water to carry off freckles, sun-burn, or pimples; . . . a curious red-pomatum to plump and colour the lips," a depilatory (such as vinegar, walnut oil, quicklime, or cat's dung), sticks or powder for cleaning the teeth, "a never-failing remedy for offensive breaths, a famous essence to correct the ill scent of the arm-pits, a rich water that makes the hair curl, a most delicate paste to smooth and whiten the hands," perfume, and a curling iron. There might also be a small box of black velvet or silk patches to stick to the face.[33] These patches, cut in circles or other shapes, and worn in such numbers that the face sometimes appeared "full of flies,"[34] were ridiculed by Addison in the *Spectator*:

> The Women look like Angels, and would be more beautiful than the Sun, were it not for little black Spots that are apt to break out in their Faces, and sometimes rise in very odd Figures. . . . I have seen a Spot upon the Forehead in the Afternoon, which was upon the Chin in the Morning.[35]

Another little box might hold false eyebrows made of mouse skin that could, in a hot room, begin to slide down an unfortunate woman's face. Those who did not shave off their eyebrows and replace them with false ones might have a tiny lead comb, or a supply of ripe elderberries, lamp black, or burnt cork, for blackening their own.[36] The dressing table might also contain "frontlets," strips of linen, leather, or paper smeared with cream and strapped to the forehead at night to combat wrinkles.[37]

Most cosmetics were made at home, though the ingredients, and some ready-made concoctions, could be purchased from shops. The recipes are often complex and, at their best, harmless, like the depilatory made of fifty-two eggshells beaten and distilled over a fire, or the perfume made of rosebuds, rosewater, benjamin, civet, and musk.[38] One recipe for a fair complexion instructed the reader to:

7.1 Costume through the century in a fictional family of gentle-women. Mary, c. 1749, wears a sacque gown with open bodice and closed skirt over oblong hoops. The sleeves of the gown have turned-back cuffs to reveal the double ruffles of the chemise sleeves. She wears a handkerchief around her neck, tied with a bow, to conceal her decolletage. Her hair is drawn back in a simple coiffure under a round-eared cap with a small peak in front, and she holds one of her gloves. (The area between her bodice and arms, though it would not have been a different color from the rest of the gown, has been shaded to show the box-pleated sacque draperies falling behind her from the neck.)

Mary's granddaughter Harriet, c. 1785, wears a large tilted hat with bow and pearls, high frizzed hair, and a gown drawn back over a cork rump, revealing low-heeled shoes. Harriet's niece Jane, c. 1800, wears a chemise dress with narrow sash, a small, classically inspired hairstyle with a wide ribbon in front and a small bun in back, and flat slippers. She carries a handbag or "indispensable."

Take of the water of nenuphar or water-lily, bean water, melon water, cucumber water, and the juice of lemons, of each one ounce; of briony, wild succory, flowers de luce, borage, and bean-flowers, of each an handful; of white pigeons seven or eight, pluck them, and cut off the heads and ends of the wings, then mince them very small, and put them, with the other ingredients into an alembic, and also four ounces of double-refined sugar, one drachm of borax, and as much camphire; the crumb of four small white loaves new from the oven, and a pint of good white wine. Let them digest in the alembic seventeen or eighteen days, after which distil the whole and reserve the water for use.[39]

Other recipes were positively poisonous, containing harmful chemicals like the white lead in face paint or the mercury in some rouges.[40]

Coats and Cloaks   Outdoors, women wore waist-length or longer cloaks. One version, called the mantle, was a long, full hooded cloak. Other protective garments included the mantlet, a deep shoulder-cape; the scarf, a large rounded wrap dangling to the waist in back and lower in front; the manteel, a smaller version of the scarf; and the pelerine, a variant of the manteel often worn with the thin dangling ends crossed over the chest and waist and tied in back. In the second half of the century, coats became more popular for women.[41]

MEN'S CLOTHING

Hair and Headgear   Most men wore their hair close-cropped, almost shaved, and covered their heads with wigs ranging in price from a guinea to £30 or so.[42] Artisans often removed the wig to work (see Illustration 9.4, where the blacksmith and his helpers are in various states of wiglessness). Wigs were usually made of human or horse hair. Human hair was best and most expensive, horse hair cheaper.[43] A gentleman dressing in the morning would wear a powdering jacket to protect his clothes and a mask to protect his clean-shaven face, while a barber greased the wig with pomatum and then applied powder, usually white or gray, with a bellows or puff.[44]

Wigs were long at the beginning of the century, when Thomas D'Urfey described beaus "In wigs that hang down to their bums."[45] Later, they shortened into simple "bob" or "scratch" styles, or grew ponytails, side curls, and "toupées"—pieces for the top of the head, brushed straight back without a part.[46] Wigs went out of fashion for good (except in the law courts) at the end of the century, when powder taxes and sympathy for French revolutionaries made short, natural hair the rage.[47]

The hat worn atop these wigs (or, often, carried under the arm) was the three-cornered cocked hat—a hat with a domed crown and a brim of varying width which was turned up in one or more "cocks." Each variation had a name: the Mathematical Cock (three equal angles), the Monmouth (an old-fashioned style, with only the back side cocked), the Denmark (high in back, low in front), the Chapeau Bras (designed only to be carried under the arm, never worn), the Nivernois Hat, and a military style later called the bicorne (turned up high in the front and back). The cocked hat was usually made of black beaver-fur felt, and was often trimmed with a button or jewels and loop, a feather, lace, braid, or a feather fringe. (For examples of cocked hats, see Illustrations 1.1 and 12.3.

If the cocked hat was the dominant style, it was not the only one. Poorer country folk wore round, uncocked straw hats. Late in the century, stylish young men adopted the jockey cap, a rounded cap with a flattened peak in the front, sometimes adorned by a buckled band, for riding. They also began to wear a round, flat-topped hat with an uncocked brim for riding and driving—the antecedent of the top hat.[48] (For working-class incarnations of the round hat, see Illustrations 11.3 and 13.2.) Another essential hat was the nightcap, which was worn throughout the century. When men took off their wigs at home at night, and before they put them on in the morning, their shaved heads felt chilly. So they wore the nightcap, a roundish, turbanlike cap with a turned up or rolled up brim and sometimes a tassel. Artisans—like the blacksmith in Illustration 9.4 or the cricketer in Illustration 10.1—also sometimes wore the nightcap in lieu of a wig while working or playing.[49]

Men's suits had three essential pieces: vest, jacket, and pants (then called waistcoat, coat, and breeches). When a man got dressed, he put on a shirt, often with ruffled sleeves and, at the throat, a jabot (frilled neck opening) or **The Three-Piece Suit** cravat (something between a tie and a scarf). The richer he was, the more glorious his ruffles and the cleaner his shirt. He also put on a pair of drawers, or linen underwear, tied at the waist and knees and sometimes fitted with a washable, detachable lining.[50] In the 1790s, out of sympathy for the French Revolution, and as part of a shift to a more "natural" mode of dress, shirt ruffles shrank and disappeared.[51]

Over the shirt he put on a waistcoat, which at the beginning of the century looked more like a coat than like the modern vest. It had long, tight sleeves, often with one wrist button left undone to display the shirt ruffles. It had a small standing collar or no collar at all, fit the body closely to the waist, then flared out over the hips in flaps, called the skirt, which were often stiffened with buckram to make them seem even fuller. A long row of buttonholes and buttons ran down the front, but usually the waistcoat was only buttoned at the waist. The waistcoat underwent a transformation in the 1720s to 1760s, losing its sleeves, growing shorter, increasing the height of the collar, gradually curving away from the midline to expose more of the thighs, and getting shorter skirts in the back than in the front. In the second half of the century, fashionable young men tended to wear waistcoats with very short skirts or even none at all. By the 1790s, the Newmarket style—square-cut in the front with no skirts—was the norm.[52]

Coats, which were worn over waistcoats, followed similar trends. They looked like larger, longer versions of the waistcoat, with fuller sleeves, slightly larger buttons, and the same collarless neck. They were buttoned only at the waist or not at all.[53] In the first half of the century, they featured flared, stiffened skirts that reached their widest in the 1740s, when a fashionable man's coattails might stretch five feet wide.[54] Sleeves ended in turned-back cuffs which were largest at mid-century, when they might be several inches deep.[55] In the second half of the century, the coat, like the waistcoat, curved away from the midline, abandoned stiffening in the skirts, and grew a collar.[56]

Working-class coats were simpler, shorter, often unlined, and less likely to have cuffs.[57] Early in the century, working men wore a loose, simple coat called a frock, and by 1730 the fashion was being imitated by the gentry for riding.[58] In the next decade, Lord Chesterfield bemoaned the sight of young men of fashion in "brown frocks, leather breeches, great oaken cudgels in their hands, their hats uncocked and their hair unpowdered."[59] In 1756 Soame Jenyns still considered the frock "a ridiculous imitation" of servile dress, but by the 1780s it could be worn almost anywhere except at Court, where the fancy, tailored coat was still required. The frock had a turned-down collar, sometimes faced with a different color or material than the coat itself.

Gentlemen going outdoors sometimes wore cloaks until about 1750, but afterward cloaks were unfashionable except on soldiers, learned professionals, and funeral goers.[60] Usually, men wore the surtout or greatcoat, which was shaped like a big frock coat. It hung below the knees with a back vent for riding and one to three broad collars called capes. From 1790 on, there was another type of outer coat, the spencer, a tailless, short-waisted, double-breasted jacket with cuffs, collar, and a few buttons in front.[61]

South of all these coats and waistcoats, and over his linen drawers, a man wore breeches. Until about 1730 they were closed in front by buttons without a fly; after that, the closure was usually a "fall," a central flap buttoned on both sides near the waistband.[62] The breeches ended just above or just below the knee; working-class breeches were tied there (see Illustration 17.3); better breeches had a slit and buttons and then a buckle at the bottom.[63] In the second half of the century, as waistcoats and coats were cut to reveal more of the breeches, men's legs became a focus of sexual attention. Breeches got tighter—so tight that some men had to be helped into them by their valets.[64] For riding, men wore leather breeches, usually buckskin. Lower artisans and such wore trousers at times, but long pants of any kind did not become fashionable until the 1790s, when some began to wear pantaloons—ankle-length tights buttoned from ankle to calf along the outside.[65]

Early in the century, it was common for coat, breeches, and waistcoat to be made of the same fabric—"a suit of ditto" was the term for such an outfit—but it became increasingly likely for the waistcoat to be of some more splendid fabric, and by mid-century cutting-edge fashion dictated a different color or material for each piece. Thus, in 1751, *The Inspector* describes "A Dandy in a black velvet coat, a green and silver waistcoat, yellow velvet breeches, and blue stockings."[66] By 1777 it was known that an "entire suit of clothes [was] hardly ever seen except upon old people, physicians, apothecaries, and lawyers."[67]

When a gentleman, fashionable or unfashionable, went home at night, he changed into a "nightgown," not a sleeping garment but a comfortable wraparound robe tied with a sash. A similar garment, a roughly knee-length coat for informal home wear, was called the banyan. The nightgown or banyan might be worn for playing cards, eating breakfast with one's family, or sitting by the fire writing letters in the evening.[68] For sleeping, a man wore a nightshirt, an example of which can be seen in Illustration 6.3.

Men wore stockings over, and later under, the breeches at the knee. A garter was wrapped twice around the stocking top and buckled or tied in place.[69] Decorations like "turn shapes" (hearts, scrolls, and other designs formed by different knitting stitches) or embroidered or knitted "clocks" began disappearing from fashionable stockings in the 1750s, but lasted for the general population to the end of the century. Middle- and lower-class men usually wore cheaper worsted stockings.[70]

Shoes and Stockings

Shoes were made of black leather, with red or black heels and buckles that fastened the shoe over the tongue. From the 1780s, men gradually began to forgo buckles in favor of shoelaces. Pumps were worn sometimes until about 1760, brightly colored slippers were worn sometimes indoors, and boots of all kinds were worn for riding, hunting, traveling, and soldiering. Boots became a little too popular for the comfort of those with more formal tastes, like Beau Nash, who, upon seeing a booted gentleman in Bath's assembly rooms, would point out, "Sir, you have forgot your horse." To protect footwear while riding, some men wore spatterdashes, which were leather or canvas coverings stretching from the ankle and top of the foot to the thigh. Farmers, laborers, and some servants wore "high-lows" (short lace-up boots); city and country dwellers alike wore pattens or clogs.[71]

An array of cosmetics and accessories completed the appearance of the well-dressed man. In addition to perfumed wig powder, gentlemen used scents and cleansers. They might rouge their cheeks and lips and darken their eyebrows, perfume their linen, use wrinkle or acne creams,

Grooming and Accessories

and, in the 1790s when male legs were prominently on display, pad their calves.[72] Fops (men who were foolishly outlandish in dress and behavior) used a host of products, including anti-freckle night masks, "Jessamine

7.2 Costume through the century in a fictional family of gentle-men. Benjamin, c. 1710, wears a full-bottomed wig, a full-skirted coat with large cuffs, an embroidered waistcoat, a sword, ruffled shirt sleeves, and stockings rolled up over the breeches. His grand-son, George, c. 1762, wears a tye wig (with side curls and a ponytail behind), frock coat, and leather breeches; compare the simplicity of his frock coat with the elegance of the laced coats in Illustration 8.2. Both Benjamin and George carry their three-cornered cocked hats. George's grandson, Henry, c. 1800, wears a double-breasted coat, short waistcoat with stand collar, and light-colored breeches. Henry wears his own hair in a "Brutus crop."

butter for the hair," cold cream, tooth powder, separate sponge and hair toothbrushes, "perfumed mouth water," silver or ivory eyebrow combs, perfumed soap, black eyebrow powder, "orange-flower water," "almond paste," and essence of Bergamot.[73]

Most men also carried or wore accessories of some kind, like a walking stick or cane, soft leather gloves, a cravat or stock (the stock being a black or white made-up neckband that buckled in back), or a handker-chief. Most men also owned or aspired to own at least one pocket watch. Some carried snuff or toothpick boxes, and purses; a few carried fans or, after 1756, umbrellas, but these latter two items were considered effeminate. Gentlemen often wore swords, though more for ceremony than self-defense, and carried whips when riding.[74]

The 18th century saw plenty of daring experiments in male costume, but the general trend was toward simplicity— **Macaronis** plainer fabrics, duller hues, slimmer lines, tighter fit, and less ornamentation. In the middle of the century, however, a group of well-traveled young men, who had been on the Grand Tour to Europe and had brought back an enthusiasm for Italian culture, art, and food, banded together and dubbed themselves the Macaroni Club. Their experiments with fashion led them to simplify some elements of male dress and exaggerate others, and their "Macaroni" style—huge club wigs, tiny Nivernois hats, short waistcoats, high red heels, parasols, inside breast pockets, striped stockings, and shoes with the buckles "within an inch of the toe"—was much satirized. Soon anyone who dressed outlandishly was called a Macaroni parson, a Macaroni soldier, and so on.[75]

CHILDREN'S CLOTHING

"How has my heart ached many and many a time," says the heroine of *Pamela* in 1740, "when I have seen poor babies rolled and swathed, ten or a dozen times round; then blanket upon blanket, mantle upon that, its little neck pinned down to one posture; its head more frequently than it needs, triple-crowned like a young pope, with covering upon covering."[76] The procedure she describes is swaddling, still widely practiced in 1740, though by the end of the century it would be "almost universally laid aside."[77] The newborn infant was dressed in a shirt, wrapped in "a square piece of cloth called a bed" from chest to feet, then wrapped round and round with a three-inch-wide woollen strip called a roller. The arms were held straight against the body by a waistcoat, and the whole bundle was covered with a blanket or mantle, a long simple garment, sometimes with separate sleeves. The head was covered with three layers of caps.[78] It was believed that this confinement made the body grow straight; certainly it made the child more subdued and easy to care for, though in some cases the child grew frantic to free itself, in which case its struggles were termed convulsions and treated as a medical condition.[79]

At about four months or so, the arms were freed from the swaddling, but the lower extremities were still swaddled for a few months. When the swaddling was removed, boys and girls alike were dressed in frocks: simple dresses with fastenings in the back, and, later in the century, a sash. A pair of fabric strips, called "hanging sleeves," dangled from the shoulders until the 1780s. Beneath the frock children wore petticoats or sometimes drawers or trousers.[80] Toddlers also wore padded caps called "puddings" to protect their heads.[81]

At about age four, boys were "breeched," or put into distinctively masculine clothes for the first time. Early in the century, they were breeched directly into adult-style knee breeches. As the century passed, however, boys were breeched not into tight knee breeches but into longer, looser breeches, which grew downward into trousers (or tighter pantaloons) by the late 1770s and early 1780s. Typically, a boy's costume from ages four to eight was a "skeleton suit," a pair of loose trousers buttoned to the outside of a jacket or tunic. Often the sash worn with the toddler frock was retained for the skeleton suit.[82] (For an example of a boy in a late-century jacket and trousers, see Illustration 14.1. Examples of children dressed more like adults can be seen in Illustrations 3.3 and 3.5.) Girls remained in the childish frock with hanging sleeves until age twelve or later. They often wore frilled caps, shoes colored to match the sash and cap ribbons, and bibbed aprons to protect the frock. Late in the century, the bibbed apron was gradually replaced by the pinafore, which covered even more of the clothing.[83]

SPECIAL-OCCASION CLOTHING

People altered their clothing for certain occasions. For weddings, white trimmed with silver was popular for both bride and groom, but up until the middle of the century, and less commonly afterward, brides wore various other colors, such as blue and lilac; one in 1714 wore a blue satin mantua and a rose-colored petticoat trimmed with silver.[84] Grooms might wear white, silver, blue, brown, or some other color.[85] A bride in a 1794 print wears a blue dress, ordinary daytime headdress, and gray jacket bodice; the groom wears a fashionable square-cut waistcoat with horizontal stripes, tight breeches, and coat.[86] The poorer the couple, the more likely they were to wear their ordinary clothes for the wedding.

Mourning clothes, too, were usually fashionable clothes slightly altered. Sometimes white but much more commonly black, clothes for mourning and funerals were cut fashionably but of dull fabric, without ribbon, lace, braid, jewels, fancy aprons, and other decorations.[87] The rich ordered new mourning clothes. Less well-off mourners might take their clothes to a dyer to have them dyed black.[88] Servants were given mourning clothes when an employer died; Parson Woodforde, upon the death of his father, gave a family servant "a black crape Hatband and buckles and a black broad cloth Coat and waistcoat."[89] Some might wear scraps of black muslin, called "weepers," on their sleeves.[90] After a period of time, which varied according to the mourner's relationship to the deceased, "first mourning" with its dull blacks gave way to "second mourning," when colors like gray, or gray or black mixed with mauve, might be worn.

Dress for Court was conservative, even backward. Long after boning had been moved from the bodice to the stays, Court women retained the boned bodice.[91] After large hoops had been discarded by fashionable women, they were still required wear at Court. And not until almost the end of the century was the king seen at a reception wearing a frock coat. But if Court clothes were out of date, they were, by way of mitigation, thoroughly gorgeous, made of velvet, brocaded silks, gold and silver stuff, and embroidered cloth. Though contemporaries complained that merchants dressed too much like aristocrats and servants too much like employers, Court dress was impossible to confuse with anything else.

8

Days, Weeks, Months, and Years: The Passage of Time

The Hours of the Day and Night are taken up in the Cities of London and Westminster by people as different from each other as those who are born in different Centuries. Men of Six o'Clock give way to those of Nine, they of Nine to the Generation of Twelve, and they of Twelve disappear, and make Room for the fashionable World, who have made Two o'Clock the Noon of the Day.

—Richard Steele

Eighteenth-century England was a curious mix of old and new attitudes toward time. On the one hand, it harbored time-conscious manufacturers anxious to squeeze every minute of effort from their employees, and laborers who gladly invested hard-earned money in pocket watches and household clocks. (The clocks themselves reflected the urge to subdivide time; until the late 17th century, most clocks had only one hand—an hour hand—and the 18th century was the first to be dominated by two-handed clocks.[1]) This was, after all, the century in which the adage "time is money" was coined in Britain's American colonies.[2] But by the standards of later centuries, 18th-century Britain was almost lackadaisical about time. Each parish church set its clock to local time, often by means of a sundial.[3] When it was noon in London, for instance, it was about 12:11 in Bristol and 12:04 in Reading. Only in the 19th century, with the development of railroads, would nationwide synchronization of clocks become necessary.[4] A significant number of people still did not own watches and measured their days by evening and morning church bells, the passage of the sun, the movement of tides, or the perpetual demands of animals and crops.

The poor were most likely to be linked to the natural rhythms of tide, crop, and sun, in part because of the expense of candles. One candle casts a feeble light. To illuminate an entire room required a huge number of candles; the poor simply could not afford to stay up late. Nor would their jobs permit them, in most cases, to sleep in as late as the gentry. Farmers, for instance, had to milk their cows, and servants had to be awake before their employers, to be ready to dress and feed them.

DAYS

Morning for working people often began before dawn. Methodist preacher John Wesley got up at four,[5] and Edinburgh chemistry professor and physician William Cullen rose at seven.[6] Robert Tatersal's bricklayer, in a poem of 1734, rises at six, dresses, eats breakfast, and gets to work well before eight.[7] By contrast, an account in the *London Magazine* from 1775 has the archetypal fashionable woman rising at ten;[8] Pope, in a caricature of fashionable life, has morning begin at noon[9] and the French traveler La Rochefoucauld notes that the typical gentleman "gets up at about ten or eleven."[10] It should be noted, however, that these late risers, like the gentry themselves, were a highly visible but small minority of the population. Most people rose at or near dawn, awakened by the sun or the local watchman thumping on their doors with his stick and crying, "Good morrow, good morrow, my masters all."[11]

After rising, dressing, and breakfasting, people began the business of the day. At noon workers paused for dinner (it was not yet called lunch). After dinner, work, walks, and visits began again. Meanwhile, those few who constituted "the fashionable World" were just beginning to appear outdoors. From noon to two P.M., Queen's Walk in St. James's Park was filled with the élite, who considered it the best place for a promenade;[12] their "morning walk" actually took place early in the afternoon.

At five, some workers, especially skilled urban workers, laid down their tools, shared a beer with their colleagues, and headed home. Others might be at their duties for some hours to come; the farmer and weaver Cornelius Ashworth, in 1782, recorded working at his weaving until sunset.[13] In London during summer, the pleasure garden of Vauxhall opened at five, and all who could afford the entrance fee were admitted to its paths, arches, pavilions, tea shops, and concerts.[14] Five o'clock was also, according to La Rochefoucauld, the dinner hour for gentlemen, who had risen only some six or seven hours before.[15]

The hours of tea, supper, and bedtime varied as much as those of rising. Farmers, craftsmen, and their wives might spend the hours after

8.1 "High Life at Noon," anon., 1769. The quality grope the maid, pass love notes, and get dunned by a tradesman. Courtesy of the Print Collection, Lewis Walpole Library, Yale University.

8.2 "High Life in the Evening, or Quality Dinner Hour," anon., 1769. Dinner was the middle meal of the day, what many people today would call lunch; note the hour on the clock. Courtesy of the Print Collection, Lewis Walpole Library, Yale University.

supper mending clothes, tidying the coal heap, and sweeping the kitchen. If they could afford a few candles, they might stay up as late as ten to do such chores.[16] In London, some took another turn in the Queen's Walk at seven,[17] while others attended a performance of the Eidophusikon (a mechanical picture) at 7:30.[18] At nine or so, gentlemen gathered at clubs and taverns to drink and gamble, staying out until at least midnight, sometimes until two or three.

WEEKS

This daily pattern was followed for most of the week. Work days technically included Monday through Saturday, and in many occupations the six-day workweek was the rule. However, in some jobs, where workers were based at home and set their own schedules, there was greater flexibility. Sunday's holiday tended, in these cases, to extend into Monday and sometimes even into Tuesday as well; those who took a long weekend in this manner were said to be observing "Saint Monday." Weavers, cutlers, cobblers, colliers, and a host of other workers spent Monday drinking, gambling, and watching cock fights, much to the dismay of employers, the gentry, and some of the workers' wives. In many areas, though, the wives and masters had fled the battle. Monday was often the day set aside for the weekly market, conferring a sort of authority on this informal holiday.

There was a price to pay, of course, for taking off an extra day or two. Wednesday, Thursday, Friday, and Saturday were days of long and grueling labor for those who honored Saint Monday. Tradition held that the loom's song on Monday and Tuesday was "*Plen-ty of Time, Plen-ty of Time*," but that by Thursday and Friday it sang, "*A day t'lat, A day t'lat*."[19] The four days of hard work in a week, in these trades, might last sixteen or seventeen hours.[20] At Guy's Hospital in London, Thursday was "taking-in day," when new patients were admitted, and Friday was the day when the hospital rules were read aloud in each ward.[21] Saturday, according to John Gay, was in London the day for serious cleaning by housemaids,

> When dirty waters from balconies drop,
> And dext'rous damsels twirl the sprinkling mop,
> And cleanse the spattered sash, and scrub the stairs.[22]

Saturday's furious activity contrasted with the enforced quiet of the following day.

For parts of the century, religious organizations policed observance of the sabbath by prosecuting offenders, but even without such interference, Sunday was unlike any other day in the week. It was, overwhelmingly, the day for church wakes—festivals to celebrate the dedication of parish churches, traditionally celebrated on saints' days, but now moved to the closest Sunday.[23] Trade and most public entertainments were banned, and foreign visitors found it a somber day; Dr. Johnson felt it was best observed not "with rigid severity and gloom, but with a gravity and simplicity of behaviour."[24] However, even if most theaters and exhibitions were closed, people found ways to enjoy themselves. Working people walked to nearby mineral spas in the morning, took the waters or simply milled about in an "unruly and unmannerly" fashion, and then walked home again at night.[25] Others went to church and then rested at home with their families.

MONTHS AND SEASONS

Market, churchgoing, and work marked the passage of the week, and other cycles and celebrations marked the passage of months and seasons. Phases of the moon were closely watched, partly for the sake of superstition (it was considered unlucky to cut hair except at the full moon, for example) and partly for practical reasons (traveling at night with a full moon was safer because it was brighter).[26] The year was delineated, for most people, by its special occasions: the king's birthday; regional fairs; the "beating of the bounds," during which a procession marked the territorial boundaries of the parish; hanging days at Tyburn; the Lord Mayor's Day in London; birthdays; trade processions, such as the weavers' parade on St. Blaise's Day; and provincial tradesmen's trips to London, often only once a year, on business.

Spring brought the culmination of the London season; Parliament's business, which had begun in November, concluded in April, and the social season ended in June.[27] Spring was also, according to superstition, the safest time to be bled for medical purposes.[28] It was the season of Easter, beginning as early as Shrove Tuesday, in February or early March, with violent football games in the streets, despite the occasional efforts of magistrates to suppress the sport.[29] On the following day, Ash Wednesday, there was an annual boxing match between Bristol's blacksmiths (and sometimes weavers) on one side, and its coopers, carpenters, and sailors on the other.[30] Six weeks later came Good Friday; there was special bread, believed to have magical healing powers, and hot cross buns, sold in the streets with the cry, "one or two a penny hot cross buns."[31] Also on Good Friday, "children took little baskets neatly trimmed with moss, and went 'a pace-egging', and received at some places eggs, at some places spiced loaf, and at others half-pennies."[32] The following Sunday was Easter, and the seventh Sunday after Easter was Whit Sunday. The days following were known as Whitsuntide and were celebrated with feasting. Lady Day, March 25, was, with Midsummer Day, Michaelmas, and Christmas, one of the days that divided the year into quarters.

8.3 "May-Day in London," drawn by Samuel Collings, engraved by William Blake, from *The Wit's Magazine* (1784), shows an annual celebration in London's Milk Street. The piles of brushes and cups symbolize the trades for which May Day was a holiday. Courtesy of the Print Collection, Lewis Walpole Library, Yale University.

Other spring holidays were pagan or secular in origin. May 28 was the birthday of George I, May 29 the anniversary of the restoration of the monarchy in 1660. On the latter day, church bells were rung and bonfires lit.[33] May Day, May 1, was a day of morris dancing, fertility symbols, flirting, chimney-sweeps' processions, a king-of-the-hill-style battle between colliers and farmers in Shropshire,[34] and dances around maypoles.

In the summer, most of the fashionable crowd left London for watering places like Epsom (where July was the height of the season) and Richmond;[35] those who remained entertained themselves at Vauxhall, and, in the last third of the century, at the Royal Academy's art exhibition.[36] Grain prices rose as supplies from last year's harvest dwindled.[37] Migratory swallows returned for the warm weather and the swarms of insects that came with summer.[38] June brought thunderstorms, the birthday of the Jacobite Old Pretender on the tenth, Midsummer Day on the twenty-fourth, and the arrival of the East India Company's fleet, laden with tea, from China.[39] August 1 was the anniversary of the 1714 accession of George I, the first Hanoverian king; the day was marked by the Dogget's Coat and Badge Race, a rowing contest held between London Bridge and Chelsea, in which the winner received an orange coat and a silver badge honoring the house of Hanover.[40] Sturbridge Fair, a huge market and festival in Cambridgeshire, began in August (and ended in September).[41] August was also usually the month of the grain harvest (though in some areas it might take place in September or even October) and of the innumerable festivals, large and small, that celebrated the generosity of nature. Once the wheat was cut, drovers began guiding huge flocks of geese through the stubbled fields, where the birds fed on stray kernels of wheat as they made their slow way from Norfolk to London.[42]

The harvest of various crops—walnuts, plums, pears[43]—continued through the autumn months, even as the rains began. Great schools of herring swam along the southwest and southeast coasts of the island. Michaelmas, September 29, was the first day of a fishing fair at Yarmouth that lasted to the end of October,[44] and the day most servants began their next year's employment. Michaelmas was also the day most agricultural rents were due, and grain prices dropped as the harvested grain, sold to pay the rents, made its way onto the market.[45] Graziers from Lincolnshire and Leicestershire sold off many of their sheep to farmers and butchers near London, and the price of mutton would drop also.[46] By October, the roads were "too stiff and deep"[47] to drive geese. The common people swarmed to the rowdy Horn Fair in Charlton, Kent, on October 19, to make fun of cuckolds and eat horned gingerbread men.[48] The fashionable crowd (if they were not at the Horn Fair in disguise), went to the horse races at Newmarket, and returned to begin a new London season. In November, Parliament returned to its business, and the people turned their attention toward the patriotic celebrations of November 5. This was a double anniversary. In 1688 it was the day William III landed in Devonshire to oust the Catholic King James II. It was also Guy Fawkes' Day, the anniversary of the failure of Fawkes' 1605 plot to blow up the Houses of Parliament. Guy Fawkes' Day was celebrated with bonfires and the hanging and burning of "guys" (effigies of Fawkes and sometimes of unpopular local residents).[49]

Winter brought, if not scarcity, then at least less bounty. Farm laborers employed during the harvest now found themselves with less or no work. Those who did have jobs or farms of their own had less to do, and the idleness, combined with the need to stay crowded indoors with one's coworkers or family, must have made people edgier. The roads worsened, limiting travel. The price of mutton rose.[50] As Christmas grew near, weavers gave their children extra work to do at the looms, and extra treats were given when the work was completed. Christmas carols were sung during the day to make the work go faster, and to help the workers to stay awake.[51] In London, street hawkers, with their loud cries, solicited buyers for rosemary, bay laurel, holly, and mistletoe. Twelve days after Christmas, the English celebrated Twelfth Night, and on January 30, fasts and prayers marked the anniversary of the execution of Charles I. February 2 was Candlemas; February 14 was St. Valentine's Day, even then a day for lovers:

> An equal number of maids and bachelors get together; each writes his or her true or some feigned name upon separate billets, which they roll up and draw by way of lots, the maids taking the men's billets, and the men the maids'; so that each of the young men lights upon a girl that he calls his Valentine, and each of the girls upon a young men which she calls hers. . . . Fortune having thus divided the company into so many couples, the Valentines give balls and treats to their fair mistresses, wear their billets several days upon their bosoms and sleeves, and this little sport often ends in love.[52]

And so the year passed, through the darkness of winter and back to spring. Shrove Tuesday football, with its cathartic violence and dirt, was just around the corner.

THE CALENDAR ACT

The 18th century was a mixture of industrial, agrarian, religious, and political cycles of time: the work day, the harvest, the sessions of Parliament. It was Parliament, in fact, that enabled the century's most dramatic restructuring of time. Passed in 1751, the Calendar Act took effect the following year, and it brought Britain into synch with the rest of Europe by switching from the Julian to the Gregorian calendar. The literati had little difficulty with the change, but there was widespread resistance in some quarters. Some feared that the consequent loss of eleven days in September of that year was unnatural; some resented missing their birthdays as a result. Some of the clergy felt uneasy about celebrating religious holidays on their "new" dates.[53] Others cited a miraculous appearance of bees on the old-style Christmas Eve (bees were believed by the superstitious to swarm at midnight on the night before Christmas) as proof that the new style was wrong.[54] There was, in the 18th century, a very modern desire to meddle with time, and, simultaneously, a very conservative desire to maintain the old rhythms of life. In the battle between clocks with minute hands and the magical swarms of bees, the minute hands would ultimately prevail, but for this century, at least, the outcome of the battle was unclear.

9

"Do What You're Bidden": Work and Wages

Raising the wages of day labourers is wrong for it does not make them live better, but only makes them idler.

—Samuel Johnson

A few generalizations may be applied to most 18th-century work: women and children were lower paid than men; children began to work quite early, as young as four or five; and the lower the family income, the more likely it came from several sources, with family members combining seasonal farm labor, textile production, factory work or some other manual labor, scavenging, or even petty crime.

Wages tended to be higher in London and in the south than in the north, though northern wages rose faster late in the century, when industrialization was well under way.[1] Workers had little recourse when they had complaints about their employers, especially when "combinations" (labor unions) were being made illegal and guilds were losing their ancient power. Some areas or trades had special tribunals for these matters; others were left with strikes and riots when perquisites were ended and wages were stagnant, reduced, or unpaid. Even in the best of circumstances, workers were often paid irregularly and infrequently—in some cases, only once a year, or when they left their employers' service. The work day might be as short as ten hours or as long as sixteen; the number of days worked varied by trade but in most cases was six per week. Unemployment rose during winter (when agricultural laborers

9.1 "The Produce of Industry," 1793, after Robert Dighton. An idealized portrait of farm life, showing some common tasks: harnessing a horse, filling a wagon with grain, feeding chickens. The family is simple but prosperous, with a good thatched roof house and plenty of cows, martins, and grapevines. Courtesy of the Print Collection, Lewis Walpole Library, Yale University.

had little to do), peace (when soldiers had little to do), and the London season (when servants and tradesmen dependent on country gentry had little to do).

FARMERS

A third of all workers in 1800, and an even larger percentage earlier in the century, were employed in agriculture.[2] In small towns, the percentage was much higher; Tilbrook, Bedfordshire, had 219 residents in 1800, 214 of whom worked the land.[3] Most of these agricultural workers were tenants who paid rent in cash or produce, or day laborers who were hired by landlords and tenant farmers. Day laborers might find work by going door to door, or by presenting themselves at "mops," or regional hiring fairs.[4] Domestic servants, especially in smaller households, helped out with harvesting and dairying, and urban workers might migrate to the countryside during harvest to make extra income. In some cases, craftsmen combined a trade, like weaving, with farming.

Farm life was especially arduous in the days before many tasks were mechanized. Grain was reaped with scythes. Sheep were shorn without electric shears. Hardened clods of earth were broken up by women armed with wooden mallets. Harvest time was jubilant, with cheers and the rumbling of laden wagons saluting the stubbled fields, and harvest was followed by feasting, revelry, and courtship. But if the harvest was poor, or if the rains came too soon and ruined the standing grain, there might be little joy. In any case, harvest was a prelude to more hard work. The poorest members of the community came through the fields to "glean," or search for stray grain dropped from the stalks during harvest. Once the grain was in, the work had just begun for the threshers, who beat the stalks against wooden planks with "Crab-Tree Staves" to shake loose the kernels of wheat, rye, or barley. It was sweaty, dusty, noisy work—so noisy, according to the poet Stephen Duck, that one could not hear the voices of one's companions.[5]

This is not to say that 18th-century agriculture remained entirely medieval in character. On the contrary, important innovations were popularized during this century. Most costly in human terms was enclosure, accomplished by expensive, privately lobbied acts of Parliament. An enclosure act took a village's commons (communally farmed open land) and parceled it out to individual owners, who could then fence the land and farm it as they chose. Particularly popular during the second half of the century, enclosure had plenty of advantages. It created employment, as the owners added ditches, fences, hedges, roads, and outbuildings to their land. It minimized overgrazing, communication of animal diseases, and misuse of the land, ended petty disputes over crops, grazing, and water, and resulted in a much greater grain output.[6] For cottagers, however, enclosure was a disaster. The Reverend Richard Warner observed, "Time was when these commons enabled the poor man to support his family, and bring up his children. Here he could turn out his cow and pony, feed his flock of geese, and keep his pig. But the enclosures have deprived him of these advantages."[7] The loss of grazing and fuel-gathering rights was keenly felt and drove many families to accept charity or to fight enclosure with vandalism and riot. Enclosure, like its close cousin, engrossing (ousting smaller tenant farmers to combine one's land into larger rented parcels), was perceived as a purely selfish endeavor.

It was the large, easily controlled parcels of land, however, that allowed owners and tenants to introduce new techniques. Some improved the soil by adding lime, clay, or fertilizers; MP Edmund Burke experimented with the relative virtues of pigeon and rabbit dung.[8] Some drained marshes or brought wasteland under the plow. Some followed the example of Lord Townshend, who advocated a fourfold rotation of crops: cereals, root crops, clover, and grasses. Townshend, a booster of turnips for the root-crop phase, earned himself the nickname "Turnip Townshend." Crop rotation enabled animals to be grazed year round rather than grazed in summer and fed scanty stored fodder in winter; this resulted in healthier animals and more continuous supplies of manure in the fields. More manure meant better soil, which led to better crops the following season, which led to even healthier animals. Another innovator was Jethro Tull, who promoted horse hoeing and planting seed with a drill he invented rather than by hand.[9] Other landowners experimented with animals rather than crops. Robert Bakewell inbred his stock for more meat and fat and less bone; he coaxed the fluffy English sheep from its lanky, hairy predecessor and influenced the thinking of evolutionist Charles Darwin and geneticist Gregor Mendel. Selective breeding and improved feeding more than doubled the average weight of calves, oxen, and sheep sold at Smithfield between 1710 and 1795.[10]

Wealthy farmers and prominent landowners could earn hundreds or even thousands of pounds a year. But in 1759, Joseph Massie thought there were about 90,000 small freeholders making from £50 to £199 per year, and another 120,000 making only from £25 to £39. He also guessed there were 155,000 tenant farmers making from £40 to £199, and 400,000 "husbandmen" and "country labourers" making £24 or less.[11] It hardly made for lavish living, and a drop in grain prices could mean real hardship. There were perquisites, like free beer during harvest, but most agricultural workers—shepherds, plowmen, hop pickers, drovers, threshers, weeders, and others—made just enough to survive.

SERVANTS

Servants made up another large class of workers. A great household might have as many as fifty servants; a middle-class household might have between two and ten. Almost everyone strove to hire at least one, but the poor could afford none at all, a serious situation when all wash was done by hand and all cooking and heating required the nurturing of fires.[12] All in all, there were perhaps from 600,000 to 700,000 domestic servants.[13]

Most servants came from the country, where at the age of sixteen or so boys went into apprenticeships or farm labor, and girls into domestic service. Servants were usually hired for a year-long term, beginning and ending at Michaelmas (September 29), and were paid yearly.[14] They found posts by getting referrals and recommendations, by going to work for wealthier relatives, or, increasingly, by using employment agencies known as "register offices."[15] Some were supplied, chiefly to inns and alehouses, by workhouses, which paid the employers a premium to take pauper girls off their hands. Such workhouse servants were especially susceptible to abuse, sexual assault, and even murder.[16]

Getting a job was less than half the battle. Keeping it was just as tricky. An employer could dismiss a servant for the slightest cause: rudeness, dishonesty, suspected theft, or even inconvenience—some landowners simply dismissed most of their country house staff when they traveled to London or abroad. Servants proven to have stolen their masters' goods were not merely fired but hanged.[17] Servants, too, often quit out of dis-

9.2 "A JORD—N for the Duke's Chamber." 1791. The Duke of Clarence's cook and chambermaids compare his mistress to a chamberpot. Courtesy of the Print Collection, Lewis Walpole Library, Yale University.

satisfaction, though for them the stakes were higher. A fired servant was due her wages to date, but one who quit was entitled to nothing. Unless she already had another post lined up, she might be unemployed for months. Her situation was especially precarious if she left her last job without a good character reference.[18] Nevertheless, turnover was high, especially in smaller households, where there was little chance for promotion; the average length of employment in two- to ten-servant households was from two to four years.[19]

Domestic service had its perks. In better-off households, servants might wear "livery"—a kind of uniform, cut in fashionable style, though usually of cheaper materials than the master's clothes. Livery conferred status within the community of servants (where, in private, servants sometimes jokingly adopted the titles of the people they served).[20] Servants also inherited clothes when employers died, or were given castoffs to wear or sell. In some cases, as with livery boys (who ran errands for the household), the clothing allowance was the only wage. However, servants given clothing by their masters were sometimes expected to give the clothes back upon quitting or being fired, and even servants given clothes on a permanent basis had to keep them washed. Some were given a washing allowance—money to cover their laundry costs—and some were allowed to have their clothes washed with their employers' laundry, but many had to pay for laundering out of their own meagre wages.[21]

There were other benefits. Servants might be remembered in an employer's will; Samuel Johnson left his manservant £70 a year.[22] Household staff got to brew their own tea from the employers' expensive leaves, then sell the twice-used leaves to the poor.[23] A few servants got a tea and sugar allowance; others got allowances for fire, candles, ale, and beer. The housekeeper usually got to keep "broken victuals"—leftover food not desired by the family, and the servants' quarters often inherited chairs with three legs, chipped or scratched dishes, and other damaged goods. Servants were often believed to spoil objects on purpose to get them for their own use.[24] There were other illicit ways of enjoying one's work: stealing from the larder or wine cellar, spying on an employer's sex life (even drilling holes in the wainscot to get a better view),[25] or—in the case of servants entrusted with making purchases—taking kickbacks in the form of "Christmas boxes" from tradesmen.[26] About one-third of servants, a disproportionate number of them male, were able to parlay their wages, perks, and experience into social mobility, becoming tradesmen or innkeepers after leaving service.[27]

One perk that came under attack in the 18th century was the taking of tips, or "vails." Visitors to a house were expected, on departing, to tip the servants, who sometimes massed in a line near the door awaiting payment. Inn servants and servants who carried packages or messages could also expect vails. Daniel Defoe estimated that an £8-a-year maid could expect £8 a year in vails, and male servants often made much more; footman Piggot Horton earned £4 a year in salary and claimed to have made £100 a year in vails. A typical tip was 1s., and if the guests paying vails were a married couple, the wife might tip the female staff, and her husband the manservants.[28] The movement against vails gained momentum in the 1760s, reached Parliament, provoked riots in 1764, retreated slightly, and made slow, steady progress for the rest of the century, yet it never quite eradicated the custom in all areas.[29] Some employers continued to sanction vails because it lessened their responsibility to pay decent wages.

Wages were certainly low. Admittedly, servants usually got food and lodging in addition to wages, but pay was often in arrears or paid in goods rather than cash.[30] Employers deducted for breakage, loans, mistakes, absence from church, holiday absences (even as little as three days at Easter and Christmas), drunkenness, and other major and minor infractions.[31] However, good servants could often bargain for raises or better jobs, and many, despite employers' resistance, insisted on "a month's wages, or a month's warning" when dismissed.[32]

Hazards and discomforts were many. Hours were long; servants were often on duty from dawn to late at night, and on call twenty-four hours a day. If they got sick, they might be fired. The only "pensions" were tenant farms at low rent, usually reserved for long-time servants to the wealthy; the average maid had no such prospects.[33] The unfortunate lived on charity after their usefulness had ended. Employers were often rude, like Lady Clavering, who threw a pair of breakfast tongs at her butler, or genuinely abusive, like the employer who had a footman suspected of theft "stripped to the waist, hoisted over the servants' hall door, and very well flogged."[34] Some masters, feeling guilty, tipped their servants after beating them.[35]

Not all employers were unpleasant. Some treated their servants handsomely; Nicholas Blundell, for example, "would visit them when [they were] ill, lend them a horse to take them home on a visit, and when any of their family died, would lend his coach for the use of the bereaved."[36] Conditions were loose enough in many households for the servants to hold private parties in the kitchen, even inviting fellow-servants from other households.[37] But even in the best households, there was no guarantee of job security, as a 1791 letter to the *London Chronicle* illustrates: "a *servant*, though never so attentive and industrious . . . lives in *fear* of not only being discarded from their service, but also of being deprived of that which is the only recommendation to his future subsistence, which recommendation consists in a good *character*."[38] The lack of a good reference from one's last employer could mean lengthy unemployment, or employment only in a disreputable household. Unemployment often meant a descent into crime, which in turn often led to disease, jail, transportation, whipping, or death. Losing one's "character" was no small threat.

Servants were expected to be celibate. Rules banning boyfriends or "followers" were de rigueur in many households, and married couples, who might value their own families more than their employers', were seldom hired. Yet women servants were considered naturally lascivious and sexually available to the master, his sons, his guests, and sometimes other servants. Maids were often young and vulnerable, separated from their family and friends in the prime of their adolescence, and faced with years of enforced chastity before they could save enough to marry. They slept in seldom-lockable alcoves, garrets, and outbuildings, and were often alone in bedchambers, lighting or tending fires, cleaning fireplaces, making beds, caring for clothing, or waiting up to undress the master when he returned from an evening abroad. Added to ample opportunity was the inducement of a bribe—masters often offered money or a gift in exchange for sex—and a threat of losing one's character. Many women succumbed out of fear, greed, despair, sexual frustration, or a combination of emotions.[39]

But if servants had plenty of reason to complain about masters, masters found reasons to complain about servants—and masters' opinions were far more likely to be recorded. Complaints ranged from trivial annoyances to profound breaches of trust. Servants, it was said, did not come fast enough when called, embezzled household funds, demanded raises, gave "pert and insolent" responses to rebukes, wasted time on errands, forgot visitors' names, left doors open or slammed them, gossiped, stole food, overspent in their departments, used poor hygiene, and refused to do anything outside their own job description.[40] Employers preferred servants who could live by the Scottish proverb, "Speak when you're spoken to, do what you're bidden, / Come when you're called, and you'll not be chidden."[41]

Men were rarer than women in domestic service; of an estimated 910,000 servants in England and Wales in 1806, only 110,000 were men.[42] Part of this discrepancy was due to earlier and higher taxes on male servants, and part was due to men's wider occupational options. Men clustered in the higher-paid, higher-status, less arduous service jobs— butler, who looked after the dining room and wine cellar, decanted and bottled wine and ale, and served liquor; groom, who took care of the horses and tack, accompanied his employer on horseback, and held the master's horse or riding jacket; coachman; footman, who waited at table and ran errands; running footman, who cleared a path for the coach on city streets; gamekeepers; steward, who managed a country estate, paid its bills, and kept the owner informed; and gardener. This was precisely why employers were taxed more for male servants—male servants cared for luxuries like wine, coaches, horses, and extensive gardens. But everyone needed female servants to do the unavoidable tasks of daily life—laundering, sewing, emptying chamberpots, dusting, hauling water, lighting fires, and shopping.[43]

Smaller households hired proportionally fewer men, and in such homes servants of both sexes were more likely to fill a variety of roles: plowman-coachman-butler, for example, or footman-groom-gardener.[44] A manservant in such a house might look after the master's clothes, attend him on visits, run errands, accompany children to school, buy and sell horses, cook, and make wine.[45]

If a household could afford only one servant, however, it was almost certain to be a woman, a "maid-of-all-work," who cooked, cleaned, gardened, milked the cows, looked after the children, and helped in the shop.[46] In larger households, maids, sometimes called "Abigails," were more likely to specialize. Nurserymaids and wet nurses cared for children. Laundry and kitchen maids were at the bottom of the hierarchy; housemaids or chambermaids were higher up. Sometimes called "spiderbrushers" after their dusting tasks, housemaids mended, made beds, closed and opened windows, tidied, served tea, swept, washed windows and stairs, oiled fireplace tools, hauled water, made fires, emptied fireplaces, polished fireplace fixtures and door locks, and emptied chamberpots.[47] Higher still in the household hierarchy were the cook, housekeeper, and lady's maid (who dressed the mistress, cared for her clothes, carried her messages, prevented or assisted her amours, and ran or accompanied her on errands). Such upper servants were most likely to get perks; the cook got to keep drippings and leftovers, the lady's maid her mistress' cast-off clothes.

LABORERS

Plenty of other occupations offered small wages and limited opportunities for advancement. Unskilled and semiskilled workers did the heavy, dirty jobs, hauling and cleaning, extracting and building. There were coal heavers, sawyers, thatchers, brick makers, donkey and hog drivers, sand carriers, ship scrapers, porters, crossing sweepers, fishermen, woodcutters, carters, shoeblacks (shoeshine boys), hackney coachmen, gravediggers, watchmen, waiters, and wheelchair-pushers. There were miners of coal, tin, and lead, who, susceptible to damps, poisonous gases, and explosions, spent their lives in

The dark inextricable maze,
Where cavern crossing cavern meets

(City of subterraneous streets!),
Where in a triple storey end
Mines that o'er mines by flights ascend.[48]

There were sawyers working in teams, bricklayers calling "Mortar!" "Bricks!" and "A line, a line!" as they wielded their trowels, lightermen ferrying goods from large ships to London's wharves, dustmen hauling dust and rubbish, dairymaids carrying pails of milk on their heads, washerwomen rising in the dark and scrubbing linen until their fingers bled into the washwater, sedan chairmen waiting in the cold for their fares to emerge from the clubs and gaming-houses, beggars stopping passersby, and canal "bankers" working in gangs building embankments and clearing drains.

A new area of employment was factory work. Men, women, and children alike were drawn to the relative job security and decent wages. In some cases, there were bonuses for especially good work, sickness insurance (paid for by mandatory employee contributions), schools for the employees' children, and even whole mill towns built from scratch with chapels, shops, and gardens. There were also disadvantages to factory work: loss of control over work hours and materials, an insistence on punctuality represented by bells and clocking in, dangerous machinery into which children sometimes had to climb to retrieve broken threads, and fines or firing for a variety of infractions, including insubordination, bringing alcohol on the premises, lateness, sleeping, talking, and idleness.[49]

The workers who attracted the most sympathy were, not coincidentally, some of the youngest. Chimney sweeps were not alone in beginning their trade at age four or five, but they worked in especially harsh conditions. They cleaned the chimneys from inside, scuttling up the flues using their feet and backs and scrubbing the soot loose with brushes. If they refused to climb, their masters prodded them with pins or fires. They faced a host of dangers, the most terrifying of which was the high-paid work of putting out chimney fires. The soot that coated their bodies and lungs also caused skin ailments, urinary infections, and scrotal cancer. To keep them from taking up too much room in the chimneys, they were fed little and dressed in few clothes, even at the height of the winter cleaning season. If they lived to the age of twelve or so, they were too big for the work and were abandoned by their employers.[50]

SOLDIERS AND SAILORS

Another job that involved long hours, miserable conditions, and low pay was military service. The size of the military varied from as few as 30,000 in peacetime to as many as 200,000 in war, not counting the militia and volunteer corps founded in the second half of the century.[51] By the end of the century, the militia, founded in 1757, numbered nearly 100,000.[52] The wartime forces were assembled in various ways: by holding recruiting drives and offering bonuses for enlistees, by commandeering merchant vessels and crews, by using press gangs to force layabouts into the army and navy, and by hiring mercenaries.

Ordinary seamen, soldiers, and militiamen were overwhelmingly poor. Officers, on the other hand, were frequently wealthy and well-connected. Under George I and George II, no Tories were awarded army commissions,[53] and even before the Georges, promotions were based on political influence. Sir Richard Steele observed in *The Spectator* that "no Man can rise suitably to his Merit, who is not something of a Courtier as well as a Soldier."[54] An extreme example was the political appointee made an ensign at age two, although most officer-track candidates waited until the ripe old age of eleven or twelve before going to sea. Sometimes they began with a letter of introduction from the king and were known as "King's Letter Boys."[55] By 1800, 38 percent of naval officers and even more army officers came from titled or landed families. Wealth was a prerequisite because commissions had to be purchased. An ensigncy, at mid-century, cost about £400, while a lieutenant colonelcy cost about £3,500.[56]

The army was admired at times, with young men aping military dress, and great victories were commemorated on everything from paintings to scarves.[57] The army was also supported by various charities. Officers lived well, and officers and men alike had the reputation of being dashing lovers. Yet the army was the least popular branch of the service. Its infantry in particular was considered a disorderly nuisance,[58] and its presence in England, especially in peacetime, was thought to be nothing short of despotism. The statesman Charles James Fox preferred to be "governed by a mob, than a standing army."[59] Furthermore, army life was not easy. Units traveled with carts and carts of baggage for officers, plus provisions, ammunition carts, herds of cattle, packhorses, cooks, laundresses, carpenters, smiths, hospital attendants and supplies, servants, traders, prostitutes, and soldiers' families.[60] The men, dressed in their heavy red wool uniforms, carried their packs, food, water, tent equipment, blankets, weapons, and sixty rounds of ammunition.[61] Their arms were flintlock muskets, clumsy weapons whose reliable range was about a hundred yards. The average soldier could load and fire his gun only two or three times a minute, juggling powder, cartridge, ball, and rod; with the bayonet fixed, loading was almost impossible and firing was highly inaccurate.[62]

There were other disadvantages. Soldiers were notoriously poorly paid. They earned 8d. a day, from which there were deductions for food, clothing, weapons repairs, the salaries of regimental officials, and the veterans' hospital. All in all, soldiers made about £14 a year.[63] In addition, they faced lice, death from sunstroke or disease, and brutal disci-

9.3 "John Bull's Progress," James Gillray, 1793. His enlistment in the army, with its nearly nonexistent pay, leads John Bull's family to sell its household goods. The soldier returns from war, with a missing eye and leg, to find his family starving and ragged. One of the pawned tools is the family spinning wheel. Though spinning was often mechanized by 1793, the image of wife and daughters handspinning at home remained a powerful ideal. Courtesy of the Print Collection, Lewis Walpole Library, Yale University.

pline that included hundreds of lashes for a single offense, up to 250 of them delivered in a single day.[64] Death and dismemberment in battle were all too common. A print called "Recruits" shows a pitiful group of recruits under an inn whose emblem is a soldier with a peg leg, a missing eye, and an arm amputated above the elbow.[65] Poem after poem describes the plight of the demobilized soldier, "with loss of leg, / Reduced from port to port to beg."[66] Between wars, officers were often reduced to half pay. Common soldiers begged if disabled, and often stole if healthy; crime rates usually went up when soldiers came home from war.

The navy, known fondly as "the wooden walls of England," was much more popular. Navy ships could be grand looking. A ship of the line had between sixty and one hundred guns, four acres of sails, and a mainmast 200 feet above the waterline and three feet in diameter at the base. Also, during war, crews shared in the loot. Captains and admirals got the lion's share, but the seamen, cooks, and stewards shared 25 percent. Sailors did not have to carry heavy packs or wear thick uniforms; they dressed lightly in caps, loose trousers, and shirts. And ships often carried special personnel, like a chaplain, or a tutor for the younger sailors.[67]

It is unclear whether a sailor's life was much more pleasant than a soldier's, however. The common sailors (though not the officers) paid the chaplain's salary out of their own, a groat a month per man.[68] Sailors, like soldiers, faced disease, death, and injury at worst, and hard work, stench, and cramped quarters at best. The food—salted meat, oatmeal, peas, butter, cheese, beer, and biscuits—was often rotten, or filled with weevils and maggots.[69] Routine perils included running aground on rocks, fire aboard ship, and ships in poor repair; in 1777, only six of thirty-five ships of the line were seaworthy.[70] Life aboard ship included glorious activities like pumping water, urinating in open tubs kept to put out fires, defecating in filthy privies smeared with other people's waste as a practical joke, and sweating for between ten minutes and half a day to perform the basic maneuver of tacking (adjusting the sails to make the most of the wind). In battle, mastering the wind became critical, as ships could fire only when they were aligned side by side. During these broadsides, the men worked the guns and hoped their own ship would not sink. A highly trained crew could, in about two minutes, remove the ropes around a gun, level the gun with the deck, remove the tompion (stopper) from the muzzle, load powder and shot, stick the gun through its gunport, prime it with more gunpowder, prepare a match, aim, fire, and swab out any stray burning material with a sponge.[71] They continued this hot fierce work sometimes for hours at a time. Sailors lived "[r]agged and lousy, hungry . . . and poor."[72]

PROVIDERS OF GOODS AND SERVICES

Some workers offered special services or skills. These workers included lice, flea, and rat catchers; knife sharpeners; tinkers, who mended pots; usurers and pawnbrokers; innkeepers; scriveners; hairdressers; shippers and haulers; barbers; gardeners; and ostlers, who cared for horses at inns.

Of those who provided goods, some made goods, some merely sold them, and some did a little of both. Among those who were principally or solely retailers were ironmongers (who sold hardware), fishmongers, fellmongers (who dealt in hides, especially sheepskins), and dealers in china, wine, brandy, carpet, "slops" (secondhand clothing), tea, and coal. A large number of shopkeepers sold clothing or textiles, including drapers, who sold linen and wool cloth; mercers, who dealt in finer fabrics like silk and velvet; and haberdashers, who sold ready-made clothes and what would today be called accessories.[73]

Small shops were frequently combined with a trade, odd jobs, or another shopkeeping trade. William Wood of Didsbury was a shopkeeper, plowman, coal dealer, moneylender, and innkeeper.[74] Even if they followed only one trade, shopkeepers were busy people, traveling long miles to purchase stock, dealing with large numbers of suppliers, bustling about on market day, receiving visits from the traveling salesmen of London firms, measuring, weighing, selling, recording transactions and any credit given, and keeping up with the regulation of certain items.[75] The sale and transportation of tea, for example, was subject to strict government oversight, and the purchase of coconuts was limited to twenty-eight pounds at a time, with the buyer's name and address recorded.[76] Despite their long hours and hard work, however, shopkeepers were usually considered greedy, and they were frequently suspected (often without justification) of taking too much profit, or of selling underweight or adulterated goods.[77]

Goods were also sold in the streets by hawkers and peddlers. Street sellers sold flowers, pies, milk, coal, pickles, apples, gingerbread, sausages, newspapers, water, rags, doormats, ballads, and more.

Craftsmen and artisans who produced goods ranged from humble journeymen employing only their spouses to master manufacturers with hundreds of workers. The average artisan probably made about £60 a year.[78] He (or, in some cases, she—usually an artisan's widow) might be a metalworker: a blacksmith, goldsmith, silversmith, nail maker, brass founder, gunsmith, file maker (an important trade when all machine parts needed to be hand filed for accuracy), copper smelter, cutler, bell founder, anchor smith, pewterer, or iron puddler. Smiths and smelters needed strength and endurance. Iron puddlers' work involved heavy lifting and intense heat, as did the blacksmith's work at the forge.[79] Other metalworkers, like typefounders (makers of printers' type) and scientific instrument makers, used a more delicate touch.

Skilled workers also included builders of various kinds: carpenters (whose emblems were plane and bench), masons, paint makers (who were sometimes poisoned by the lead they used), plasterers, shipbuilders, joiners (who built boxes, sea chests, furniture, and the like), and plumbers. Plumbers sometimes constructed and repaired lead pipes, but they more commonly built lead coffins or worked as glaziers, making windows.

There were makers of household goods: potters, tanners and leather workers, coopers (who made barrels), wheelwrights, tallow chandlers (who made candles and soap), basket weavers, glassblowers, printers, publishers, bookbinders, and makers of rope, brushes, paper, and toys. Some in the luxury trades made goods that were purchased principally

9.4 "The Blacksmith lets his Iron grow cold attending to the Taylor's News," from *Oxford Magazine*, June 1772. A blacksmith's shop showing a great bellows operated by a rope, and the other trappings of the smith's trade: forge, anvil, hammer, tongs, and horseshoe. Courtesy of the Print Collection, Lewis Walpole Library, Yale University.

by the wealthy. These artisans included upholsterers, coach builders, jewelers, perfumers, cabinetmakers (including Thomas Chippendale, George Hepplewhite, and Thomas Sheraton), japanners (those who lacquered furniture), sword-hilt makers, and saddlers. There were thousands of watchmakers, mostly in London; there were clockmakers all over the country, most of whom ordered parts from Birmingham and assembled the clocks in their shops.[80]

Food workers included sugar refiners, maltsters (who roasted barley into malt), distillers, butchers (who wore distinctive aprons), and brewers. Millers took in grain from the grower, who paid a toll in kind—a certain percentage of the flour by weight, taken from the best flour in the center of the hopper. This toll was most advantageous to the miller—and most resented by the grain's owner—when flour prices were high. The grain's owner was seldom present for the actual milling, instead dropping off a certain amount of grain and returning later to pick up a certain amount of flour. Some customers suspected that, while they were absent, the miller substituted rotten or otherwise inferior grain or, worse yet, foreign substances—"Accorns, Beans, Bones, Whiting, Chopt Straw, and even Dried Horse Dung"—for their own good grain.[81] Food riots often began with a siege on the local mill.

TEXTILE AND CLOTHING TRADES

In an age when even a handkerchief or a petticoat was a significant investment for an ordinary worker, the clothing trades were of great importance. Most cherished was the wool trade, which was regulated by protective legislation from the moment of shearing. It was illegal, for example, to shear sheep fewer than four miles from the sea, lest the wool be smuggled out of the country.[82] Once gathered, the wool was carded and combed, then spun into yarn, and finally woven into cloth.

Much of this work was done in the home, with women and children carding and spinning while men wove, and at the century's beginning this work was all done by hand. Over the next hundred years, the process gradually became mechanized. Hand spinning and weaving survived in some areas, and the cottage industry was hardly eliminated. It was threatened, however, and the workers knew it. In many areas, they reacted to the introduction of machinery with rioting, vandalism, and arson.

Wool was not the only fabric produced in England. At one point, there were 12,000 silk weavers, although they suffered from French competition after the Seven Years' War, and there were thousands of cotton spinners and weavers as well.[83] There were plenty of workers ready to turn these fabrics into clothing: stay makers (makers of corsets), straw plaiters, lace makers, tailors (who sometimes worked door-to-door),[84] mantua (dress) makers, glovers, stocking knitters, breeches makers, calico printers, collar makers, and dyers. Shoemakers were sometimes called cordwainers, after their work with "cordovan" leather, or Crispins, after their patron saint, St. Crispin; in some shoe shops, there might be well over a hundred workers, each focusing on a different task—measuring, cutting, stitching—in an assembly-line fashion.[85] Women worked to some extent in most of these trades, but they dominated only a few. About 25 percent of working women were seamstresses, and they were the majority of milliners.[86]

APPRENTICESHIP AND GUILDS

Other changes were under way in the skilled trades. Traditionally, to learn a trade one left home and paid a fee to live in the home of a master artisan as his apprentice. Apprentices received no salary and worked hard, but they were fed and clothed and given the opportunity to learn the trade. They were bound to the master's service for a fixed number of years, usually seven, and were expected to be celibate during that time. Plays and prints warned apprentices to be honest and diligent, but apprenticeship was not easy, and there were cases of masters mistreating and even killing their charges. Running away meant the end of one's hopes in the trade, but for some it was preferable to staying; the runaway apprentice was a common figure. Those who stuck it out became jour-

Table 9.1
London Livery Companies

Mercers	Merchant Taylors
Grocers	Haberdashers
Drapers	Salters
Fishmongers	Ironmongers
Goldsmiths	Vintners
Skinners	Clothworkers

Note: London's Lord Mayor had to be a member of one of these twelve guilds.

neymen, then masters themselves with shops of their own once they could afford the setup costs. A large workshop or factory might cost hundreds or even thousands of pounds to equip, but some trades were cheaper to enter; a sailmaker's workshop could be rented for as little as £16 a year.[87]

The governing body of a trade was its guild or, in London, its livery company. Traditionally, it controlled entry into the trades to prevent overcompetition. In some provincial towns, the town corporation performed this duty, selling the "freedom" of the town, or the right to pursue a trade within its limits. In York, for example, a shopkeeper's freedom cost £25. Some towns had a sliding scale to allow poorer artisans or merchants to pay less for the freedom.[88]

During the 18th century, the old system of guilds and apprenticeship began to dissolve. Declining trades had no desire to limit entry; upstart trades had no long-standing traditions. Legislation governing apprenticeship and work conditions was repealed, town corporations ceased in some cases to enforce their licensing policies, and apprenticeships were reduced in many cases to five years or even three. In the 19th century, apprenticeship disappeared altogether.[89]

MERCHANTS AND INDUSTRIALISTS

Wholesalers were not unknown before the 18th century, but they were a far less meaningful presence in 1700 than in 1800. In 1700 much of what people ate was produced locally and bought at the town or village market. By 1800 the explosion of urban populations meant that livestock and produce had to be raised in the country and transported to the cities. To move the huge quantities of fuel and food that cities, especially London, demanded, a large body of middlemen emerged: warehousemen, brokers, drovers, and graziers who fattened and resold livestock.[90]

Middlemen were despised by most people, but factory owners, like "the iron chieftain" Matthew Boulton or "vase-maker general to the universe" Josiah Wedgwood, were lauded and emulated. Factories were still too new and marvelous, and their environmental impact still too uncertain, to be feared or hated. The increasing numbers of steam engines became popular tourist attractions. Furthermore, in a nation that valued commerce, it was hard to resist the allure of the successful manufacturer. Some of the big iron and textile magnates employed hundreds or even thousands of workers and had personal fortunes in the hundreds of thousands of pounds.[91]

Expansion of empire meant new markets to be exploited, as well as new sources of raw materials. Merchants, some of them "certainly far wealthier than many sovereign princes of Germany or Italy,"[92] financed the ships that carried Scandinavian timber, American furs and tobacco, African ivory, Indian tea, and British cloth. Banking, a brand-new occupation in 1700, employed more and more people as trade and agricultural improvement necessitated the use of credit.

PROFESSIONALS

The growing middle class was swelled in part by an increase in professional occupations. There were scholars of various kinds, including tutors and schoolmasters; the latter supplemented their often meager salaries by boarding pupils or collecting fees for extra services. Some turned to the written word, becoming authors, poets, journalists, or translators. "Writing," said Defoe, who had plenty of experience in the field, "is become a very considerable part of the English commerce."[93] The old system of aristocratic patronage of authors was in decay, replaced by the practice of publishers paying for the copyright to a work. While there were plenty of hack writers making very little, there were also a few who were very well paid. Samuel Johnson made £1,575 for his *Dictionary*, Adam Smith £500 for *Wealth of Nations*, Alexander Pope £4,000 each for his translations of the *Iliad* and the *Odyssey*, and Christopher Anstey £2,000 for his *New Bath Guide* (which was so successful that the publisher, as token of thanks, returned the copyright to Anstey after only five years).[94]

The visual arts, too, offered increasing opportunities for employment. The wealthy required the services of sculptors, silhouettists, enamelists, and painters; a decent painter got between £15 and £20 for a portrait of a face; prominent artists, like William Hogarth, Thomas Gainsborough, George Romney, John Constable, William Blake, and Sir Joshua Reynolds, got far more for their works. Hogarth made £12,000 from his series *The Harlot's Progress*.[95] The wealthy also employed other professionals: lawyers, architects, auctioneers, canal engineers, clergy, decorators, and surveyors. In 1759–1760, Joseph Massie thought lawyers made (or at least spent) about £100 a year, clergymen £50 to £100, and scholars and scientists £60.[96]

GOVERNMENT WORKERS

Government service proved unremunerative for the many and extremely lucrative for the few. Many local offices like magistrate and constable were technically unpaid, though constables were sometimes hired substitutes. Other jobs, like beadle, watchman, turnkey, and revenue officer, offered low salaries and few, if any, raises. Radical author Tom Paine was once an exciseman, who complained on behalf of his colleagues about their terrible work conditions and wages; he was later fired for suspected smuggling, to which many excise officers resorted to make ends meet.[97] Such minor officials were quite numerous. There were over 1,500 full-time and part-time customs officers in the Port of London alone in 1718, and 14,000 paid revenue collectors in 1782, a number comparable to the number of clergy in England and Wales.[98] Jail keepers, or wardens, made varying salaries according to the size and prominence of their institutions. The keeper of the Litchfield City Gaol, for example, made £2 a year, while his counterpart at Newgate made £200.[99] Massie thought there were 16,000 civil officials making between £50 and £79 a year, a wage well above poverty level but hardly lavish.[100]

Many government workers were independent contractors. Legal clerks and copyists, for example, were paid by the page, and they quickly learned to write large and leave generous margins.[101] Workhouse masters were paid a set fee per pauper—in St. Marylebone it was 18d. per week—and expected to buy all they needed from that sum, pocketing the difference.[102] Jailers operated on a similar basis, augmenting their salaries with prisoners' fees. Contractors were not always honest, and indeed, in the spirit of free enterprise, were not even expected to be so. An anonymous poem of 1775 illustrates the glee of a man who has gotten a government contract to handle local street lighting. He chortles to his wife that he'll cheat the parish by quadruple-charging for the number of men in his employ, under-oiling the lamps and blaming the shortfall on thieves, and stealing the lamps himself and charging the parish for their replacement.[103]

Some government posts were clearly sinecures, awarded to political cronies or relatives and requiring little if any actual work. If the job necessitated real work, it was subcontracted to a deputy for much less than its true salary. Government offices had few employees—the Admiralty had eight clerks, and the Treasury a staff of twenty-three, in 1743, and the Home and Foreign Offices each had staffs of nineteen in 1792 [104]— and acts of Parliament periodically reduced their number. More than 1,000 jobs were associated with the royal household, many of which were reserved for the wealthy and well connected.[105] Sinecure holders often held two or three posts at once, since there was little work involved, and increased their salaries by collecting fees and bribes, obtaining grants or loans from the government, or embezzling public funds. The annual pay-off for a clever gentleman of the bedchamber, comptroller of the pipe, paymaster general, secretary of state, or Teller of the Exchequer could run into the thousands of pounds.

Table 9.2 lists income earned by members of various professions. It should be remembered in reading this table that there was no income tax, and that many employments offered perquisites not included in wages. Farmhands often got an allotment of cheap grain; craftsmen sometimes got scrap materials; servants ate their employers' food and might have the right to old clothes or used tea leaves. Where an area of England or a particular time period is specified in the source, it is indicated.

Table 9.2
Income by Profession

Job	Income	Term	Place	Date
Agricultural laborer	1s.	day	Surrey	c. 1727–87[106]
	6s. 6d.	week	Lancashire	1767–70
	10s. 1d.	week	Lancashire	1794–5
	8s.	week	Buckinghamshire	1767–70
	7s. 4d.	week	Buckinghamshire	1794–5
	7s. 9d.	week	—	1767–70[107]
Apothecary	£150–£300	year	London	1797
Baker	£60–£300	year	London	1797[108]
Baronet	£1,500–£4,000	year	—	—[109]
Beadle	£20	year	—	—[110]
Bishop	£300–£7,000	year	—	—[111]
Blacksmith	1s. 6d.	day	Erddig, Wales	1784[112]
Bookseller	£200–£600	year	London	1797
	£80–£350	year	York	1797[113]
Brewer (prominent)	£8,000	year	—	c. 1800[114]
Brewery superintendent	£500	year	—	—[115]
Butler	£10	year	—	1773
	£25	year	Erddig, Wales	1774[116]
Cabinetmaker	£100–£200	year	York	1797[117]
Carpenter	1s.–1s. 6d.	day	Erddig, Wales	1779[118]

Job	Income	Term	Place	Date
Carter and digger	8s.–9s.	week	Oxfordshire	late century[119]
Chair carver	£4	week	—	—[120]
Chandler	£40–£400	year	London	1797[121]
Clergy	£50–£199	year	—	1759[122]
Chaplain	£35	year	Newgate Jail, London	—
Curate	£15–£20	year	—	—
Dissenting	£120	year	—	c. 1801
Fleet parson	£1	week	London	—
Parson	£400	year	—	—[123]
Coachman	£8	year	Erddig, Wales	1725
	£20	year	Erddig, Wales	1776[124]
Collier	15s.	week	Newcastle	—[125]
Compositor	24s.	week	—	—[126]
Confectioner/ fruiterer	£80–£150	year	York	1797[127]
Cook	£40	year	—	—[128]
Cutlery worker	13s. 6d.	week	Sheffield	—[129]
Doctor	10s.	per visit	—	—
Prominent	£1,000	year	Derby	—
Prominent	£12,000	year	London	—[130]
Draper	£100–£500	year	London	1797
	£100–£400	year	York	1797[131]
Excise officer	£50	year	—	most of the century[132]
Factory worker— button- making—child	1d.–2d.	day	Birmingham	1758[133]
Factory worker—rope- twisting—child	3d.–4d.	day	Bridport	—[134]
Footman	£6–£8	year	—	early to mid-century
	£14–£7	year	—	1771[135]

Table 9.2 (continued)

Job	Income	Term	Place	Date
Glover	£120	year	London	1797[136]
Gravedigger	1s.	per burial	St. Marylebone, London	—[137]
Grocer/ greengrocer	£40–£600	year	London	1797
	£100–£350	year	York	1797[138]
Haberdasher	£500	year	London	1797
	£60–£250	year	York	1797[139]
Hairdresser	£40–£80	year	London	1797[140]
Haymaker	1s. 4d.	day	Islington	pre-1775
	1s. 6d.	day	Islington	post-1775[141]
Hosier	£500–£700	year	London	1797[142]
Housekeeper	£28	year	—	—[143]
Industrialist or factory owner (clothier)	£10,000–£40,000	year	Wiltshire	early century[144]
Innkeeper	£50–£79	year	—	1759[145]
Jeweler	£3–£4	week	—	—
	£150	year	York	1797[146]
Journeyman	2s. 6d.	day	London	1775[147]
King	£200,000	year	—	—[148]
Laborer	1s. 6d.	day	London	1775
	7s. 3d.	week	—	1737
	8s. 3d.	week	—	1777[149]
	£25	year	London	c. 1700
	£15 10s.	year	West Country	c. 1700
	£11 5s.	year	North	c. 1700[150]
Lawyer	£80–£199	year	—	1759[151]
Lord Warden of the Cinque Ports	£4,000	year	—	late century[152]
Maid, of all work	£2–£6	year	—	—[153]
Lady's	£6	year	Erddig, Wales	1725
Laundry	£2 10s.	year	Erddig, Wales	1725[154]

Job	Income	Term	Place	Date
Mantuamaker	£60	year	London	1797[155]
Mercer	£70–£50	year	London	1797[156]
Military officer	£80–£99	year	—	1759[157]
Admiral	£122,000	prize money from capture of Havana	—	1761[158]
Naval dockyard worker	2s. 6d.	day	—	—[159]
Optician	£400	year	London	1797
	£300	year	York	1797
Pawnbroker	£200	year	York	1797[160]
Peer	£2,500–£40,000+	year	—	—[161]
Post-boy (hired with chaise)	up to £5	week	—	—[162]
Printer	£1–£3	week	—	—[163]
Saddler	15s.	week	—	—[164]
Sailor	24s.	month	—	until 1797
	£15–£24	year	—	1759
	30s.—35s.	per voyage	Newcastle-to-London collier	—
	£3. 5s.	per voyage	ship importing timber from Norway	—
First mate	£5	month	aboard East Indiaman	mid-century
Captain of mail packet	£104–£1,000	year	—	—[165]
Secretary of State	£6,000–£9,000	year	—	mid-century[166]
Sedan Chairman	1s.	hour	London	—
	1 guinea	week	London	—[167]
Shoemaker	2s.	day	—	1780s[168]
Shopkeeper	£45	year	—	early century
	£40–£600+	year	London	1797[169]
Silversmith	£300–£500	year	London	1797[170]

Table 9.2 (continued)

Job	Income	Term	Place	Date
Soldier	£14 or less	year	—	1759[171]
Spectacle framemaker	£49 9s. 4d.	year	Wolverhampton	—[172]
Spinner	8s. 7d.	week	—	—[173]
Squire	£300–£5,000	year	—	—[174]
Stationer	£200–£900	year	London	1797[175]
Staymaker	£80–100	year	London	1797
	£80–£150	year	York	1797[176]
Stocking knitter	10s.–30s.	week	—	1783[177]
Surgeon	£3	month	aboard East Indiaman	mid-century
Prominent	£15,000	year	London	—[178]
Tailor	£100	year	London	1797
Journeyman	21s. 9d.	week	—	—
Prominent	£3,000	year	London	—[179]
Teacher	£60, plus fees	year	Tiverton	early century
	£600	year	—	c. 1801
	£12	year	Mayfield parish, Sussex	—
	£10–£20	year	—	—
	£150	year	—	c. 1801[180]
Tea Dealer	£60–£300	year	York	1797[181]
Theater Manager	£3 6s.	day	London	c. 1749
	£600	year	York	1797[182]
Tobacconist	£70–£150	year	York	1797[183]
Turnpike Surveyor	£20–£30	year	—	—[184]
Turnpike Toll-Collector	£50	year	—	1799[185]
Washerwoman	6d.–8d.	day	—	1739[186]
Watchman	1s. plus tips	night	London	—[187]

Job	Income	Term	Place	Date
Weaver, on home loom	£3	week	Lancashire, Derbyshire	late century[188]
Silk	£2–£3	week	Spitalfields	early century[189]
Wet Nurse	£25	year	—	mid-century[190]
Whipmaker	£60–£200	year	York	1797[191]
Wholesaler, Prominent	£800	year	—	c. 1801[192]

TIMELINE

1710	The first successful enclosure bill comes before Parliament.
1720	Parliament passes an act against labor combinations (unions).
1726	Combinations are outlawed in the woollen trade.
1740	Parliament outlaws the appropriation of work materials by employees, attacking long-standing traditions that granted scrap materials to workers.
1744	Parliament passes another act against combinations.
1777	Lord North taxes male servants. The base tax is one guinea per manservant, with a higher rate for bachelors and a lower rate for families with children.
1779	Hundreds of stocking frames are smashed by workers fearful of mechanization and anxious to obtain a minimum wage.
1783	The tax on male servants is raised, and hiring female servants is taxed for the first time.
1788	Work conditions for chimney sweeps are regulated.
1799	Organizing in combinations for the purpose of improving wages and conditions is outlawed as conspiracy by act of Parliament.[193]

10

"What Joy Was Mine!": Entertainment

Stitched half a wristband, read the text,
Pouted and dined, dressed, looked divine,
Made an excuse, got Ma to back it;
Went to the play, what joy was mine!
    —Charles Dibdin, "The Lady's Diary," 1798

SPORTS

As befitted a population employed mostly on the land and sea, the English were outdoorsy. A few dabbled in archery, and at least one late-century aristocrat was fond of pole-vaulting.[1] In the winter, people strapped or screwed skates to the bottoms of their shoes and took to the ice.[2] Gentlemen pushed ladies in swings but were cautioned by the *Spectator* to preserve their companions' modesty: "The lover who swings his lady is to tie her clothes very close together with his hat-band before she admits him to throw up her heels."[3] Water sports of various kinds increased in popularity during the century. People swam, and awnings called "bathing machines" or "Modesty Hoods" were invented to conceal women bathers as they emerged from the water in wet flannels. Some swimmers used buoyant chest "girdles" made of cork or bladders to help keep them afloat.[4] For those who preferred to get less wet, there was pleasure boating on rivers or the ocean, sometimes with the purpose of fishing or picnicking, or participating in or observing regattas or rowing competitions.[5]

Fishing and Hunting

Fishing was relaxed enough to be considered appropriate for genteel women, but it could also be enjoyed by those of lesser means. A twig pole, a horsehair line, and a little cow brain or a few fish eyes for bait was all that was really required.[6] Hunting was a more complex social issue. There was a strict property requirement for hunters. Hunters had to own land worth £100 a year or lease land worth £150 a year before they could hunt anywhere, even on their own land. Poorer people hunted, of course, sometimes with a qualified hunter's companionship or permission, but more commonly as poachers.[7] The rich guarded their privilege fiercely. It became suspect for a laborer to own a dog or a gun, tougher penalties were legislated for poaching, and some landowners set out vicious mantraps to snare and wound those who trespassed on their property.[8]

Early in the century, the classic prey was the deer, or game birds hunted with guns or hawks. But country squires turned increasingly to the pursuit of foxes and hares, breeding horses and dogs especially for the purpose, founding hunt clubs, and popularizing riding wear for all casual occasions. Even bird hunting became an organized social pursuit. Gentlemen nurtured flocks of birds on their land, then arranged for "beaters" to drive the birds toward a waiting group of hunters, who competed to kill the most game.[9] Country squires were much teased about their obsession with the hunt; and the frock coat, riding boots, pack of dogs, and enthusiasm for horses became part of their iconography. The squire in Alexander Pope's "Epistle to Miss Blount"

> . . . visits with a gun, presents you birds,
> Then gives a smacking buss and cries,—No words!
> Or with his hound comes hollowing from the stable,
> Makes loves with nods, and knees beneath a table;
> Whose laughs are hearty, though his jests are coarse,
> And loves you best of all things—but his horse.[10]

Riding and Racing

Men and women alike rode for pleasure, although women rode sidesaddle, with their legs draped over the horse's left side and their torsos and heads facing forward. The left foot was in a stirrup; the right leg was held up by a support built into the saddle.[11] Men alone were the jockeys and the principal patrons of horse racing, which came into its own as an organized sport in the 18th century. The Jockey Club, which codified racing rules, was founded in Newmarket in the early 1750s, but continuous records of races were kept as early as 1709.[12] Grandstands were built, racing colors were adopted, and classic races—like the Oaks, named for Lord Derby's house at Epsom—were founded.[13] Some horses, like Dragon and Eclipse, became famous. Jockeys, too, became well-known. Tregonwell Frampton,

Dragon's jockey, was called by Daniel Defoe, "the oldest, and as some say, the cunningest jockey in England." Joseph Rose, in great demand, rode at Lincoln, Richmond, and Manchester on three consecutive days in September 1764, a feat of riding in itself in the days of slow transportation and bad roads.[14]

Not all approved of races, perhaps because such spectacles drew working people away from productive labor. Methodist preacher William Seward denounced them in the same breath with "balls, assemblies, whoredom, and drunkenness,"[15] and Parliament passed an act in 1739 designed "to restrain and prevent the excessive Increase of Horse Races."[16] The act was ineffective, and working people continued to flock to races of horses, donkeys, even (as a joke) turkeys and geese.[17]

Humans raced, too, and plenty of people enjoyed a good foot race, either as participants or spectators. Fairs and holidays often included a foot race of some kind, like a "smock race" between women competing for a chemise or other item of clothing. Facetious races of a sort might also be held. People might chase a greased pig, or hop in sacks, or hold a blindfolded wheelbarrow race.[18]

Various team and field sports were played in England— the newest and most fashionable was cricket. One foreign visitor found it perplexing. "I will not attempt to describe this game to you," he wrote, "it is too complicated."[19] Cricket cut across class and gender lines. Lords, ladies, and laborers alike played the game. Rules were drawn up; gamblers bet furiously on matches, innings, and even individual balls; and spectators came in huge numbers (20,000 for a match between Kent and Hampshire in 1772).[20] The "Hambledon men" dominated the game for most of the second half of the century,[21] and the Hambledon women were no slouches either. A 1745 newspaper article reported on the "greatest cricket match that was ever played in the south part of England" between the women of Bramley and Hambledon. Hambledon won, 122 to 119, before the biggest crowd "that was ever seen on such an occasion. The girls bowled, batted, ran and caught as well as any men could do in that game."[22] Cricket even affected the royal succession when, in 1751, the forty-eight-year-old heir to the throne, Prince Frederick, was hit on the head by a cricket ball and killed, which enabled his son to become George III.

Other Sports

Other sports included tennis, golf, lawn bowling, skittles (skittle alleys were often attached to taverns),[23] "Shovel-board" (shuffleboard), quoits, and ninepins.[24] The ultimate crowd-pleasing game, however, was football, in which the teams were each the size of a crowd. Casual pickup games were small enough, but hundreds of players might be enlisted on each side for big inter-parish matches or Shrove Tuesday games, and the two goals might be a mile or two apart. Rules varied locally, emphasizing kicking, throwing, and carrying to different degrees; some used a

10.1 "Cricket," drawn by F. Hayman, engraved by Benoist, 1743. The verse begins, "To exercise their Limbs, and try their Art . . ." Courtesy of the Print Collection, Lewis Walpole Library, Yale University.

small hard ball, while others used a leather-covered bladder; some matches were relatively civil, while others got quite violent, with shin-kicking and turning other players head over heels.[25]

In the East Anglian version called "camping," the goals were 150 to 200 yards apart. One player tossed a cricket-sized ball in the air and darted away while the two teams of ten to fifteen players tried to grab it. The player who got the ball ran with it toward his goal, pursued by the opposing team and helped by his own teammates. He could throw the ball to a teammate but not hand it off; he must carry the ball between his goals but could not throw it there. He got a point, called a "notch" or "snotch," for a goal, and lost a snotch for being caught with the ball. When a snotch was scored, the two teams faced off again for the ball. A game was usually to seven or nine snotches and took two to three hours to play. "Rough-play" camping involved boxing, while "civil-play" permitted wrestling and kicking only. The Derby version of football had goals two miles apart and, in the early 19th century, involved as many as a thousand players. It usually devolved into a brawl in the middle of the River Derwent; creative tactics were encouraged, such as unstuffing the ball and smuggling it to the goal under someone's clothing.[26] If cricket involved everyone and emphasized fair play, football was emphatically a game for the masses and emphasized whatever worked.

PERFORMANCES AND SPECTACLES

More sedate entertainments included various kinds of shows. People of all kinds enjoyed the theater, performing plays at home **Plays** and patronizing traveling companies and established stages. The century produced a host of popular plays by George Colman, George Lillo, Hannah More, Sophia Lee, Richard Brinsley Sheridan, and Oliver Goldsmith, but the century's most significant play was John Gay's *The Beggar's Opera*, first produced in 1728. With its lower-class criminal characters, its street songs, its pointed political satire, and its traditional melodies, it was guaranteed to appeal to the working class and to alienate those in power. Like Henry Fielding's novel *Jonathan Wild* and other 18th-century works, *The Beggar's Opera* pointed out that poor criminals got hanged while rich ones got elected. It was not a message that Prime Minister Robert Walpole, in some people's eyes the biggest thief of them all, wanted to hear on opening night, when he saw himself caricatured as "Robin Bagshot." Walpole had to swallow the insult for the time being, but in 1737 he got his revenge with the passage of the Licensing Act, which toughened the laws making actors subject to arrest as vagrants and also required that all plays be reviewed and licensed by the Lord Chamberlain.[27]

Walpole was not the only enemy of the theater. Playgoing was denounced by many. On a rigorous "spiritual barometer" printed in 1800, it falls between "free association with carnal company" and "private prayer totally neglected" on the scale of iniquities.[28] Some towns, to keep the contagion from their doorsteps, got local acts of Parliament passed against theaters, or had their magistrates ban traveling shows.[29]

Noted actors included Peg Woffington, Anne Oldfield, Catherine Clive (a playwright as well as an actress), Sarah Siddons (the greatest actress of the last quarter of the century), Anne Bracegirdle (who retired in 1707), Charles Macklin, and Colley Cibber (also a theatrical manager, mediocre poet laureate, and a leading example of the stilted, traditional style of acting). Greatest of them all, however, was David Garrick, who popularized more natural speech and gestures onstage. Author of several plays of his own, he pushed Shakespeare, editing the slower plays, introducing more faithful versions of *King Lear* and *The Tempest*, and supporting the Shakespeare Jubilee in 1769, a nationwide celebration of the Bard. Garrick's trip abroad in 1765 was considered "one of the greatest national calamities that could befal us."[30]

Garrick was also the comanager, from 1747 to 1776, of one of the great

London theaters: Drury Lane, twice renovated and partially wrecked by riots in 1743, 1750, 1755, 1763, 1770, and 1776. Garrick barely averted another by obeying the audience's command to apologize on his knees for a scheduling error.[31] Another of the great London houses was the Haymarket, and the third was Covent Garden, which could seat 22,000 patrons per week in 1762. From 1700 to 1800, it produced 3,212 plays, or an average of about one every eleven days.[32] There were no shows that ran for thousands of performances. When Sheridan's *The Duenna* managed a run of seventy-five nights in 1775, it was England's longest-running play ever.

Theatergoers were a miscellaneous crowd. The "Persons of Quality, and . . . Ladies and Gentlemen of the highest Rank" sat in boxes, some of which were located on the stage. The "Persons of Quality" could, and sometimes did, hold conversations with the actors or cross the stage to talk with friends. In the pit, the area at ground level in front of the stage, sat "the *Judges, Wits,* and *Censurers* . . . the *Squires, Sharpers, Beaus, Bullies* and *Whores,* and here and there an extravagant *Male* and *Female Cit.*" Above them, in shallow galleries a few seats deep, sat "the Citizens' Wives and Daughters, together with the *Abigails,* Serving-men, Journey-men and Apprentices."[33] At Drury Lane, for Samuel Johnson's play *Irene,* a seat in a box cost 5s., in the pit 3s., in the first gallery 2s., and in the upper galley 1s.[34]

The theater opened at about 3:00 P.M., candle-lit performances began at about 5:00 or 6:00. The well-to-do, still eating their late and lesiurely dinner, would send servants to buy and hold seats for them until their arrival. There would be a principal play and various interludes and afterpieces, most of them involving music or dance. Workers, stuck at their jobs until after the mainpiece began, could buy half-price tickets to see the third act plus the afterpieces which ran until about 10:00 P.M.[35]

Theater audiences were rude. They bought oranges, either inside or outside the theatre, and dropped seeds and peels onto the people in the pit. They threw rotten fruit and vegetables at the stage and at other members of the audience. They laughed and talked; Joseph Addison lamented in 1709 that a contortionist, "a Monster with a Face between his Feet," obtained more respectful silence than "some noble Tragedy."[36] They rioted when the play displeased them. But the actors often gave as good as they got. At the Haymarket in 1786, the actors noticed that the audience was ridiculing four fantastically dressed women in the audience, who had adorned themselves with gargantuan headdresses, handkerchiefs, and nosegays. Four actresses improvised similar accessories, then came onstage to salute the unfortunate women, who were driven from the theater by the resulting roars of laughter.[37] There was nothing passive about going to a play.

10.2 "The Country Concert," C. L. Smith, 1794. The instruments include ket-
tledrums, trumpet, bassoon, and cello. Courtesy of the Print Collection, Lewis
Walpole Library, Yale University.

Music, so often a part of plays and afterpieces, also stood on
its own. Opera was popular, and Italian opera dominated in the   **Music**
first half of the century. Great composers came to England as
well. Wolfgang Amadeus Mozart toured, as did Joseph Haydn in 1791;
George Frideric Handel came to stay, setting up residence and drawing
a crowd of 12,000 for a rehearsal of his *Fireworks Music*.[38] Wealthy people
also held private parties to hear chamber music played in their homes,
while the less well-off went to music festivals, sang hymns in church,
paid ballad singers to warble the latest tunes, or joined church bands,
chamber music clubs, or choral clubs.

Displays of unusual or trained animals were always pop-
ular. In one act, birds pretended to march with toy guns,   **Performing**
then held a mock execution of another bird by firing squad;   **Animals**
the "shot" bird fell down on cue, then stood up to march
out with his comrades.[39] Various impresarios offered camels, panthers,
lions, baboons, and exotic birds for public inspection. Philip Astley specialized in equestrian shows. A marmoset danced on command, dogs
danced, hares played music, birds told time and played cards, bees performed tricks and returned to the hive at a pistol shot. The Learned Pig

of the 1780s was, wrote Robert Southey, "in his day a far greater object of admiration to the English nation than ever was Sir Isaac Newton."[40]

Art Shows There were various other kinds of shows as well. Waxwork figures of celebrities and historical figures could be seen in Mrs. Mills's, Mrs. Salmon's, Mrs. Goldsmith's, Benjamin Rackstrow's, and other less famous collections. Salmon's, the most notable collection, endured throughout the century and featured, at various times, the execution of Charles I, a Canaanite sacrifice of children to Moloch, English prophet Mother Shipton (who was rigged to kick each patron on departure), three Cherokee chiefs, and Antony and Cleopatra. Rackstrow's had a Chinese mandarin, a dwarf, a giant, another Mother Shipton, and a model of an eight-month-pregnant woman showing the circulatory system, heart, and lungs. It also had non-wax curiosities: a mummy, stuffed crocodiles, death masks, shells, bones, fish, fetuses, and placentas. In the 1770s, American sculptor Patience Wright also showed her work; her figures were so lifelike that Lady Aylesbury spoke to a wax housemaid Wright had sculpted.[41]

Painters, too, displayed their work. Paintings were shown at London's Foundling Hospital from 1740 and at the annual Royal Academy exhibition from 1769.[42] The Society for the Encouragement of the Arts held a show in 1760 that drew an estimated 20,000 people,[43] and there were three major shows in 1770, provoking Horace Walpole to observe, "[I]t is incredible what sums are raised by mere exhibitions of anything; a new fashion, to enter at which you pay a shilling or half a crown."[44] At such exhibitions, paintings were shown clustered tightly on the walls, with nearly every available square foot covered by images. At the print sellers' shops, too, where many went to peruse and buy the works of William Hogarth, Thomas Rowlandson, James Gillray, and others, lots of images competed for the viewer's attention. A few painters sought more of a monopoly on the audience. John Singleton Copley held showings of individual paintings—*The Death of the Earl of Chatham* in 1781 and *The Floating Batteries at Gibraltar* in 1791—that netted him thousands of pounds. Robert Barker constructed a special building to display his masterpiece, a 360-degree painting mounted on curved walls; the word he invented for it, "Panorama," and the idea itself, were soon adopted by others.[45]

Other artists and artisans showed their work, usually at their homes or shops. There were shows of stained glass, needlework, pictures burned into wood with hot pokers, pictures made with shells, and architectural models. At one watchmaker's shop, there were various tiny carvings that could be viewed through a magnifying glass, including a coach small enough to be drawn by a flea and a camel that could pass through the eye of a needle.[46]

People flocked to anything that promised to be inter-
esting, ready to believe in the most outrageous marvels.   **Other Shows**
Balloon ascents seemed no less remarkable than a talking
"centaur" (actually a legless man attached to a stuffed horse body).[47] Fed
up with the public's gullibility, the duke of Montagu, in 1749, wagered
that he could draw an audience for virtually anything, no matter how
implausible. Accordingly, he advertised that he would creep into a quart
bottle and then sing a song from inside it. A huge crowd assembled at
the New Theatre in the Haymarket, then rioted when it realized it had
been tricked; the duke won his bet.[48]

The same people who came to see the Duke no doubt paid to see other
types of performers: magicians, clairvoyants, rope walkers, clowns, and
snake handlers. They flocked to exhibitions of giants, like the "wonderful
tall Essex woman" or 8 foot, 4 inch Charles Byrne, whose skeleton sold
for £500, and Patrick Cotter O'Brien, who had himself buried in a twelve-
foot-deep grave of rock, brick, and iron bars to avoid a similar fate. They
showed similar enthusiasm for midgets and dwarfs, hermaphrodites and
androgynes, people with bizarre birth defects or missing limbs, "noble
savages" from Africa or America, and people who ate fire, cats, stones,
or raw flesh.[49] They viewed semaphore systems, guillotine models, a
four-horse carousel, a traveling house sheathed in plate iron, naumachia
(mock battles with model ships), shadow plays, puppet shows with
"Punch and His Wife" (sometimes named "Joan," and not consistently
named "Judy" until the end of the century), magic-lantern shows,[50] and
colorless fireworks shot into the air or set off on the ground to form suns
and fountains of sparks.[51] They saw mechanical pictures that incorpo-
rated moving figures like ships, coaches, and people, and sometimes
special lighting or sound effects.[52] For a penny, one could see a peepshow
or "raree-show." The raree-show man would carry a box with one to
four sets of eyeholes. The customer looked through the apertures to see
one or more scenes inside, which were usually designed to fool the eye
into perceiving them as full-sized. Some raree-shows even had moving
figures.

GATHERING IN PUBLIC

Many of the aforementioned pastimes and wonders found their
way to local celebrations and gatherings. Though they were being   **Fairs**
increasingly suppressed by gentry and entrepreneurs miffed at
the loss of work time, wakes, holiday feasts, and fairs were important in
the lives of working people. Potter Josiah Wedgwood's attitude was typical: "Our men have been at play 4 days this week, it being Burslem Wakes.
I have rough'd and smooth'd them over & promised them a long Xmass,
but I know it is all in vain, for Wakes must be observed though the world

Publish'd according to Act of Parliament March 3, 1748.

A View of the *GREAT FIRE WORKS* on account of y̆ *GENERAL PEACE.*
Exhibiting the Curious Piece of Architecture *erected on that Occasion, the* 3 Fire Suns, *the middlemost*
22 *feet, the other* 10 *feet in Diameter,* 12 Fire Trees, *and that perticular Grand Scene of the Fire Works,*
called the Girandola, *which is the firing at Once* 6000 Rockets *of half a pound of Powder each.*

This Elegant piece of Architecture is 410 *long &* 104 *feet high, is Embellish'd with the Statues of Justice, Prudence, Fortitude,*
Clemency, Vigilence, Piety on the Front, on the top of the Building are 6 *Statues, representing Jupiter, Bacchus, Ceres, Pomona, Vesta &*
Fidelitÿ, under the Great Arch on a Pedestal, is the Statue of Peace holding the Olive branch over Neptunes head. Over the Arch is paint-
ed in Bas Relievo His Majesty presenting peace to Britannia, the Bas Relievos on each side of the Arch, one represents Neptune drawn
by Sea Horses, the other the Triumph of Mars. This grand Fire work will last about 3 *hours, and it is computed twenty five tuns*
weight of Gunpowder and combustibles will be consumed.
    Printed for Tho: Bowles in St Pauls Church Yard — & John Bowles at the black horse in Cornhill.

10.3 "A View of the GREAT FIRE WORKS on account of ye GENERAL PEACE," 1748. Courtesy of the Print Collection, Lewis Walpole Library, Yale University.

was to end with them."[53] The wake was an annual celebration of the parish church's founding, traditionally held on the Sunday after the church's saint's feast day. Often, the feasting and celebration carried over into the following day or week. A fair was a longer revel, lasting two to six weeks, though few people, besides pickpockets and prostitutes, would attend every day. The fair's ostensible purpose was business—selling wool, buying livestock, or hiring servants—but its real business was entertainment.

A wake or fair might feature any or all of the following: courting, dancing, wrestling or other combats of strength and agility, races, hot-hasty-pudding-eating contests, combats between animals, music, plowing contests, raffles, raree-shows, menageries, and bell ringing. There would be festive foods, like gingerbread, nuts, or roast pork. There might be Morris dancers, all male, performing in lines and figures with bells strapped to their lower legs and big sticks that smacked against each other at certain parts of the dance. Fairs were also frequented by peddlers of trinkets and medicines, professional gamblers, trick riders, tightrope walkers, tumblers, and acrobats.[54] William Wordsworth, in 1802, described Bartholomew Fair as a "Parliament of Monsters" filled with

> . . . Albinos, painted Indians, Dwarfs,
> The Horse of knowledge, and the learned Pig,
> The Stone-eater, the man that swallows fire,
> Giants, Ventriloquists, the Invisible Girl,
> The Bust that speaks and moves its goggling eyes,
> The Wax-work, Clock-work

and puppet shows, as well as musicians playing the hurdy-gurdy, the fiddle, the kettledrum, and the trumpet.[55] Forty years earlier, it was much the same: crowds pressing in each direction, fiddles, flutes, "Fifes, trumpets, drums, bagpipes, and barrow-girls squeaking," hornpipe dancing, a Punch reenacting the Gunpowder Plot, rides, a camel, a "learned dog that can tell all his letters," and food, food, food—plum porridge, black pudding, oysters, pease porridge, fried sausages, "Wine, beer, ale and cakes."[56]

Fairs offered young people a venue for courtship. So did assemblies and balls. The assembly was simply a ball held at a public venue, with an admission fee for each partici-

Assemblies and Balls

pant. The price of admission kept out the really poor and sorted people roughly by class, shunting lesser tradesmen and their ilk to the cheaper assemblies at Wapping, Deptford, and Rotherhithe, and reserving the genteel City and London assemblies for the wealthy. Defoe was a firm opponent of "the new mode of forming assemblies so much, and so fatally now in vogue,"[57] but he was ignored. For genteel young

10.4 "The Cotillion Dance," J. Collet, James Caldwall, 1771. Two musicians in a raised box play while the dancers form a circle with joined hands. Courtesy of the Print Collection, Lewis Walpole Library, Yale University.

women, it was a heady experience to dance, to be admired, and, no doubt, to whisper with friends over the merits of particular gentlemen. For their parents, the idea must have been appealing as well—a chance for their daughters to mingle publicly and decorously with men and so make better and happier marriages. Parents could fulfill their responsibilities to find a good match and to supervise chastity while enjoying a hand of cards or a glass of punch and the conversation of their peers. Assembly rooms were the chief attraction of spas like Bath.

In time, variations on the ball developed. Working people held their own dances: servant Jack Beef, in the 1760s, went to "a Ball of Blacks,"[58] and Dudley Ryder, a Hackney linen-draper's son, went to winter dances in the local schoolroom.[59] The wealthy turned to the *fête-champêtre*, a pastoral party with "shepherds and peasants, druids and dryads, fairy lights, rustic sports and games."[60] The type of ball that most terrified moralists, however, was the masquerade. The anonymity (or pretended anonymity) of one's dance partner could be arousing, dangerous, or embarrassing, and the masquerade was accordingly embraced by the daring and condemned by the prudent.

CLUBS AND SOCIETIES

Some people enjoyed themselves by finding others with similar interests or temperaments and forming a club. Clubs had existed before, but now they became so popular at every social level that they were a principal aspect of 18-century life—though perhaps we should say 18th-century male life, since few clubs were open to women. Most clubs were short-lived and casually organized. Some had a specific purpose, while others existed purely as an excuse to talk, drink, and gamble.

The principally social clubs evolved from a 17th-century institution, the coffeehouse. Men gathered in these dirty, smoky rooms to drink coffee, read newspapers, entertain friends, and discuss politics. By 1714 there were hundreds of them in London alone, each with its own character and clientele. Lawyers and authors, including Joseph Addison, Sir Richard Steele, Alexander Pope, Jonathan Swift, Thomas Gray, Dr. Samuel Johnson, and Oliver Goldsmith, gathered at the Grecian; clergymen at Child's; artists at Old Slaughter's; marine insurers at Lloyd's; stockbrokers at Jonathan's (which became the Stock Exchange in 1773), Man's, or Garraway's (which also attracted doctors and apothecaries); military men at the Little Devil; and fops at Ozinda's. The Golden Lyon was owned by Thomas Twining of tea-selling fame. Don Saltero's, in Chelsea, housed London's first public museum. The Leicester was the site of an attempted murder of one magistrate, Thomas de Veil, by another named Webster, whose corruption had been betrayed to the Lord Chancellor by de Veil.[61]

Coffeehouses were supplanted by another all-male, and more exclusive, institution: the gentlemen's club. The most fashionable examples, clustered on St. James's Street and Pall Mall, were White's (est. 1736), Crockford's, and Almack's (est. 1762). In 1764 Almack's membership split into two new clubs, Boodle's and Brooks's, while the Almack house remained headquarters for the Ladies' Coterie (which admitted men as well as women) and the Macaroni Club. The chief activities of these clubs seem to have been conversation and gambling. Horace Walpole called Brooks's a place "where a thousand meadows and cornfields are staked at every throw, and as many villages lost as in the earthquakes that overwhelmed Herculaneum and Pompeii."[62]

Another important social club was that of the Freemasons, whose religious tolerance, aura of secrecy, and fashionable yet diverse membership made them eminently popular. Their first Grand Lodge was founded in 1717, and 206 London lodges were in existence by the late century. Most of the male royals were among their membership by 1800. The Prince of Wales himself was the grand master from 1790 to 1813.[63]

There were other clubs whose chief purpose was pleasure. There were lottery clubs, sodomites' clubs, flagellants' clubs, and book clubs. There was the Hell-Fire Club for notable rakes and, farther down the social scale, a club described in 1770 as consisting of "servants, journeymen, and apprentices. On these evenings [of their meetings] every member laid down fourpence, for which he had music and a female gratis."[64]

Some clubs were political in nature. These included the 1760s Tory club, Wildman's; game associations founded in the 1750s by landlords anxious to protect their hunting rights against tenants; debating societies like London's Robin Hood Club or Ye Antient Society of Cogers; the Society of the Supporters of the Bill of Rights, which argued for reform and paid the legal bills of its hero, John Wilkes; the Yorkshire Association and the Society for Constitutional Information, which worked for redistribution of Parliamentary seats; and a host of reform societies founded in the wake of the French Revolution, the most notable of which was the London Corresponding Society.[65] Sometimes ethnic groups formed clubs to promote their culture or support their communities. Thus, there were clubs for blacks, for the Welsh, and for Scots.[66]

Other clubs were dedicated to a particular purpose. There were religious clubs for the establishment of Sunday schools, the suppression of vice, and "the Propagation of the Gospel in Foreign Parts."[67] There were scientific and mathematical societies, charitable groups, and commerce clubs, like the Society of Arts or the Laudable Association of Anti-Gallicans, which gave out prizes for inventions or achievements helpful to British trade. There were sports clubs, like the Toxophilite Society (a club for archers, established in 1781);[68] musical clubs; gardening clubs; and antiquarians' clubs. There were literary societies, like Dr. Johnson's Literary Club at the Turk's Head Tavern or the Falstaff Club at the Boar's Head Tavern (in which each member took the name of a Shakespearean character). There were even ugly clubs, farters' clubs, and surly clubs.

ARTS AND LETTERS

Fairs and club meetings were not daily events. Most of the time, people had to amuse themselves. They drew, painted, talked, and told stories. Women embroidered or played music on pianofortes and spinets. They wrote in their diaries or scribbled poetry or autobiographies, activities not confined to the wealthy. Though literacy was certainly higher among the rich, it was high enough generally to create a fair number of working-class authors. Literate people could also read, to themselves or to their families and friends, and the 18th century witnessed an unprecedented consumption of reading material: histories, biographies, magazines, scandal sheets, newspapers, pornography, political tracts, sermons, collections of folklore and ballads, and poetry. Even relatively humble homes might have a Bible and an almanac; *Old Moore's* almanac alone sold 100,000 copies a year.[69] Such homes might also hold a few of the burgeoning number of cheap reprints, pirated editions, and remainders sold by aggressive publishers. And even journeymen and children read chapbooks like *Tom Thumb*, *Jack and the Beanstalk*, *Guy of Warwick*, *Pleasant Conceits of Old Hobson the Merry Londoner*, and *The Nine Worthies of London* (a collection of tales of livery-company role models). There was poetry, too, for every taste, from doggerel verse to epics (and mock epics, like Pope's *Rape of the Lock*) to romantic celebrations of nature and the innate innocence of childhood (like Wordsworth and Coleridge's *Lyrical Ballads*, which came out in 1798). Sometimes working-class people had surprising taste in literature; the foreign pastor Moritz found a Derbyshire saddler who was as knowledgeable about Homer and Virgil as "a doctor or master of arts from Oxford," as well as a widowed landlady whose favorites included John Milton.[70]

Another newly popular genre was the novel, which was invented in the 17th century but was finding its mass audience in the eighteenth. Sometimes it was epistolary—written in the form of letters between the characters—as was the hugely popular *Pamela* by Samuel Richardson. Sometimes it was satirical, like Henry Fielding's epistolary parody *Shamela*, which turned Richardson's virtuous servant Pamela into a greedy, calculating trollop. Sometimes it pretended faintly to be nonfiction, as with Fielding's *History of Tom Jones* or Daniel Defoe's *A Journal of the Plague Year*, or autobiography, as with Defoe's *Moll Flanders* and *Robinson Crusoe*. Sometimes it educated young women about etiquette and courtship; Frances Burney's novels, including *Evelina* and *Camilla*, were of this ilk. Sometimes, in the second half of the century, it was Gothic—often set in the Middle Ages and full of ruined abbeys, mysterious castles, leering uncles, corrupt priests, ghosts, tombs, and creaking staircases. The fad was started by Horace Walpole's *Castle of Otranto* and mastered by Ann Radcliffe in such novels as *The Mysteries of Udolpho* and *The Italian*. The most sensationally lurid of the Gothics was *The Monk*, by Matthew Lewis, which concluded, spectacularly, with a rape and murder in a tomb and the escort of the chief villain to hell; it was so popular and notorious that its author never shook the nickname "Monk" Lewis. Novels, read widely by the middle class, could be purchased (for fairly considerable sums) or borrowed from for-profit circulating libraries—390 of them by 1800—usually run by booksellers.[71]

Circulating libraries stocked mostly nonfiction, but they did their biggest trade in current fiction and plays.[72] It was the fiction that made them controversial, for it was widely believed that ephemeral romances were

10.5 "Beauty in Search of Knowledge," 1782. The typical customer, a young lady, is about to enter a circulating library. Courtesy of the Print Collection, Lewis Walpole Library, Yale University.

ruining young women by raising their expectations of marriage, encouraging premarital sex, and wasting their time. Sir Anthony Absolute, in Richard Sheridan's *The Rivals*, expresses a popular sentiment when he calls the circulating library "an evergreen tree of diabolical knowledge." Sheridan apparently shares Sir Anthony's fashionable distaste, for he gives the patrons of such libraries names like Lydia Languish, Sukey Saunter, and Lady Slattern Lounger. Lydia, who yearns for books like *The Reward of Constancy*, *The Fatal Connection*, *The Delicate Distress*, and *The Innocent Adultery*, cannot love a man unless there are "romantic" obstacles of class and fortune between them.[73] The *Evangelical Magazine*, less subtle than Sheridan, denounced novels as "instruments of abomination and ruin" and the mind that enjoyed them as "contaminated, and totally unfit for the serious pursuits of study, or the delightful exercises and enjoyments of religion."[74] Vicesimus Knox thought that Laurence Sterne's *Sentimental Journey* was likely to lead innocents to "disease, infancy, madness, suicide and a gibbet."[75] It was the rare soul who offered a defense of novels or the women who read them.

SONGS

People also entertained themselves with songs—at home, at Christmas when groups went caroling, at work to keep in time with one's fellows or to stay awake, in the streets to attack political foes, at church, at fairs, in taverns, and even at an army's surrender. There were songs for Masons, for particular trades, and for commemorating battles. Some celebrated literary characters like Queen Dido or Robinson Crusoe. There were songs for dancing, like "Jumping John," "The London Prentice," and "The Joyful Days Are Coming." Often, songwriters, instead of devising a new tune for every song, would simply fit a new set of lyrics to an old tune. Thus, one piece of music was known variously as "Stingo," "The Oil of Barley," "Cold and Raw," "The Mother Beguiles the Daughter," and "The Country Lasse."[76] It was a practice carried to Britain's colonies, which is why the American song "My Country, 'Tis of Thee" and the British song "God Save the King" have the same melody.

There were political songs, like the abolitionist "The Negro's Complaint," which began life as a poem by William Cowper;[77] "The King Shall Enjoy His Own Again," a Restoration song retooled in various forms to celebrate the Hanoverian succession;[78] and songs against taxation, like "Britannia Excisa" and "The Income Tax" (the latter of which helpfully provided information on the amount paid by people in each income bracket—above a hundred pounds a year, "nothing less than a tenth will suffice, / Sing tantara rara one tenth").[79] "God Save the King," first published in 1742 and first performed publicly in 1745, began its life as a Jacobite song but was wholeheartedly appropriated by the Hanoverians during the Scots invasion of '45, with George II's name planted in the second line:

> God save our noble King
> God save great George our King.
>   God save the King.
> Send him victorious,
> Happy and glorious,
> Long to reign over us,
>   God save the King.[80]

"The Roast Beef of Old England," excerpted in Chapter 15's epigraph, was another popular patriotic song, as were "Heart of Oak" and "Rule, Britannia," with its chorus, "Rule, Britannia, Britannia, rule the waves: / Britons never, never, never will be slaves."[81]

Since songs were often sung in taverns, there were many with drinking themes. Other songs dealt with love, sex, and courtship. There were "sa-

tyrical Ballads" about the faithlessness of women, the perfidy of government, the incompetence of generals and admirals, and the worldliness
of the church. "The Country Garden" (also known as "The Vicar of
Bray") makes fun of a clergyman who has preached Divine Right under
Charles II, popery under James II, "Old principles" under William III,
opposition to occasional conformity under Anne, and Whiggery under
George I; the chorus for each shift of doctrine proclaims,

> And this is law that I'll maintain
> Until my dying day, Sir,
> That whatsoever King shall reign,
> I'll be the Vicar of Bray, Sir.[82]

More serious religious songs included the hymns "Rock of Ages" and
"Amazing Grace," both written in this period.

GAMBLING

Most people loved to gamble. They played hazard, a complicated dice
game, or EO, a form of roulette. They bet on races, cricket, boxing
matches, political events, births, and drinking contests. They even bet on
deaths. It was possible to buy insurance on another person's life, to bet
that George II would be killed in battle when he went to war in 1743,
and to wager on whether wounded boxers or accident victims would
recover from their injuries.[83] Sometimes, people offered to perform risky
tricks in order to win money. For example, in 1736, a Nottinghamshire
man bet he could walk over the flooded River Trent— on the handrails
between its two bridges.[84] About forty years later, another man bet he
could dive at Plymouth in a homemade submarine and surface twelve
hours later. Twelve hours elapsed, and more, and it became clear that
he had drowned. When raising the vessel was later discussed, Pall Mall
coffeehouse patrons bet on how his body would be positioned when
found.[85]

Gambling was enjoyed by rich and poor alike. Horace Mann and shopkeeper Thomas Turner both bet on cricket. Mann bet (and lost) £1,000
on a single match, while Turner wagered a half-crown's worth of
punch.[86] Small-stakes games played by working people included crown
and anchor and a coin game called pitch-and-hustle, later called pitch
and toss.[87] The rich wagered on their animals in two-horse races or
sweepstakes (where all participants anted a sum toward the winner's
purse, an 18th-century innovation).[88] Side bets by nonparticipants could
send the total amount wagered into the tens of thousands of pounds. At

the gentlemen's clubs, huge sums were gambled—£70,000 in one night at Brooks's[89]—resulting in frantic economies by the unfortunate. A 1701 poem speaks of a knight who, having lost big at dice, sends word home to chop down the estate's trees and sell the timber.[90] If nothing else, high-stakes games made for good stories. The Parliamentarian Charles James Fox lost £15,000 in one night alone; in 1774, he played nearly twenty-four hours straight and lost £11,000; two days later, he won £6,000. He had lost £140,000 by his mid-twenties.[91]

The government's position on gambling was contradictory. It had no desire to penalize its own members by attacking gamblers. Thus it aimed most of its ineffective antigaming statutes at the working-class proprietors of gaming houses.[92] However, the government also ran and authorized lotteries, thus sanctioning gambling on a grand scale. The British Museum and Westminster Bridge were founded by lotteries, and Cox's Museum and the Adam brothers' Adelphi building were sold by lottery. The national lottery, run with varying frequency throughout the century, began with a minimum ticket price of £20, with a top prize of £10,000. Later, the ticket price was halved and the top prize doubled. Since tickets were so expensive, people clubbed together to buy shares of a single ticket and paid for the ticket in installments. Drawings took place over a forty-two-day period at London's Guildhall, with interest and speculation increasing as the contest neared a conclusion.[93]

INDOOR GAMES

Card and board games, whether or not they were accompanied by gambling, were played by servants, King George III, and almost everyone in between. Many people played backgammon, draughts (checkers), cribbage, and chess. Card players enjoyed ombre, a three-person game played without the eights, nines, and tens in the deck; quadrille, a four-person game similar to ombre that overtook ombre in popularity in the second quarter of the century and was in turn ousted by whist, brag, basset, put; Pope Joan, played with the eight of diamonds removed, and with eight piles of counters or coins to be won for the playing of various cards or combinations; *vingt-et-un* (twenty-one); loo, a game with a pot divided according to the number of tricks taken by each player; all-fours; and piquet.

Other indoor games included billiards and parlor games akin to charades, with puzzles of some kind and guessing by the assembled company. One game played by educated men was that of "capping verses." One player would recite a line of Latin verse. His opponent would have to think of another line of poetry that began with the last letter of the previous selection.[94]

10.6   "Playing the Game at Quadrille, from an original Painting in Vauxhall Gardens," c. 1750. A maid carries a tea-tray; a black servant stands in the background. Courtesy of the Print Collection, Lewis Walpole Library, Yale University.

DEATH AND INJURY

The torture and killing of animals and fights between humans were a prime source of entertainment. Thus, in 1730, a showman advertised "a mad bull to be dressed up with fireworks and turned loose in the game place, a dog to be dressed up with fireworks over him, a bear to be let loose at the same time, and a cat to be tied to the bull's tail."[95] Some impresarios staged dog fights, or tied an owl to the back of a duck to see the duck dive in fear and half-drown the owl, or hung a goose head down from a tree or a pair of poles, greased its neck, and gave people turns trying to pull off its head while riding underneath. Children's games included shooting flies with small guns, sewing a string to a mayfly to keep it on a leash, and "conquering," or pressing snails against each other till one shell broke.[96] Some towns held bull runs, letting a single bull loose in the streets to be hounded by unarmed men.[97]

One of the most popular sports was cockfighting. Participants of all classes came to the cockpit with sacks holding their prize roosters, whose wings and tails had been clipped and whose legs were fitted with long sharp spurs called gaffles. Amidst a roar of betting, two cocks were placed in the ring and pushed at each other until they began to fight. "Then it is amazing," wrote one spectator, "to see how they peck at each other, and especially how they hack with their spurs. Their combs bleed terribly and they often slit each other's crop and abdomen with the spurs." Battle continued until one of the birds stood crowing on its dead opponent's body. Individual pairings were most common, but the most spectacular competition was the Welsh main, a tournament of thirty-two birds, with the survivors of each pairing advancing, until only one bird was left alive.[98] Boswell, who saw a cockfight in December 1762, thought the birds battled "with amazing bitterness and resolution. . . . One pair fought three quarters of an hour."[99]

Another popular spectacle was the "baiting" of an animal by tying it up and sending dogs against it. The most popular animal for such contests was a bull. In fact, in some places, it was illegal for a butcher to slaughter a bull without first making it the subject of such sport. The bull's horns were attached to a fifteen-foot-long rope that was staked to the ground at the other end. Owners held their dogs by the ears and released them one at a time. Each dog tried to bite the bull's muzzle or neck, gripping once it found such a hold until it tore out the piece in its mouth, died, or was pulled off the bull by the owner. The bull, in return, tried to flip the dog into the air with its horns, with the intent of breaking its back when it fell. To prevent this, the spectators tried to catch the dogs, often using long poles held at an angle to form a kind of slide. In badger baiting, the object was to bet on the number of times a skilled dog could make the badger come out of a box. In bear baiting (a rare sight, as bears were not abundant), the bear defended itself by standing up on its hind legs and batting at the dogs, or by rolling over the dog when one found a grip. Baiting of animals was attacked by a few, but often supported by the local gentry; Nicholas Blundell, in 1712, offered a bull to bait and a collar to the dog that performed best.[100]

Shying at cocks was particularly popular at Shrovetide and involved a rooster attached to a stake by a rope. Contestants threw a stick at it from about twenty yards away, paying a fee for the privilege, usually about twopence for three throws. If they succeeded in knocking the bird down, running forward, and grabbing it before it could stand, the cock was theirs. The new owner sometimes continued the game, pocketing the fees of the remaining contestants.[101] From about midcentury, cock throwing was banned in various towns.[102]

Contests between humans were considered good fun as well. Cudgeling, backswords, and singlestick, all of which involved combat with sticks, ended when blood was drawn (and, in one case, ran down an inch). In cudgeling, the combatants each had two sticks, one to hit the opponent and one, covered with a bowl-shaped wicker shield, for defense. Singlestick, as the name implies, allowed only one stick per fighter, with the unused hand tied behind the back. In all these sports, the chief targets were places that bled easily—scalp, teeth, nose, and so on.[103]

Wrestling was a common sport as well, as was boxing. Though boxing was technically illegal, it survived through aristocratic patronage, with gentlemen attending bouts, sponsoring favorite fighters, and offering prizes. Contests were fought with bare-fisted punches and head butts, in as many as thirty rounds. Women as well as men boxed, usually fighting other women, but sometimes battling men as well.[104] Some boxers, like "Gentleman" John Jackson, Tom Molineux, Bill Richmond, and Daniel Mendoza, became quite famous.

OTHER FORMS OF ENTERTAINMENT

Not all pleasures were violent, of course. People increasingly enjoyed travel and tourism, journeying to the Continent, to medieval ruins, to the Welsh mountains, to the British Museum, and to the Peak and Lake Districts. Those who could not travel enjoyed faraway places vicariously through travel literature. People also visited each other for pleasure, conversing, dining, or sharing a pot of tea. What John Strype called "the more common sort" enjoyed bell-ringing demonstrations; whistling, grinning, smoking, plowing, eating, and yawning contests; "lying at Alehouses"; watching parades and other street spectacles; and cheese rolling. Some villages had their own traditional pastimes. One held a "scrambling" for ale and meat pies. In Northumberland, at Christmastime, musicians and sword dancers traveled from house to house, performing in hopes of a tip; when they got one, they fired a gun in salute to the generous householder. Children spun tops and played leapfrog, hopscotch, and marbles.[105] Poor or rich, there was joy to be had.

TIMELINE

1720	The Theatre Royal is built in the Haymarket in London.
1728	John Gay's *The Beggar's Opera* is first performed.
1730	Colley Cibber is made poet laureate.
1731	The *Gentleman's Magazine* begins publication.
1732	William Hogarth issues *A Harlot's Progress*, a popular series of paintings and engravings.
	Vauxhall Gardens opens.
	Covent Garden theater is built.
1733	Hogarth issues *A Rake's Progress*, showing the consequences of sexual folly in men.
1737	The Stage Licensing Act imposes censorship on the theater.

Publisher Elizabeth Cooper issues the *Muses' Library*, the first general anthology of English poetry.

1740   Samuel Richardson publishes the immensely popular novel *Pamela*, about a lady's maid whose determined chastity wins her the heart and hand of her squire employer.

James Thomson writes the song "Rule Britannia."

1747   Hogarth issues *Industry and Idleness*, a series showing the different fates of two apprentices.

1749   Henry Fielding publishes *The History of Tom Jones*, a comic novel about a foundling adopted by a country squire.

1759   Laurence Sterne publishes the novel *Tristram Shandy*.

1764   Horace Walpole publishes the novel *The Castle of Otranto*.

1768   The Royal Academy is founded. Its annual art show will become a major social event.

1769   The Shakespeare jubilee is held.

1770   Oliver Goldsmith publishes the poem *The Deserted Village*.

Tobias Smollett publishes the novel *Humphry Clinker*.

Young poet Thomas Chatterton commits suicide.

1771   Henry Mackenzie publishes the novel *The Man of Feeling*, which fuels the trend toward expressing and feeling strong sentiment.

1773   The *Encyclopaedia Britannica* is published.

Oliver Goldsmith's play *She Stoops to Conquer* is first published.

1775   Richard Sheridan's play *The Rivals* is first performed, at Covent Garden.

1776   England's leading actor and stage manager, David Garrick, retires. He is replaced as manager of the Drury Lane theater by Sheridan and two partners.

Historian Edward Gibbon publishes the first volume of his *Decline and Fall of the Roman Empire*.

1777	Sheridan's play *The School for Scandal* is first performed, on May 8.
1778	Novelist Frances Burney publishes *Evelina*.
1780	London's magistrates close all tavern skittle alleys.
1787	The Marylebone Cricket Club is founded.
1789	William Blake publishes *Songs of Innocence*, a collection of poems.[106]

11

"The Turnpike Roads of the Kingdom": Transportation and Communication

> I wish with all my heart that half the turnpike roads of the Kingdom were plough'd up, which have imported London manners, and depopulated the country—I meet milkmaids on the road, with the dress and looks of Strand misses.
>
> —John Byng, 1781

In 1785, when wooden ships were still moved by canvas and wind, when riverboats were propelled by oars or sails or harnessed horses on the banks, and when the fastest pace on land was the ten miles an hour of a well-mounted equestrian, a singular event occurred in London. Or, rather, it occurred *over* London, when an Italian adventurer named Count Zambeccari rose below a hydrogen-filled sack in the city's first manned balloon flight. London went balloon-crazy, as balloon ascents multiplied and a balloon voyage was made across the English Channel. Fashions and coaches were named after balloons, and the English dreamt of speed. Their dreams seemed realized when, three years after Zambeccari's flight, a workable steamship was constructed. The physician Erasmus Darwin immediately conjured up a vision of a steam-driven airplane. But the effective use of steam for transportation would have to wait for the 19th century, and powered air travel would have to wait for the 20th. The 18th century would see speed of a kind, but its basic means of transport would be as they had been for centuries: foot, ship, and horse.

SHIPPING

Since England was an island nation, ships carried much of its cargo to other parts of Great Britain as well as to colonies and foreign lands. British merchant ships—8,000 of them at the time of the Seven Years' War[1]—imported and exported goods from spices and flax to beer and nails. They served in wartime as privateers and as sources of experienced seamen for the British Navy. Some caught seals (over 100,000 a year) for their oil and pelts. Fewer caught whales, which would not become really profitable for the British until late in the century; but the so-called Greenlandmen, who served on Arctic whaling ships, were universally acknowledged as the toughest the nation could provide.[2]

Some of the most profitable traffic was in passengers, willing or unwilling: landowners sailed to the West Indies, slaves were transported from Africa, indentured servants headed from Britain to America, and convicted felons were conveyed to America and later to Australia. Slavers typically got about 4 percent of the sale price of each slave; those transporting felons to Australia got £17 7s. 6d. per convict. With the third fleet of prisoners, this payment was restricted to convicts delivered alive and well.[3]

For foreign trade and travel, ships were the inevitable means of transport, and even for domestic coastal trade they were often the fastest means available but hardly as swift as could be desired. Convoys from North America typically arrived only twice a year, in the spring and in the fall and, while the journey "downhill" to Europe took about three to five weeks, the journey "uphill" to North America, against the Gulf Stream and the prevailing winds, took two to three months.[4] Trips to and from the West Indies were limited to one a year by the hurricane season.[5] An analysis of shipping costs reveals much the same situation as for speed: it was not cheap, but sea vessels were often the best or the only way.

Table 11.1
Cargo Costs by Sea

From	To	Price and Unit	Notes
Hull	London	10s. / chaldron of coal	peacetime
		14s. / chaldron of coal	wartime
West Indies	England	£3–£4 / ton	peacetime
		£9–£12 / ton	wartime
Virginia, Maryland	England	£5–£7 / ton of tobacco	peacetime
		£15–£21 / ton of tobacco	wartime

Bay of Bengal	England	£20 and up / ton of silk and cotton manufactures
Mediterranean	England	£5–£5. 10s. / ton
Portugal	England	£2 / ton[6]

Hazards of sea travel included docks and harbors in poor condition, inadequate maps, foreign privateers, storms or fires at sea, disease, falls from rigging, suffocation in the hold's foul air, wounds, and malnutrition.[7] The mortality rate for seamen on Liverpool and Bristol slave ships was 20 percent.[8] Add to these dangers some more ordinary inconveniences: lack of privacy, long voyages (two to three years in the case of many Mediterranean traders), and delays in sailing due to storms or the assembly of convoys.[9] Crowding was so severe that soldiers being transported by ship had to sleep "spoon fashion," lying on one side with their bellies against their neighbors' backs; periodically someone would yell, "About face!" and they'd roll, more or less in unison, onto their other side.[10]

Navigation was still a rough science at best. Latitude was easily determined, but no one had yet thought of an accurate way to reckon longitude. A Board of Longitude was established in 1714 to award a prize for a solution, but only in 1759 did John Harrison develop his chronometer, and even after the chronometer was tested by Captain Cook years later, its adoption by the merchant fleet was slow. Most merchant captains navigated by dead reckoning, and they calculated their speed with a log—a floating device attached to a line and tossed from the ship. As the ship moved away, a string tied with knots at specific intervals unwound. After a given number of seconds, the device was pulled back in and the number of knots counted. This, in theory, gave the number of nautical miles per hour—or "knots"—that the ship was traveling. In practice, the reading could be altered by currents and wind. As a result, many captains had only a general idea of where in the ocean they were.[11]

Still, some advancements were made in shipping during the 18th century. Towns invested in wet docks, lighthouses, and warehouses.[12] Seamen began the practice, which continues today, of identifying ships by their type of rigging. Barques, brigs, ketches, schooners, sloops, and others were classified according to the number of masts and the arrangement of sails. Early in the century, the steering wheel was introduced, and improvements in rigging gave vessels better maneuverability close to the wind.[13] Life on board ship was not horrible for everyone. Officers in particular stood to gain from their voyages, because in addition to their modest salaries, they often received the right to ship a specified amount of cargo for their own profit. Conditions were best aboard East Indiamen; one third officer, who served on the *Plassey* in 1768–1769, dressed well and had a spacious, painted cabin amply stocked with books and furniture.[14] For him, at least, sea travel was not only a necessity but a pleasure.

RIVERS AND CANALS

Within England, much of the country was accessible to river transport. It was slow, but cheaper than hauling goods overland and free of many of the hazards of the ocean. Rivers, however, had their own problems: flooding, ice, drought, erosion, obstructions caused by garbage and mills, and unregulated tolls charged by local landowners.[15] Navigable miles rose from about 960 in 1700 to about 1,400 in 1750,[16] but by mid-century most of the obvious river-improvement schemes had been enacted. Besides, local farmers, fishermen, and millers often objected strenuously to plans to alter the courses of rivers.[17]

An answer was discovered by the duke of Bridgewater and his engineer, James Brindley, who built a man-made waterway—a canal—to carry the duke's coal from his Worsley mines to Manchester. Over the next forty-three years, the Worsley mines, thanks largely to the canal, became 118 times more profitable.[18] During the 1760s and 1770s, canal development boomed; it stagnated during the American Revolution, then rebounded gloriously in a period of "Canal Mania" during the early 1790s. By 1790 navigable waterways had been extended to 2,223 miles.[19] Alongside the canals ran towpaths, where draft horses harnessed to the barges pulled malt, metal ore, slate, fertilizer, pottery, and, above all, coal, widening markets, leveling prices nationwide, and stimulating industry. Canal and river hauling was incredibly cheap, averaging as little as 2½d. per mile.[20] The obvious disadvantage of the canals was that they could not possibly go everywhere.

LAND TRANSPORTATION

What did go everywhere—or nearly everywhere—were the roads, but the roads were atrocious. They were potholed, narrow, rutted, dusty in summer, impassably muddy in winter, indistinguishable in places from the surrounding countryside, often unmarked by signs, poorly drained, and the resort of highwaymen. Nevertheless, goods had to be conveyed to buyers, despite the fact that land carriage cost twice as much as river transport.[21] Animals had to be driven from pasturage to slaughter. For these purposes, people used the roads.

Only the poorest people walked such roads. Most of those who walked were no doubt honest enough, but there was a common perception that they were beggars or criminals, and they were routinely refused service at inns.[22] Even in London, where walking might seem justified, the rich preferred to be shielded from the smells and filth of the streets. Therefore, they hired others—sedan chairmen—to do their walking for them. The sedan chair was a box mounted on rails, lined with cloth inside, and opened by means of a hinged top and doors. It was often summoned by a footman, who would call, "Chair! Chair!" and wait for competing chairmen to come running. The passenger sat inside while two men, one in front and one behind, carried the chair by holding the horizontal rails. It was common knowledge that chairmen preferred to carry ladies, who were lighter than gentlemen. An advantage of the sedan chair was that, unlike a coach, it could be brought directly into the house, allowing the passenger to disembark in private. Also, London's 400 sedan chairs could legally use the sidewalks and thus help avoid traffic jams.[23]

The sedan chair was impractical for long distances, and in such cases, manpower was replaced by horsepower. Plenty of goods were moved by mounted riders or by packhorses laden and led by a man afoot. Packhorses were especially useful in mountainous places or in other regions where the roads were bad. One such place was Somerset in the first half of the century, where horses made runs of about fifteen to twenty miles, each horse carrying about 250 pounds.[24]

Riding and Hauling

Horses could drag even more when harnessed together and hitched to a wagon or cart with its load sheltered by a collapsible canvas cover. The general appearance was much like that of the American pioneers' Conestoga wagon, except that it was perhaps twice as tall as the horses and equipped, after 1753, with nine-inch-wide wheels, which were believed to be gentler on the roads. It was drawn by four to eight horses, who were led by a walking wagoner, and sometimes even carried a few passengers too poor to pay for a stagecoach. Despite having a top speed of about two to three miles per hour, it was sometimes optimistically called a "flying waggon."[25] It must have seemed so to manufacturers, for a six-horse wagon could legally haul six tons of goods, making it approximately five times more efficient than six packhorses.[26]

In some cases, this kind of transport added little to the cost of goods. For example, wool carried overland from Bristol to East Anglia, early in the century, rose in cost only 15 percent due to transportation costs.[27] With coal, however, the price increase was much greater. In one 1738 case, hauling it three miles raised its price 66 percent.[28] Many haulers

11.1 "The Female Orators," drawn by John Collet, engraved by M. Rennold-son, 1768. A well-dressed man emerges from a sedan chair while two lower-class women hold a loud argument. Courtesy of the Print Collection, Lewis Walpole Library, Yale University.

objected to canal development at first, fearing barges' low rates would drive them out of business, but they soon found they could cooperate with canal transport, delivering goods to and from the barges and going where canal boats could not. Some owned both boats and horses; Pick-ford's had ten canal boats and fifty wagons by the 1790s.[29] By the end of the century, even small towns had a good system of carrier services. Rates were set by competition or by justices of the peace (JPs).[30]

Coaching   Just as no one who could afford to ride would walk, no one who could afford to ride in a coach would ride in a wagon.

There were various coaches for hire: the thousand or so hackney coaches that served London as taxis;[31] the omnibus, intro-duced in London at the end of the century;[32] the post chaise or post coach; and the stagecoach or diligence. The post chaise was the most expensive form of long-distance hired coach, chiefly because it was fast and relatively private. Usually it took the form of a closed chariot, bought from a previous owner by the postmaster who hired it out. It had no seat for a driver; instead, it was piloted by a postboy (often a fifty- or sixty-year-old man in a red or yellow jacket) who sat on one of the horses. Three features made the post chaise quick: the light construc-tion of the chariot, the fact that it seated only two passengers and a small

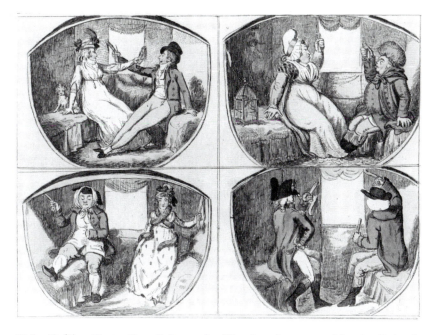

11.2 "Jolting Preventives," drawn by Woodward, engraved by Cruikshank, 1797. In four panels, various travelers adopt positions to keep themselves from being hurled about the inside of a carriage. Courtesy of the Print Collection, Lewis Walpole Library, Yale University.

amount of luggage, and the fact that it traveled almost universally at a gallop. It must have been exciting to see a post chaise galloping down the Great North Road with a furious clatter of hooves and wheels, and a terrifying, jolting experience to sit inside such a vehicle as it rattled, springless, over every bump and rut.[33] The stagecoach was cheaper because it was slower—about four miles per hour—and more crowded. Four to six passengers sat inside; additional riders sat on top of the carriage.[34] Stagecoaches often left as early as 2 or 3 A.M. and were populated with a variety of disagreeable traveling companions who stank, farted, swore, vomited, and flirted their way across the countryside.[35]

There were certain constants to travel in hired coaches. First, any hired staff, such as coachmen, guards, and postboys, would expect tips whenever their duty shift was finished. Second, there would be periodic stops to exchange tired horses for fresh ones. Third, there would be stops to allow the passengers to eat and sleep, and the cost of food and lodging on the road added significantly to the price of a trip. Sir Walter Scott, for example, made a journey from Edinburgh to London, on which food, lodging, and incidentals cost him more than nine times as much as coach hire.[36]

Table 11.2
Fares for Hired Coaches

Hackney Coach	London	1s. per 1½ miles
Highflyer	London to York, 1790	£2 10s. inside the coach, £1 5s. outside
Mail Coach	London to York, 1790	£3 3s. inside, £1 11s. 6d. outside
	London to Ipswich, 1796	£1 1s. inside, 10s. 6d. outside
Post Chaise	1757–81	4 wheels, 2 horses, 9d. per mile
	Oxford to Castle Cary, Somerset, 1774	£4 8s.
	1793–99	4 wheels, 2 horses, 1s. per mile
Post Coach	London to Exeter, 1781	£1 18s.
Stagecoach	—	2d.–3d. per mile plus tips for guards and coachmen[37]

Coaches were hardly perfect. Carriages, private or hired, were taxed during the century, increasing costs to coach owners. Coaches also meant traffic jams, the expense of hiring additional servants or tipping the staff of a hired stagecoach, and a rapid multiplication of horses (and their manure) on city streets. Yet traveling by coach, or, better yet, owning one's own, was an increasingly important measure of status. In 1712 the Lord Mayor of London stopped riding to his installation ceremony on horseback and began riding there by coach.[38] By mid-century, when Charles Johnstone satirically declared a carriage to be "so indispensably necessary to procure respect, that no eminence in science, no practice of virtue, is held in esteem" without one, there were 7,250 private coaches and carriages in London alone. The number would double by 1765.[39] Coaches permitted easy social visits, tourism, business trips, and even sexual liaisons: "the undulating motion of the coach, with the pretty little occasional jolts, contribute greatly to enhance the pleasure of the critical moment, if all matters are rightly placed."[40]

The rich invested in vehicles they could drive themselves: the four-wheeled phaeton, including the 1790s "highflyers" with the seat perched above wheels four to five feet in diameter, and pulled by two to six horses; the curricle, a two-wheeled vehicle drawn by two horses abreast; and a variety of other two-wheeled carriages, including gigs, whiskeys, and hooded gigs or buggies.[41] They also bought coaches meant to be driven by coachmen: two-seater chariots, four-seater town coaches, landaus, barouches, and broughams. A new coach might cost well over £100, plus another £30–£90 for a pair of matched horses. Used coaches could be had for less—as little as 25 or 30 guineas—and some people made use of "contract hire," in which a service provided the coach and some upkeep for a fixed period of time.[42]

Of course, fashion alone could not account for the increase in coach travel. A number of factors, each of which encouraged the others, combined to make coaching faster, cheaper, and more convenient. The introduction of springs for stagecoaches in about 1760 made them more comfortable, safer at faster speeds, and acceptable for outside passengers. More changes of horses reduced travel times (and, noted critics, increased the number of horses eating grain that could have been fed to the poor). Some coaches began traveling at night on trips between one and two days long, to reduce travelers' inn expenses. The variety and number of services also expanded, offering travelers a wide range of speeds, departure times, and costs. By 1769, Salisbury had 126 weekly departures, mostly from inns, provided by forty different coaching men or companies.[43]

The factor that contributed most to the coaching boom was the gradual improvement of the roads. At the beginning **Turnpikes** of the century, roads were the sole responsibility of the parish through which they ran. The local JP appointed a surveyor, who was forced to serve for one year without salary. The surveyor, usually a person of no experience with road repair, had one week to inspect the roads and some additional time to prepare a report for the justices at Quarter Sessions. He then appointed and supervised laborers. By law, farmers with holdings worth at least £50 and people who owned horses or plows had to provide a cart, a pair of horses or oxen, and two men. Those of lesser means had to supply one man or themselves. All these "statute laborers" had to report for six consecutive eight-hour days a year, for which they were not paid. Statute labor was not popular, and statute laborers worked in lackluster fashion when they showed up at all. In theory, they could be fined for absence, but JPs were reluctant to impose fines.[44]

This system was supposed to provide for all road work—laying gravel, clearing obstructions and trash, clearing drains, and fixing bridges—but by the 17th century it was clear that local taxes would have to be raised to supplement statute labor. By the 18th century, it was apparent that even the combination of taxes and statute labor was insufficient. Winter dissolved the roads into pitted seas of mud. Travelers thrown from their horses or coaches risked being drowned in the potholes.[45] Certain stretches, like on the London-to-Kensington road in 1736, simply became impassable to wheeled traffic. Daniel Defoe reported that each tree cut for a ship's mast took two to three years to arrive at Chatham, for "once the rains come, it stirs no more that year, and sometimes a whole summer is not dry enough to make the roads passable."[46] Travelers themselves only made things worse by carrying overly heavy loads, dragging sledges and wood against the road surface, or equipping their vehicles with narrow, spiked wheels.[47] Even where wheeled traffic was possible, it slowed appreciably in winter, and not until the 1770s did most coaching services abandon seasonal schedules.[48] Parishes where the volume of traffic or number of road miles was out of proportion to the wealth or number of residents were unable to keep the roads in good repair.

The answer, hit upon in the 17th century but barely used until the 18th century, was the turnpike, or toll road, which forced users to help pay for maintaining the roads. A parish that felt itself unable to repair its roads with statute labor and the rates alone submitted petitions specifying the problems and the section of road affected. Counterpetitions, if any, were reviewed, and usually the bill went to Parliament and was passed.

The first turnpike acts, until 1714, authorized "justice trusts," in which the local JPs retained their jurisdiction over the roads and had their powers extended. They were now allowed to set up toll gates, pay small "rewards" to surveyors who performed well, hire toll collectors, dissolve the trusts before their statutory terms were up, and mortgage the tolls (i.e., raise money for immediate repairs, using later tolls to repay the creditors with about 4 percent interest). Surveyors still had to serve or pay a £5 fine, unless they were peers, members of Parliament, or clergymen; they still served for one year; and they still selected road workers who were forced to provide labor, though now the laborers were paid a minimum wage.[49]

The justice trusts quickly betrayed their shortcomings. Surveyors were still inexperienced, forced labor still did not work, and the justices themselves were too busy with their other duties to pay enough attention to the roads. Therefore, beginning in 1707, and exclusively after 1714, turnpike management was awarded not to JPs but to private trustees, and the administration of the trusts was altered. Surveyors were now paid, offered a choice of whether or not to serve, and not limited to one-year terms. Statute labor was supplemented by paid labor and by contract labor hired for special tasks. In some cases, trusts "farmed the tolls," meaning they auctioned the right to collect the tolls. The contractor then paid the trust the agreed-upon amount and got to pocket any toll surplus.[50]

Turnpike acts specified the powers and duties of trusts. Trusts were typically granted a lifespan of twenty-one years.[51] They could purchase land adjacent to the roads, build side gates to keep evaders from sneaking around the tollgates, and, from the late 1740s, build entirely new roads. Trustees could lower the tolls only with the creditors' permission; they could raise the tolls only by obtaining a new act of Parliament.[52] The JPs, who were often trustees themselves, regulated the amount of statute labor owed the trusts, fined evaders, awarded compensation to landowners whose property was damaged by road work, and punished tollgate vandals.[53]

Toll schedules were complex, varying from trust to trust and by the type of vehicle or creature using the road. Pedestrians, for example, were free, while driven beasts were not; in 1761–1762 the Gloucester-Birdlip Hill Trust charged 10d. a score for cattle and 5d. a score for sheep and hogs.[54] Vehicles that used more horses and vehicles with narrow wheels were charged more, in the belief that these factors increased damage to the roads. Some trusts charged higher rates, as much as 50 percent higher, during the wet winter months. There were lower rates or exemptions for certain types of traffic—coal wagons in some places, tourists in Bath, haulers of road materials, mail horses and coaches, churchgoers, funeral goers, clergy on parochial business, and soldiers and their baggage carts.[55] Many of these measures benefitted locals, who were already paying their share in the form of rates and statute labor. Other tactics served them as well: discounts for frequent users, free passage at the trust's second gate if one paid at the first, and free same-day returns through the same gate.[56]

Some users tried to evade the tolls. They went into neighboring fields to avoid the gates, used other people's tickets, bullied the collectors, unhitched their extra horses before passing through the gate, or, in extreme cases, destroyed the tollgates. The trusts invented various ways of dealing with these offenses: installing weighing engines to ensure that the tonnage limits were observed, instituting large fines (up to £5), installing side gates to prevent circumvention of the tollgate, locking nearby fences and gates, and prosecuting some offenders.[57] Destruction of tollgates was made a capital offense in the mid-1730s.

Most people, however, realized that turnpikes were both necessary and potentially profitable, and the system spread rapidly. It entrenched itself most quickly in the heavily traveled roads around the capital, where the Great North Road alone had five turnpike trusts by 1720.[58] In that year the turnpikes formed a spidery, broken network around London, with some little sproutings, in most cases just single lines, around some provincial towns. A huge boom between 1750 and 1770 nearly quadrupled the total turnpike miles. By 1770 there were more than 500 trusts and more than 13,000 miles of turnpikes that crisscrossed the map.[59]

The turnpikes had multiple effects. In many cases, they leveled prices by ending local monopolies. Travel times were cut for goods, troops, and passengers. Coach departures and destinations multiplied, as did mileposts, signposts, and road atlases. Horse breeding intensified. Winter travel became faster and, in some cases, possible.

Table 11.3
Travel Times to London by Coach

Point of Origin	Date	Time
Bath	1700	50 hours
	1800	16 hours
Bristol	1754	2 days
	1800	less than 12 hours
Edinburgh	1700	256 hours
	1800	60 hours
Manchester	1700	90 hours
	1788	28 hours
Newcastle	1754	6 days
	1783	3 days
Norwich	1700	50 hours
	1800	19 hours[60]

THE MAIL

Turnpikes had another effect as well: the faster carriage of mail. They did not, of course, affect overseas mail, which had long been deposited by senders at coffeehouses or taverns and picked up by merchant ships before departing. Official mail packets, ships of eighteen guns with crews protected by law from naval impressment, moved currency, letters (usually folded up without an envelope and sealed with melted wax), government dispatches, news, and sometimes smuggled goods, and were as prone to do a little privateering as to be accosted by privateers themselves. If attacked, they were to throw the mail overboard and sink it. A letter to America might cost 3s. 7d. to send and take from two to seven months to arrive.[61]

For mail within Britain, turnpikes had a profound effect. For most of the century, mail was delivered slowly and haphazardly. Some people no doubt hand-carried their letters or had their servants do so. Peers, MPs, and their fortunate friends got franking privileges, and they could thus send mail for free. For everyone else, London had a penny post, but it was alone in this advance until 1765, when the Post Office Act was

POST-MAN

11.3 "Costume of the Lower Orders of the Metropolis 1800: Post-Man." The Postman carries a portfolio for letters and a bell to announce his presence. Courtesy of the Print Collection, Lewis Walpole Library, Yale University.

passed. Before 1765, sending a letter the shortest allowable distance outside London cost 3d., and sending a letter halfway across the country was prohibitively expensive for most consumers. The postmaster sent out mounted postboys, who took two days to deliver mail from Bath to London, while the stagecoach took only seventeen hours. The system was hard on the postboys, hard on the horses, and hazardous for the mail, since the postboys were unarmed and susceptible to highwaymen.[62]

A better method was found in 1784 with the first special mail coach, which made the Bath-to-London run in sixteen hours, at an average speed of about seven miles per hour. The red, maroon, and black mail coaches carried a coachman, a guard, four inside passengers, and no more than one outside passenger.[63] The passengers' fees kept down the cost of mail while increasing revenue, a strategy that could not have worked without the improved road conditions that made rapid wheeled traffic feasible. The coaches ran in any weather (unlike stagecoaches, which halted in bad weather) and ran on the same schedule year-round.[64] The coaches carried a tool kit (though not, unfortunately, a spare wheel) and sent mail ahead with the guard on horseback if there was a serious accident. The system was not flawless. Coachmen were prone to picking up unofficial passengers along the way, delaying the mail and pocketing the passengers' fees themselves. But the century saw progress, and by 1791, mail coaches had traveled an astounding 17,619,280 miles.[65]

PERIODICALS

The mail-coach system had several effects, one of which was the gradual standardization of time around the country. Another was the more rapid standardization of culture, as publications homogenized the countryside. London's first daily newspaper, the *Daily Courant*, was founded in 1702. A host of others followed: the *Morning Post, Lloyd's List*, the *London Advertiser*, the *Gazette*, the *Morning Chronicle*, the *Public Advertiser*, the *London Courant*, the *Times*, and many more. There were six dailies by the 1730s, fourteen morning papers by 1790.[66] Provincial towns followed suit; there were fifty provincial papers by the 1780s.[67] Papers broadcast matrimonial scandals, political news, reports of crimes, lists of stolen property, advertisements for products and jobs, and prices of goods at market. They were devoured eagerly by their readers. Only a few thousand people might actually buy a successful provincial paper, but they would share the paper with others or read it aloud to coworkers and friends. Whether it happened at the coffeehouse or workplace (as in Illustration 9.4, where a blacksmith's shop shuts down to hear the news), the reading of the newspaper was an event.[68]

Newspapers, however, were not the only way of getting news and culture. A new type of periodical, the magazine, was also enjoying its first real success. About 250 of them were published during the century, some intended for a general audience, some for a specific group. There were magazines for men's issues, women's issues, fashion, politics, religion, and pornography. Circulation might be very small, especially early in the century when distribution was slow and the magazine habit in its formative stages, but the *Gentleman's Magazine*, in the 1730s, might sell 10,000 copies. Other magazines included the *Tatler* and the *Spectator*, the *Ladies' Diary*, the *London Magazine*, the *Scots Magazine*, the *Connoisseur*, the *Town & Country Magazine*, and *Bon Ton Magazine*.[69] The reading public also consumed a host of annual periodicals and ephemeral publications: almanacs, political ballads, handbills, cartoons, and pamphlets like radical Tom Paine's. Such publications, along with turnpikes and canals and imperial conquests, fed the nation's growing desire to go more places, see more things, get somewhere faster, absorb more information, become more fashionable, ship goods farther, and do all these things at a better price.

11.4 "Country Characters: Barber," drawn by Woodward, engraved by Rowlandson, 1799. The barber is so absorbed by the newspaper and its word from Amsterdam that he cuts his client's nose with the straight razor. Working people were as fascinated by newspapers as the gentry were. Courtesy of the Print Collection, Lewis Walpole Library, Yale University.

TIMELINE

1555	Parishes are made responsible for the upkeep of roads within their boundaries and are authorized to require parishioners to provide labor for this purpose.
1663	The first toll road in England is authorized.
1691	The parish's right to levy rates for road repair, first authorized in 1654 as a temporary supplement to statute labor, is made permanent.

1695	The second toll road, or turnpike, is authorized.
1701	The first provincial newspaper, the *Norwich Post*, is founded.
1702	London's first daily paper, the *Daily Courant*, is established.
1707	The first true turnpike act, with the turnpike administered by trustees rather than by the local justices of the peace, goes into effect.
1741	An act of Parliament allows turnpike trusts to install weighing engines to ensure compliance with weight limits.
1753	The Broad Wheels Act is passed, which grants toll reductions to vehicles with wide wheels.
1759	The duke of Bridgewater's Worsley canal is begun, giving rise to the canal age.
1773	The General Turnpike Act allows all trusts to lease or reduce tolls, to build side gates, to buy land compulsorily, and to arrange for some road work to be done by subcontractors.
	All trusts are extended five years in exchange for building weighing engines.
1788	London gets its first evening newspaper.
	London's *Daily Universal Register*, founded in 1785, changes its name to *The Times*.
1797	The Manifest Act, requiring ships to carry a full manifest of cargo, is passed.
1799	London gets its first Sunday newspaper.[70]

12

"The Main Business of the Life of Man": The Economy

There was never from the earliest ages a time in which trade so much engaged the attention of mankind, or commercial gain was sought with such general emulation.

—Samuel Johnson

I was this day through Cheapside, the Change, etc. . . . the sole cause of that vast concourse of people, of the hurry, and bustle they were in, and the eagerness that appeared in their countenances, was the getting of Money, and whatever some divines teach to the contrary, this is true that it is the main business of the life of Man.

—Industrialist Jedediah Strutt, 1767

In 1700 day-to-day financial transactions were conducted in much the same way as in the Middle Ages. Most goods (except in London) were produced, purchased, and consumed locally. Farmers and butchers brought their wares to the closest weekly market, selling to large households and small. Shops dealing in specialty items were rare and their pool of customers limited; the local blacksmith, draper, and grocer dealt with the same clients year after year and had little need or inclination to fight for new business. Aggressive competition was deemed a vulgar violation of the centuries-old guild-based sense of brotherhood in a trade, and considered unnecessary when everyone who mattered could generally agree on a "fair" price.

Traveling long distances to conduct business was a daunting prospect. Without a widespread system of banking and credit, travelers had to carry all the funds they needed, in cash, over roads infested with highwaymen. Those who fell victim to crime, or other reversals of fortune, could not count on insurance to repay their losses. There were few banks, and thus few places to save one's money. Surplus funds had to be hidden around the house or reinvested in household goods or land. Capital for entrepreneurial ventures, such as the opening of a store or workshop, had to be obtained from friends or relatives, since there was no such thing as a small-business loan.

BANKING, CREDIT, AND INSURANCE

Over the next hundred years, many of these conditions changed. Turnpikes and canals lowered freight costs, which reduced prices and made it easier for middlemen and distributors to buy goods from all over Britain. Consumers thus had a wider selection of products at lower cost, but the rise of shops selling this merchandise, and offering credit, meant the decline of the weekly market and its ready-money purchases. More shops meant more competition, which led to advertising and inventive marketing strategies. Better marketing induced even common people to yearn for luxury items like clocks, watches, and teapots; more competition between shopkeepers meant that buyers could, in theory at least, influence prices and selection with their purchasing power, and the consumer economy was born.

The rise of credit was encouraged by the insufficient supply of coinage throughout the century. So scarce were copper and silver coins that many people, especially poorer farmers and servants in smaller households, probably possessed Mint-issued money only rarely. A workman might labor for weeks or months, buying his daily necessities at a petty shop on credit and repaying his debt when his wages were paid or when the harvest came in. His employer, in turn short of cash, might pay not in the coin of the realm but in produce or paper notes payable in the future. This chronic shortage was due in part to an overvaluing of silver, which made it unprofitable to produce silver coin.[1] The value of the coins available was further reduced by years of wear, and by outright clipping—cutting off the edges of the coins for the value of the shavings.

Private enterprise attempted to fill the void left by the Mint's failure. Issuing one's own coins was technically illegal, but in certain circumstances, given the need for some sort of currency, it was tolerated. Tradesmen, including ironmongers and innkeepers, issued their own tokens, redeemable at their places of business.[2] For less respectable coiners, who actually counterfeited government currency, penalties could be severe. In 1771 counterfeiting copper coin was made a felony,[3] and several

Table 12.1
English Currency in the 18th Century

4 farthings	=	1d. (1 penny)
2 halfpennies	=	1d.
4d. (fourpence)	=	1 groat
12d.	=	1s. (1 shilling)
2.5s	=	1 half-crown
5s.	=	1 crown
20s.	=	1£ (1 pound)
21s.	=	1 guinea

Note: Paper money was issued by the Bank of England in £10, £15, and £20 notes; a £5 note was added in 1794.

counterfeiters were executed, including "King" David Hartley, whose gang had killed a local excise officer.[4] Though the government was willing to punish coiners, it was reluctant to address the root of the problem. No major attempt was made at recoinage between 1693 and 1773, and when the currency was finally recalled and reissued in 1773–1776, the emphasis was on gold coin. Little was done to improve the supply or value of silver or copper money.[5]

Credit was therefore a necessity. Some sources of credit predated the 18th century and continued to be utilized. Shopkeepers allowed some customers to buy goods on credit and even extended cash loans on occasion. Goldsmiths, silversmiths, and attorneys held deposits and offered loans as well. Loans could also be obtained from friends, relatives, and sometimes from one's religious group. A nursery rhyme from the early years of the century, naming an occupation for each letter of the alphabet, says that "U was a Usurer took Ten *per Cent.*"[6] This can hardly be considered a reliable indicator of interest rates, but it does indicate that a loan provider of some kind was a recognizable, even an archetypal, local figure. Yet these small-time lenders could not supply the range of services, or the size of loans, offered by banks.

Bank interest averaged about 3 percent,[7] and banks offered a somewhat more secure harbor for deposits than did local tradesmen. They also provided mortgages, issued promissory notes or paper money, and dealt in checks and bills. The first banks were founded in London, and London remained the financial capital of the nation. Banking was not a new concept there—Childs Bank was founded in 1560, Hoare's in 1672, and the Bank of England in 1694—but the 18th century saw an explosion in the number of London banks, from a handful in the first decade of the century to nearly eighty by 1800.[8] Even more remarkable was the growth in banking outside London. In Edinburgh, Norwich, Birmingham, and dozens of other cities, new banks were founded. In 1750 there were twelve banks outside London, in 1797, 290.[9]

Another helpful development for business was the growth of the insurance industry. Like banking, insurance was not an entirely new idea. Insurance against fire and shipwreck had been available since about the 1680s. But, like banking, insurance first became commonplace in the 18th century. The idea of insurance was also embraced by workers, who formed "box clubs" to provide death and disability coverage.

Eighteenth-century insurance was still rough around the edges. Some "assurers" were no better than con men, and the primitive state of actuarial calculations caused many an honest enterprise to end in bankruptcy. However, despite fraud and miscalculation, the insurance industry thrived, encouraging entrepreneurial risk taking and, in some cases, meaning the difference to a poor family between burying a relative in a coffin with a headstone and burying him in one of the mass graves known as "Poor's Holes."

THE STOCK MARKET

From 1680 to 1720, Londoners invested in a horde of joint-stock companies. In 1695 there were ninety-three such ventures in England.[10] Daniel Defoe was suspicious of the stockbrokers:

> Some in clandestine companies combine,
> Erect new stocks to trade beyond the line:
> With air and empty names beguile the town,
> And raise new credits first, then cry 'em down.[11]

Such skepticism was widespread, but caution was banished in the second decade of the 18th century, when thousands saw what they perceived as a sure thing.

It began in 1711, when the earl of Oxford formed the South Sea Company to trade with South and Central America. The public, anxious to get rich quickly, snatched up shares of the company, spent extravagantly in expectation of eventual profit, and talked of nothing but "stockjobbing." The stock peaked in 1720, then plummeted sharply. The whole enterprise, noted contemporaries, was as insubstantial and fragile as a bubble. The frenzy for stocks collapsed in a matter of minutes, as the South Sea Bubble turned would-be magnates into debtors, and amateur stockjobbers into outraged opponents of the entire idea of joint-stock companies. The company's directors were held responsible for its failure, and government officials tainted by association with the "bubble" were forced from office. Parliament, led by Prime Minister Robert Walpole, passed the Bubble Act, which did more than any other one piece of legislation in the 18th century to cripple business. The Bubble Act forbade the formation of joint-stock companies, except those sanctioned by royal charter or act of Parliament. Royal charters were notoriously difficult to obtain, so only a few companies, including the East India Company, were founded in this way. Private acts of Parliament were costly and time-consuming processes.

There were several ways to raise capital to start a business. One was to have the money in hand already, like John Pinney, who made a fortune of £340,000 in trade with the West Indies, starting with a mere £70,000 of his own.[12] A second strategy was to obtain capital from relatives or friends. This worked well enough for the journeyman blacksmith eager to establish his own shop, or the weaver seeking to buy a spinning machine to increase his output, but it was inadequate for larger ventures, such as the Dowlais iron works, which required starting capital of £4,000, or a substantial spinning mill, which could cost about £15,000.[13] For this sort of venture, the easiest method of raising starting capital would have been to offer stock in the company.

But the Bubble Act, and the psychological wounds inflicted on the nation by the South Sea Bubble itself, all but closed this third route to funding. Potential investors remained skittish throughout the century. When market reversals occurred, there were always fears of another bubble-like crash and gloomy evocations of the original bubble.[14] Even very rich men hesitated to sink their funds into companies based on new ideas, and entrepreneurs were forced to obtain capital from friends or from their own savings, a process that often took years longer than joint-stock funding.

In such a hostile environment, it may seem remarkable that Britain's Stock Exchange survived at all. However, there were always comparatively safe government stocks to be traded, and the 1790s saw a cautious renewal of interest in investing. From 1698 brokers met at Jonathan's Coffee-House in Change Alley, which in time became the site of the London Stock Exchange. There, according to Voltaire, one could see "a Jew, a Mohammedan, and the Christian deal with each other as if they were of the same religion, and give the name of infidel only to those who go bankrupt."[15] Such extensive cooperation between members of different religions was rare in Europe, and it was encouraged for the simple reason that it fostered commerce, and commerce made people rich, and rich people could buy all the marvelous stuff that commerce made available.

SHOPPING

This, truly, was the first age of marvelous stuff—or, at least, marvelous stuff for the middle and lower middle classes. Increased consumption was due in part to colonialism and industrialization, which made a wider range of goods available at lower prices, and in part to the tactics of savvy shopkeepers and manufacturers, who created demand through advertising. Advertisers exploited the desires of consumers by promising either an irresistibly good bargain or instant status. The undisputed master of the latter tactic was potter Josiah Wedgwood, who touted the use of his goods by royalty and knew what separated successful products from failures: "*Fashion,*" he declared, "is infinitely superior to *merit.*"[16] Fashion certainly brought swarms of customers to his London showroom, and the fashion for acquiring piles and piles of marvelous stuff gradually changed the way the nation did its shopping.

Shopping, in 1700, revolved around the weekly and yearly cycles of the market and fair. Not every town was authorized to hold a weekly market; even by mid-century, there were only about eight hundred market towns in England and Wales combined.[17] Thus, the market drew buyers and sellers from the town itself, nearby villages, and the surrounding countryside. Farmers brought produce and livestock to sell: horses, bark for tanning, pigs, puddings, honey, flowers, herbs, grain, milk, malt, vegetables, fruit, butter, cheese, eggs, poultry, oysters, fish, and bread. Of these, dairy goods, eggs, fruits, vegetables, and poultry were likely to be sold by the women of the family, who customarily kept their profits for household expenses or personal trinkets.

More prominent farmers paid a fee, or toll, to set up an official booth within the market limits, while smaller producers, and most of the women, set up unofficial stands just outside the market grounds. The town shops, particularly the butcher's, prepared for their market day, the heaviest day of the week by far. Then a swarm of people (by 18th-century standards) descended on the booths and stalls: men eager to spend the proceeds of their grain sales on small beer, women anxious to buy cloth and ribbons and new pans, cooks and maidservants sent to the market by their employers, butchers' and grocers' apprentices making deliveries, courting couples, entertainers, gamblers, poor women banding together to buy a sack of wheat, children, and the market clerks and officials who made sure that procedures were followed.

It was a day of bustle, noise, laughing, shouting, the sound and stench of animals, the equally daunting stench of the unwashed plowmen and drovers nearby, the scratching hum of a fiddler's jig, and the buzzing of flies fresh from the meat and vegetable stands. When prices rose, the market might also witness riots or smaller gestures of defiance, as when, in 1766, a farmer who raised his price for butter was attacked by "an old woman" who "clapped one hand around the nape of his neck and with the other smeared his face with butter."[18]

The market, however, was not destined to thrive. Not every town that needed a market had one, and getting the right to hold a market was not especially easy. Markets also required a direct exchange of cash for goods, and coin was in short supply. Furthermore, most of the poor, and thus perhaps half of the population, could not afford to buy a whole sack of flour at once, or a whole flitch of bacon. They needed to buy a pound of flour, perhaps, or a half pound of cheese, and market-stall holders scorned to sell such small quantities.[19] The market was also held only once a week, but many people preferred or needed to buy their goods each day, sometimes twice a day. Finally, the market declined because the growth of the economy meant that more and more farmers were selling their produce, not to individuals at the market, but to middlemen. The middlemen then held the grain till prices were higher and shipped it to London, or even overseas, since at times there was a government bounty for grain exports.

Traditionalists hated the new system. They wanted the old way of marketing, in which farmers brought all their grain to market, sold for a prescribed period to small buyers, and only then made larger sales to licensed dealers. But increasingly, farmers brought only token quantities of grain to market. The rest had been sold already, sometimes before it had even been harvested. Laws forbade selling standing grain, or selling by "samples," or holding back grain in expectation of higher prices, but the laws were enforced only occasionally, when crowd violence or the mood of the local magistrate dictated.[20] More commonly, buyers at the markets saw loads of wheat but were told, " 'Tis sold."[21] By the 1790s, the market as the chief source of food and useful goods was nearly extinct.

What took its place? There were certainly other retailers, even at the beginning of the century. There were, for example, licensed hawkers, who paid a fee to the government for the right to travel by foot or by horse who sold goods. There were, for most of the century, between 1,300 and 2,300 of these at any one time, selling mostly cloth, ribbons, and related items. There were also peddlers, who required no license, as they sold exempted goods like printed papers and food, and traveling craftsmen, including "tinkers, coopers, glaziers, plumbers, and harnessmenders."[22] Hawkers and peddlers were especially prominent in London, where almost everything that could be bought, including fruit, fish, and

PEDLER

12.1 "Costumes of the Lower Orders of the Metropolis 1800: Pedler." The pedler holds out a case of trinkets for sale. Courtesy of the Print Collection, Lewis Walpole Library, Yale University.

coal, was "bawled in frequent cries through all the town."[23] However, though the number of licensed hawkers rose and fell, there was no increase dramatic enough to explain the decline of weekly markets. In fact, hostility to the hawkers from other retailers resulted in legislation increasing hawkers' license fees and restricting their methods and areas of business.[24]

What replaced the market was not the hawker but the shop. Shops offered convenience for town and village dwellers because they were open on days when the market was not, and in places where markets were not held. They offered credit. They would sell small quantities of food, enough for one meal. They also carried items that the markets did not, like tea and sugar. They did not quite replace the market when it came to fresh meat, vegetables, poultry, and fruit, but they did carry these items to some extent.[25] In all other areas, shops triumphed.

They did so by introducing a variety of new tactics. Some exploited snob appeal, like Covent Garden's Edward Archer, who styled himself in his advertisements "Tabbinet and Poplin Mercer to Her Majesty and His Royal Highness the Prince of Wales."[26] Advertising itself was a new strategy. Early in the century, with few newspapers in existence, and those boasting only a small circulation, advertising made little sense, but as newspapers and newspaper readers proliferated, it became useful to put one's name before the public. Some merchants' ads printed prices for current specials or noted the inferior quality of their rivals' goods.

Retailers found other ways to attract new customers and keep their old ones. They offered discounts for cash rather than credit purchases, delivered goods free of charge within certain areas,[27] marked items with price tickets (an 18th-century innovation), shopped and arranged shipping for customers in distant parts of Britain,[28] and sent circulars to customers, alerting them to special items for sale.[29] Most of all, especially in London, they lured customers with the bright, glossy, irresistible appearance of the shops themselves. Passersby marveled at the candlelit interiors, the bowfront windows, the displays under glass, the gilded decorations, and the sheer variety of merchandise of London's shops. The German philosopher Lichtenberg described his walk through Cheapside: the "shops . . . seem to be made entirely of glass; many thousand candles light up silverware, engravings, books, clocks, glass. . . . The street looks as though it were illuminated for some festivity."[30]

Wholesalers, too, became more aggressive. They sent traveling salesmen, price lists, and order cards to provincial shopkeepers,[31] and some offered goods ready packed, as did a tea wholesaler who distributed his product in one-, half-, and quarter-pound packages.[32]

Shops were everywhere, even in small towns and villages, where the local tailor or brickmaker or wool comber might keep a small general shop on the side. England and Wales as a whole had more than 140,000 recorded shops and may actually have had twice that many, if one includes shops too small to be taxed.[33] Small towns and villages supported at least the basic types of shopkeepers: drapers or mercers, who dealt in cloth; petty chandlers, who sold food as well as candles, soap, and hardware; grocers, who tended to sell specialty food items; alehouse and inn keepers; ironmongers; apothecaries; and a host of tea dealers. Large towns and cities might add to the basic shops those of clock and watchmakers, booksellers and stationers, confectioners and fruiterers, perfumers, wig makers, opticians, whip makers, carpet and wallpaper sellers, newspaper vendors, print sellers, seedsmen, gunsmiths, glovers, cartographers, florists, fan makers, auctioneers (Sotheby's was founded in 1744, Christie's in 1762), hosiers, and other specialists. There were also "toy shops," some of which indeed sold children's toys, but most of which were devoted to "fans, china, lacquer ware, tea, silks, brocades, watches, snuff boxes, cutlery, purses, heads of canes, trinkets and baubles."[34]

A typical general shop would carry at least the basic necessities of life: wheat and barley flour, bread (both large quartern loaves and manchets,

The Beaux Disaster.

We Sparks whose Merit lies in Dress,
Take warning by a Beau's Distress:
Whose Boxing, Eye, & ill turned Wigs,
Featured with Butchers to engage.

But they unused of affronts to brook?,
Have hung poor Prittle, on a Hook.
While foul Disgrace, spread in their,
The Butchers Sweet, & Ladies stare.

Judge wav'ring yr Sops most strike you,
How can you think yr Fair will like you.
Women of Sense, in, Men despise
The Futicks, they in, Monkeys prize.

12.2 "The Beaux Disaster," 1747, shows the open butchers' stalls of Holywell Street in the Strand, London. A beau is being hung on a butcher's hook. Courtesy of the Print Collection, Lewis Walpole Library, Yale University.

12.3 "Hero's recruiting at Kelsey's; _____ or _____ Guard-Day at St. James's," James Gillray, 1797. Soldiers eat fruit jellies at a confectioner's shop. The wares for sale include fruits, candy, and jellies. Courtesy of the Print Collection, Lewis Walpole Library, Yale University.

or small wheaten loaves), tea, coffee, sugar, treacle (molasses), tobacco, cheese, bacon, patent medicines such as "Daffy's Elixir" and "Dr. Anderson's True Scots Pills," candles, butter, salt, soap, rice, raisins, currants, figs, pepper, cloves, mustard, and starch. Full-fledged grocers carried a more extensive selection of food. They sold cocoa, including several varieties of brand-name "patent chocolates"; hops; fresh meat; wine and liquor; "all kinds of Poultry either in the feathers or ready for the spit";[35] soups and sauces; ginger and cinnamon; quinine; almonds; curries; sausages; coconut; and dried fruit, oranges, and apples.

There were other establishments that dealt in food and drink as well. England had about 50,000 inns and taverns.[36] Sellers of ale were thus nearly as common as sellers of tea. In the excise year 1764–1765, England and Wales combined had 32,234 licensed tea dealers, despite the inroads made by smugglers into their trade, the license fees, and the daunting bureaucracy involved in the retailing of tea.[37] The lowering of tea duties late in the century enabled legal dealers to compete more successfully with smugglers, however, and the number of licensees rose to more than 56,000 by 1801.[38] There were hordes of small tradesmen who dealt in tea as a sideline, as well as numerous larger firms, most notably Twinings.

COST OF LIVING

Ironically, the rise of shops coincided with a general decline in earning power among the laboring classes. In the second half of the century, wars, increased population, a few disastrous harvests, and the growth of the national debt contributed to increases in prices and farm rents, without an equivalent increase in wages. Inflation was particularly steep during the 1780s and 1790s. The result was that, for many people, even the necessities of life became difficult to afford. An 18th-century writer estimated that, in 1737, the average laboring couple made 7s. 3d. a week and spent 6s. 5d. for food, shelter, and clothing, but that by 1777 their income had risen to only 8s. 3d., while their expenses were now 9s. 10d.[39]

Tables 12.2 through 12.7 detail the costs of some of the items on which 18th-century people spent their money—both basic items and, for the 20 to 25 percent of the population with "disposable income" of at least £30 per year,[40] some of the pricier luxuries.

The most resented expenses, without doubt, were taxes. There were direct taxes, chiefly on land; the land tax varied between 5 and 20 percent, hovering near 20 percent most of the time, but based on increasingly outdated land valuations. (Catholics paid a double land tax.[41]) There was no income tax until 1799, but there were numerous indirect taxes on services and commodities. Most were levied on luxuries, but some, on necessities like salt and soap, penalized the poor with special severity. There were turnpike tolls and stamp duties, customs duties on imports, and excise duties for domestically produced goods. Cider, beer, tea, chocolate, coffee, carriages, auctions, male servants, sugar, glass, silver plate, posthorses, hair powder, newspaper advertisements, malt, dogs, candles, leather, paper, starch, wine, and tobacco were all taxed at one point or another during the century. Taxes on alcohol or related products—beer, cider, malt, gin—were especially likely to provoke riots, and excise officers were reluctant to collect certain taxes in certain areas, for fear of arousing popular discontent.

In addition to Parliamentary taxes, there were county rates, assessed and collected by the local magistrates for road maintenance, prisons, street lighting, and charitable relief. There were also tithes—customary fees or percentages of the harvest paid to the parish's Anglican priest. For Dissenters, there were tithes to the Anglican church they never attended and additional donations to the church they did attend. The English, in short, were heavily taxed, far more so than the French peasantry or the American colonists who rebelled in the third quarter of the century.

Table 12.2
Cost of Living: Taxes and Fees

3d.	duty per gallon on gin sales, midcentury
5 s.	stamp tax on marriage licenses and certificates
10s.	tax on gold watches (one in each household exempt), July 1797–March 1798
18s. 2d.	tax on a shopkeeper with 7 windows and an annual rent of £6, in 1797
£1	duty per gallon on gin sales, 1736–1743
	license to distill gin, midcentury
1 guinea	annual tax per male servant, introduced 1777
£1 5s.	average Englishman's tax bill at the time of the American Revolution
£4	average tax assessment for all shopkeepers in York, 1797
	annual license fee for a hawker on foot, until 1785 and after 1789
£8	annual license fee for a hawker with one horse or other beast, before 1785 and after 1789
£12 14s.	tax on a shopkeeper with 23 windows, an annual rent of £50, a dog, and a servant, in 1797[42]

If taxes were the most onerous part of the Englishman's budget, food was, for most people, the largest. About two-thirds of the family income was expended on food and drink, and the majority of that was spent on bread and beer. In hard times, meat and vegetables would be neglected in favor of more bread.[43] Most of the populace thought of money in terms of the food it would buy. Shopkeeper Ignatius Sancho wrote to a correspondent, "I cannot afford to pay five pence for the honour of your letters;—five pence is the twelfth part of five shillings—the forty-eighth part of a pound—it would keep my girls in potatoes for two days."[44]

Table 12.3
Cost of Living: Food and Drink

1d.	a bun at the Chelsea Bun House, London, 1711
	enough gin to get drunk; "dead drunk" cost twopence
1.25d.	one pound of barley flour, 1787

1.75d.	one pound of wheat flour, 1786–8
3d.–3.5d.	quart of beer (later 3.5d.)
3.5d.	one pound of treacle (molasses), 1795–6
4d.	one pound of butcher's meat, such as veal, pork, beef, or lamb
	two mackerel in London
4.5d.	one pound of wheat flour, 1795
6d.	one pound of tobacco
7d.	one pound of sugar, 1795–6
8d.	one pound of bacon, 1795–6
9d.	one pound of "Muscatel Raisins" in London, 1790
10d.	one pound of butter, 1780s and 1790s
1s.	a "Cream Cheese" in York, 1782
	price set by an Oxford mob on one pound of butter, Sept. 1800
1s. 6d.	price of a chicken in London, 1755
2s. 3d.	price of a chicken in London, 1785
2s. 4d.	six pounds of cheese at a Didsbury grocer's, 1787
2s. 6d.	one pound of "fine French fruit" in London, 1790
4s.	approximate price of one pound of low-quality tea, late 1780s and early 1790s
4s. 6d.	one pound of brand-name cocoa, 1786–7
12s.	approximate price of one pound of high-quality tea, early 1790s
15s.	average monthly grocer's bill of Didsbury laborer "Ould William Chase," 1780s
£59 13s.	1795 food expenditure for household of Rev. Laurie of Newburn, Fifeshire
£65	load shipped from a London grocer to Scotland's Sir Robert Menzies, including 66 lbs. of tea, 400 lbs. of sugar, 14 loaves, 100 lbs. of hops, dried fruits, nuts, spices, and rice[45]

Note: There was some variation, even in the same year, from town to town or even from merchant to merchant. Bread, for example, ranged in price widely (from about 5d. to 1s. 2d., depending on the size and quality of the loaf, and on the year and region).

Shelter and clothing devoured most of the rest of the laborer's budget. From 10 to 20 percent of the family income might go toward renting a house or farm. Rents, like food prices, shot up in the latter half of the century, rising as much as 50 percent between 1750 and 1790.[46]

Table 12.4
Cost of Living: Shelter

.25d.	cost per acre to the earl of Westmorland for four hundred acres of Whittlewood Forest, 1718
2d.	cost per night of a bed in a gin-shop, 1751
10s.	right to pasture a horse "in the Comonable Places in the ffields" in Hellidon, Northamptonshire, 1744
£2	weekly rental of genteel London lodgings
£3	house rent for an Oxfordshire rural laborer, last quarter of the century
£22	annual rent on Boswell's modest but comfortable London house
£20–£60	approximate annual rent of "handsome large houses" in Stratford in the early 1720s
£5,000	annual upkeep on Wentworth Woodhouse, home of the Marquis of Rockingham.[47]

Most of the rest of the lower-class budget was spent on clothing, chiefly on shoes.

Table 12.5
Cost of Living: Clothing

2d.	one yard of cheap lace edging
3s. 2d.	one yard of good poplin, 1791
3s. 6d.	pair of women's calf leather shoes at Loxham's Shoe-Warehouse, Leeds, 1791
5s. 6d.	pair of men's calf shoes at Loxham's, Leeds, 1791
£4 10s.	annual clothing budget for spectacle framemaker with total income of almost £50
£7 10s.	annual clothing budget for Oxfordshire rural laborer and his family, near the end of the century, including coats, shirts, shoes, and other items
£12 14s.	wholesale cost of 168 yards of crape.[48]

If there was anything left over, it could be spent on household goods, entertainment or other services, or travel.

Table 12.6
Cost of Living: Possessions

1.5d.	provincial newspaper
3d.	one yard of wallpaper
4d.	needle
6d.	sheet music—"a ribald song" about three Cherokee chiefs, 1762
	three ounces of Dr. Benjamin Godfrey's Cordiall, a patent medicine
	one installment of a serialized novel
1s.	a box of Dr. Anderson's True Scots Pills, a patent medicine
1s. 3d.	good-quality wooden stool
7s. 6d.	copy of a complete new novel
15s.	Oxfordshire rural laborer's annual expenditure on soap and candles, near the end of the century
£1	cottager's cheap clock
£2 7s.	smallest of three models of Thomas Todd's portable patent washing machine, which could, one retailer claimed, "wash as much in one hour as 3, 6, or 10 women"
	plain longcase clock, Wrexham, c. 1755–1774
£6	second-hand spinning machine, a "forty-spindle jenny of the best sort"
£16	approximate worth of a gentleman's mare, Wales, 1770
£43 17s. 6d.	new gates and locks at Erddig estate in Wales, 1781[49]

Table 12.7
Cost of Living: Entertainment and Other Services

.5d.	charge for a ballad-singer to sing one song
1d.	charge to view a peepshow or "raree-show," a miniature display inside a box
	minimum postage for a letter sent and delivered in London
1.5d.	per ton charge to haul twenty-five tons of coal on a barge on the Trent and Mersey canal

3d.	minimum postage for a letter sent or delivered outside of London
	catalogue of the museum of curiosities at Don Saltero's coffeehouse
6d.	tip customarily paid to clerk and sexton to act as marriage witnesses
	admission to a bear-baiting spectacle
	spectator's admission to the Marylebone Cricket Club
1s.	admission to most prominent art shows
	pre-written sermon for busy (or lazy) clergymen
	admission to the pleasure gardens at Vauxhall
	admission to Mrs. Salmon's, the best waxworks in London, 1763
	fee for a sedan chair for an hour
2s.	cost of a scalped ticket to the British Museum, 1784
3s.	a better seat at the Eidophusikon, a mechanical picture with special light and sound effects (the less expensive seats were 2s.)
	three months' worth of piped water service to a London home
7s. 6d.	approximate minimum fees for a clandestine marriage
£1 1s.	fee for a sedan chair for a week
£1 1s. 4d.	marriage license
£2	approximate cost of membership in a circulating library; some only charged a guinea
£10	cost of hiring a substitute to take one's place for militia service
£24	approximate yearly cost of a private tutor
£5,000	three-year Grand Tour to France, Italy, Germany, and the Netherlands[50]

When expenses exceeded income, there were few options. Charity might be forthcoming from the parish or from a sympathetic friend or relative. One might turn, if desperate, to crime. More commonly, debtors were thrown into prison, forced to pay for much of their own upkeep, and held until their creditors were satisfied; habeas corpus could not be invoked on a debtor's behalf. The harshness of the law was ameliorated somewhat by occasional amnesties, charities founded to free debtors, and the reluctance of creditors to deprive debtors of a means of repayment. However, the spectre of debtors' prison—the disease, the filth, the shame—was enough to drive some men to desperate measures, even suicide, for the more the economy changed, the more vigorously the debt laws were enforced, for in a world of credit, banks, coiners, forgers, insurance cheats, and stock bubbles, it was crucial to maintain faith in the system and to encourage the belief that debts would be repaid at all costs.

TIMELINE

1694	The Bank of England is founded.
1711	The South Sea Company is formed.
1720	The Bubble Act is passed.
1763	Baring's merchant bank is established.
1776	Adam Smith writes his *Wealth of Nations*.
1784	The Commutation Act reduces the tea duty from more than 119 percent to 12.5 percent. It will be raised to 20 percent in 1795. Reducing the duty finally makes legal dealers competitive with smugglers.

13

"Robbers, Burglars, etc.": Law and Order

All persons who shall for the future suffer by robbers, burglars, etc., are desired immediately to bring or send the best description they can of such robbers, etc., with the time and place and circumstances of the fact, to Henry Fielding Esq., at his home in Bow Street.
— ad placed by magistrate and novelist Henry Fielding

In some respects, the 18th-century English justice system was highly advanced. It afforded the accused strong protections, including strict evidentiary rules, jury trials, and the revered principle of habeas corpus, which banned imprisonment without trial. In other respects, the system was haphazard and chaotic. Patchwork jurisdictions, judicial improvisation, uneven enforcement, widespread corruption, and an almost complete lack of police protection plagued participants and observers alike. The fact that Henry Fielding had to print the above advertisement, instructing people to report crimes, says a great deal about the inadequacies of 18th-century pursuit and punishment. Why report a robbery if there was no one to whom to report it, or if the local constable was in league with the thieves, or if one could go to the fence who led the thieves to buy back one's property at discount rates?

A similarly relaxed attitude was adopted by the criminals themselves, who were rarely professionals. More often, they were demobilized soldiers or struggling workers who stole during hard times. They knew, as did everyone, that a hangman's noose was the prescribed sequel to many a conviction, but they also knew that the chances of being detected, arrested, and vigorously prosecuted were slim. Even if they were convicted, a sympathetic jury might undervalue the stolen goods to avoid imposing a death sentence, or a pardon might be granted at the last minute, or a death sentence might be commuted to transportation to the colonies.

TYPES OF COURTS

Two principal types of law were practiced, canon (church) law and common law, in two distinct types of courts. The church courts, however, were of decreasing importance. Each diocese had a Consistory Court, which heard cases dealing with tithes, probate of wills, defamation, Sabbath breaking, and marriage,[1] but the Consistory Courts had few enforceable penalties, which were largely limited to penance or excommunication.[2] Canon law cases could be appealed to a higher court—in the case of south England, the Court of Arches—and beyond that, to an ad hoc High Court of Delegates selected by the Lord Chancellor, and beyond that, to the Commission of Review, convened extremely rarely, and serving essentially as an appeal to the Crown. Appeals to the higher levels of the system were quite rare. The High Court of Delegates, for example, heard only about one case every three years at mid-century.[3]

Common law concerned itself with debt, credit, and criminal violations. Many cases of this type were handled on the spot by the local magistrate; more serious cases might await trial at the county's quarter sessions or the twice-yearly arrival of the circuit-court justices for the assizes, which handled juried, capital trials. The high courts of common law were Common Pleas, which dealt with civil disputes between individuals, King's Bench, which handled criminal cases, and Exchequer, which concerned itself with debts to the Crown. There was also another high court, the Court of Chancery, which adjudicated a third type of law, equity law, and governed trusts, alimony, and the wardship of orphans and the insane.[4] By far the busiest of these courts, at least from 1760 on, was King's Bench, which handled most high-level common law cases.[5]

The judicial system was far from tidy and consistent. Not all areas of the country were administered by typical magisterial courts. Some had manorial courts deriving from the ancient privileges of some long-dead landowner. Where magistrates presided, they might or might not know anything about law; they might be "trading justices," who sold favorable rulings for cash or sexual favors. Magistrates dealt out justice anywhere it suited them, from their homes or a local pub as often as from a courtroom. Miscellaneous courts, long-standing or ad hoc, served specific needs: the Lord Mayor's Court in London heard complaints by freemen against City employers; the Cambridge magistrates held court at Sturbridge Fair to chastise unruly fairgoers on the spot; and special com-

13.1 An illustration of a courtroom by Isaac Cruikshank (1796) shows Lord Chief Justice Bacon, lawyers, jury, and the prisoner in the dock. The prisoner, whose surname is Hog, pleads (or perhaps, given the *sang froid* of many eighteenth-century criminals, jokes), "My Lord I hope your Lordship have mercy on me as we must be related on account [of our] names Hog & Bacon." His Lordship replies, "Aye that may be very true, but a Hog can never be Bacon until he is hung." Courtesy of the Print Collection, Lewis Walpole Library, Yale University.

missions were sometimes established, like the one that prosecuted food rioters in four counties in 1766.[6]

MAGISTRATES

Most courts were headed by magistrates, the vertebrae of the judiciary. The parish magistrate was, by statute, a propertied man and unsalaried. This was supposed to place him above bribery and reduce "jobbery," the awarding of magisterial benches as political sinecures. In practice, it did not work. In London, magistrates were notoriously corrupt.[7]

If there was no salary, why did anyone want the job? First, lack of salary did not mean lack of income. In addition to bribes, there were perfectly legal—though not always ethical—ways of making a few pounds. For instance, prisoners could be set free on bail by paying 2s. 4d., which the magistrate was authorized to keep. Some justices found this a perfect excuse to round up innocent people for the sake of the bail fees. Sir Thomas de Veil, a Westminster magistrate who was by no means the worst of the lot, used to boast that he made £1,000 a year from his supposedly unpaid position.[8] De Veil's successor, Henry Fielding, found that a more ethical administration of the Westminster bench had its price.

> By composing, instead of inflaming, the quarrels of porters and beggars (which I blush to say hath not been universally practised), and by refusing to take a shilling from a man who most undoubtedly would not have had another left, I had reduced an income of £500 a year of the dirtiest money upon earth to little more than £300, a considerable portion of which remained with my clerk; and indeed, if the whole had done so, as it ought, he would be but ill-paid for sitting almost sixteen hours in the twenty-four in the most unwholesome, as well as nauseous air in the universe.[9]

Fielding's answer was to apply for, and eventually receive, a regular salary from the government, though this was kept quiet to avoid the appearance of jobbery. As for the rest of his colleagues, Horace Walpole called them "the greatest criminals of this town."[10] Money was one reason to become a magistrate.

Another was power. Fielding was accurate in describing the job as demanding, especially in London where magistrates saw an unending stream of lice-infested, diseased prisoners. Justices of the peace (JPs) had a long list of duties that only grew with time. They oversaw apprenticeships, road upkeep, taxation, alehouse licensing, market practices, wages, prices, and the poor law. They swore in constables, dispersed riots, licensed fairs and other public amusements, issued arrest warrants, made arrests themselves, took statements, and interrogated suspects. Also they acted as judges, without juries, mediating disputes between neighbors, and, alone or in petty sessions, sentencing those they deemed guilty of drunkenness, vagrancy, profanity, poaching, petty larceny, assault, bastardy, and other crimes.[11] The staggering array of largely unremunerative duties, plus the fear of being sued for wrongful arrest or assault by a thief's or a rioter's lawyer,[12] plus the awareness of serving as a natural lightning rod for civil disturbances—the magistrate's house was one of the first places rioters went—made the job seem thankless, demanding, irritating, and undesirable. On the other hand, it offered unparalleled power over one's community, so much so that when clergymen began to take JP posts under Lord Hardwicke, there was an outcry over giving any one man a monopoly over both temporal and spiritual power.[13] Most 18th-century people never saw a judge in the Court of King's Bench, imposing though such a man might be. Many, however, knew their local magistrates, whose authority influenced how they worked, played, drank, and fought.

LAWYERS

Another authority figure was the lawyer, no more popular then than now. Fear and loathing of lawyers pervades 18th-century art and literature, from satirical and often vicious prints to John Gay's argument that

A fox may steal your hens, sir,
A whore your health and pence, sir,
Your daughter rob your chest, sir,
Your wife may steal your rest, sir,
  A thief your goods and plate.

But all this is but picking,
With rest, pence, chest, and chicken;
It ever was decreed, sir,
If lawyer's hand is fee'd, sir,
  He steals your whole estate.[14]

Samuel Johnson, on this as on almost all other subjects, had an opinion as well. Of a member of the profession, he reportedly said that "he did not like to speak ill of any man behind his back, but he believed the gentleman was an *attorney.*"[15]

The law was nonetheless considered a good career for younger sons of the gentry. It was far more gentlemanly than trade, brought one into contact with well-bred clients, and could lead to high income, perhaps even the Lord Chancellorship. Joseph Massie, in 1759, thought there were 12,000 lawyers making between £80 and £199 a year. Above that income, however, he does not distinguish between professionals and the landed idle, labeling everyone "gentlemen or esquires and titled," but presumably some of these were better-paid lawyers.[16] Of these thousands of lawyers, more than 25 percent lived in London.[17] Almost all lawyers were attorneys, who handled mortgages, civil litigation, wills, and such, and sometimes provided banking and brokerage services. An act of Parliament passed in the first half of the century required them to be registered and to meet certain minimum qualifications, but they were held in perpetually lower esteem than barristers, who argued criminal cases before the courts. There were few barristers, and they did not have to pass an examination. They did have to wait for a place in the small circle of about 400 lawyers who monopolized the bar, and their admittance was symbolized by the right and requirement to dine at the Inns of Court with their colleagues once a day.

THE COURTS

Court procedures varied in formality. Even the illustrious King's Bench did not acquire its own cramped courtroom until 1760; up to that time, it was held in an open part of Westminster Hall. Some of its business was conducted at the Guildhall, which did have a separate courtroom.[18] Prisoners, in some areas of the country, might wait months for the assizes; in parts of England, assizes were held as much as seven years apart.[19] When prisoners arrived at court, sometimes after walking miles in chains to the courtroom, they might notice a sprinkling of herbs, sometimes strewn between prisoners and court officials to hinder the spread of disease.[20]

Some elements of the legal system remain all too familiar today—for example, the practice of filing civil suits as a way to force a settlement. Others seem alien. For nearly a third of the century, court proceedings were not even conducted in English, but in Latin, with some terms of French descent thrown in for good measure. Many of the Latin terms, such as *alibi* (elsewhere) and *amicus curiae* (friend of the court) remain in use to this day. Another alien aspect of the courts was their attitude toward married women. A wife was a *feme couvert* ("covered woman," one of the French-descended terms), subsumed in her husband's legal identity. She could not be sued for debt; her husband was responsible for her bills, and he could thus order tradesmen not to sell to her, even if his income came from her property or profession. If she committed a crime in his presence or at his instigation, he bore the brunt of the penalty because she was presumed to be under his control.[21]

Procedures differed between common law and canon law courts. In canon law courts, there was a judge but no jury, and parties were represented by special civil lawyers called proctors. All statements and questions to witnesses were submitted in writing. Only at the end of the case did both proctors appear before the judge to speak and to hear the verdict. No testimony from the principal parties was permitted, as they were deemed too biased to be reliable, and two witnesses were required to prove that a particular act had taken place. In common law courts, things were quite different. Testimony was oral, delivered in court, with oral cross-examination. In many cases, there was a jury, and testimony from the principal parties was permitted. One witness to an act was sufficient.[22] In both canon and common law courts, unlike in American courts, blacks could testify against whites.[23]

Criminal prosecutions—for example, of pickpockets—would almost always be brought by an individual, who had to pay 2s. for the indictment, as well as legal costs.[24] The defendant's counsel could call character witnesses, and the charges might be dismissed on various grounds, even a misspelling of the defendant's name in the indictment.[25] Many witnesses, juries, and judges could be bribed. There were few prosecutions for perjury; as a result, there were professional witnesses who specialized in supplying whatever testimony was needed.[26]

LAW ENFORCEMENT

Like prosecution, the duties of patrol and arrest were largely left to public service and private enterprise. Each parish had a constable or two—Westminster as a whole had 80, metropolitan London as a whole about 1,000—who, in theory at least, were selected from the parish's citizens to serve for one year without pay. They were expected to maintain their regular trade and perform their constabulary duties in their spare time.[27] In practice, virtually no one of means ever served, choosing instead to hire a substitute from a force of paid professional constables. Substitutes were paid as little as possible, and thus their advantage in experience was often offset by their susceptibility to bribery. At times they even encouraged disorder, as when they participated in burnings in effigy of the radical author Thomas Paine.[28] In any case, they were helpless in the face of the increased numbers, mobility, and anonymity of urban populations. It was simply too easy for criminals to vanish.

Informers and thief takers were another element of Britain's private enterprise law enforcement system. They earned a bounty for every criminal convicted with their assistance—for example, £5 for illegal gin dealers, £40 for highwaymen or burglars, £10 for sheep stealers, and £1 for army deserters.[29] Sometimes the reward included a "Tyburn ticket" exempting the holder from parish service, which could be kept or sold. Both informers and thief takers avoided antagonizing powerful criminal gangs. Some thief takers, like the notorious Jonathan Wild, were criminals themselves. They discovered that the best and safest money was to be made by luring children or bumpkins into a small theft and then "apprehending" them. The system was expensive for the government, futile at catching professional criminals, and occasionally perilous for the informers, who were rolled in the mud or pitched into the Thames.[30]

Other means of law enforcement were equally haphazard. London had paid watchmen, called "Charlies," who earned about a shilling a night. They cried the hours, woke people who needed to rise early, helped drunks home for 6d. apiece, and got drunk themselves. On occasion, they supplemented their income by working for burglars.[31] Westminster had about 300 Charlies; metropolitan London, about 2,000.[32] The parish beadle also had limited law enforcement responsibilities, mostly in the form of rousting vagrants.[33] Sometimes, whole neighborhoods grew impatient with the inefficiency of the thief takers, informers, constables, and Charlies, and they issued their own rewards for the capture of local bandits. Parliament, too, offered special rewards on occasion.[34]

The idea of a professional police force was vigorously resisted even by law-abiding citizens, who saw it as a first step toward tyranny. As

WATCHMAN

13.2 "Costume of the Lower Orders of the Metropolis 1800: Watchman." Henry Fielding, in *Amelia*, called the Charlies "poor, old, decrepit people," though this one seems hearty enough. Courtesy of the Print Collection, Lewis Walpole Library, Yale University.

late as 1785, the Lord Mayor and aldermen of London fought such a proposal, terrified of living "under the scourge of such a system."[35] Consequently, the core of the London police force was assembled without public knowledge. In the early 1750s, Henry Fielding organized a force later known as the Bow Street Runners. Armed with cutlasses (and pistols for the officers), the Runners were paid a guinea a week—which came from the secret service fund—plus reward money.[36] After Fielding's death, the Runners were coordinated by his blind half-brother, magistrate Sir John Fielding.

CRIME

Despite inadequate or nonexistent police protection and state prosecution, criminals were arrested in substantial numbers for both minor and major offenses. In the former category were such crimes as embezzlement, minor vandalism such as destroying fences, forgery (a misdemeanor until 1771), manslaughter, attempted murder, perjury, breach of promise, swearing, trading on Sunday, keeping unlicensed alehouses, homosexuality, *very* minor thefts, failing to support one's family and thus leaving them dependent on the parish, and performing abortions. Capital crimes, which rose in number from 50 in 1689 to about 200 in 1800, included poaching (if a gun was fired at a gamekeeper), counterfeiting, forgery, sheep stealing, killing a cow, looting, theft or robbery of even small items (for pickpocketing, goods over 1s. in value, for shoplifting 5s. worth, for burglary or "house-breaking" 40s.), associating with gypsies, entering land with intent to kill rabbits, chipping stone from Westminster Bridge, bigamy, major vandalism (against turnpikes, fishponds, silk looms, machinery, and hop binds), and theft of a master's goods by a servant.[37]

PUNISHMENT

With so many crimes carrying a death sentence, it might be supposed that the English were executed in huge numbers. The numbers were significant—about 1,200 Londoners over the course of the century, about 20 a year in the late century in London and Middlesex combined, and as many as about 200 a year in England and Wales together[38]—but not nearly as large as they might have been, for several reasons. The first was that no administrator of the law expected to catch and punish all criminals. Enforcement was by random example. The English even took pride in their non-enforcement of many laws, citing it as proof of their free society. Second, many felt compassion for those sentenced to hang (who could by law be as young as seven, but who were in practice usually no younger than fifteen), and either refused to prosecute or, if on a jury, acquitted or undervalued stolen goods to avoid imposing the death penalty. "They who would rejoice at the correction of a thief," said Samuel Johnson, "are yet shocked at the thought of destroying him."[39] Third, judicial and royal pardons and commutations were often handed out for reasons of politics or public relations. And fourth, literate prisoners could plead "benefit of clergy," a holdover from the Middle Ages when only clergy were likely to be able to read. A prisoner could read the 51st Psalm, known as the "neck verse" for its power to ward off the noose, as proof of clerical—or at least protected—status. Many an illiterate thief must have memorized the neck verse for this secular purpose.

Capital punishment came under severe scrutiny in the 18th century. Almost everyone agreed that some executions would act as a deterrent; nevertheless, crime seemed to be out of control, with highwaymen robbing on the roads alone or in pairs, footpads (thieves on foot) robbing in dark alleys, "mudlarks" and their accomplices robbing from ships,

Death Penalty Controversy

wool smugglers intimidating and even murdering excise officers, and pirates operating in the English Channel. The question, then, was how and when to execute for maximum effect. Johnson defended public executions, as did politician John Wilkes, who said privately that he thought they engendered a militarily useful contempt for death.[40] Henry Fielding, like many others, opposed public executions because he thought they created too much pity for the condemned. A writer in *Fog's Weekly Journal* in 1737 considered death too merciful a fate, since "We are condemn'd to death by Nature," and advocated hard labor instead.[41] Fielding and William Eden both wanted to reduce the number of capital crimes, and Martin Madan wanted pardons to be used less frequently.[42]

Jail For non-capital crimes, there were plenty of punishments available, but jail was not among the preferred options. Jails were used primarily as holding places before trial, or places of confinement for short sentences. Few people, except debtors, were jailed for years at a time. Only toward the end of the century did reformers turn to long jail terms in state-of-the-art prisons with solitary confinement cells. Still, even in the early 1770s, only between 2 and 3 percent of Old Bailey sentences were prison terms. The few new-style prisons were not built until the 1780s and 1790s,[43] although the 1770s saw the first "hulks," hard-labor prison ships anchored in the Thames.[44] Most prisons continued to operate on old-fashioned lines. Male and female prisoners often mingled freely during the day. The women sometimes sold their bodies for money or for the hope of getting pregnant; "pleading one's belly" stalled execution. Lice, disease, noise, crowding, and dirt were plentiful; fresh straw for bedding was not.

Alcohol was available, like almost everything else, for a price. Wardens (who might pay up to £5,000 for the keepership of a large jail) and jailers operated on a free-enterprise system, seeking to squeeze the largest possible fees from their inmates. They charged for private rooms, gin, beer, bedding, removal of chains, freedom to walk or live outside the prison, and food beyond the standard allowance, which was often solely bread or, as at the Fleet and the Marshalsea, nothing at all. Alehouse keepers or other small businessmen could set up "prisons," which often housed only one or two prisoners. The sheriffs who were ostensibly responsible for inspecting conditions performed this duty sloppily. And Parliament, prior to the efforts of reformer John Howard, acted seldom and halfheartedly on prisoners' behalf. Indeed, the prisoners, when they were not dying of "gaol fever," entered enthusiastically into the commercial spirit of prison life. When a new prisoner arrived, his predecessors gathered around to demand a cash payment, called "garnish." (Garnish at Newgate was 5s. 6d. for felons, 2s. 6d. for debtors.) If the fee was not forthcoming, they took his clothes, calling out, "Pay or strip!" Once acquitted, a prisoner could not leave jail until he had paid all his fees.[45]

If the authorities worried little about prisons until the 1770s, it was be-

13.3 "Newgate," 1799. An exterior view of the prison. Courtesy of the Print Collection, Lewis Walpole Library, Yale University.

cause they had no need. There was already an obvious dumping-ground for those whose crimes were too seri-ous for a couple of months in jail, but not serious enough to merit execution. Such convicts could be loaded on a boat and shipped to America, chiefly to the southern **Transportation and Corporal Punishment**
colonies, where they often wound up as cheap labor on tobacco planta-tions. This punishment, called transportation, was sometimes for a lim-ited time, like seven years, and sometimes for life. Transportation enabled England to get rid of felons, supplied the colonies with workers, and gave the felons themselves a chance to avoid both the noose and the often-fatal diseases of jail. For many convicts, it provided a fresh start, especially since many of them were not guilty of particularly hei-nous crimes. In one case, two women were sentenced to be transported for breaking into a house at night and stealing 10d. worth of flour. Yet it was not a perfect solution. Transported (or "lagged") convicts some-times returned illegally and committed more crimes, despite the fact that illegal return was a hanging offense. And the destination for convicts was, as it happened, not available indefinitely. In the 1770s, the American colonies rebelled, ending transportations there for good. Late in the 1780s, transportation began again, but this time the destination was Aus-tralia.[46]

Even for minor crimes, judges were reluctant to impose jail sentences. Instead, they preferred to impose public pain, shame, or discomfort. Sometimes this meant the pillory, a wooden frame that locked the head and hands in place. People exposed in the pillory were tormented by the crowd, sometimes for fun, sometimes out of genuine resentment of the crime. It was not unusual for the person pilloried to suffer death or maiming as a result of being pelted with stones, food, dirt, dead animals, and trash. Those not pilloried were sometimes branded, though the brander could be bribed to use a cold iron. Another common punishment was public flogging, and it was a holiday of sorts when women, particularly prostitutes, were flogged. Crowds would gather to see these women stripped to the waist and beaten.

Execution The holiday mood only intensified when a hanging was scheduled. In London, the procession began every six weeks at Newgate with the condemned—most of them younger than twenty-one—being loaded onto an open cart, accompanied by their coffins. They made their slow way westward to Tyburn, where the triangular gallows awaited them. On the way, they stopped at taverns, drinking heavily and promising to pay the bill "when they came back." The crowd, which included workmen, pickpockets, food vendors, and apprentices on holiday (much to the dismay of their employers), drank too.[47]

At Tyburn the crowd stood or paid for the privilege of sitting in the wooden grandstands, called "Mother Proctor's Pews."[48] The cart moved beneath the gallows where there were final speeches from the condemned, perhaps a last-minute reprieve, and prayers from the chaplain; then nooses were placed around the doomed necks. Then "away goes the Cart, and there swing my Gentlemen kicking in the Air." Hawkers began selling the alleged dying utterances of the hanged, which were usually composed and printed before the execution, timely sale being far more important than factual accuracy. Sufferers from disease snatched at the bodies, believing them to possess magical powers. Entrepreneurs waited for the right moment to make off with the rope, which could be sold in pieces as a souvenir. Friends of the hanged lingered, trying to support them long enough to cut them down (which worked on at least one occasion), yanking on their legs to shorten their suffering (since 18th-century hanging had no drop to break the neck and death was by slow strangulation), and defending their bodies (sometimes with fierce violence) from the surgeons, who had a right to dissect ten Tyburn corpses per year and claimed any corpse not purchased by the family.[49]

In some cases, the bodies were violated according to the nature of the crime. Jacobites' heads were, until 1777, severed and displayed on spikes at Temple Bar. Sometimes whole bodies, often shaved, disemboweled, or coated with tar or tallow, were hung in chains near the symbolic scene

13.4 "The Idle Prentice Executed at Tyburn," Hogarth, 1747. Note the gibbet, the gingerbread vendor in the right foreground, the cart with the coffin, Mother Proctor's Pews, and the woman already hawking the prisoner's dying speech. The carriage carries the Ordinary of Newgate; atop the carriage is a man, probably the executioner. Executions were usually held at 8 a.m. on Mondays and might draw as many as 100,000 spectators. Courtesy of the Print Collection, Lewis Walpole Library, Yale University.

of their crimes—along roads for highwaymen, near the Thames for pirates, mutineers, and deserters.[50] Far from being shocked by such displays, the crowds positively demanded them. They sometimes rioted if denied a hanging, for example by the suicide of the condemned. In one such case they seized the dead body and "dragged his guts about the highway, poked his eyes out, and broke almost all his bones."[51] Tens of thousands gathered at Tyburn for the express purpose of seeing death, suffering, bravado, and cowardice. The crowd increased for the hangings of notorious murderers, like Lord Ferrers, who murdered his steward and went to the noose in a gorgeous suit of white and silver. It also loved the hanging, drawing, and quartering of traitors.

Henry Fielding, who saw so much so clearly on this subject, brushed aside claims that executions frightened would-be thieves. Instead, he thought, executions merely accustomed thieves to the idea of death. He knew already, though it would take the rest of the nation some time to agree, that there were many answers to questions of crime: fewer capital offenses, professional patrol and enforcement, reduction of the causes of crime (like addiction to gin), and prompt reporting of crimes.

TIMELINE

1693	Parliament offers a £40 reward for captured highwaymen, and thief takers come into existence.
1718	Parliament authorizes transportation of felons to the colonies.
1725	The notorious head of a band of thieves, Jonathan Wild, is hanged.
1731	English is made the official language of British courts.
1736	The case of *Middleton v. Croft* establishes the supremacy of common over canon law.
1739	Notorious highwayman Dick Turpin is executed.
1748	Henry Fielding becomes a Westminster magistrate.
1750	Henry Fielding publishes *An Enquiry into . . . the late Increase of Robbers*.
1752	Parliament agrees to compensate poor citizens who prosecute criminals.
1754	Parliament authorizes compensation for poor witnesses in trials.
1758	Sir John Fielding publishes his *Account of the Police*.
1760	Lord Ferrers is hanged.
1765	Sir William Blackstone begins his landmark *Commentaries on the Laws of England*.
1771	William Eden publishes *Principles of Penal Punishment*, in which he argues for fewer capital crimes.
1774	Two largely ineffective acts of Parliament are passed to improve jail conditions.
1776	The Hulks Act authorizes prison ships on the Thames.
1777	Prison reformer John Howard publishes his *State of the Prisons*.
1779	Branding is abolished.
1780	Several prisons, including Newgate, the Fleet, and the Clink, a debtors' prison in Southwark, are wrecked in London's Gordon Riots.

1783	Public executions are moved from Tyburn to New-gate.
1785	Martin Madan publishes *Thoughts on Executive Justice,* which concludes that the problem with the death penalty is uneven enforcement.
	An attempt to found a 225-man police force in London is defeated.
1790	The execution of women by burning is abolished.
1792	A police force is established in Manchester.
1817	Public flogging of women is abolished.[52]

14

"A Progeny of Learning": Education

I would by no means wish a daughter of mine to be a progeny of learning; I don't think so much learning becomes a young woman; for instance, I would never let her meddle with Greek, or Hebrew, or algebra, or simony, or fluxions, or paradoxes, or such inflammatory branches of learning—neither would it be necessary for her to handle any of your mathematical, astronomical, diabolical instruments. But . . . I would send her, at nine years old, to a boarding-school. . . . Then, sir, she should have a supercilious knowledge in accounts.

—Mrs. Malaprop, in Richard Sheridan's *The Rivals*, 1775

The above speech from *The Rivals* was considered amusing to 18th-century playgoers because Mrs. Malaprop misuses a number of words within it, not because Mrs. Malaprop's idea of female education is so limited. The debate over what should be taught in school, and, indeed, who should go to school at all, was an energetic one, particularly in the middle and later parts of the century. There were disagreements about the essential nature of the child, discipline, curriculum, and the ultimate purpose of education.

Methodist schoolteacher Mary Fletcher, in 1764, explained that her job was "to fit them for good servants" and "to inure them to labour, early rising, and cleanliness." Fifteen minutes' recess was allowed for health's sake, but "[w]e never use the term play, nor suffer any to give those toys or playthings, which children are usually brought up to spend half their time playing in."[1]

INFORMAL EDUCATION

Throughout the period, all education was run by private industry or supported by private subscriptions or endowments. The government felt no responsibility to educate any or all of its future citizens, and as a result many children never went to school. These children learned from a variety of sources, including lectures by itinerant scientists, almanacs, parental tutelage, shop signs, nursery rhymes, church sermons and decorations, instruction by trade masters or journeymen, and advice from neighbors and relatives. Girls imbibed moral wisdom, or so their mothers hoped, while embroidering samplers:

> Patience is a virtue
> Virtue is a grace
> Both put together
> Make a pretty face.[2]

Some children were encouraged to learn the alphabet by eating it:

> To master John the English maid
> A hornbook gives of gingerbread;
> And, that the child may learn the better,
> As he can name, he eats the letter.[3]

Others, both adults and children, took advantage of a booming market in cheap books. They learned from dictionaries, fairy-tale chapbooks like *Jack and the Beanstalk* and *Tom Thumb*, educator Anna Letitia Barbauld's *Hymns in Prose for Children*, publisher John Newbery's primers and picture books, and Wallis's *Educational Cards for the Amusement of Youth*.[4]

TUTORS

Those who could afford a more organized approach to education often hired tutors for their children. A private general tutor could be hired for about £20 to £30 per year, or roughly twice the cost of a middling boarding school.[5] There were hosts of these personal teachers in England: French governesses, dancing masters, drawing masters, singing instructors, and music teachers. Tutors were sometimes clergymen or artisans who could find no other employment, but in other cases they were quite distinguished talents; the astronomer and professional musician William Herschel, for example, gave private lessons in Bath during the 1760s.[6]

Those who hired tutors were sometimes, but not always, members of the upper class. Freed slave Olaudah Equiano, a working man, hired tutors to teach him hairdressing, mathematics, and music.[7]

SCHOOLS

Schools were founded and bankrupted with sometimes dizzying frequency, and a school in existence in 1710 might well be out of business by 1715 or 1720. A particularly gifted teacher or headmaster, or the presence among the students of the heir to a title or a fortune, might draw hordes of fee-paying pupils. A few years of financial mismanagement, a theological dispute with a sponsoring religious body, or the presence of too many poor local youths in the school, could cause the school to close its doors. Hackney, Hoxton, and Warrington academies, despite their heydays of fame and prestige, were among those that folded.[8] The lifespan of smaller schools, often composed of one teacher and as many students as he or she felt able to instruct, was even shorter. When the teacher died, fell out of favor, found a better job, or moved away, the school disappeared.

There was also no standardization of curriculum from one school to the next. Depending on the type of school, the focus might be on Anglican doctrine, accounting, or Greek poetry. Schools for the poor were almost always charitable ventures, founded to train pious servants and workers who would stay sober during work, and opposed by those who feared that literacy would make the rabble "fractious and refractory."[9] The rich and middle class, however, were often won over to the idea of such schools; they were a good Christian institution, they demonstrated the generosity of the founders, and they kept potentially idle children busy, especially on Sundays, when they might otherwise be lounging about causing mischief. For the poor, the lure was some sort of education, however scanty, free or at low cost, sometimes with free uniforms in an age when clothing was a significant portion of the family budget. To call the curriculum of such schools unambitious is being overly kind, though no doubt the founders thought it quite adequate for future servants and laborers: reading (though not always writing), religion, discipline, obedience, personal hygiene, a little arithmetic, sewing for the girls (sometimes in place of the arithmetic),[10] and deference to authority. To teach them not to pilfer the goods of their future employers, the pupils recited couplets like, "It is a sin/To steal a pin,"[11] and they participated in scripted exchanges like the one below:

Question: Is it honest for workmen to waste and destroy the materials and implements which they make use of?

THE COUNTRY SCHOOL MISTRESS.

14.1 "The Country School-Mistress," drawn by J. Saunders, engraved by B. Duterrau, 1797. A country schoolmistress helps her pupil to learn the alphabet. Courtesy of the Print Collection, Lewis Walpole Library, Yale University.

Answer: No.

Question: Who do these things belong to?

Answer: Their Master.

Question: Whose eyes see you when your master is not by?

Answer: God's.[12]

William Cobbett thought such lessons worse than useless—a daily course of instruction in "the rudiments of servility, pauperism and slavery."[13]

Yet, in some cases, parents had no choice. They could, in certain places, be denied poor relief if they refused to send their children to the local Sunday School.[14] Some employers insisted on Saturday or Sunday school for their child laborers.[15] The exact number of children attending charity and Sunday schools is open to debate. Sunday school attendance may have been as low as 69,000 or as high as 250,000.[16] In addition to the Sunday schools and the village charity schools, there were schools in workhouses, at London's Foundling Hospital, and afloat on the Thames to teach poor boys to be sailors. There was even a school to teach poor blind children to support themselves by weaving baskets.[17]

At the top of the social scale, the curriculum was entirely different. Expensive boarding schools like Rugby, Winchester, Eton, Westminster, and Harrow could cost as much as £50 a year. Here pupils were taught Greek, Latin, grammar, composition, the works of John Milton and other English authors, oratory, and history. There was also some lesser emphasis on geography, mathematics, fine arts, fencing, and modern foreign languages like French and Italian. There was also, as critics of these "public schools" pointed out, gambling, drinking, homosexual dabbling, and ruthless cruelty. Henry Fielding called them "the nurseries of all vice amd immorality."[18] The boys were frequently unruly and even violent; the militia once had to storm Eton, the Riot Act was read at Winchester in 1770, and at Rugby the students put gunpowder in the headmaster's study.[19] Nonetheless, wealthy parents sent their sons to such schools in increasing numbers, mostly because of the social connections that could be made in youth and exploited later in life. By 1800, 70 percent of English peers had attended Eton, Westminster, Winchester, or Harrow.[20]

Between the handful of élite public schools and the vast numbers of charity schools lay a middle ground occupied by miscellaneous grammar and "dame" schools, attended chiefly by the children of tradesmen and artisans. Most grammar schools were run by ordained ministers and unemployed intellectuals; most dame schools, by women (hence the name). Teachers had a wide range of ability and training. They taught whatever would bring in the most pupils: a little religious doctrine, a little Latin, and plenty of comparatively useful knowledge—reading, writing, geography, accounting, shorthand, science, law, business correspondence, French, navigation, and drafting. Teachers made money both from tuition fees and from boarding students, often in their own homes. Such a school, depending on whether the students boarded or not, and on how many "extras" were supplied, might cost from £10 to £20 a year.[21] The pupils would study for a few years, then leave to be apprenticed or to go into the family business. Schoolmasters, who wore academic gowns as a sign of authority, made about £10 to £20 per annum.[22]

TEACHING METHODS

There were some constants in the educational system, but most of them were undesirable. Almost all students learned by rote. If they were asked questions, it was usually only in the context of catechism or drill, in which the expected reply was practiced over and over. Students rose, turned, sat, and often spoke in unison, cued by hand gestures or the sound of a bell.[23] They were taught as often by older pupils as by their adult instructors, and they often had to rise early and study or sleep in cold rooms. Boys of seven or so wept at being sent off to boarding schools; once at school, they were tormented and enslaved by older boys until they grew old enough to abuse and enslave others. Teachers joined in the torture; beatings were the primary method of discipline in such a huge majority of schools that the practice may with very little exaggeration be called universal. Outcries against "this Custom of educating by the Lash"[24] were wholly ineffective. Nonetheless, many adults managed to look back on their school days with some affection, and to remember with nostalgia the minutiae of school days: the satchels in which they carried their books, the primers read through a protective layer of thin transparent horn, the secret nicknames and jokes at the teacher's expense.

WOMEN'S EDUCATION

Girls were more likely than their brothers to be educated at home, but many did go to school. The debate over whether and how much they were to be taught raged as fiercely as that over educating the poor, and for much the same reason. Most experts wanted to teach them enough to be really useful, but not enough to give them ambition. Religious authors like James Fordyce and Hannah More warned of the frivolity of female education, but stopped short of advocating a serious program of academic study for girls; instead, they recommended more religion, more attention to domestic skills, and fewer novels. More went so far as to recommend works of philosophy but stressed that reading really talented authors would have the benefit of discouraging aspiring women writers, by demonstrating how hopelessly inferior were their own talents. She also hastened to describe the ultimate purpose of a woman's education:

> The chief end . . . is to qualify them for the practical purposes of life. Their knowledge is not often like the learning of men, to be reproduced in some literary composition, and never in any learned profession; but it is to come out in conduct. A lady studies, not that she may qualify herself to become an orator or a pleader; not that she may learn to debate, but to act. She is to read the best books, not so much to enable her to talk of them, as to bring the improvement she derives from them to the rectification of her principles, and the formation of her habits. The great uses of study are to enable her to regulate her own mind, and to be useful to others.[25]

More also opposed training girls in music, on the grounds that in ancient Greece such arts had been the province of courtesans.[26] Even Mary Wollstonecraft, who surely would have called herself a feminist if that term had been in use at the time, was a prisoner of the boundaries of the debate. Though her *Vindication of the Rights of Woman* was greeted with horror by conservatives like More, it, too, justifies educating women on the grounds of making them more useful at home:

> It is generally acknowledged that they spend many of the first years of their lives in acquiring a smattering of accomplishments; meanwhile strength of body and mind are sacrificed to libertine notions of beauty. . . . Can they be expected to govern a family with judgment, or take care of the poor babes whom they bring into the world?[27]

Poets, too, joined the debate. Sarah Fyfe Egerton taunted men who opposed educating women, saying "They fear we should excel their sluggish parts,/Should we attempt the sciences and arts," and, later, "We will our rights in learning's world maintain;/Wit's empire now shall know a female reign."[28] Mary Leapor responded at mid-century with that age-old attack: the caricature of learned woman as unattractive and unloved;

> The damsels view her with malignant eyes,
> The men are vexed to find a nymph so wise:
> And wisdom only serves to make her know
> The keen sensation of superior woe.[29]

Despite the fears of the conservatives and the ambitions of the radicals, women's education remained decorative and superficial. A middle- or upper-class girl's curriculum, whether at home or at boarding school, consisted of some combination of reading, writing, sewing, knitting, drawing, etiquette, posture, dancing, religion, French, singing, playing an instrument, cooking, and supervising servants. There were many learned and accomplished women in 18th-century England, most notably the circle known as the Bluestockings, but it was certainly not by design.

UNIVERSITIES

Girls were not admitted to the great public schools (or to most grammar schools). Nor were they allowed to attend any of Britain's universities. England had only two—Oxford and Cambridge—whose students, drawn largely from public-school rolls, were either men of leisure seeking polish and companionship, or future clergymen on scholarships. All were Anglican. Both Oxford and Cambridge boasted some formidable intellects among their faculty and students, but enrollment remained fairly low (not quite 200 new students per year at mid-century Oxford[30]), and instruction was of little practical use, consisting usually of Latin and Greek, with some philosophy and a smattering of science. Neither had written exams until the end of the century. They were, for the most part, comfy clubs based on patronage and privilege. The best universities in Britain—and, arguably, in the world—were in Scotland, where the medical training in particular was superior.[31] After leaving university, it was customary for a young man of wealth to go abroad on a Grand Tour, spending thousands of pounds for up to three years of travel in France, Germany, Italy, and elsewhere.

LITERACY

Though there was no substantial reform of the educational system in the 18th century, there was expansion. Schools multiplied, and literacy rose, albeit slowly. At mid-century, about two-thirds of men and one-third of women could sign their names,[32] a basic indicator of writing (though not reading) skills. Since reading is usually mastered more easily than writing, it seems fair to guess that somewhat more than those proportions of men and women could read at least a little. Literacy rates rose with income; male literacy was nearly universal in the middle class and above.[33] The proliferation of newspapers, magazines, cookbooks, almanacs, and cheap editions of religious works and novels testifies to a large population of readers. Those who could not read were often read to by literate friends and relatives, but being able to read for oneself was a distinct advantage, even in humble occupations. The housekeeper at Erddig in Wales, for example, who was paid only £10 a year, had to keep a written account of the linens, make note of payments to local merchants, and record the distribution of pocket money to her employers' children.[34] To do all this, she had to be able to read and write, as did a growing percentage of her fellow Britons. Education, if no better in 1800 than in 1700, was both more common and more necessary for survival and success.

TIMELINE

1701	Not quite 35 percent of English peers have attended Oxford or Cambridge.
1711	London and Westminster have at least 100 charity schools teaching at least 4,000 students.
1723	Bernard Mandeville publishes an *Essay on Charity and Charity Schools*, in which he asserts that the poor should not receive too much education, lest they acquire ambitions above their station.

The Society for the Promotion of Christian Knowledge, a prime supporter of charity schools early in the century, reports that there are 1,329 such schools outside London.

1724   Winchester, the oldest public school in England, has thirty-five fee-paying pupils.

1774   A plan to reform the examination process fails at Cambridge.

1785   The Sunday School Society is established to promote the founding of Sunday schools.

1799   Hannah More publishes *Strictures on Female Education*.

More than 60 percent of English peers have attended Oxford or Cambridge.

15

"The Roast Beef of Old England": Food and Drink

When mighty roast beef was the Englishman's food,
It ennobled our hearts, and enriched our blood;
Our soldiers were brave, and our courtiers were good.
  Oh, the roast beef of old England!
  And oh, for old England's roast beef!
        —*The Roast Beef of Old England*, R. Leveridge

Roast beef, simply prepared, and in great quantities, was indeed the quintessential British dish. A club devoted to beef eating was established in 1735. Songs were written about the glories of beef. And William Hogarth, who would die in 1764 shortly after consuming a beefsteak dinner, in 1749 painted a group of gaunt, enfeebled Frenchmen in *The Gate of Calais*; he portrays them as enslaved by their religion and starved for the freedom and strength represented by a monumental piece of imported English beef.

Yet beef, while often consumed, was not as universal a diet as Hogarth might have liked. Many could not afford to eat meat on a regular basis, and for them the giant haunches of beef were the stuff of daydreams, not dinner. At the opposite end of the economic scale, the rich (or so their accusers claimed) were eating less beef, and in less straightforward fashion. French sauces and fancy dishes, some claimed, were replacing the traditional roast beef on the tables of the wealthy.

INGREDIENTS AND TECHNIQUES

It is true that, for those who could afford them, more types of food than ever before were available. Expanding trade, especially with colonies, brought new items to the table or reduced the price of old ones: pineapples, curries, ginger, molasses, cinnamon, macaroni, vermacelli, figs, pistachio nuts, truffles, rum, cocoa, rice, tea, coffee, pepper, sugar, olives, anchovies, Parmesan cheese, almonds, peacocks, and ortolans. There were plenty of home-grown ingredients as well. One of the century's most popular cookbooks, Hannah Glasse's *The Art of Cookery Made Plain and Easy*, lists over 160 different ingredients organized according to the months in which they were in season. While hardly comparable to the selection at a modern-day grocery store, it is a respectable list, and in some ways (particularly with regard to seafood and wild game) more varied. Under poultry, for example, she includes pheasant, partridge, rabbit, hare, leveret, woodcock, snipe, dottrel, turkey, chicken, pigeon, duckling, duck, goose, plover, wheat-ear, teal, widgeon, and lark.

In addition to fresh meats, vegetables, and fruits, cooks could obtain bread, butter, eggs, raisins, hams, potted meats, sausages, sago, mineral waters (including a new brand manufactured by a Dr. Schweppe),[1] "Spanish juice" (licorice), honey, tamarind, nutmeg, tapioca, morels, ready-made sauces,[2] and a variety of cheeses: cream cheese, Cheshire, Stilton, and, of course, Cheddar, called by Daniel Defoe "the best cheese that England affords, if not, that the whole world affords."[3] Some of these ingredients could be conveniently combined in a new dish named for its inventor, the Earl of Sandwich. Despite these options and innovations, however, English cooking remained simple. Voltaire claimed that the English had a hundred religions and only one sauce, and he was not far wrong. In fact, they had two sauces: white (cream-based) and brown (gravy). There were no red sauces because tomatoes were believed to be poisonous and were cultivated for their appearance only.

Differences between 18th-century cooking and modern cooking might begin with tomatoes, but they hardly end there. Glasse's cookbook, and its emphases, make the differences clear. Her first chapter, on shopping, brings to life a world in which adulterated bread and milk, spoiled meat, and vegetables contaminated by "night soil" (human waste) were commonplace, and in which government regulation of food was virtually nonexistent. Her admonitions to shoppers make it clear that butchers often substituted one animal for another, cheap cuts for expensive ones, and spoiled meat for fresh. She gives instructions for testing the color, texture, and smell of the meat to establish its provenance. One example, for venison, reads,

Try the haunches, shoulders, and fleshy parts of the sides with your knife, . . . and in proportion to the sweet or rank smell it is new or stale. With relation to the other parts, observe the colour of the meat; for if it be stale or tainted, it will be of a black colour, intermixed with yellowish or greenish specks. If it be old, the flesh will be tough and hard, the fat contracted, the hoofs large and broad, and the heel horny and much worn.[4]

Grocers evidently cheated, too, to judge from her notes on buying butter:

[T]aste it yourself at a venture, and do not trust to the taste they give you, lest you be deceived by a well-tasted and scented piece artfully placed in the lump. . . . If it be a cask, it may be purposely packed, therefore trust not to the top alone, but unhoop it to the middle, thrusting your knife between the staves of the cask.[5]

Even when the food was fresh, it would have looked odd to modern eyes. Meat was open to the air and the flies. Birds were sold with the heads on. Eggs were not cartoned but packed by the customer in bran or salt.

The preparation of food was also more hands-on and comprehensive. Glasse's instructions for roasting a pig begin with how to kill it: "Stick your pig just above the breast-bone, run your knife to the heart."[6] They continue with how to clean, de-hair, gut, and dry the carcass. Because few prepared foods were available, cookbooks included information on pickling, preserving, brewing beer and cider, fermenting wine, and making cheeses, hams, and sausages. There are also recipes that would seem out of place today—the 1796 edition of Glasse's book contains recipes for bug repellent, varnish, cattle medicine, cosmetics, a cleaner for gold and silver braid, and "cures" for plague, mad-dog bite, consumption, and colds.[7] It must be remembered that even middle-class housewives could afford few books on housekeeping for their own use or their servants' and that this juxtaposition of dinner menus and cattle remedies was not odd to the woman in charge of kitchen, nursery, sickroom, and dairy.

Cookbook instructions were rather imprecise. In part, this is a question of measurement; ingredients are often given in vague terms—"a handful," "a little," "a lump." Recipes relied on the cook's vision or experience: "when the smoak begins to draw to the fire, and they look plump,"[8] or "when it is enough."

Other differences are perhaps less fundamental but more startling. Eggs were a common thickening agent; one recipe calls for asparagus to be served with a boiled sauce of oil, water, vinegar, salt, pepper, and eggs.[9] A recipe for orange jelly includes isinglass (gelatin), orange juice, cinnamon, mace, "as much sugar as you find requisite," and eight egg whites.[10] The limitations of the kitchen fire made broiling and boiling far easier than baking; a recipe for "Pigeons Transmogrified," therefore, calls for the birds to be seasoned with salt and pepper, wrapped in puff pastry, then in cloth, and boiled for an hour and a half.[11] There are also recipes for cuts of meat that modern cooks seldom use: ox palates, tripe, calves' and pigs' feet, sweetbreads, ox cheek, stuffed udder, heart, tongue, hogs' ears, cocks' combs, calf's head, sheep's head, lamb's head—Glasse gives nine animal-head recipes, including the particularly ominous-sounding "calf's head surprize."

SNACKS AND TREATS

Between meals, or on special occasions, people of both great and small means treated themselves to special foods. Street and fair vendors sold gingerbread, cheesecakes, nuts, oysters, shrimp (sold near Sadler's Wells and eaten from handkerchiefs, the shells dropped by the eater into the street as he or she walked), oranges (an especially popular snack at the theater, where those in the upper tiers dropped the peels onto the pit-dwellers below),[12] and pig-shaped pastries with currant-filled bellies and currants for eyes.[13] Children were fond of raisins, cakes, sugarplums, figs, and pudding. An 18th-century pudding was not what modern Americans would call pudding; it was instead a conglomeration of suet, flour, dried fruit, and spices, wrapped in a cloth and boiled. Foreign visitor Henri Misson said, tongue in cheek, that it was "a Manna better than that of the Wilderness, because the People are never weary of it. Ah, what an excellent Thing is an *English Pudding! To Come in Pudding Time*, is as much as to say, to come in the most lucky moment in the world."[14]

Some foods were associated with particular events or places. The pleasure garden of Vauxhall was famous (or infamous) for its ham sandwiches. Bartholomew Fair featured "Plum-porridge, black-puddings, and op'ning of oysters," "Fine sausages fried," "Wine, beer, ale, and cakes," and especially roast pork.[15] At St. James's, strollers could buy "warm milk served directly from the cow."[16]

DIET OF THE LABORING CLASSES

Some people could not afford these treats, or even fresh meat, more than once a week. What meat they bought was the cheapest cuts: old fowls, tough mutton, lean beef with no visible fat, tripe, or chine (the backbone with some attached flesh). By far the most popular meat for laborers was bacon, which was easy to store, to cook, and to buy in small quantities.[17] Cooking time was an issue, since fuel could be expensive.

Most of the laboring diet was bread. White bread was preferred by all classes, but those who could not afford white flour grudgingly ate bread of whole wheat, rye, barley, or maslin (a mixture of grains).[18] In Scotland and the northern English counties, like Lancashire and Yorkshire, oatmeal often replaced bread, especially at breakfast. A poem written around 1776 describes a bread substitute, improvised by northern housewives when they could get no yeast, made of flour and cream only.[19]

Other staples of the laboring diet were cheese,[20] treacle (molasses, used as a cheap alternative to sugar), greens from the garden or market, potatoes (especially in the northern counties), dumplings, broths, stews, small beer, and tea. Eggs and milk were consumed rarely. On special occasions, there might be something extra on the table: a hoarded bottle of wine for a visit from the landlord, "spiced bread or potato custard . . . and probably an extra piece of beef"[21] near Christmas, and roast beef, goose, and chickens for a wedding feast.[22]

Servants in middle- and upper-class households ate well most of the time, since they ate much the same food as their employers. Other segments of the laboring population ate much worse, even to the point of chronic malnutrition. An unskilled worker might eat worse than the unemployed inmate of a workhouse. Jonathan Swift wrote in 1727 of Irish families who sustained themselves "upon buttermilk and potatoes."[23] While there was very little actual famine in England, especially compared with Continental Europe, hunger and poor nutrition were certainly common enough.

DIET OF THE MIDDLE AND UPPER CLASSES

Artisans, merchants, shopkeepers, prosperous farmers, and members of the professions could expect more variety and bounty in their diet. The family of a Yorkshire weaver in about 1730 would have eaten all the foods found in poorer households, plus oat cakes, mutton, and home-brewed ale.[24] A middle-class breakfast, eaten at about eight A.M., would have included tea with sugar, coffee, hot chocolate (perhaps a patent brand like Churchman's), and buttered bread toasted over the fire.

Dinner, served at about two or three P.M., was the principal meal and might last several hours on festive occasions. It featured several dishes, including a choice of meats, meat pies, soups, vegetables, fish, salad, jellies, and, in more affluent households, fruit. On March 6, 1795, Parson Woodforde ate "for Dinner a Couple of boiled Chicken and Pigs Face, very good Peas Soup, a boiled Rump of Beef very fine, a prodigious fine, large and very fat Cock-Turkey roasted, Maccaroni, [and] Batter Custard Pudding."[25] Samuel Johnson, as a country-house guest, ate leg of lamb stuffed with flour and raisins, chopped spinach, beef sirloin, turkey, figs,

15.1 "French Happiness/English Misery," 1793. A classic piece of anti-French propaganda and a primer on archetypal English cuisine. The Frenchmen are delighted because they've found a frog to share amongst four starving men. Their water jug is broken, and everywhere there are symbols of tyranny and famine. The English, in contrast, are "miserable" only from being surfeited with food—brimming pots of beer, pink roast beef being cut with lascivious relish, and a huge spotted pudding. Patriotic mottoes, including "O the Roast Beef of Old England," are pinned to the walls. Even the dog is fat. Courtesy of the Print Collection, Lewis Walpole Library, Yale University.

grapes, and peaches.[26] Some dinners, especially those eaten while traveling, were quite simple. Defoe ate a dinner in Dartmouth of pilchards (a kind of fish) broiled with pepper and salt, consuming seventeen of them with a servant and one other companion.[27] Like Defoe, Johnson, and Woodforde, all who could afford to do so ate voraciously; a roast goose was thought to be "too much for one, and not enough for two."[28] After the dinner, in genteel households, the women retired from the room, while the men remained in the dining room to smoke pipes and drink heavily.

Late in the afternoon, people stopped to take tea, which came into its own as a separate meal in this century. It consisted chiefly of tea and some form of bread—usually hot rolls or muffins with butter in winter, cold rolls or "slices of bread ... as thin as poppy leaves"[29] with butter in summer. Supper, eaten shortly before retiring, was a light meal of cold meats, boiled eggs, salad, or other simple fare.

The rich ate all their meals at later hours, and they ate more food, better cuts of meat, and sometimes more complex, French-influenced dishes. An upper-class dinner might feature venison, ham, turkey, cod, pigeons, lobster, sweetbreads, crab, pheasant, turtle, turbot, duck, or salmon as well as the ubiquitous chicken and beef. There might also be root vegetables, asparagus, tarts, syllabubs, jellies, blancmange, fruit pies, cheesecakes, out-of-season fruit, cream, sweetmeats, truffles, "marigolds in porridge,"[30] and copious and varied alcoholic beverages. The rich could also afford more spices, and they began to hire French or French-influenced cooks to create showy dishes. Numerous critics opposed the "fricasee," the "rich ragout of snails," the "larded quail,"[31] and the "costly and pernicious Sauces"[32] of the French chef.

OTHER DIETS

Such quibbles were irrelevant to the vast majority of the English, whose diet was simple and monotonous. Patients in hospitals ate bread, beef, beef broth, beer, pottage, and "Ale Cawdle"[33]—an unexciting menu, but served in substantial quantities. Some of the worst-fed Britons were those imprisoned for debt, who were not legally entitled to any food at all. Some prisons provided them with about a pound of bread a day, but any supplementary sustenance had to come from their families, friends, or handouts from passersby. On the prison ships of the Thames, the daily ration for six prisoners was half a bullock's head, four pounds of biscuits, water, and broth with bread and oatmeal in it.[34]

Some people, chiefly travelers and unmarried men, chose to eat away from home at pubs, inns, taverns, coffeehouses, shops, and tea gardens. Travelers at coaching inns could not expect anything fancy—cold meats, salads, cheese, wine, punch, and eggs were standard fare, and the diner would have to assemble the salad himself at his table.[35] In some cases, customers could purchase their own food and bring it to an inn's cook to have it prepared, as Defoe did with his dinner of pilchards. City taverns and coffeehouses were the resort of single men, merchants and professionals conducting business, club members who held their meetings there, and literary types like Sir Richard Steele, who wrote to his wife, from a tavern, that he would join her "within half a bottle of wine."[36]

Some ate on foot. Poet Robert Southey knew of a pastry shop where customers "took up buns or biscuits" from the open window "as they passed by and threw their pence in, not allowing themselves time to enter."[37] Others bought from food stalls or wandering piemen.[38] There were also full-fledged restaurants: chophouses like Dolly's Beefsteak House[39] or the "breakfasting Places" mentioned by Miss Giggle in Catherine Clive's *The Rehearsal*, who calls them "all so immensely superb, that I can't touch my Breakfast at home."[40]

BEVERAGES

All this food had to be washed down with something, and nonalcoholic choices were few indeed. Fruit was so expensive that the mere idea of fruit juice (other than cider, which was usually hard cider) was too profligate to be imagined. Milk was often adulterated. Water was usually unsafe to drink, especially in London, where the Thames was both reservoir and sewer, and where public water was carried to the home (or, for most people, to numerous public pumps) by poisonous lead pipes. Coffee was expensive—the poor drank a substitute made of horse chestnuts—and, according to Continental visitors, poorly made; one called English coffee an "atrocious mess of brown water."[41] This left tea, drunk without milk.[42] It was drunk by all social classes, from dukes to the simplest dairymaids, who bought used tea leaves from rich people's cooks and used and reused the leaves themselves. Those who could not afford cheaper teas or genteel leftovers bought adulterated blends. Enterprising souls even sold tea by the cup to haymakers during harvest.

Since tea had little nutritive value, and since it was expensive, many opposed its use by workers. The Reverend John Clayton called it "this shameful devourer of time and money";[43] reformer Jonas Hanway blamed it for the unhealthy pallor of the nation's chambermaids.[44] Their arguments, however, were ignored. Women whose husbands disapproved of their tea drinking would even collude with the local shopkeeper to disguise their purchases in the accounts.[45] Tea consumption rose dramatically during the century. The East India Company imported 67,000 pounds in 1701, and about 8 million by 1801. Smugglers brought in even more, perhaps twice as much.[46]

Teas were either green or black, and they came in many varieties and levels of quality. Strong types, like green "gunpowder tea" or black pekoe, were blended with hyson or "bloom tea," which were generally weaker. Congou was the most popular type; bohea, the cheapest and least fashionable, was drunk on its own mostly early in the century when prices were high. Later in the century, it was more commonly mixed with congou to form an intermediate blend called "congou kind."[47] Early in the century, affluent customers had their own personal blends mixed for them by their tea dealers.

Those who were not drinking tea drank alcohol, usually to excess. Rich men boasted of their ability to drink two, or even four, bottles of wine apiece at dinner. In one heroic, appalling incident, two men reportedly drank ten bottles of champagne between them.[48] Westminster Quarter Sessions, until 1763, convened in the Hell pub, near the House of Commons.[49] Tipsy magistrates were such a problem in general that "the Mutiny Act specified that courts martial must be held *before* dinner."[50] Sir Robert Walpole's wine budget for one year at his seat in Norfolk was

£1,500, and in this he was only living out the fantasies of numberless country squires, who, according to Lady Mary Wortley Montagu, spent every evening "with what liquor they can get." Porters, carriage drivers, nurses, hospital patients, and prisoners were routinely drunk; indeed, some of the smaller jails were actually located in alehouses.[51] Workers drank on breaks and during work, consuming as much as four quarts of ale a day.[52]

Henry Fielding called gin "the principal sustenance (if so it may be called) of more than a hundred thousand persons in this metropolis."[53] If he exaggerated, he did so only mildly; if he did not, one in seven Londoners was addicted to gin. Yearly gin consumption ran into the millions of gallons, perhaps as much as six gallons per person per year. Known as "strip me naked," "Hollands" (because the English learned to use essence of juniper from Dutch distillers), or "geneva" (because the French word for juniper is *genèvre*), gin was attractive principally because it was strong and cheap. It sold for a penny a quartern, a quartern being a quarter pint or half a cup. Accordingly, the shops sometimes advertised that one could get "drunk for a penny" and "dead drunk" for twopence. For three pennies more, a double bed of straw could be rented to sleep off the effects of the gin. Strangers—men, women, and children—bunked together, as many as fifty-eight in one room, overwhelming one visitor with their stench.[54] Fielding believed that "should the drinking of this poison be continued in its present height during the next twenty years, there will be by that time few of the common people left to drink it."[55]

Gin was controlled for most of the century by legislation, but the laws were not always designed to minimize consumption. The distilling industry was a powerful one, and in 1750 it absorbed about half the output of the nation's wheat fields.[56] This kept the demand for grain high, which pleased the farmers. Nonetheless, in 1729, Parliament put a five-shilling-per-gallon tax on home-distilled spirits, tightened licensing requirements for alehouses, and imposed a license fee of £20 to sell gin. It was unenforceable and encouraged the sale of new liquors not specifically covered under the law, which the public nicknamed "parliament brandy." In 1733 the law was repealed, making it possible for virtually anyone to distill or sell gin. The very minor restrictions and duties left in place could be evaded easily. The consequence was a huge increase in the sale and consumption of gin, and in 1736 Parliament tried again, placing a twenty-shilling-per-gallon sales tax on gin and all other spirits and reimposing a retail license fee, this time £50. The public responded by draping tavern signs in mourning, ridiculing the law in a play called *The Deposing and Death of Queen Gin*, and gathering in the streets to shout "No gin, no king."[57]

The 1736 act was energetically flaunted. Spirits were sold as "Cholick Water," "Tom Row," "Make Shift," and "Ladies' Delight." Those who informed on the illegal dealers were dunked in mud or in the Thames.[58]

Like the 1729 act, the one of 1736 was largely useless and was repealed in 1743; in the seven years of its life, only three £50 licenses had been issued.[59] Further acts of 1743 and 1751 restricted sales by distillers and shopkeepers, and this, combined with naturally rising grain prices, gradually reduced spirit consumption. The gin problem became less urgent in the second half of the century. Throughout the century, though, attention was paid to the licensing of alehouses, the other chief outlet for workers' drink. And drunkenness remained a misdemeanor, but it was not meant for the "two-bottle" men of leisure enjoying their claret with dinner and their champagne in the evening. The threat of being hauled before a justice of the peace and sentenced to the stocks[60] for drinking during church hours on Sunday was intended, like the gin laws, to keep bricklayers and coachmen healthy, sober, and ready to work when the sun rose.

There were always a few who were ready to condemn not just gin but alcohol in general. Usually they did so for religious reasons, but their reforming zeal went unrewarded, especially after the first few decades of the century. Abstemious folk like the physician Erasmus Darwin, who drank nothing but water, and prison reformer John Howard, who was both teetotaller and vegetarian, were hardly in the majority. Even Dr. Johnson, who condemned public drunkenness, objected to it largely on the grounds that it made stupid men more likely to air their foolish opinions instead of allowing the wiser members of the company (like himself) to hold the floor. He himself preferred to drink in private and believed that drink was the only thing that could make a person perfectly happy in the present moment.[61]

Tippling was celebrated in songs, like "Come Let Us Drink About,"

> Wine cures the gout, the cholic, and the tisic,
> And is for all men the very best of physic.
>
> He that drinks small beer, and goes to bed sober,
> Falls, as the leaves do, that die in October.
>
> But he that drinks all day, and goes to bed mellow,
> Lives as he ought to, and dies a hearty fellow.[62]

It was celebrated in plays, and even in epitaphs; Rebecca Freeland's, from 1741, read

> She drank good ale, good punch, and wine
> And lived to the age of ninety-nine.[63]

Attitudes toward drink became slightly more negative toward the end of the century, as part of a general conservative trend. Diners who guzzled to excess were treated with less tolerance. Women encouraged the substitution of tea for alcohol as an evening beverage. Even the hospitals, long the home of drunken patients and drunken staff, began to reform.

Drinkers had ample choices available to them. There was, of course, beer; the inmates of Marshalsea Prison drank 600 pots of it on one day alone in 1775.[64] Greenwich Hospital allotted fourteen quarts a week to each patient.[65] Early in the century, the pub-goer had a choice of ale, beer, or twopenny (a cheap beer that sold for twopence a quart); half-and-half, meaning half beer and half twopenny; or three-thread, meaning a mixture of ale, beer, and twopenny. Three-thread was eventually premixed and sold in one cask as "entire," later called "porter" from its popularity with London porters. Especially rich, strong porters were known as "stouts."[66] Sometimes beer was served heated, to judge from the assertion of Sir William Forbes that "a bottle of beer . . . is made brisker by being set before the fire."[67] Beer was manufactured by a multitude of small brewers and home brewers, as well as more than a hundred London brewers like Thrale's and Whitbread. The big manufacturers alone produced more than a million barrels a year.[68]

Cider was drunk by many, especially in Herefordshire, Kent, and the western counties. Some Gloucestershire workers were rumored to be capable of drinking a gallon of the stuff in a single draught. Because it was sometimes made in lead containers, it was dangerous even in smaller amounts.[69]

Wine was the drink of the upper and upwardly mobile middle classes. They drank champagne, claret (red wine, usually from France), port (cheaper than claret, since import duties were lighter for Portuguese than for French products), sack (white wine from Spain or the Canary Islands, often quite sweet, and increasingly replaced by port), brandy, burgundy, cherry-brandy (the specialty of the house at the Bermondsey tea garden and spa),[70] and other types, including Sheraaz, Zante, Lissa, and Calcevella. Sometimes wine was served "burnt," with some of the alcoholic content removed by fire; burnt champagne was an archetypal drink for a society lady's evening at Vauxhall.[71] The type of wine drunk in a particular household varied according to income, but also according to politics; Jacobites drank French wines as a statement of support for France, which harbored the Pretenders, while Whigs, to express the opposite sentiment, drank port. Some preferred their wine mixed with other substances. Punch, a popular beverage, was brandy mixed with citrus fruit and sugar. Possets and syllabubs mingled wine with warm milk.

As for hard liquor, there was gin, West Indian rum, and, in Scotland chiefly, whisky. Sailors aboard ship sometimes drank what they called "two-water grog," made of one third rum and two thirds water.[72]

Alcohol, in whatever form, was certainly England's drug of choice. There was some use of laudanum, a little recreational ether sniffing, and a great deal of consumption of pipe tobacco and snuff. Pipes and snuff were enjoyed at all levels of society, from the simple pipe of a shopkeeper to the bergamot snuff of fops and the gold, silver, ivory, tortoiseshell, or mother-of-pearl snuff boxes of the wealthy.[73] But it was beer, rum, gin, whisky, brandy, punch, and wine that accompanied meals, sometimes replaced meals, and gave a significant number of Britons a daily dose of inebriation.

The stereotypical view of British food in this era—beef, beer, pudding, and tea—is hardly the whole picture. There was a greater variety of food for the upper classes, and a greater dependence on bread among the poor, than that quartet implies. But it is, perhaps, the British ideal of that century, the diet that Francophobes terrified of snails and sauces would choose for their countrymen, the diet celebrated in the songs of the day, and the diet that a poor woman, feeding her children on water porridge and garden greens, would have wanted for her family if she could have scraped together the money.

RECIPES

The recipes below may be used to reconstruct an 18th-century English dinner. The recipes, adapted from Hannah Glasse's *Art of Cookery*, represent a considerably abridged menu. Glasse recommends serving three courses, each containing ten to twelve main dishes, with appropriate side dishes. In her menus, fruit dishes, cheesecakes, and the like are served in the second and third courses, along with meats and vegetables brought to the table at the same time. Desserts to accompany this meal could include almost any poached or stewed fruit or an English pudding.

Petit Patties (or Pasties)
Makes 18

1 lb. lean ground beef

½ lb. bacon, cut into small squares

1 medium yellow onion, finely minced

6 mushrooms, finely minced

2 tablespoons dried parsley

½ teaspoon dried marjoram

½ teaspoon salt

½ teaspoon black pepper

1 17 ¼ oz. pkg. frozen puff pastry (2 sheets)

2 egg yolks

Water

Thaw puff pastry according to package directions and preheat oven to 400 degrees.

Brown ground beef and bacon in a medium saucepan over moderate heat. Cover a plate with a few paper towels and remove the meat to this plate with a slotted spoon. Reserve the fat from the pan, placing it in a heatproof container.

Place 1 tablespoon of the reserved fat into the saucepan and raise heat to medium-high. Cook the minced onions until they soften and begin to turn golden, about 5 minutes. Add the mushrooms and cook for 1 minute more.

Lower heat to medium-low. Add the parsley, marjoram, salt, and pepper. Stir. Return the beef and bacon to the pan and stir for about a minute.

Cut each sheet of puff pastry into nine squares and roll each to about half its original thickness. Place about 2 tablespoons of beef filling in the center of a square. Fold it into a triangle and pinch the edges closed. Place it on a well greased or nonstick baking sheet and repeat with the other 17 squares.

Stir the egg yolks together with 2 tablespoons water in a small bowl. Brush egg yolk mixture over the pasties and bake 10 to 12 minutes, or until golden brown.

Chestnut Soup
Serves 6 to 8

[Glasse's original recipe called, at the end, for removing everything but the broth and chestnuts, then using the resulting soup to stew small birds. I have simplified it by leaving out the small birds and leaving in the chicken and vegetables.]

50 chestnuts

6 cups chicken broth

6 cups beef broth

1 half slice bacon, cut up

1 lb. boneless skinless chicken thighs, cut into 1-inch pieces

1 onion, coarsely chopped

1 carrot, peeled and sliced into ¼-inch rounds

1 ½ tablespoons thyme

½ teaspoon mace

2 tablespoons dried parsley

½ tablespoon dried marjoram

½ teaspoon black pepper

1 tablespoon butter

1 cup French bread (preferably the heel of the loaf) cut into ½-inch cubes

Salt

6 to 8 slices of French bread

3 tablespoons butter, softened

Preheat oven to 425 degrees. Place chestnuts on a baking sheet and pierce the rounded side of each with the tines of a fork. Roast 15 minutes. Allow to cool, then use a nutcracker and your fingers to remove the smooth outer shell and feathery inner husk. The nuts inside should be golden brown and somewhat pliable.

Place 2 cups chicken broth and 2 cups beef broth in a medium saucepan. Bring to a boil. Add the peeled chestnuts and reduce heat, simmering, covered, till nuts are tender, about 30 minutes.

Meanwhile, put the bacon, chicken, onion, carrot, thyme, mace, parsley, marjoram, black pepper, and 1 tablespoon butter into a large saucepan or soup pot. Cook over moderate heat, stirring occasionally, until chicken is browned and onion is translucent, about 10 to 15 minutes. Add the cubed French bread, the chestnuts and their cooking liquid, and the rest of the chicken and beef broth. Raise heat and boil until reduced by one-third.

While the soup boils, spread the sliced French bread on both sides with the softened butter and brown each side in a pan over moderate heat. Set each slice of bread in a bowl.

When soup is reduced, ladle into bowls over the browned French bread.

Roast "Pigeon"
Serves 2

[Glasse calls for pigeons in this recipe, but I have substituted the more readily available Rock Cornish hens.]

1 cup packed, coarsely chopped parsley

1 half stick cold butter (4 tablespoons), cut into 8 pieces

½ teaspoon salt

½ teaspoon pepper

2 Rock Cornish hens

Flour (about ¼ cup)

1 tablespoon butter, cut in 8 pieces

Preheat oven to 450 degrees. In a medium bowl, use fingers to mix together the parsley, half stick of butter, salt, and pepper until the mixture sticks together in one ball. Divide the ball into two equal pieces.

Wash hens and pat dry; remove giblets if present and discard. Stuff each with half the parsley mixture and use a skewer to close the opening. Place hens in a roasting pan and dust generously with flour, covering all exposed surfaces. Dot each hen with ½ tablespoon of butter cut into four pieces.

Put hens into the oven and immediately reduce oven temperature to 350 degrees. Roast for about 45 to 60 minutes, or until the thigh juices run clear when the skin is pierced with a knife. Baste the birds every 15 minutes with the pan juices.

Before serving, remove the skewers and stuffing, and place stuffing to one side of the plate as a garnish.

Green Salad
Serves 4 to 6

1 small head lettuce, washed and cut up

1 cup watercress leaves

1 cucumber, peeled and sliced ⅛-inch thick

20 mint leaves

Dressing

⅛ cup olive oil

⅛ cup balsamic vinegar

¾ teaspoon salt

In a salad bowl, mix the dressing ingredients well. Add the greens and toss to coat with the dressing.

Fried Potatoes
Serves 4 to 6

4 to 5 small potatoes, peeled, washed, and sliced crosswise ⅛-inch thick

4 tablespoons butter

¼ cup white wine

½ tablespoon brown sugar

Heat 2 tablespoons of butter over medium-high heat in a large non-stick skillet. When the butter is bubbling, add potatoes and sauté until they begin to brown around the edges and the butter is absorbed, about 10 minutes.

Raise heat to high and add the remaining 2 tablespoons of butter. Sauté potatoes until golden with some brown spots, about 5 minutes. Add wine and sugar and boil until almost all liquid is gone and potatoes are moist, about 4 or 5 minutes. Serve hot.

Mashed Parsnips
Serves 6

4 medium parsnips

2 tablespoons butter

½ to 1 cup milk

½ cup cream

Set a large pot of salted water on the stove to boil. Peel parsnips and cut off tops and bottoms. Cut the remaining portion of the parsnips crosswise into 2-inch-long sections. The larger sections from the upper portion of the parsnips may need to be sliced in half.

Boil parsnips until tender, about 10 to 15 minutes. Drain and place them in a heatproof bowl with ½ cup milk, the cream, and the butter, and mash them until they are thoroughly mixed but still a bit chunky. Add more milk as necessary.

Beef Olives
Serves about 8

[These have no olives in them but are so named because when rolled they vaguely resemble stuffed olives. Hannah Glasse recommended stewing "some mushrooms, truffles and morels, force-meat balls and sweetbreads, cut in small square pieces, (and) some ox-palates" along with the beef "olives," but this version leaves them out.]

8 boneless beef steaks (like flank steak or round tip) ⅛-inch to ¼-inch thick, 4 to 6 inches wide, and about 8 to 10 inches long

1 lb. bacon

2 egg yolks

4 tablespoons vegetable oil

2 tablespoons butter

2 tablespoons flour

1 can beef broth (14 to 16 ounces)

1 cup white wine

2 tablespoons lemon juice

lemons for garnish (optional)

Forcemeat:

1 lb. ground beef

1 cup finely chopped fresh parsley

1 tablespoon dried marjoram

½ tablespoon dried thyme

¼ teaspoon nutmeg

¼ teaspoon mace

Zest of 1 lemon (yellow rind only, with no white pith, shredded with a zester or carefully cut off and sliced thin with a knife)

½ teaspoon salt

¼ teaspoon pepper

Make forcemeat by combining all its ingredients in a bowl. Divide forcemeat into equal portions, one for each slice of beef steak.

Lay out one steak. Brush with egg yolk. Cover with two or three slices of bacon and brush again with egg yolk. Spread one portion of forcemeat over the bacon. Starting with one of the short sides, roll up the beefsteak and pin it together with a few toothpicks. Repeat with the other slices of beef.

Heat oil over medium-high heat in a wide pot with a lid. When the oil is hot, put in the "olives" and brown them on all sides. Remove them to a plate.

Melt the butter in the pot and add flour, stirring well. Add beef broth and white wine. Return the "olives" to the pot, reduce to a simmer, and cover. Cook for one hour, turning the "olives" occasionally.

Add the lemon juice. Serve on a platter with the sauce from the pot and, if you choose, slices of lemon.

16

"I Love a Mob": Behavior

[J]udged by French standards, the English, and especially the women, seem lacking in polite behaviour. All the young people whom I have met in society . . . gave the impression of being what we should call badly brought up: they hum under their breath, they whistle, they sit down in a large armchair and put their feet on another, they sit on any table in the room and do a thousand other things which would be ridiculous in France, but are done quite naturally in England.

—Duc de la Rochefoucauld

The 18th century had a sense of the immediacy of bodily functions, sexuality, dirt, pain, and cruelty. Daily behavior—rich and frequent swearing, brawls, duels, riots, noisy public flatulence, medieval table manners, the eating of nuts and oranges by members of Parliament during the speeches of others, and the vicious humiliation of wrongdoers—emphasized the present tense, the satisfaction of immediate needs and whims. There was, however, a trend late in the century toward a different mode of behavior, identified by a new term, first coined in 1785: "respectability."[1]

SWEARING

The century's gloriously varied swearing was condemned by moral tracts, outlawed by act of Parliament, combated by reforming societies, and chastised in the *Spectator* as "foolish" and "unnecessary."[2] Yet it continued. A 1700 tract claimed that "many dare reckon it Breeding to Swear."[3] Hospital patients swore, as did servants, militia units (which Jonathan Swift facetiously claimed would each swear 300 oaths in eight hours), women, and peers.[4] Only in the 1770s did standards begin to change, at least among the gentry. Those who swore used softer terms, and "she-dog," "pregnant," "stomach," "small-clothes," and "chemise" replaced ostensibly coarser terms like "bitch," "big with child," "belly," "breeches," and "smock."[5]

For most of the century, however, people of all ranks swore heartily. Many of the terms they used were sexual in nature: son of a bitch, son of a whore, you bitch's baby, son of a whore of Babylon, bastard, hussy, and slut (though slut usually specified a woman who was messy or dirty rather than sexually overaccessible).[6] Many of these terms were rendered incompletely in print to spare the delicate: w—e, b—h, and the ever-popular f**k or f—k. Variations on the term included f—k-finger and f—k-fist, applied to female and male masturbators respectively.[7]

Terms for body parts and functions were also popular: piss and fart (which only became vulgar from about mid-century), bloody (which meant only either "sanguinary" or "exceedingly" till mid-century and gained increasing vulgarity over the next hundred years), cack, shit, and ass or arse. A typical usage of the last is in a 1793 handbill which attacks a well-paid peer "for setting his Arse in the House of Lords and doing nothing."[8]

Other popular curses involved religious or quasi-religious themes: Lord, Jesus, God damn it, damn me, By Jupiter, Devil hang you, damn my eyes (or heart, or limbs, or blood—an especially low-class category of oath), damn ye, by the Lord, Hell and the devil, by Christ, by Heaven, God's flesh, God's fish, Good God, my God, what the devil, the devil take me, and be damned to you.[9] "I don't care a damn" appears in print by 1766 and was probably in use well before that date, and the popularity of this class of cursing may be judged by G. C. Lichtenberg's observation that if cities were named after the first words heard by a visitor, London's name would be "Damn it."[10] Many religious oaths were softened by leaving out letters in print, as in G—d or L—d; others were made milder by deliberate mispronunciation or substitution. Thus God, God's wounds, and similar oaths became Odds fish, Odds bob, Odso, egad, Odds bodikins, ecod, Gad so, by gad, 'ounds, zounds (pronounced zoonds, not zownds), oons, Odsbud, who the deuce (instead of devil), Gadzooks, and O Lud![11] Even these substitutes were often too harsh for late-century auditors, who preferred rabbit it, smite my timbers, splice my old shoes, or something equally innocuous.[12] A midcentury advertisement for a museum offers a sampling of inoffensive exclamations:

To be seen Gratis . . . the greatest Collection of your oh Laws and Lackadazees! Oh Dears! Goodlacks! Bless mees! Oh la! Dear mees! Heyday! Believe me! Dear la! Ods me! Hah! Odso! Looke-there! Aye Eh! Hi! Oh! Umph! Well I vow! See there now! Well-a-day! So they say! Well to be sure! Nay-but-there! Dear Heart! For my Part! Pon-my-Honour! I protest! Pon-my-Word! I'm amaz'd! Pon-my-life! I'm surprized! Who would think it? I'm astonish'd! Who cou'd a thought it? Take my word for 't! I-never-see-the-like! Didn't I tell yo so? 'Tis-very-fine! That-ever-any-Body-saw! . . . Note, a large quantity of oh Jemminies! Are lately arrived.[13]

FIGHTING

If words failed, there were always fists. French visitor Henri Misson averred, "Anything that looks like a fight is delicious to an Englishman."[14] Brawls were common. The spa and music venue Lambeth Wells was closed down because of the constant fighting there, and, early in the century, Londoners feared to walk the streets after dark because of the beatings given to passersby by a gang of wealthy youths called the Mohocks.[15] Hospital patients slugged each other, workers hurled missiles at each other, theatergoers threw rotten oranges at the stage, masters beat slaves, parents beat children, husbands beat wives, and men dressed for the royal court were "pelted with mud by the mob, while the gentlemen look[ed] on and laugh[ed]."[16] Entertainment such as boxing, cudgeling, bullbaiting, cockfights, and hunting reinforced the atmosphere of violence.

RITUALIZED VIOLENCE: DUELING

Gentlemen were expected to defend their or their dependents' honor if necessary, and some men genuinely enjoyed a good fight. A slighting comment about one's courage, a gambling debt, an insult to a woman, or a little teasing over an exaggerated story could give cause for a challenge. Journalists were in especially grave peril, as a duel was quicker than a libel suit, and the author of a printed criticism might find himself "called out" by the subject of the article.[17]

The duel was supposed to be an upper-class affair. Common tradesmen were not supposed to challenge gentlemen; if they did so, their courage might be noted but their challenge declined. It was also frowned upon for soldiers of different ranks to challenge one another.[18] Yet the forms of dueling were observed by ordinary people, who instituted special etiquette and the use of seconds in fistfights, and who called a knife fight a "chivy duel."[19] Sometimes the entire ritual was duplicated, as in

16.1 "Modern Honour," Matthew Darly, 1771. A pistol duel. Courtesy of the Print Collection, Lewis Walpole Library, Yale University.

1780, when two black footmen with white footmen as seconds held a pistol duel behind Montagu House.[20] Some of the chief figures of the century were engaged in one or more duels: the duke of Grafton, Lord George Germain (who dueled with a fellow MP), essayist Sir Richard Steele (who fought a Captain Kelly in 1700), playwright Richard Brinsley Sheridan (who fought two duels), the duke of Hamilton and Lord Mohun (who killed each other in 1712), the duke of York, radical politician John Wilkes (shot in the stomach in a 1763 duel with a government official), and Whig politician George Tierney (who fought a pistol duel with Prime Minister William Pitt in 1798).[21] The Prince of Wales himself was challenged by the Duke of Newcastle in 1717.

Some men practically specialized in dueling. Soldiers were especially prone to dueling, and despite military regulations against the practice, it was winked at by senior officers and even by royalty. George II privately confided that a lieutenant involved in a dispute ought to "fight or forfeit his commission; otherwise all the other officers would be likely to refuse to serve with him."[22] "Tyger" Roche, who became notorious for picking fights with Scotsmen while traveling to India, and "Fighting" George Fitzgerald, who fought more than thirty duels, eleven of them by the age of twenty-four, were both army officers.[23] Fitzgerald, whose prowess and temper were the stuff of legends, met his match one day when a duel nearly erupted over some insulting looks at a woman. The woman's defender, who ended this "Vauxhall Affray" before anyone was killed, was the Reverend Henry Bate, a clergyman, boxer, greyhound breeder, art critic, playwright, and (thanks to his journalistic endeavors) duelist, known as "the fighting parson." In the end, a substitute for Fitzgerald boxed Bate and lost.[24] Not all the best duelists were soldiers.

In theory, a duel was rigorously constrained by etiquette. It was a living monument to the superior courage and politeness of the gentry that their quarrels could be convened, distilled to a few minutes of tension and bloodshed, and dismissed as finally and cordially as a formal dinner. In practice, things sometimes got messy, especially when one gentleman's code of honor found itself in conflict with another's. In general, however, the procedure was as follows: an insult of whatever kind was given, a politely worded challenge delivered by the challenger's second, the challenge accepted or declined by way of the other party's second, and a time and place arranged. To minimize the number of spectators, the place selected was usually on the outskirts of the city, and the time was usually at or near dawn.

The challenged party selected the weapons. Swords favored the young and the skillful. A duel with swords typically ended when the first blood was drawn.[25] Pistols were a little more arbitrary due to their inaccuracy, encouraged a pause for reflection while the duelists went home to get weapons, and required that the adversaries stand quite still, without trembling, and with their bodies turned sideways to present the smallest possible target.[26] In the interim, both parties had some time to put their worldly affairs in order.

When they arrived at the place specified, their seconds began to work. Seconds made sure swords were the same length, that pistols were loaded with equal amounts of powder, that neither party was facing into the sun, and that (in the case of pistols) the distance between the shooters was agreed upon. If they were doing their job properly, they were also urging a peaceful settlement, usually in the form of an apology for the original insult. Some seconds, however, did the opposite, encouraging the parties to complete the duel.[27] If no apology was offered, the duelists saluted each other and began.

For a duel with pistols, the combatants walked to their marks. They had to be close enough to see each other's faces. The shorter the distance, the more dangerous and gentlemanly the duel, and the more the conditions favored an amateur. The typical distance was twelve paces, or about twenty yards.[28] At a prearranged signal—a word or a dropped handkerchief—the men fired. If neither was wounded, a second shot was customary.[29] In the event that one man was wounded, a surgeon, placed a short distance away by the seconds, was summoned. If one party died, the other might flee the country or be arrested, though successful prosecutions were extremely rare.[30] They were most likely when one party had behaved dishonorably, by attacking in the heat of the moment, for example, instead of setting a date and time through seconds.

In some cases, duels were declined or subverted. A man might decline to offer or accept a challenge on the grounds of rank, or because he had an ungentlemanly advantage in skill, or because he preferred to seek justice in the courts. Or he might satisfy his own sense of honor, and simultaneously admit guilt or convey contempt for his opponent, by firing his weapon wide or into the air. Some men simply disapproved of dueling, a position that was increasingly widely held. Many moralists attacked the practice. Steele, a former duelist himself, later ridiculed the idea that "it would be a Satisfaction to be run through the Body. . . . Most of the Quarrels I have ever known, have proceeded from some valiant Coxcomb's persisting in the Wrong, to defend some prevailing Folly, and preserve himself from the ingenuity of owning a Mistake."[31]

RITUALIZED VIOLENCE: RIOTING

The duel was a genteel means of settling a private grievance, but for most people, it was useless. They had larger concerns: food, taxes, land, wages, community standards, traditional pleasures, and political rights. Barred from voting, they expressed themselves through mass demonstrations, and their theoretical right to do so was hardly challenged until quite late in the century. The duke of Newcastle defended the practice with pride: "I love a mob; I headed a mob once myself. We owe the Hanoverian succession to a mob."[32] Sometimes, especially in the countryside where the local landlords had nearly infinite powers of reprisal, the methods were furtive: threatening letters, bricks thrown through windows, harassment of livestock, vandalism of orchards or fences.[33] Sometimes, the action was more public. Groups of men and women marched to a focal point—the market, the bakery, the mill, a magistrate's house—perhaps carrying symbols of their grievances or targets. An effigy might be burned or hanged, a house or shop looted. Often, the crowd simply wanted to be sure that its demands were heard by someone in authority.

While the gentry sometimes sympathized with the frustrations of the mob, looting and destruction of property were despised. Accordingly, Parliament passed a Riot Act to address the problem of disorderly gatherings. The Act contained a proclamation to be read aloud to any group of twelve or more disorderly persons:

> Our Sovereign Lord the King chargeth and commandeth all Persons, being assembled, immediately to disperse themselves, and

peaceably to depart to their Habitations, or to their lawful Business, upon the Pains contained in the Act made in the first Year of King George, for preventing Tumults and riotous Assemblies. *God Save the King.*[34]

Once this proclamation was read, the official in charge (usually a justice of the peace or constable) was permitted to order troops to fire on the crowd. Although the Riot Act was certainly read at times, magistrates were reluctant to call out troops for a variety of reasons: sympathy with the protestors, fear of appearing to have lost control of the situation, anxiety about having soldiers in town afterward, and fear of public reaction. Often, "riots" could be defused "by gentlemen going out & desiring to know what they wanted & what they wd have, apprising them of the consequences, & promising them" that steps would be taken to address their grievances.[35] After the riot, there might be some token prosecutions, but often the arrested parties were not indicted or convicted, or they were let off with light sentences.[36]

Riots (or, more accurately, protests which sometimes became riots) took place for a variety of reasons. There were food riots when prices rose, with crowds descending on millers or bakers to force a reduction in the price of grain or bread, or on shippers to prevent grain from being exported. Women were often prominent in food riots; a 1740 uprising against grain exports was led by "General" Jane Bogey.[37] The middle and upper classes tried their best to suppress such activity; a 1795 poem by Hannah More satirizes a rabble-rousing Tom Hod, who wants to "kick up a bit of a riot" and praises Jack Anvil, who espouses hard work, meek subservience, abstinence from tea and whiskey, and a willingness to leave the big issues to king, Parliament, and a charitable gentry.[38] Nevertheless, there were plenty of real-life Tom Hods, and plenty of riots—250 of them in England, Scotland, and Wales in the years from 1794 to 1796 alone.[39]

There were also riots over taxes, especially taxes on staples like malt, ale, and cider; enclosure of common land; wages and working conditions; restrictions on the sale of gin; censorship of the theater; being robbed at brothels; and the suppression of May Day festivities.[40] Deprivation of any expected pleasure could spark a riot, as in August 1749, when a scheduled horse race at Tothill-Fields was not held. The spectators were "so enraged . . . that they pulled down the Starting-post, Booths, Benches, etc. and made a large Bonfire with them in the Middle of the said Fields."[41] There were riots against the building of turnpikes and against the use of machinery in the textile industry. There were even personal "riots" or public demonstrations against members of the community: wife beaters, scolds, adulterers, quarrelsome spouses, mismatched spouses (for example a very old husband and very young wife), spouses married for money, homosexuals, and those who engaged in unfair business practices. In various areas this practice was called "rough music," the "skimmington" or "skimmerton," and other names. It usually involved a mocking procession of some kind, with effigies or stand-ins for the targets of the abuse, shaming songs or rhymes, and loud noises. In some cases, the targets or their proxies might be ridden through town on a pole, a cart, or a donkey; being bounced along on the pole in this fashion was called "riding the stang."[42]

The great mass of people, being both disenfranchised and also keenly interested in politics, often chose to make political statements through demonstration, protest, and riot. Elections could turn violent, as they did at Tiverton in 1754, when troops attacked the crowd with swords and bayonets; one particularly bloodthirsty lieutenant, who had begged to be allowed to fire on the rioters and make "the fellows hop like peas," was swarmed by women who deprived him of his sword, to his perpetual humiliation.[43] Supporters of the demagogue John Wilkes held gatherings that sometimes swelled into riots, which frightened the authorities into firing on the crowd.[44] The worst urban riots of the century were the Gordon Riots, which ostensibly began as a pro-Protestant demonstration and erupted into a weeklong siege against Catholics, distilleries, prisons, and the Bank of England. The mob, which numbered in the tens of thousands, set fire to Lord Chief Justice Mansfield's house, Newgate jail, the King's Bench jail, the Clink, and the Blackfriars Bridge tollgates, among other structures, and there were hundreds of deaths and arrests.[45] Twenty-five rioters were later hanged, and the episode put a good solid horror of riot into even the most mob-friendly hearts among the gentry. Combined with the French Revolution a few years later, the Gordon Riots ended any sort of widespread public sympathy for mass demonstrations.

STRIVING FOR GENTILITY

Increasing distrust of riot was not the only change in behavior over the course of the 18th century. It was also becoming increasingly important to seem genteel, and people studied books and the behavior of others to learn to be ladies and gentlemen. They read Lord Chesterfield's *Letters to His Son* (despite Dr. Johnson's judgment that it taught "the morals of a whore and the manners of a dancing master").[46] Girls' schools taught manners and deportment as well as French and geography.[47] The polite person was supposed to be sensitive to the plight of the unfortunate, a good conversationalist, susceptible to strong feelings, inoffensive, discreet, courteous, frugal, religious, apolitical, calm, modest, interesting, and, above all, *natural*. Conduct-book authors were infuriatingly fond of prescribing an exhaustive series of behaviors and then advising one in the strongest terms against any sort of affectation.

NO POPERY or NEWGATE REFORMER.

Tho' He says he's a Protestant, look at the Print,
The Face and the Bludgeon, will give you a hint.
Religion he cries, in hopes to deceive,
While his practice is only to burn and to thieve.

16.2 "No Popery or Newgate Reformer," Gillray, 1780. Buildings burn behind a Gordon Rioter, who wears a "No Popery" cockade and cries, "Down with the Bank." Courtesy of the Print Collection, Lewis Walpole Library, Yale University.

The rules for behavior listed in conduct books offer two kinds of information. First, they tell us what the behavioral ideals of the time were; second, they tell us what sorts of commonplace errors people made. For example, rules regarding table manners show that a well-bred person ate quietly and at a moderate pace, used a napkin and silverware, placed the spoon across the cup to signal "No more tea, thank you," and did not scratch or spit at the table. Conversely, they show that lesser mortals ate fast and noisily, spitting, sniffing the food before eating it, propping their elbows on the table, picking their teeth, blowing their noses, touching the food with their hands, drinking tea from the saucer rather than the cup, and shouting "Drink up, man!" or some such unwelcome encouragement to the slower imbibers.[48]

Good conversationalists listened well, spoke modestly, refrained from expressing vehement opinions, contradicted tactfully, avoided pedantry and jargon, respected their listeners' beliefs and professions, and avoided double entendres. Jokes about people present in the room were acceptable, according to Henry Fielding, as long as the joke was about a minor or imaginary flaw, or about a "weakness" that was actually a virtue. An acceptable joke, for example, might be to scold one's host teasingly for his imprudent expenditure, listing as evidence the generous courtesies and amenities provided for his guests. Bad conversationalists, then as now, were argumentative, laughed too often at foolish things, bored their listeners, dominated the conversation, betrayed confidences, gossiped, interrupted, made cruel jokes, boasted, and droned on about work.[49]

Polite people also made allowances for rank and sex. Certain things that could be said with perfect propriety in front of gentlemen were considered unsuitable to say to a lady. And the same person would behave differently in different groups. Thus Dr. Thomas Fuller, in 1731, advised his readers, "Among thy Inferiors, thou shalt be sure of Respect; therefore it's good to be a little familiar. Amongst thy Peers thou shalt be sure of Familiarity; and therefore it's good a little to keep State." Because there was power behind precedence, Fuller also warned, "If thou art cheated by a great Man, lose thy Money, and say nothing."[50] Inferiors were likewise expected to show deference through various gestures, depending on the greatness or meekness of the people involved: bowing or curtseying, taking off one's hat, standing in a superior's presence, tugging at the front of one's hair or touching the knuckles to one's forehead.[51]

On one hand, there was a kind of subtle leveling influence at work: more people laid claim to respectable titles such as "Esquire," "Mr.," "Mrs.," and "Madam," and instead of long introductions in polite society, there was one bow to the company at large when a man entered and none when he left.[52] On the other hand, only so much equality and ease could be tolerated. British soldier Captain John Bowater said of Americans that

> The Natives are such a Levelling, underbred, Artful Race of people that we cannot Associate with them. . . . I met a man of very good property a few days ago who had a Complaint to make and I refer'd him to Lord Percy. I heard him enquire at his Lordships door for Mr. Percy. Thinking him Ignorant I stept up & told him again Lord Percy. He replied to me he knew no Lord but the Lord Jehovah.[53]

This lack of deference would have been intolerable in England.

Gentility was especially necessary in public places, which were often crowded and dirty. It was a polite gesture to "give someone the wall," meaning to let them walk nearest the buildings on the sidewalks. This was an important courtesy, since the gutters were full of mud and refuse, and maids frequently emptied dirty water from the upstairs windows and balconies. The person given the wall was less likely to be spattered with something unsavory. It was important to greet acquaintances politely (though, by mid-century, men had stopped kissing each other as a greeting, preferring a handshake or bow).[54] Workers greeted each other at their work, referring to older people as "father" or "mother" even if they were not related; for example, a "Countryman" seeing a wheelwright of his acquaintance greeted him "with the usual Compliment, *Good-Morrow Father Wright, God speed your Labour*."[55] On the street people were advised not only to yield the wall to strangers, superiors, and women, but also to push through the crowd using elbows only, not hands; to step out of traffic when stopping with acquaintances, rather than blocking the sidewalk; and to make way for "the groping blind" and the porter panting beneath his load.[56] They were also to adopt genteel positions for hands, face, feet, and torso for walking, conversing, bowing, giving or receiving objects, and dancing, but of course they were also to remain "easy, natural, unstudied."[57]

It was not easy to be perfectly polite in the 18th century, any more than it is today, but the consequences then were certainly more severe. Great and humble alike had methods of enforcing their codes of behavior: social ostracism, the duel, the fistfight, the skimmington, and the stang. It was a small world, and, rough and vulgar though it could be, it would not and could not tolerate certain transgressions.

TIMELINE

1715	The Riot Act takes effect.
1736	Londoners take part in Gin Act riots over increases in the price of liquor and in the Rag Fair Riots over the importation of Irish labor.
1744	London footmen riot over the importation of French footmen and lay siege to the house of the Bow Street magistrate.
1745	Parliament imposes fines or imprisonment for swearing and a £10 fine for taking God's name in vain in a theatrical presentation. The act is ineffective, and vigorous swearing persists.
1763	Thousands of journeymen silk weavers riot in Spitalfields.
1767	Dockers' wives in Portsmouth riot over the loss of a perquisite, the right to glean scrap wood from the yard.
1773	The Vauxhall Affray pits the Reverend Henry Bate against George Fitzgerald.

1774   Lord Chesterfield's *Letters to His Son*, an influential
             guide to genteel behavior, is published.

1775   Rioting seamen hold Liverpool for three days in Au-
             gust, with some fatalities.

1780   The Gordon Riots take place in London.[58]

17

"One Foot Within the Grave": Health Care and Hygiene

The Patients shall not Swear or take Gods Name in Vain nor Revile nor miscall one another, nor strike or beat one another.
—From the rules of St. Thomas' Hospital, 1754

Imagine that you are sick in the 18th century. You are running a high fever, feeling lightheaded, and beginning to develop blotches on your skin. Your mother has dosed you with some cheap patent medicines. She has tried poultices and some sort of nasty-smelling broth. Time passes, and a man with a cane and a sword feeds you more bad-tasting medicines. You think you hear him say that one is made of spiders. You are dimly aware of warm water and a pain in your arm, and you turn your head to witness the sight of your blood running from a vein in your elbow into a bowl. "Ah, good," you think, being an 18th-century person, "everything that can be done is being done."

In the 18th century, "all that could be done" was very little. Physicians knew, even at the beginning of the century, about the circulation of the blood. They had some understanding of anatomy but only a few effective treatments, like quinine, ipecacuanha, and, later, inoculation. They could diagnose few diseases with accuracy; that which was not plague or smallpox was likely to be classified loosely as a "fever." They were aware that drinking water contaminated with feces was bad, but more because the idea was disgusting than because anyone had studied the connection between drinking water and disease. They were ignorant of the role played in disease by parasites like lice and fleas. Because it was expensive to call in a doctor (about 10s. at least for a visit),[1] most people waited until they had exhausted every other resource. Doctors therefore often saw only the most desperate cases. As a result, most people believed that doctors were as likely to kill their patients as to heal them. Needing to do something dramatic, or for lack of anything better to do, or because they really believed it would work, doctors resorted to visible but useless or even harmful measures—bleeding, dosing with dangerous drugs, raising blisters on the skin, and inducing vomiting. Joseph Addison, in the *Spectator*, called physicians "a most formidable Body of Men: The Sight of them is enough to make a Man serious, for we may lay it down as a Maxim, that When a Nation abounds in Physicians it grows thin of People."[2]

MEDICAL PRACTICIONERS

Physicians   Physicians, who were considered gentlemen, could carry swords as proof of their genteel status, and they sported gold-topped canes (sometimes hiding a vial of vinegar as a disinfectant) and special wigs. If he were successful, a physician might make thousands of pounds a year. It was the promise of status and income that motivated some to follow the path to the top: years of study at Oxford, Cambridge, or Trinity College in Dublin, followed by a lengthy exam in Latin and membership in the Royal College of Physicians, which entitled one to practice in London. Then, one took a wife to gain the respectability required to attend fashionable women, taught paying pupils at one of London's hospitals, bought a nice house in the West End, stole other doctors' patients and fees, and perhaps amassed a collection of medical specimens.[3]

In reality, however, few physicians followed this course. Oxford and Cambridge were rotten places to study medicine, and they graduated very few doctors. The universities of Edinburgh and Glasgow offered better training, educated surgeons as well as physicians, and admitted Dissenters.[4] The Royal College, moreover, was small, with only forty-five full members in 1745.[5] Furthermore, it was possible to evade the university process entirely. Except in a few places with long-established barbers' or physicians' guilds, like London, York, Newcastle, and Bristol, no examination was necessary to practice medicine. Not a few physicians were clergymen who had switched professions.[6] Also there were plenty of medical practitioners who did not claim to be physicians at all.

Surgeons   Just below the physician on the hierarchy of respectability was the surgeon. Descended from the medieval barber-surgeon who cut hair and flesh alike, the surgeon performed operations and drew blood, neither of which the lofty physician was

17.1 "Physical Advice," John Nixon, 1784. A doctor examines a gouty patient by looking at his tongue and taking his pulse. Courtesy of the Print Collection, Lewis Walpole Library, Yale University.

expected or permitted to do. Surgeons tended to get stuck with jobs that no physician would have tolerated, serving aboard ships at war and in prisons. Medically, their training was often even worse than physicians'. William Hunter, one of the century's greatest surgeons, was allowed access to only two cadavers during his entire medical education.[7]

Rudimentary education was only one of the obstacles to successful surgery. Because there were no reliable anesthetics, surgical patients were usually given alcohol or opium beforehand. Furthermore, little was known about infection. Medical practitioners rarely washed their hands, even when they had come directly from another patient. Even if they knew little of its causes, however, they knew that infection existed, and that it quite frequently killed the patient. Therefore, surgery was exceedingly rare, and surgical procedures (other than bleeding) were few, limited to trepanation (drilling a hole in the skull to relieve pressure against the brain), tonsilectomy, lithotomy (the removal of bladder stones), excision of skin and breast cancers, and amputation. The surgeon, with his paying students and a few dressers or other assistants, would work extremely quickly, while the patient sweated, struggled, or fainted. The blood dripped freely off the wooden operating table into a box of sawdust kicked around as needed or onto the floor, beneath which might be several more inches of sawdust to soak up the seepage. Shipboard surgeons worked in even worse conditions, in small lantern-lit rooms rocked by the waves. All surgeons strove to minimize the time that an incision lay open. A bladder-stone removal by the reigning expert, William Cheselden, could take thirty seconds to one minute; the amputation of a leg by an expert took two to four minutes. Nevertheless, due to the prevalence of infection, almost one in five of Cheselden's lithotomy patients died.[8]

Apothecaries, Midwives, and Quacks
Below the surgeon in status was the apothecary, who dispensed drugs. Middle- and working-class people who could not afford physicians consulted apothecaries instead. Well below the apothecaries were the midwives and nurses, overwhelmingly female, and trained outside the university system, since women could not attend universities. Nurses in particular were accused of thievery, drunkenness, and licentiousness. They were drawn chiefly from the working class and were domestic servants as much as medical staff. The largest group of nurses were mothers and daughters, whose typical duties included caring for sick relatives. Occasionally a woman achieved success as a surgeon or bonesetter—the bonesetter Sally Mapp was celebrated in song and caricatured in a Hogarth print—but this was the exception rather than the rule.

Sharing the bottom muck with nurses and midwives were the quacks. Some of them were anonymous incompetents, like the physician in George Crabbe's poem "The Village,"

> A potent quack, long versed in human ills,
> Who first insults the victim whom he kills;
> Whose mur'drous hand a drowsy bench protect,
> And whose most tender mercy is neglect.[9]

Others became quite famous, like Joshua Ward, whose patent medicines were used by all sorts, including the Royal Navy;[10] the oculist "Chevalier" Taylor; and "Doctor" Katterfelto, who traveled with a bunch of black cats in a coach drawn by six black horses.[11] In his show, Katterfelto projected the microscopic contents of a drop of water onto a large wall, sold patent medicines and phosphorus matches, gave gambling advice, and shot sparks from his fingers using what appears, in a contemporary engraving, to be an early Van de Graaff generator. Dr. James Graham promised men virility and fertility. Two guineas admitted one to his Temple of Health and Hymen, which featured liveried doormen, lectures on sexual health, opulent furnishings, scantily clad "Goddesses of Youth and Health," and the "Celestial Bed." A night's stay in the twelve-foot-by-nine-foot bed cost an additional £50, and its combination of glass pillars, "balmy and ethereal spices," statues, music, pivots, magnets, and silk sheets was guaranteed to produce "immediate conception" and "Superior ecstasy." Horace Walpole, unconvinced, called Graham's temple a "most impudent puppet show of imposition."[12]

HOSPITALS

Hospitals, founded by wealthy subscribers, served orphans, women in labor, and the indigent and working-class ill. In terms of reducing the patients' mortality, they accomplished little. Disease was poorly understood. All hospitals were haunted by vermin, especially lice, which clung to walls, beds, patients, and doctors' coats.[13] At Chelsea and Greenwich Hospitals, patients captured their lice and pitted them against each other in races.[14] Furthermore, until about the last quarter of the century, there was no London hospital with a lavatory; in 1774 Guy's got a common privy, in 1788, a set of indoor water closets. In most hospitals for most of the century, the waste of patients and staff was collected in buckets and carried through the hospital (down a back staircase, at St. Bartholomew's) to a cesspool located terrifyingly nearby. In warm weather especially, the stink of it must have wafted through the wards.[15] Linens, when they were provided by the hospital rather than the patient, were minimal. Even late in the century at Guy's, the patient was issued five sets of sheets but got a refund for the unused ones, and had to pay 3d. for extra sets.[16] Surely some patients, too poor in the first place to afford at-home care, slept in dirty sheets to save money. Nevertheless, hospitals did serve certain purposes. They got sick servants out of the household where they might infect their employers or require time-consuming nursing care. They made an effort to bolster population by serving children, pregnant women, useful workers, and military personnel. And they provided training opportunities for physicians and surgeons, who competed actively for hospital posts.[17]

The behavior of patients was closely scrutinized by the hospital, and their labor was utilized on occasion. At Guy's Hospital, late in the century, "prophane or Lewd Talking," corroborated by two witnesses, meant no food for one day after the first offense, and for two days after the second offense. After the third offense, the patient was discharged, cured or not. At St. Thomas' Hospital, patients were forbidden to "Swear or take Gods Name in Vain," and at both St. Thomas' and Guy's, prayers

17.2 "The Quacks," 1783. A satirical duel between James Graham and Doctor Katterfelto. Courtesy of the Print Collection, Lewis Walpole Library, Yale University.

were required at mealtimes, bedtime, and waking, and Scripture was read aloud in each ward on Sunday. The rules of Guy's in 1797 also indicate that patients were expected to assist the nurses in all sorts of ways: helping weaker patients, cleaning the ward, fetching coal, and other tasks. Failure to help, or deliberate absence at the time a job was assigned, could lead to discharge.[18] A penetrating sense of one's status as a humble petitioner for health care was present from admission to discharge; patients had to apply for permission to enter the hospital, often with a letter of recommendation from a subscriber, and received a certificate of discharge—a kind of written pat on the head—reminding them of their profound obligation to the hospital. In at least one hospital, only patients who had attended chapel to offer thanks to God for their renewed health could receive such a certificate.[19]

The "undeserving" or unreferred poor used dispensaries, which became increasingly popular as the century passed. Dispensary staff saw patients, diagnosed ailments, dispensed drugs, and sent the patients on their way. By 1800, 50,000 people a year were being treated by such institutions.[20] Other health care systems, formal and informal, also existed. A sick person might be cared for by neighbors, by a company doctor in some of the new mill towns, by a workhouse, or by a private society that offered health benefits, such as a trade guild or an inoculation society.[21] If he were very unfortunate indeed, he might be in prison, where the hygienic horrors were far worse than in hospitals and homes. Some prisons had a surgeon on staff; some did not. Even those that did, like Newgate, suffered devastating waves of typhus, spread by lice and known in this context as "jail fever." In the "Black Sessions" of 1750, infected prisoners and their lice were brought from Newgate to the Old Bailey, where their parasites found new hosts. More than forty people present in the courtroom that day died of jail fever, including judges, jurors, and court officials.

HYGIENE

Lice could be found everywhere, from the dingiest jails to the most aristocratic dinner parties. Wooden bedsteads provided them with homes. Window taxes encouraged the bricking up of old windows and discouraged the installation of new ones, making houses darker and mustier and more hospitable to head and body lice.[22] They were especially common in crowded places—hospitals, prisons, and military camps—but could be seen in cleaner and more genteel surroundings as well. Fleas were common, too, as were the mites that cause scabies. Conditions improved later in the century when iron bedsteads began to replace wooden ones and when brick and stone

Vermin

houses, more resistant to rats, replaced some of the old wood and plaster ones.[23]

Cleanliness Parasites thrived in part because personal cleanliness was not a priority. Places of crowding and infection were sometimes cleansed with sulphurous smoke or doused with vinegar,[24] and those who feared contagious disease washed with vinegar or inhaled its fumes. Frequent, full-body washing, however, was rare, and most people preferred to rinse their hands and faces; fashionable ladies did so by collecting the morning dew on their handkerchiefs. Even if they had wanted to, most of the working classes could not have afforded to bathe scrupulously because soap was expensive and often heavily taxed.[25] Washing clothes was difficult early in the century, before cheap and washable cotton replaced wool as the dominant fabric. In Samuel Johnson's youth, shirts were changed once a week. The rich could afford to mask their odor with perfumes; the poor had to get used to the smell or suffer.

It was not just the skin that smelled, but the mouth as well. There were plenty of ways to clean the teeth, and dental care was part of the morning ritual for some at least. *The Tatler* of April 12, 1709, refers to a young man "washing his teeth" and "rubbing his Gums."[26] The well-off chewed cinnamon, cloves, honey, orange peel, and other substances to sweeten the breath, and many used tooth powder or abrasive sticks to clean the teeth, or a new invention—the toothbrush.[27] Yet yellow or black teeth, crooked teeth, and foul breath remained commonplace.

Though people in general gradually grew more fastidious, offensive personal habits were rife. People ate with their hands, spat, wiped their hands on their clothes instead of napkins, belched, farted, and blew their noses into their hands.

Human Waste Indoor plumbing was rare, and relieving oneself was a clumsy process at any social level. The rich, in their country or town houses, used chamberpots—glorified buckets—which were then carried by servants to a cesspool. In the city, the cesspool was often in the garden or basement, and was emptied periodically by a night-soil man, who would load the contents into a cart to be carried away to the country. The traditional after-dinner departure of the ladies in fashionable households, leaving the men alone in the dining room for further conversation and drink, was at least in part a toilet issue. The women, upon leaving, would head for "close stools" where they could relieve themselves privately, while the men could often open a sideboard or a sliding wall-panel to retrieve a chamberpot. Then they urinated, often without interrupting their toasts and arguments.[28] In the country, there might be chamber pots or "jordans" for nighttime emergencies and a "necessary house" for all other times. (Jordans can be seen in Illustrations 9.2 and 6.3.)

Toilet paper, as a purposely designed product, lay in the future. In the meantime, most used scrap paper; Lord Chesterfield described a man who routinely tore a few pages from a book of Horace, read them while defecating to illuminate his mind, then used them to clean his backside and "sent them down as a sacrifice to Cloacina."[29] Small children and the poor, especially in cities, simply relieved themselves wherever they were—against buildings, in alleys, or even in the middle of the street. A poem about schoolboys says that they

> Then squatten down with hand beneath each knee,
> Ne seeken out or secret nook or wall,
>
> . . .
>
> And may no carl their innocence deride,
> While they p—ss boldly in the face of all;
> Turning unawed their vestments small aside.[30]

Not until the last quarter of the century would a reliable water closet be constructed, and even then it remained a luxury item.[31] Sloppy disposal of human waste, along with contamination by garbage and animal waste, made some food, and virtually all milk and water in some places, dangerous to consume. Those Londoners with indoor plumbing seldom drank what came through their pipes and allowed it to settle for a few days before using it.[32] Not everyone could avoid tainted water or food, however, especially soldiers and the poor. They succumbed in great numbers to bacterial infections like typhoid fever and dysentery. Tea, in this context, was literally a lifesaver. Though it offered no real nutritive value, it required boiled water and thus killed many infectious agents.[33]

HEALTH CARE IN CHILDHOOD

Every person's contact with medical care begins at birth. In the 18th century, if labor did not progress, or began too early or too late, mother or child or both were often doomed. Practitioners could sometimes shift a baby from a transverse or breech position; some used forceps to extract the baby's head. Caesarean sections were performed rarely, usually only when the mother had died during delivery or seemed certain to do so, since the resulting abdominal infection was almost 100 percent fatal.[34]

There were changes in obstetrical care besides the introduction of forceps. Chief among them was the shift from female midwives to male obstetricians (or "man-midwives"). The fashion for man-midwives was vigorously contested by their female counterparts, led by Sarah Stone, Elizabeth Nihell, and others, who cited female modesty, overuse of forceps by man-midwives, and the superior skill of female midwives. Nevertheless, male doctors had attained supremacy in the field by the end of the century, and many of them became quite well-known, including

William Smellie (attacked by Nihell as "a great horse-godmother of a he-midwife"), who designed a life-size model for teaching purposes; the quack Paul Chamberlen, who sold "Celebrated Anodyne Necklaces" as magical charms for lying-in; and John Maubray, who thought birth defects were caused by perverse sexual practices and believed women could give birth to demons.[35] The shift to male practitioners did not, however, reduce the incidence of "childbed fever"—puerperal fever brought on by infection, introduced into the womb by dirty hands or implements. Puerperal fever continued to claim even the lives of women with uncomplicated deliveries. Of sixty-five women who delivered babies at one London hospital between November 30, 1769, and May 15, 1770, nineteen contracted puerperal fever, and fourteen died.[36]

Those who survived the ordeal of birth had some of their hardest work ahead of them. Childhood ailments claimed a large number of children before their fifth birthdays (60 percent in London in 1764),[37] and those illnesses that failed to kill often scarred or attracted treatments that were even worse. A child might have to survive teething problems, tapeworms, chicken pox, whooping cough, smallpox, lead poisoning, thrush, measles, and mumps, while being bled, swaddled, and dosed with belladonna, syrup of poppies (opium), quinine, rum, gin, brandy, laxatives, and patent medicines. They wore amulets of such ingredients as mistletoe and elk's horn, had hare's brains smeared on their gums while teething, and were given enemas for worms. A particularly drastic worm remedy involved inserting a piece of pork on a string into the rectum and drawing it out slowly to lure the worms. Some diseases could be cured, it was thought, by a sudden fright, such as riding on a bear, having a gun fired nearby, or "Giving the patient a part of some disgraceful animal, as a mouse, &c., to eat, and afterwards informing him of it; and so forth."[38]

DISEASE AND ACCIDENT

Specialized care was little better. Eyeglasses existed for those who could afford them, but many eye problems were treated with home remedies like poultices of rotten apples, patent medicines like William Read's "styptic water," or cauterization. Lost eyes could be replaced with glass ones.[39] If something went wrong with one's teeth, dentists hand-drilled cavities—as always, with no anaesthetic but alcohol—and filled the resulting holes with molten tin, lead, or gold. Where a dentist was unavailable, a farrier might pull the tooth (and might also serve as the local bonesetter).[40] False teeth could be had, made of bone, ivory, gold, porcelain, wood, or the purchased teeth of the poor, but such teeth were expensive and, held in place by awkward spring mechanisms, sometimes fell out of the mouth.[41] Tooth problems could also result in infections; 780 Londoners ostensibly died in 1774 from dental problems.[42]

17.3 "The Country Tooth-Drawer," R. Dighton, 1784. The local farrier, identifiable by the horseshoes and tools on the wall and floor, yanks a tooth as he and an assistant hold the patient still. Courtesy of the Print Collection, Lewis Walpole Library, Yale University.

Still, far fewer people died from festering teeth than from infectious disease. There were few remedies or palliatives for contagious illness. For venereal or "Foul" diseases, a common treatment was "salivation," in which the patient was dosed for days or even weeks with toxic quantities of mercury, in either ointment or pill form. The treatment caused drooling (sometimes as much as three pints per day), swollen gums, and loosening of the teeth.[43] Treatment of contagious disease remained largely ineffective; however, some progress was being made in the area of prevention. Gradually, writers, physicians, and reformers became aware of the effects of crowding and sanitation on public health. Furthermore, one of the century's great killers was being brought under control.

Early in the century, Lady Mary Wortley Montagu, a noted intellectual and author, traveled to Turkey and saw women digging into smallpox pustules and poking the contaminated instruments into healthy people. Told that this procedure prevented the healthy individuals from contracting smallpox themselves, she brought the technique back to England and began campaigning for its adoption. Her own son was one of the first to be inoculated, and tests on prisoners and charity-school pupils followed. Eventually, two daughters of the future George II were inoculated, giving the practice a royal seal of approval. However, inoculation sometimes resulted in infection or a full-blown case of smallpox rather than a minor, immunizing illness. Later in the century, Edward Jenner learned that a milder illness, cowpox, offered the same protection against smallpox infection, and the procedure became much safer.[44]

Diseases of malnutrition were also rife. Starvation was rare, but so was a healthy, balanced diet. Lack of vitamin C caused scurvy, especially aboard ship where fresh fruits and vegetables were scarce. Scurvy caused exhaustion, swellings, spots, trembling, and a delay or reversal in the healing of wounds. Although it was known to be dietary in origin, it was late in the century before effective substances, like sauerkraut and lime juice, were used to combat it.[45] Vitamin D or calcium deficiency caused rickets, whose sufferers, principally children, developed enlarged livers and heads and bent, crippled spines and limbs.[46] The exceptionally malnourished contracted jaundice.

A host of other perils awaited people of all classes: industrial accidents, farm accidents, gout, poisoning as a result of toxic cosmetics, cancer, dropsy, rheumatism, ulcers, itches, infected feet, and the inevitable amputations and maimings of wartime service. The inventive spirit of the time rose to the occasion, producing not only glass eyes and false teeth but guide dogs, playing cards for the blind, wheelchairs, special beds for invalids, trusses, and prosthetic limbs.[47]

SPAS

Sufferers from various diseases sought remedy or relief at one of England's numerous mineral spas or seaside retreats. Coastal resorts, where one could drink or bathe in the seawater for health's sake, included Brighton, Margate, and tiny Freestone, which attracted farmers and small tradesmen.[48] At Southampton, the ladies' bathing dresses (still extraordinarily demure by modern standards) shocked reformer Jonas Hanway,[49] but no doubt the ladies did feel more vigorous and healthy after removing some of their constricting garments and getting a little exercise wading in and out of the sea.

Women were also often the prime urgers of spa visits because the spa towns offered them social diversions second only to London's. Spa towns included Tunbridge-Wells, patronized by the Prince of Wales early in the century, long a resort of the aristocracy; Epsom; Malvern, whose waters were supposed to be useful for eye problems;[50] and Leamington, whose waters were recommended for mad-dog bites.[51] The queen of them all, though, was Bath. There the seeker after health could visit the Pump Room to drink the town's famous mineral waters, jostling a crowd of "reeking" fellow-sufferers—"unwashed beaus" and "foppish slovens foully fine"—to sip from a cup fresh from the mouth of the previous user. If she preferred to bathe in the waters, she put on bathing clothes. In the water, she got perhaps her only full-body bath that year, aside from any other spa baths she might take, and she joined a crowd of others similarly dirty, whose filth floated off and swam in the water nearby. The water also held skin flakes and urine. A disgusted poet in 1737 wrote that "All (from the porter to the courtly nymph) / Pay liquid tribute to the swelling lymph."[52]

HOME REMEDIES

Many people, perhaps most, chose to treat their ailments at home. Some chose commercial remedies: bottled Malvern waters, Goddard's Drops, Dr. Anderson's True Scots Pills, Carminative Windexpelling Pills, Mrs. Stephens' "Medicine for the Stone" made of ingredients that included egg shells and snails, Daffy's Elixir, Steel's cake for rheumatism, Dr. Bateman's Pectoral Drops, and Dr. Hooper's Female Pills.[53] George Washington and George III alike took Dr. James's Fever Powders, to which prison reformer John Howard was addicted; playwright Oliver Goldsmith probably died from them.[54] Dr. Joshua Ward's drops and pills, widely used at mid-century, were composed chiefly of antimony and wine.[55]

Some invested in home health manuals, which contained largely useless and possibly quite dangerous advice. Others relied on folk remedies or blind instinct. They ate soap for stomach troubles,[56] touched hanged men to cure goiter and swollen glands,[57] drank hawthorn tea[58] or asses' milk, made charms of babies' amniotic sacs, drank their own urine for ague or snails' tea for a sore chest, rubbed their eyes with black cats' tails for styes, and ate eye of pike for toothaches, pigeons' blood for apoplexy, tortoise blood for epilepsy, cockroach tea for kidney ailments, puppy and owl broth for bronchitis, and spiders for fever.[59] Confirmation, christening, and Good Friday bread were all believed to possess magical powers.[60] Methodist founder John Wesley advised swallowing three pounds of quicksilver, one ounce at a time, to untwist the bowels, and placing celandine leaves under the foot to cure jaundice.[61] Another "cure" for jaundice was burying an egg, hard-boiled in the patient's urine and pricked with a pin, in an anthill. Still another was consuming nine live lice.[62] Not all home remedies were useless, however. Quinine, dung poultices, foxglove (digitalis) for heart problems, and cod-liver oil had medical benefits.[63] In some cases, faith in the remedy, or fortuitous timing, may have lent some "cures" an appearance of efficacy: one gentleman, dying of dropsy, supposedly averted his fate by consuming "a boiled chicken entire and five quarts of small beer."[64]

MENTAL ILLNESS

Remedies for mental illness were no better. Increased attention to feelings and sentiments, especially from the 1760s on, led Britons to examine how much emotion, and what kind, was normal and acceptable. Suicide was common and feared to be on the increase, especially after some high-profile cases. Suicide was less likely to be thought of as sin or the result of demonic possession, and more likely to be considered the outcome of a deranged mind. Yet because suicides were still thought to rise again as ghosts, they were often buried at crossroads, with a stake driven through the heart.[65]

The causes of mental illness were a matter of debate. Some thought that insanity was bodily; others, a distinct minority, thought it was purely mental in origin. Treatments were blunt, unpleasant, and usually of no actual benefit. They usually consisted of immersion in water, prayer, purging, bleeding, blistering the skin, trepanning (boring a hole in the skull), or enemas.[66] More often, simple confinement was the goal, and inmates were sometimes chained or tied to make sure they stayed put. The interior of a madhouse such as London's Bethlehem Hospital (Bedlam) was a sight to behold, and many did. Bedlam was one of London's principal tourist attractions; until 1770, visitors could pay for admission and a tour, during which guards and visitors alike goaded the inmates to view their violent reactions. Nuts, fruit, cheesecakes, and beer were sold, to the tune of "rattling of Chains, drumming of Doors, Ranting, Hollowing, Singing," and a distinctive uproar that spread like a wave through the asylum when the inmates became outraged at the treatment one of their fellows was receiving.[67] Some inmates fought back by hurling the contents of their chamberpots.[68] Bedlam's occupants were lightly dressed in both summer and winter and lived in unheated rooms, often with only a pile of straw for a bed.[69]

A reaction against the conditions of madhouses and the exhibition of the insane took place in the second half of the century. St. Luke's Hospital, founded in 1751, explicitly forbade exposing "the patients . . . to public view."[70] Parliament involved itself in the question in 1774 when it required madhouses to be licensed by the College of Physicians in London and by JPs in the provinces. The Madhouse Act further provided for inspections, a doctor's certificate for admission, and records of admission, treatment, and discharge.[71]

DEATH

Death was a close and constant companion. Birmingham businessman William Hutton received a straightforward appraisal of his chances when, as a child, he lost both his parents. "Don't cry," his nanny told

17.4 "The Hospital of Bethlehem," drawn by I. Maurer, engraved by T. Bowles, 1747. An exterior view. Courtesy of the Print Collection, Lewis Walpole Library, Yale University.

him. "You will soon go yourself."[72] His case was not unusual; average life expectancy fluctuated throughout the century, but it usually hovered in the low- to mid-thirties. This, of course, includes those who died in droves while young: children, soldiers and sailors at war, and women giving birth. Those who made it past their young adulthood often led quite long lives.

When death came, it was attended by as much ceremony and display as the family resources permitted. Funerals could be expensive, entailing fees for the beadle, porter, pallbearers, gravedigger, and others, as well as mourning clothes for family and servants alike. Alms were also traditionally distributed to the poor at such a time.[73] The funeral began with a viewing of the corpse, which was usually dressed in a white wool shroud, with its head resting on a wool pillow and covered by a white flannel cloth. The Burial in Wool Act, intended to increase the wool trade, mandated that graveclothes be of wool. Rich families who wanted to circumvent the law had to pay a £5 fine to dress their dead in beautiful clothes, silk stockings, and expensive shoes. The very poor, who could not afford wool shrouds, avoided graveclothes altogether and covered the naked corpse with flowers or hay.[74]

In a genteel family, guests would be issued engraved invitations to the funeral. The guests would receive tokens, including leather gloves (sometimes black for the principal mourners and white for everyone else), mourning rings of varying worth (sometimes containing a bit of the deceased's hair), decorative knots of black ribbons, and a sprig of rosemary, which symbolized remembrance.[75] The procession to church and churchyard would include the parson, wearing a long black gown; an attendant called a mute, who held a black-draped staff; a "feather-man" carrying a "lid of feathers," a tray of black ostrich plumes that he balanced on his head; mourners and attendants on foot, on horseback, or in carriages; and the coffin itself, carried in a hearse drawn by black horses. The coffin was covered with a long fabric covering called a pall (hence "pallbearer"), decorated with the family's coat of arms and topped with several black plumes.[76] The church bells announced the gender and age of the dead, tolling three times for a child, six times for a woman, and nine times for a man.

The poor had only three or four bier carriers in their regular clothes. Even the cost of a small child's funeral—about two guineas[77]—might be beyond them, and their dead were commonly disposed of in mass graves called "poor's holes," left open to the elements until filled to capacity.[78]

Unfortunately, the troubles of the world did not end with death, or even with burial. "Resurrectionists" who supplied cadavers to medical schools sometimes unearthed recently buried coffins and stole the bodies inside. To thwart such grave robbers, families buried bodies extra deep, or buried them in metal or metal-lined coffins, or posted guards, or even, on occasion, booby-trapped the gravesites.[79]

If death was a more assertive companion in the 18th century than today, it was sometimes a less terrifying one. The coarse, straightforward wit of the times accompanied people not only to coffeehouses and clubs but to gallows and graves. One-legged comedian Samuel Foote's epitaph in Westminster Abbey reads,

> Here lies one Foote, whose death may thousands save,
> For death has now one foot within the grave.[80]

TIMELINE

1676	Bethlehem (Bedlam) Hospital for the insane is completed.
1719	The London area, which at the beginning of the century had only two hospitals, gets a third, Westminster Hospital.
1721	Lady Mary Wortley Montagu introduces smallpox inoculation to Britain.
1725	Guy's Hospital is built in London.
1729	The Edinburgh Royal Infirmary, Britain's first hospital outside London, is built.

1735	The first provincial English hospital is built in Bristol.
1739	The first successful Caesarean section in Britain, in which both mother and child survive, is performed by Irish midwife Mary Donally.
1745	Surgeons flee the ancient Company of Barbers and form their own Company of Surgeons.
1746	London gets two smallpox hospitals, one for regular patients and one for those being inoculated.
	London's Lock Hospital for sexually transmitted diseases is founded.
1749	The British Lying-In Hospital, Britain's first maternity hospital, is built in Covent Garden.
1750	Dr. Richard Russell publishes *A Dissertation on the Use of Sea Water in the Diseases of the Glands*, the founding text of the vogue for finding health at the seashore.
1751	St. Luke's Hospital for the insane is founded.
1752	William Smellie publishes his influential *Treatise on the Theory and Practice of Midwifery*.
1760	Elizabeth Nihell publishes a *Treatise on the Art of Midwifery*, which attacks male midwives, chiefly for their overuse of forceps.
1769	London builds its first dispensary for poor children.
1774	The first national medical register is issued.
	The Madhouse Act is passed.
1778	A surgeon is knighted for the first time in English history.
	Joseph Braham patents a ball-cock flush toilet, selling 6,000 by 1797.
1780	Quack Dr. James Graham opens his Temple of Health and Hymen in London.
1793	Scottish surgeon John Hunter, who studied fetal development, nasal and olfactory systems, the repair of Achilles tendons, and other anatomical questions, dies.

1795	The Royal Navy mandates the provision of lime juice on all its ships to combat scurvy, a measure espoused in 1754 by James Lind in his *Treatise on the Scurvy*.
1796	Edward Jenner infects a healthy boy with cowpox, then tries unsuccessfully to infect him with smallpox, proving that immunity to the milder disease also confers immunity to the more severe one.
1798	Jenner publishes the results of his smallpox studies in *An Inquiry into the Cause and Effects of the Variolae Vaccinae*.[81]

18

Religion

[E]very man is the worse looked upon & the less trusted, for being thought to have no religion . . . a wise atheist (if such a thing there is) would, for his own interest, & character in the world, pretend to some religion.

—Lord Chesterfield

Religiously, England was an anomaly. It had a state-sanctioned church, like France, yet, unlike almost every other nation in Europe, it allowed minority religions. However, it stopped short of the policy of the Netherlands (and, later, the United States), which was to allow complete freedom of worship. England still imposed civil or financial penalties on Catholics, Jews, Moravians, Methodists, Quakers, and all other non-Anglicans; it merely stopped short of jailing, torturing, exiling, or executing them.

There was a good deal of popular support for religious belief, among Anglicans, Catholics, and Dissenters alike. Religious tracts and books sold well. Religious music was similarly popular; the hymn today known as "Rock of Ages," originally titled "A Living and Dying Prayer for the Holiest Believer in the World," was written during this period, in 1776. There was also a common impression that to doubt the essential goodness of religious faith and practice was to offend society as a whole.

Yet for most of the century, with the singular exception of the success of Methodism, the nation seemed to linger in a state of spiritual inertia.

Anglicans were bored by clergy who seemed more interested in tithes and fox hunting than in hellfire and salvation. Dissenters, without the motivating force of fierce, organized persecution, grew increasingly lax. Religion remained a powerful force in daily life, but genteel culture was dominated by the ideas of rational religion, of God as a distant creator rather than a day-to-day miracle worker, and of emotionalism or "enthusiasm" in religion as distasteful and vulgar. One ought to have faith, and plenty of it, but one ought not to make too much fuss about it, or make anyone else feel guilty about enjoying a comfortable, worldly life.

THE ANGLICAN CHURCH

Anglicans were, in the eyes of the law, those who subscribed to the Thirty-Nine Articles of the faith and who took Anglican communion. They were the majority of the people as a whole, and the vast majority of the ruling class. The majority religion's dominance was reinforced by the names by which it was known: the *Anglican* Church, the Church of *England*. To be anything but a member of the established church was, by definition, to be un-English. Everything about Anglicanism reinforced its special ties to the state. Oxford and Cambridge, government posts, and the governing corporations of towns were still closed to non-Anglicans. Anglican clergy could, in theory at least, preach anywhere they liked, in a church, a field, or a private home; Dissenting ministers were limited to the pulpits of licensed Dissenting chapels. Even the basic unit of local government itself, the parish, was identical to the basic unit of the religious hierarchy. Whether one belonged to it or not, one was affected by the politics of the established church.

For example, even non-Anglicans had to pay tithes, a kind of tax, to the parish priest. In some areas, these annual payments were made in coin, but traditionally, especially among the poorer members of the parish, payment was made "in kind" out of the harvest produce. Tithes were often loathed by parishioners, and in some extreme cases there was sabotage in an attempt to undermine the system. In one case in 1779, in which the tithes were paid in quantities of milk, the churns containing the milk were hidden, delivered on the wrong day, or adultered with urine and pig feces.[1] In some parishes, tithes were replaced altogether by a fixed sum, called a composition or *modus*. This system made it easier in some ways for both parishioners and parson, but as inflation worsened late in the century, members of the clergy living on fixed compositions suffered. Where tithes were the basis of payment, the clergy usually benefited from Parliamentary enclosure of lands, since enclosure bills usually allotted the parson one-seventh of the enclosed land in lieu of tithes. The parson could then farm this land himself or lease it to tenants.[2] The land from which a parson derived his income was known as the "glebe."

The parson's duties were not particularly onerous. He performed marriages, christenings, and funerals; delivered a sermon each Sunday and rarely at any other time; visited the sick and dying, usually only when he was sent for and less often on his own initiative; and socialized with the local squire. He was assisted by a clerk, who recorded baptisms, marriages, and deaths; two lay churchwardens, who supervised church property and the distribution of alms; and often by at least one curate, a low-paid member of the clergy not fortunate enough to have a living of his own. All too often, the bulk of the parson's duties actually fell on the curate, who worked hard, lived meanly, and seldom had enough money to marry well if at all. Much was written about the plight of curates, but little was done. A plan to assist the lowest-paid clergy, enacted early in the century and known as Queen Anne's Bounty, was successful in a very small way but was unable to counteract inflation's effects. Curates made from £10 to £40 per year, compared to the hundreds earned by parsons and the thousands earned each year by some bishops.

Bishops were responsible for overseeing the functions of the diocese, ordaining clergymen, and licensing curates. They also had the right to sit in the House of Lords. Aristocratic families were overrepresented at this level of the church, but they were never in the majority. In 1800 six of the twenty-six bishops were the sons of peers.[3] Influence, as always, was useful. Brownlow North, half-brother of Prime Minister Lord North, was made dean of Canterbury, bishop of Lichfield, bishop of Worcester, and bishop of Winchester in turn, all by the time he turned forty; his sons and grandson were granted lucrative church posts as well. The grandson became registrar of Winchester diocese when he was a mere seven years old.[4]

Distaste for such string pulling was only reason that the power of the Church was waning. Its governing body, Convocation, was dismissed in 1717, and, for all practical purposes, it remained dissolved for the rest of the century.[5] The ecclesiastical court system, which dealt with such matters as marital separations and nullifications, and which regulated the conduct of clergy, was being used less frequently.[6] In practice, even penance and excommunication were imposed reluctantly, for fear punished parishioners might turn to Dissent or even to Catholicism. On a personal level, the church failed to move the emotions of the well-fed gentry who came late to services and left early, or the servants and farm tenants who came to church only to please their masters. It failed to preach at all to many far-flung communities of workers, who later proved all too receptive to Methodism.

Problems of the Church

Part of the Anglican Church's problem was that it was composed, in large part, of men who wanted genteel status and a good annual income, rather than men who felt a genuine calling. A middling farmer or tradesman found that sending his son to a university to be trained for the clergy was one way of allowing the family to rise in the world. Certainly, much of one's success in the church was attributable not to religious fervor but to luck, family connections, the influence of friends, and political affiliation. Wealthy or noble families inherited or purchased advowsons (the right to name the new occupants of vacant religious posts) and usually granted such positions to younger sons, other relatives, or faithful family supporters.

There was also a certain detachment of priests from their flocks. It was permissible and common for a parson to be a pluralist, holding the livings of two or more parishes which were sometimes widely scattered. As a result, "[a]bout a quarter of parishes did not have a resident minister."[7] In fact, it was this tendency to pluralism that made curates so necessary. One could not preach on the same Sunday in two parishes a day's ride apart, so the curate was enlisted to deliver the sermon on many occasions. The most common complaints were that the clergy were stingy, uncharitable, hypocritical, and neglectful of their spiritual duties. Thomas Holcroft lamented,

> The priest often preaches
>   Against worldly riches;
> But ne'er gives a mite to the poor,
>   Well-a-day![8]

Even if every parson had been generous, virtuous, and diligent, there were simply too few churches in the right places. England's population underwent profound changes in the 18th century, with the number of people growing overall and their distribution shifting. The result was that in parts of the south, churches built to house hundreds had only dozens of worshippers, while in the industrializing north, there was a staggering ratio of worshippers to seats. Some communities had no parish church at all. Manchester had only one in 1750, though its population was some 20,000. The problem was no better in London, where Dissenting chapels would outnumber Anglican churches by the early years of the nineteenth century. In just one of its parishes, Marylebone, there were 40,000 residents in 1800, and one 200-seat Anglican church.

The shortage of church seats in booming areas was due primarily to three factors. First, building new churches required money, and Parliament was always reluctant to spend. Its most aggressive attempt to address the problem was its 1711 London Churches Act, which was intended to provide for the erection of fifty new churches. Instead of fifty serviceable churches, however, ten splendid ones were constructed, and a shortage of pews remained. The second problem concerned the pews themselves. There were two types in 18th-century churches: the plain

18.1 "The Sleeping Congregation," Hogarth, 1736, retouched 1762. An Anglican congregation is unmoved by the parson's sermon. Courtesy of the Print Collection, Lewis Walpole Library, Yale University.

bench pews familiar to most American churchgoers and the more expensive, lavishly upholstered box pews, owned by wealthy families. The box pews took up enormous amounts of space that could have been used for several bench pews, but box pews were owned by the families, not the church, and they could not be removed without the permission of the owners. The owners, conscious of their status, were hardly eager to volunteer their box pews for destruction.

Perhaps the most significant deterrent to church building, however, came from within the church. Parsons, after all, derived their income from tithes. Tithes, in turn, were directly linked to how much the parishioners made in a year, and how many parishioners there were in each parish. It would have been a foolish parson indeed who suggested carving up his own parish and yielding half his profitable flock to a rival.[9]

The 18th century was also a uniquely secular age, an age in which reason and science were given unprecedented importance. Fashionable society seemed bored by church, even if it believed collectively in God. Those who could afford to snub the parson often did so, attending church haphazardly, sleeping during the sermons, and swearing outside church with relative impunity. (Swearing and Sabbath breaking were still technically illegal.) The occasional brave soul even declared him- or herself an atheist, as did London tailor Francis Place;[10] such a declaration, a century or two earlier, would have resulted in the most vicious persecution, but in the 18th century it was merely distasteful to some, a curiosity to others, and a rational conclusion to a few.

Throughout the 1700s, people of all kinds noted, usually with dismay, the lack of faith around them. In the early years of the century, Joseph Addison complained, "There is less appearance of religion in England than in any neighbouring state."[11] Daniel Defoe, in 1702, wrote of London, "No city in the spacious universe/Boasts of religion more, or minds it less;"[12] the situation was to worsen measurably in the years that followed. In 1714 seventy-two churches provided daily services in London, but by 1732 the number had shrunk to forty-four.[13] In 1736 the bishop of Durham, Joseph Butler, claimed that "religion is more and more wearing out of the minds of men." To him, it seemed that the number and "zeal" of "those who call themselves unbelievers" was on the rise, and he concluded, "The deplorable distinction of our age is an avowed scorn of religion in some and a growing disregard of it in the generality." Methodist founder John Wesley agreed, "Ungodliness is our universal, our constant, our peculiar character."[14] Of course, there has never been an age in which the custodians of religion were perfectly satisfied with the faith and behavior of their followers, but there was some justification in this case for these views.

Whether the church deserved the attacks upon it is open to some debate. To be sure, the average clergyman was a worldly man, concerned with his income and status, enjoying a glass of good wine, and perhaps, like Parson Woodforde, not above buying a little smuggled tea.[15] Only a few were truly scandalous or eccentric, like Laurence Sterne, author of the controversial and risqué novel *Tristram Shandy*; Henry Bate, a playwright, boxer, editor, and dog breeder; and Martin Madan, whose public endorsement of polygamy effectively ended his career.[16] A number of parsons distinguished themselves through their extra-clerical endeavors. Clergymen used the relative leisure of their position to become antiquarians, naturalists, historians, agriculturalists, legal scholars, chemists, and archaeologists.

CATHOLICISM

There were plenty of rival sects eager to take advantage of the Anglican Church's lassitude; however, the most visible rival was in many ways the least able to seize its opportunities. Since the 16th century, the Church of England had been waging a war of public relations against "papists" and it had quite decisively won. Papists were almost universally believed to be superstitious, treasonous, and idle (owing to the larger number of religious holidays in the Catholic calendar).[17] Toleration was fashionable in some circles, but anti-Catholic bias remained strong. It was reinforced by Jacobite attempts in the first half of the century to return a Catholic monarch to the British throne and waned somewhat with the failure of the Jacobite cause.

Even late in the century, the law treated Catholics unequally. They paid a double land tax. They could not hold public office or military commissions. They could not succeed to the throne of England. They could not vote or own weapons. If they chose to be educated in a foreign country (a logical course of action given that they were forbidden to attend the British universities), they could be forced to forfeit their property. They could not purchase land. Their priests were treated as felons under the law.

These last three disabilities were removed in 1778 by the Catholic Relief Act, and the popular response was, if not swift, certainly terrible. Scots rioted so vigorously that the act could not be enforced. In England, Lord George Gordon's Protestant Association organized a march to Parliament on June 2, 1780, which swelled to "upwards of 50,000 true Protestants"[18] and quickly turned violent. For nearly a week, the mob burned and pillaged the homes, chapels, and businesses of Roman Catholics, then turned to other targets. The riot was halted only by a royal proclamation on June 7, the reading of the Riot Act on June 8, and repeated firing into the crowds.

In the face of such hatred, Catholics could hardly hope to capitalize upon the inertia of the established church. At best, they might hope to maintain their numbers and earn, little by little, the respect and tolerance of their near neighbors. Maintaining numbers alone was difficult: in 1720, England had 115,000 resident Catholics; by 1780, there were only 69,000.[19] About a third of these lived in Lancashire, where there were 23,000 Catholics in 1767. Another 11,000 lived in London.[20] Most Catholics were country gentry who found the legal restrictions especially irksome and the temptation to turn Protestant especially strong. Late in the century Catholicism became associated with Irish laborers working in England.

METHODISM

It was not Catholicism that attracted those on the Anglican fringe, but Dissent, and the most successful new Dissenting or Nonconformist sect of the 18th century actually began as a part of the Anglican Church. Brothers John and Charles Wesley, with other divinity students, founded the Holy Club at Oxford in 1729 and were joined in 1732 by George Whitefield. They developed a system of devotion, charity, and evangelism that came to be known as Methodism. In 1739 Whitefield was denied a pulpit from which to preach his unorthodox views, but he turned the setback into an advantage, taking his message directly to the people in a series of open-air sermons. John Wesley joined him in field preaching, delivering about 40,000 such sermons between 1739 and 1791, and traveling nearly 25,000 miles on his journeys through England.[21] Wesley tried earnestly to keep the Methodist movement within the Church of England. A Tory, a royalist, and a stout opponent of Dissent, he insisted that Methodists attend Anglican services. Only in 1784, seven years before his death, did he begin ordaining his own priests, in defiance of the Anglican Church, and then only because Anglican bishops had refused for years to ordain Methodist candidates.[22]

Methodism, as it operated under Wesley, was thoroughly autocratic. Each "class" of a dozen or so worshippers was headed by an appointed leader. The classes belonged to larger "bands," segregated by sex and marital status, which sent delegates to an annual conference. The conference was not designed for discussion or debate but for the issuance of decrees by Wesley himself, who reinforced his commands by visiting the local congregations personally, or by sending a lay preacher in his stead.[23]

Wesley's vision was of poor, itinerant, evangelist priests—which offended clergymen with comfortable livings and good wine cellars—and spiritually enthusiastic, even ecstatic, congregations. Sermons, full of the agonies of hell and the unfathomable joys of heaven, were designed to evoke emotion rather than abstract theological speculation. Enthusiasm for any cause was a target of mockery in the 18th century, and enemies of the new sect harped on the supposed frenzies of worshippers. Wesley was also at odds with genteel intellectual fashion: he believed firmly in the existence of witches and, despite the trend toward revering the innocence of childhood, thought children were best raised with little or no play and plenty of good old-fashioned flogging.

Methodism was quite successful, in large part because it targeted the groups usually overlooked by the tithe-conscious church—the supposedly "ungovernable" Kingswood Forest colliers and Cornish tinners,[24] the poor workers of industrial cities and suburbs, servants, and women. One of the most notable leaders of Methodism in the 18th century, in fact, was a woman, Lady Huntingdon, who, by virtue of her social position and firm will, did more than any other person to make Methodism acceptable to the gentry. By late in the century, Methodism was well-established; there were only 24,000 Methodists in 1767, but 77,000 by 1796.[25] The number may seem small compared to the number of Anglicans in the nation, but Methodism's rapid growth unsettled the majority.

Methodism met with all sorts of opponents. Some merely expressed disgust for it; hymn author Augustus Toplady called it "an equal portion of gross heathenism, Pelagianism, Mahometanism, popery, Manichaeism, ranterism, and antinomianism."[26] The duchess of Buckingham despised its insistence that even aristocrats were sinful, a view she found "highly offensive and insulting and at variance with high rank and good breeding."[27] Many a professional or amateur theologian published a tract denouncing "Pope John," as Wesley's enemies called him. William Hogarth painted a vicious satire (a sequel to his milder satire of a sleeping Anglican congregation) that lumped George Whitefield's chapel together with various famous religious hoaxes. Evan Lloyd composed "The Methodist," a poem that accused workers of abandoning their duties to become useless and deceptive lay preachers. "The bricklay'r," he says, "throws his trowel by,/And now builds mansions in the sky."[28]

Some found stronger means of opposition. Magistrates read the Riot Act to sermon attenders, encouraged mobs to harass Methodists, and, in at least one case, had a lay preacher impressed into the military. Employers dismissed servants who attended Methodist meetings. Mobs, especially in the 1740s, threw bricks and stones at Methodist preachers; the first to die as a result was William Seward, who was killed at Hay on Wye in 1742. Even after the violence subsided and Methodism became more widely tolerated, mobs sometimes disrupted services by playing games and music directly outside or by releasing dogs among the worshippers.[29] This behavior was typical of 18th-century England's religious majority; it was fine to let others be different, as long as they were reminded occasionally who was in power.

DISSENT

The laws regarding Dissenters, like those regarding Catholics, granted tolerance but not full civil rights. The Toleration Act gave them the right to set up their own chapels, though they still had to pay Anglican tithes. They could also (unlike Catholics) set up their own religious academies, carry weapons, and vote. But unless they were willing to take Anglican communion once a year, they were barred from holding public office by the Test and Corporation Acts. Most Dissenters with political ambitions chose occasional conformity, and in some areas Dissenters developed powerful political machines. Nonetheless, by the end of the century, Dissenters had grown increasingly impatient with Parliament for failing to award them equal citizenship. Throughout the century, too, they faced the same kind of harassment as Catholics and Methodists, though usually to a lesser extent. Riots started for other purposes often turned to the homes and businesses of Dissenters, and there was public disapproval for any Dissenting sect that seemed too enthusiastic.

If the Church of England primarily served the gentry and Methodism the poor, Dissent aimed at the prosperous and growing middle class. In general, Dissenters were Whiggish and urban, and likely to be professionals, intellectuals, entrepreneurs, weavers, and reformers. Their ministers were usually hired by church elders, who were among the most prosperous members and who sometimes paid a guinea a year for the privilege of a vote. The congregation paid its ministers directly, and wealthy members of the meeting, like wealthy Anglicans, sometimes bought box pews in front for their families. Since Dissenters also had to pay tithes to the Anglican parish priest, whether they attended his services or not, Dissenting ministers often received paltry pay and had to take second jobs.

The sheer number of openly practiced faiths in England, particularly in London, was both dazzling and baffling to contemporaries. Membership in such sects was always in flux, as one group was seduced from plainness to worldly trifles, or as another split over doctrine, or as another gained members by force of oratory. There were Congregationalists (or Independents) and Baptists, who doubled in number between 1750 and 1790;[30] Quakers, noted for their plain dress, their requirement that members marry within the faith, their use of "thee," and their shocking tendency to let women preach; Moravians, who inspired the Methodists in the 1720s but split with them in the 1740s; Sandemanians; Antinomians; Swedenborgians; Muggletonians; Unitarians, whose liberal faith, popular with scientists, writers, and educators, rejected miracles and the Trinity; Presbyterians, from whose ranks Unitarians originally emerged; Lutherans; Calvinists; and Arians. There were also the fleeting fringe groups led by individual prophets or lunatics, depending on the perspective of the observer: Druid cults and millenialism like that of George Bell, who predicted the end of the world on February 28, 1763, or of Joanna Southcott, who claimed she would give birth to the son of God and who sold "seals" that guaranteed entrance into heaven.

Dissent was highly successful by some measures; by 1812 its chapels outnumbered parish churches in London, 256 to 186.[31] Yet a relaxation of Anglican oppression actually made Dissent less attractive to some, and the civil rights associated with the majority religion seduced many Dissenters from more austere faiths. When the century began, there were four main groups of "Old Dissenters": 179,000 Presbyterians, 59,000 Congregationalists, 58,000 Baptists, and 38,000 Quakers.[32] Some of these sects lost membership over the course of the century, including the Quakers, whose number had decreased to 20,000 by 1800.[33] Hampshire had only two Presbyterian chapels in 1812, down from forty in 1729.[34] However, Nonconformists were hardly extinguished. Some older sects which had lost members in midcentury regained some of their losses, and some newer sects rose from fringe to mainstream status.

JUDAISM

Eighteenth-century England was also home to perhaps 20,000 Jews, most of whom lived in London's East End.[35] Most upper-class Jews were Sephardim; most lower-class Jews, Ashkenazim. They were specifically exempted from certain laws that would have required compliance with Anglican ritual, for example the Marriage Act of 1753, and from time to time, despite laws to the contrary, they even held public office. Jews were sometimes defended by MPs like Edmund Burke, who declared, "If Britons are injured, Britons have armies and laws to fly to for protection and justice. But the Jews have no such power and no such friend to depend on. Humanity then must become their protector and ally."[36] Even though anti-Semitism probably declined over the century, there were still plenty of instances of Jews being "hooted, hunted, cuffed, pulled by the beard and spat upon."[37] A Jewish Naturalization Act, passed in 1753 and designed to offer citizenship to individual Jews by later acts of Parliament, was met by virulent anti-Semitic tracts and mob demonstrations. It was repealed in 1754. A few Jews, like the wealthy financier Sampson Gideon, renounced their faith in order to further their ambitions, and a few Anglicans, like the Lord George Gordon whose Protestant Association started the Gordon Riots, converted to Judaism. Overall, though, the Jewish community remained closed, intact, and relatively stable.

THE ROLE OF RELIGION

People of all faiths were daily reminded of the presence of religion. Religious tracts, pamphlets, magazines, sermons, novels, chapbooks, and almanacs were reliable sellers. Religious books of one kind or another were the largest segment of publishers' lists,[38] with the Bible and John Foxe's *Book of Martyrs* available in a variety of editions. Rioters used Biblical imagery in their threats and demands. The church or chapel was no longer the sole center of community social life, but the chief holidays were still those associated with the church—Good Friday, Easter, Christmas, Twelfth Night, and Shrove Tuesday. Especially in Dissenting communities, the chapel might also be a financial center, distributing small loans to businessmen.

For most, the sabbath was Sunday, and even those who failed to attend services knew that Sunday was special: most work and travel ceased; George III put an end to Court dinners on Sunday; drinking alcohol during church hours was forbidden, with the penalty being time in the stocks;[39] and public entertainments, such as the display of a working guillotine at the Haymarket in 1793, were banned.[40] Though increasing numbers of people regarded Sunday as a day of play rather than prayer, prayer was a ritual for most "respectable" people each day.

For the middle and upper classes, religion often stimulated charity and reform. Various sects, acting alone or in cooperation with each other, founded charity schools, monitored prison conditions, worked for the abolition of slavery, ministered to the sick in hospitals, published tracts for the poor, prosecuted sabbath breakers and blasphemers, and opposed pornography and prostitution. For the lower class, religion meant the opportunity to benefit from the aforementioned charities, but it also meant the suppression of some of their favorite pastimes—drinking, gaming, and riotous fairs and festivals.

Religious or quasi-religious superstitions abounded. According to tradition, christening prevented illness, confirmation cured rheumatism, Good Friday bread had magical healing powers, putting any book but a prayer book on top of a Bible was bad luck, and saying one's prayers at the foot of the bed was bad luck as well.

Eighteenth-century England was a religious nation, in that almost everyone subscribed to a faith and was affected on a daily basis by religion. It was, however, a nation inclined to secularism, with science, overall lack of interest in worship, a largely indifferent government, and the materialism of the Anglican clergy each playing a part in the heyday of "rational religion." Few civil rights victories were achieved during the century by the minority religions, but there were no significant net losses of rights either; the established church lost some battles and won others but largely held its ground without torture, mass imprisonments, or authorized pogroms. It was a time and place, compared to, say, medieval France, or 18th-century Spain, or late 20th-century Iran, of astounding diversity of religious views. Jew and Gentile, Catholic and Protestant, Methodist and Anglican, Quaker and Baptist, and even the occasional Muslim, Druid, and atheist lived together with some mutual harassment but, for the most part, without killing each other. It was no small achievement.

TIMELINE

1689	The Toleration Act is passed.
1717	Convocation is prorogued.
1718	The Occasional Conformity Act (1710) and Schism Act (1714), which penalized Dissenters, are repealed.
1723	The Crown establishes a fund for the support of Dissenting ministers.
1729	The first Methodist meetings are held at Oxford.
	George II announces that he will favor men of genteel birth in assigning clerical livings.
1736	Repeal of the Test and Corporation Acts is defeated.

The Quaker Tithe Bill is defeated. It would have given summary authority to local magistrates in cases of Quakers who refused to pay Anglican tithes, sparing the Quakers long and expensive lawsuits in higher courts.

William Warburton publishes his popular and influential tract, *Alliance between Church and State*, a defense of the links between the Anglican Church and government.

1748	Lady Huntingdon's house is opened for Methodist preaching.
1753	The Jewish Naturalization Act is passed (repealed 1754).
1766	Evan Lloyd's satire *The Methodist* is published.
1774	Theophilus Lindsey's Unitarian Chapel is opened.
1778	The Catholic Relief Act is passed.
	The *Arminian Magazine*, the official publication of Methodism, is founded.
1789	The Great Synagogue is built in London for German and Polish Jews.
1791	John Wesley dies.
1829	Legislation allows Catholics to vote for the first time since they were disfranchised in the late 17th century.

19

Orreries, Dephlogisticated Air, and Spinning Jennies: Science and Technology

Everything yields to experiment.

—Josiah Wedgwood

Before the 18th century, a potter like Josiah Wedgwood would probably have had no interest at all in scientific method. By 1800, however, science and its proponents had changed dramatically. Interest in science spread widely among professionals, laborers, and women, with the result that many of the century's scientists made their living by other means. Erasmus Darwin was a physician, Joseph Priestley a Nonconformist clergyman, James Watt an industrial entrepreneur, astronomer John Michell a church rector, chemist James Keir a glassmaker, and chemist John Dalton a tutor. And technological achievements led to the industrial revolution, which altered work patterns unchanged for centuries.

Science was producing amazing results so rapidly that the popular imagination was almost overwhelmed by the pace of change. To keep up, people bought encyclopedias, scientific journals, and foreign scientific texts in translation. Encouraging invention became a patriotic cause. The government permitted inventors to patent their devices, and private organizations offered prizes for useful inventions, sometimes with the stipulation that they remain unpatented and therefore available to British industry as a whole. People went to lectures, watched displays of electricity, ogled steam engines, developed an appreciation for the natural world, marveled at creatures and plants from all over the world, and believed as readily in plausible nonsense as in scientific fact. A rapping ghost, a woman giving birth to rabbits, and a substance with negative weight permeating flammable objects were no less remarkable, even to people of learning, than a loom that did the work of fifty people, a new planet in the sky, or water created by an electric spark. It would take time and experiment to separate the false from the true.

PHYSICS AND CHEMISTRY

Those who studied physical phenomena and forces—they were not yet called physicists—began the century with a knowledge of vacuums, gravity, inertia, and acceleration. Their instruments included barometers, thermometers, and pendula. They supposed, as many had before them, that matter was composed of very small particles called atoms, though the structure of the atom was much debated. John Dalton, for example, thought that each element's atoms were made of fundamentally different material, surrounded by a layer of heat whose thickness was inversely related to density. A gaseous substance's atom, therefore, would have a thick layer of heat keeping it at a distance from other atoms, while a solid would have only a thin layer of heat around its atoms.[1] Physicists and mathematicians alike revered the memory of Sir Isaac Newton, who was eulogized in a 1727 poem for his work on the relationship of moon and tides, gravitational forces, comet trajectories, sound waves, and optics.

> But who can number up his labours? who
> His high discoveries sing? When but a few
> Of the deep-studying race can stretch their minds
> To what he knew[2]

Newton, however, did little important work in the 18th century. The most significant developments of the 1700s were in the study of electricity: Benjamin Franklin's discovery of its relationship to lightning in 1749 and his invention of the lightning rod, which George III ordered installed on the Buckingham Palace roof;[3] Priestley's work with the attraction and repulsion of electrical charges; and Priestley's discovery, verified by Henry Cavendish in 1784, that an electrical spark could create water from oxygen and hydrogen.[4]

The harnessing of electricity was to revolutionize the way in which experiments were performed, and in chemistry a revolution was under way. Chemists had for centuries believed that the four basic irreducible elements were Earth, Air, Fire, and Water. At the beginning of the 18th century, they also believed that a substance called phlogiston was found in flammable bodies. Materials would burn until all their phlogiston was gone, or until the surrounding air was too saturated with phlogiston to absorb any more.

These beliefs were largely eradicated by century's end. Air, for example, was discovered to be composed of several different kinds of gases (which were still often called "airs"). In 1727 Stephen Hales discovered that solids, when heated, released "fixed air." He collected the released gas by feeding it into an upside-down vessel filled with water. The gas ran into the vessel, displacing the heavier water, and rising to the top of the vessel. This technique was later refined by William Brownrigg, who devised a simple "pneumatic trough" that allowed gases to be moved from one flask to another;[5] by Cavendish, who displaced mercury instead of water, to solve the problem of some gases being water soluble; and by the French chemist Antoine-Laurent Lavoisier, who constructed his own highly accurate gasometer.[6]

Although Hales had isolated a gas, he did not realize that it was not elemental air. Soon others began to isolate and describe different kinds of gases. Scottish chemistry professor Joseph Black discovered carbon dioxide (CO_2); because it would not support combustion, it was long known as "phlogisticated air" (air so saturated with phlogiston that flammable bodies could not release any more into it). Many erroneous theories about carbon dioxide were advanced, including Lavoisier's that it caused combustion and Priestley's that it killed plants. Priestley, proven wrong by his friend Thomas Henry, repeated his experiments and discovered that plants actually thrived in the presence of CO_2 but also required sunlight. Continental scientists, at the end of the century, built on this information to construct a theory of photosynthesis.[7]

Other gases discovered in the second half of the century included chlorine, oxygen (called "dephlogisticated air"), carbon monoxide, hydrogen chloride, hydrogen ("inflammable air"),[8] argon,[9] nitrogen (called "mofette" or "azote" by Lavoisier),[10] and nitrous oxide. Oxygen in particular was interesting because it supported combustion, leading Lavoisier to theorize that it contained heat, or "caloric," and that it "burned" carbon-based foods within the body to heat animals and produce CO_2. With mathematician Pierre Laplace, Lavoisier verified his theory of respiration using a guinea pig (giving rise to the phrase "guinea pig" as a generic term for the living subject of an experiment).[11]

The theory that water was an element was disproven as well. Priestley noticed that oxygen and hydrogen, ignited with an electric spark, yielded water. Cavendish duplicated Priestley's findings and reported this to the Royal Society, though there was debate for years over the composition of water. Lavoisier thought it a compound of hydrogen and oxygen; Watt, a combination of "pure air and phlogiston"; and Cavendish, hydrogen and oxygen deprived of their phlogiston. In 1789 two Dutch chemists synthesized and then separated water using electricity, which resolved the matter for most scientists.[12]

At about the same time, the phlogiston theory was coming under attack. The idea that phlogiston was contained in all flammable bodies was plausible only if burned materials *lost* weight as the supposed phlogiston was released into the air. In the 1770s it was established that roasted metals actually *gained* weight. The phlogistonists then invented all sorts of preposterous arguments to explain how a loss of phlogiston could cause a gain in weight. Some thought phlogiston was incorporeal, others that it had negative weight, and others that it somehow buoyed up the flammable materials that contained it.[13]

Lavoisier became skeptical of the phlogiston theory. He concluded that the heat and light released came from the oxygen in the air, not the phlogiston in the metal. In 1785 he launched an all-out attack on phlogiston itself:

> Chemists have made phlogiston a vague principle, which is not strictly defined and which consequently fits all the explanations demanded of it. Sometimes it had weight, sometimes it has not; sometimes it is free fire, sometimes it is fire combined with an earth; sometimes it passes through the pores of vessels, sometimes they are impenetrable to it. . . . It is a veritable Proteus that changes its form every instant![14]

Within about ten years most prominent British scientists had rejected the phlogiston theory. Chief among the diehard phlogistonists was Priestley, who would hold to the discredited theory all his life.[15]

Discounting phlogiston meant that substances like iron and silver could be considered elements. In the 1780s, Lavoisier and others proposed a revised chemical nomenclature, identifying the known elements and basing the names of compounds on their composition. Until this point, substances had derived their names from several languages, including Arabic, Latin, and Hebrew, and from their taste, smell, color, place of origin, discoverer, or use. Thus, copper acetate was "Spanish green"; sulphuric acid, "oil of vitriol"; and zinc oxide, "flowers of zinc." Lavoisier's list of thirty-three elements, published in 1789, contained some errors, such as the inclusion of light and silica as elements, but it was a great improvement nonetheless, and by the end of the century it was widely adopted by British scientists.[16]

The phlogiston controversy was certainly lively, and the isolation of gases was of great importance, but these were not the only preoccupations of British chemists. Some experimented with producing sodium carbonate and sulphuric acid.[17] Robert Boyle, Robert Hooke, and astronomer Edmond Halley studied the salt content of seawater, and Joseph Black studied specific heat capacity—that is, the amount of heat retained by different substances—and latent heat, or "the amount of heat required to bring about a change of state; for example to change boiling water into steam, or ice into water at the freezing point."[18]

ASTRONOMY

Astronomy struggled against a basic lack of precision. Astronomers began the century with telescopes, though not particularly large ones. They accordingly began to map the skies, a difficult procedure because no one knew how far away the stars really were. Astronomer Royal John Flamsteed compiled a catalogue of 3,000 stars,[19] and his successor Halley tracked the orbits of comets, theorizing that sightings in 1531, 1607, and 1682 were of the same comet. It reappeared as he predicted in December 1758, well after his death, and was named for him. The greatest sky-charters of the century were William Herschel and his sister, Caroline. William catalogued 848 double stars and 2,500 nebulae;[20] Caroline discovered eight comets and, in 1790, revised Flamsteed's catalogue.[21]

The Herschels were assisted in their efforts by the improvements made in astronomical equipment. Several noteworthy makers of scientific instruments worked in England, including John Bird, George Graham, and Herschel himself, who built large telescopes, including a massive forty-foot reflector with a forty-eight-inch mirror that weighed half a ton. The second night after its installation in August 1789, the telescope revealed a new moon around Saturn. Herschel, who had recently submitted a paper to the Royal Society, dashed off an addendum to the president, Sir Joseph Banks: "P.S. Saturn has six satellites. 40-feet reflector." Herschel was already famous for finding new bodies in the solar system. It was he, in 1781, who discovered a sixth planet, which he wanted to name Georgium Sidus (George Star) in honor of George III. Others suggested Neptune, Neptune de George III, Neptune de Grand-Bretagne, and Herschelium, before most astronomers agreed to call it Uranus. It was sixty years before all the alternates were abandoned, and to this day there are two symbols for the planet.[22]

Those not engaged principally in charting the skies studied a variety of other phenomena, including sun spots,[23] the velocity of light, the influence of gravitation on light,[24] the shape of the universe, the shape and nature of the Milky Way, the small "nodding" of the Earth on its axis caused by the moon's gravitational pull, and the possibility of the existence of other galaxies. While exact distances to the stars could not yet be determined, some rough guesses about distance were made. William Herschel determined, from the apparent motion of a selection of stars, the direction in which the solar system moves through the universe.[25]

19.1 "Sir William Herschel Exhibiting His Great Telescope to George III at Slough," John Inigo Richards, 1782. Herschel climbs a scaffold to demonstrate the workings of the telescope, which is apparently kept outdoors. Courtesy of the Print Collection, Lewis Walpole Library, Yale University.

He also determined that there were two types of nebulae—those composed of a cloud of gas lit by a single star, and those composed of groups of stars that appeared to inferior telescopes to be large white blobs.[26]

LIFE SCIENCES AND GEOLOGY

Later in the century, popular interest shifted from physics, astronomy, and chemistry to earth sciences, such as botany and zoology. Early in the century, Sweden's Karl Linnaeus had revised the taxonomy of these sciences, and Captain James Cook's voyages, with the wealth of species they brought to British attention, spurred enthusiasts to collect and classify specimens. Naturalist Sir Joseph Banks, who accompanied Cook's first voyage, returned with about 30,000 plant and animal specimens, discovered about 2,400 new plant and animal species (including the Australian shrub *Banksia*, named for him), and became one of the most famous people in Britain. It was the amazing abundance of new species he found at one Australian spot that prompted Cook, in 1770, to name it Botany Bay.[27] A nationwide interest in the study of plants was stimulated by these discoveries, as well as by George III's personal interest in the subject,[28] the obvious agricultural and economic benefits, and a fashionable respect for nature.

Studies of animal life usually tried to fit animals and their behavior into a Divine plan. Fossils seemed to point to the change and extinction of species, but this was felt to be inconsistent with the Christian story of creation, and the idea of a species differentiating into an entirely new species was only tentatively proposed, at century's end, by a distinct minority.[29] The general assumption was that all species had existed since the Flood, so little attention was paid to what animals might have been like in the past. Instead, there were studies of how animal populations were maintained, how animals reproduced, and how animals interacted with their environment. The last subject was of particular interest to farmers, who routinely killed the birds in their fields, in the belief that the birds were eating the crops. Richard Bradley, an observer in the early part of the century, urged them not to do so because he had noted that the birds also ate harmful insects.[30] The increasing interest in animal life led to popular displays of fleas under microscopes[31] and to the invention of the butterfly net.[32]

Cook's voyages contributed as much to geography as to botany and zoology. His first voyage took him to Brazil, Tahiti, Bora-Bora, New Zealand, Australia, Jakarta, and South Africa,[33] and he successfully used the new chronometer invented by John Harrison. This device, designed to win a £20,000 prize, allowed time on board ship to be compared to the time at the Greenwich Royal Observatory, and thus enabled calculation of the ship's longitude. Cook's voyages also disproved theories of a huge undiscovered southern continent of comparable size to the northern ones. While Australia was a spectacular discovery, it hardly served to "balance" the globe. By 1800, though the polar regions and the interiors of Africa and the Americas remained largely uncharted, the world's coastlines had been mapped and the shape of the earth itself better described.[34]

In geology, the chief controversy was over the mechanism by which mountains were formed. It had been observed that mountains were often composed of a granite core, covered with sedimentary layers of increasing thickness towards the base. Neptunists claimed that the granite was older than the sedimentary layers, which had been deposited by the primeval Flood as it receded. Plutonists claimed that the granite was newer, thrust up from below the sedimentary layers by volcanic activity, with the upper sedimentary layers being eroded to reveal the granite core at the summit.[35]

THE IMPACT OF SCIENCE AND TECHNOLOGY

Power Sources Not everyone debated the origins of mountains, of course, but science and technology in general had an definite effect on everyday life. At the beginning of the century, power sources were limited. Grain and textile mills, pumps, and bellows, had to be driven literally by horsepower, windmills, or water-wheels, each of which had its drawbacks. Waterwheels, for example, yielded the greatest and most consistent power, but they could be used only where there was a suitable river.[36] Fossil fuels had yet not been widely exploited, and the iron industry alone annually used 300,000 loads of timber, mostly oak, which was first laboriously converted into charcoal and then burned to smelt iron from ore. With England's timber resources in serious jeopardy, the Darby family of Coalbrookdale developed a technique for smelting iron using coal (coke) instead of charcoal. The technique spread slowly, partly because the Darbys carefully guarded their secret process, and partly because charcoal prices remained low. When prices rose, coal became more popular, and it was the dominant blast-furnace fuel by 1800.[37]

Coke smelting, which allowed iron parts to take more stress, improved the quality of the iron produced, Landowners all across Britain hunted on their property for coal, and, if they found it, feverishly constructed mines and built canals to transport the coal to iron foundries. The problem was that coal mines could be dug only so deep before they filled with water, and the pumping systems available early in the century were inadequate to the task. It was a fortunate conjunction indeed that placed a coal mine just the right distance from a river to turn a waterwheel to power a pump. There were similar problems with the bellows used in the blast furnaces.

Fortunately, several inventors developed steam-driven engines capable of driving air and water pumps. Thomas Savery's engine, a water pump demonstrated in 1699, created a vacuum inside an iron vessel by passing steam through it and then cooling the outside of the vessel with water. The vacuum drew water up through a pipe, and then more steam was used to drive the pumped water out into a trough. Savery's engine did not achieve wide usage because it worked by means of atmospheric pressure and thus limited the effective length of the pipe to ten meters (not much use for deep mines) because the poor quality of early 18th-century iron limited the strength of the vacuum vessel and because the repeated heating and cooling of the vessel wasted energy.[38] Thomas Newcomen improved on Savery's design by building a five-horsepower engine in 1712. It had a beam with a piston on one end and a pump rod on the other. Steam was pumped under the piston and cooled to create a vacuum, pulling the piston down and pumping water up.[39] From 1715 to 1733, ninety-four of these engines were installed in Great Britain,[40] and the design remained dominant until the last quarter of the century. It was cheap, ran on poor-quality waste coal from the mine it served, could be adapted to drive a waterwheel,[41] and could be easily and safely enlarged to raise more water to a greater height.[42] It was still not tremendously efficient, but a large version built by John Smeaton generated seventy-six horsepower.[43] Mine shafts could now be driven as deep as 100 fathoms.[44] More coal enabled more smelting at higher temperatures, yielding better metal, and thus more and better parts for more and better engines. Mining, smelting, and engine design thus drove each other; each improvement in one area led to greater efficiency in the others.

This interaction was encouraged by the invention of an even more efficient, but more expensive, steam engine by James Watt. However, steam power became popular largely despite, rather than because of, Watt and his partners. Watt feared a fatal boiler accident and the injury it would do to his engine's reputation. Therefore, he deliberately avoided building the type of powerful, high-pressure engines that would ultimately come to replace the old waterwheels and horse gins for good.[45] His desires were thwarted by his competitors, who began to turn out high-pressure engines. By the end of the century, there were more than 2,000 steam engines in Great Britain, most of them in mines, quarries, and textile mills,[46] with others being used to grind flour, pump water, and perform other industrial tasks. Poems lauded the steam engine and its creators, floridly describing the workings of "boiling cauldrons" propelling mine-drowning water "foaming to the sky."

> Sagacious Savery! Taught by thee
> Discordant elements agree,
> Fire, water, air, heat, cold unite,
> And listed in one service fight;
> Pure streams to thirsty cities send,
> Or deepest mines from floods defend.
> Man's richest gift thy work will shine;
> Rome's aqueducts were poor to thine![47]

The Textile Industry

By contrast, the developments in the textile industry attracted both positive and negative attention. Carding machines were invented by Lewis Paul in 1748 and Richard Arkwright in 1775.[48] Spinning moved from the human-powered wheel to spinning machines with rollers; the first, invented in 1738 by Lewis Paul and John Wyatt, spun thread "Without the tedious toil of needless hands,"[49] though it was never a commercial success. Better machines were Arkwright's "water frame," patented in 1769, and James Hargreaves' "spinning jenny," patented in 1770. In 1779 Samuel Crompton invented a spinning "mule," which could process cotton twenty-five times faster than hand spinners. By 1795 power mules with multiple spindles were processing cotton about seven times as fast as Crompton's original machine.[50]

Weaving, too, was being mechanized. Moving the weft thread across the loom, a time-consuming process done by hand, and limited by the weaver's speed and the length of his arms, was sped up and made more efficient by John Kay's fly shuttle, which sent the bobbin zooming across the loom from one box to another.[51] Clergyman Edmund Cartwright designed a power loom in the 1780s. By the end of the century, textile making as a cottage industry was on its last legs, as machines became too big and expensive to be owned by individual spinners and weavers.

The mechanization of spinning and weaving was one of the wonders of the 18th century, but there were others. Inventors were creating new types of candle holders, fire escapes, thermometers, pneumatic brakes for shipyard cranes,[52] carriages, farm tools, lathes, umbrellas, roller skates, wheelchairs, and musical instruments.[53] William Addis invented the toothbrush; others designed dumbwaiters, bellpulls,[54] and the "teagle"—the world's first elevator.[55] Civil engineer John Smeaton, after studying the trunks of trees, devised the shape of the modern lighthouse and planned the first successful offshore model.[56] Well might a Birmingham resident of 1757 write, "Almost every Master & Manufacturer hath a new invention of his own, & is daily improving on those of others."[57]

Science as Work and Play

Science was becoming more central to British life. Scientific careers multiplied, and more engineers, surveyors, cartographers, instrument makers, and inventors were to be found in England than ever before. Parents, especially in the middle class, demanded that more practical learning, including science, be taught to their children. Despite the objections of critics like James Fordyce, who insisted that women were naturally unsuited to the sciences, a number of scientific books were aimed at women, and the *Ladies Diary*, a women's periodical, posed challenging mathematical problems to its readers.[58] Children's author Sarah Trimmer suggested replacing the "romantic nonsense" of fairy tales with the solid substance of natural history.[59]

Chemistry, botany, and a host of other specialties became chic hobbies. Wealthy men and women, including Sir Ashton Lever, the duchess of Bedford, the dowager duchess of Portland, and Sir Hans Sloane, collected all sorts of specimens: fossils, pigs born with eight legs, crocodiles, monkeys, scorpions, chameleons, foreign costumes, medals, coins, plants, butterflies, fetuses, minerals, coral, seashells, and animal skeletons. Sir Hans Sloane's collection became the core of the British Museum, opened in 1759, and not nearly so accessible to the public then as it is today. To keep away the riffraff, visitors had to buy tickets in person, giving name, social rank, and address, and wait an indefinite period of time before receiving the tickets. This could, in some cases, take months.[60]

Hobbyists also bought scientific toys and instruments—microscopes, telescopes, terrestrial and celestial globes, and orreries. Orreries, named for Charles Boyle, the earl of Orrery, who owned one of the best, were models of the solar system that moved to illustrate planetary orbits, eclipses, and the like.[61] Science enthusiasts also formed clubs and societies to further their interests including the Linnaean Society, a natural history society established when Briton James Smith purchased the late Linnaeus's collection of specimens;[62] the Royal Society of London, which had the most prestige but deferred to social rank as much as to scientific genius;[63] the Royal Institution, which focused on educating the public about science;[64] the Spitalfields Mathematical Society, whose membership was limited to seven squared;[65] the Literary and Philosophical Society of Manchester; and the Lunar Society of Birmingham, which met once a month at the full moon. The Lunar Society's members included Matthew Boulton, James Watt, Josiah Wedgwood, Joseph Priestley, James Keir, Erasmus Darwin, and inventor-educator Richard Lovell Edgeworth.[66]

Many attended scientific lectures and demonstrations, some of which later proved to be fraudulent, like the "automaton" chess player who concealed a human player. Even these frauds, however, served a purpose because they demonstrated how absolute was the public's faith in science and machinery. It was after observing this chess player that Edmund Cartwright decided to construct a power loom, chiding some gentlemen from Manchester who asserted that the task was too difficult: "Now, you will not assert, gentlemen, that it is more difficult to construct a machine that shall weave than one which shall make all the variety of moves which are required" in the game of chess.[67] Mass-produced cloth, steam trains, air travel, and, ultimately, a machine that *can* play chess and win can all be traced back to the 18th century and its profound faith in the value of experiment.

TIMELINE

1676	The Royal Observatory at Greenwich is completed.
1687	Sir Isaac Newton publishes his *Philosophiae naturalis principia mathematica*.
1702	Thomas Savery describes his steam engine in *The Miner's Friend*.

1704	Newton publishes his *Opticks*.
1713	William Derham's *Physico-Theology* argues that animal reproduction rates are balanced by life span, predation, and natural hazards.
1717	The Spitalfields Mathematical Society is founded.
1719	Edmond Halley replaces John Flamsteed as Astronomer Royal.
1727	Stephen Hales publishes *Vegetable Staticks*, which reports his discovery of "fixed air" in solids.
	Newton dies.
1733	John Kay invents the fly shuttle.
1741	Dutchman Hermann Boerhaave's influential *Elementa Chemiae* (1732), which asserts the existence of Aristotle's four elements, is translated into English.
1746	John Roebuck and Samuel Garbett of Birmingham, after observing that lead is not dissolved by sulphuric acid, build a lead-lined chamber to mass-produce the acid.
1753	The British Museum Act creates the British Museum, though it will not open until January 1759.
1754	The Society of Arts is founded to offer prizes to inventors.
1755	John Smeaton designs the world's first successful offshore lighthouse.
1766	Joseph Priestley expounds his Law of Inverse Squares, stating that the attractive or repulsive force between two electrical charges diminishes as the inverse square of the distance between them.
1767	James Hargreaves invents his spinning jenny, but he does not patent it until 1770.
	Priestley publishes a *History and Present State of Electricity*.
1768	Captain James Cook begins his first voyage and returns in 1771. On board are Sir Joseph Banks and botanist Daniel Solander.

1769	James Watt patents his steam engine.
	Richard Arkwright invents the water frame.
1774	Priestley announces his isolation of oxygen, which he calls "dephlogisticated air."
1776	Cook's second voyage begins.
1778	Sir Joseph Banks becomes president of the Royal Society.
1779	The world's first iron bridge is built over England's River Severn.
	Samuel Crompton's mule is invented.
1781	On March 13, William Herschel discovers the planet Uranus.
1784	Watt defines the unit of horsepower as the power required to lift 33,000 pounds one foot in one minute.
1785	French chemist Antoine-Laurent Lavoisier attacks the phlogiston theory.
1787	The first iron ship is built.
1789	William Herschel discovers Saturn's moon Enceladus.
1796	Priestley defends the phlogiston theory in *Considerations on the Doctrine of Phlogiston*.
1797	The influential *Journal of Natural Philosophy, Chemistry and Other Arts* begins publication.
1799	The Royal Institution is founded.
1800	Humphry Davy publishes *Researches, Chemical and Philosophical; Chiefly Concerning Nitrous Oxide . . . and its Respiration.*

Notes

CHAPTER 1

1. Roy Porter, *London: A Social History* (Cambridge, Mass.: Harvard University Press, 1995), 156.

2. Roy Porter, *English Society in the Eighteenth Century* (New York: Penguin Books, 1990), 112, 173; Barbara Tuchman, *The First Salute: A View of the American Revolution* (New York: Alfred A. Knopf, 1988), 146.

3. Porter, *English Society*, 108.

4. Paul Langford, *A Polite and Commercial People: England 1727–1783* (Oxford: Oxford University Press, 1992), 32.

5. Linda Colley, *Britons: Forging the Nation 1707–1837* (New Haven, Conn.: Yale University Press, 1992), 199.

6. Kirstin Olsen, *Chronology of Women's History* (Westport, Conn.: Greenwood Press, 1994), 86.

7. Colley, *Britons*, 202.

8. Quoted in ibid., 200.

9. John Gay, *The Beggar's Opera* (1728), quoted in Langford, *A Polite and Commercial People*, 23.

10. E. P. Thompson, *Customs in Common: Studies in Traditional Popular Culture* (New York: New Press, 1993), 31.

11. Porter, *English Society*, 100.

12. *Middlesex Journal*, 1769, quoted in Porter, *English Society*, 99.

13. Langford, *A Polite and Commercial People*, 703.

14. Porter, *English Society*, 125.

15. Ibid., 106; also Christopher Hibbert, *Redcoats and Rebels: The American Revolution Through British Eyes* (New York: Avon, 1990), 115.

16. Porter, *English Society*, 346; Colley, *Britons*, 318.

17. Colley, *Britons*, 51; Porter, *English Society*, 111.

18. Colley, *Britons*, 109.

19. Ibid., 111.

20. Colley gives the total number of seats as forty-four (p. 49), Langford as forty-two (p. 712).

21. Porter, *English Society*, 109, 111.

22. Langford, *A Polite and Commercial People*, 181–2.

23. Quoted in Porter, *English Society*, 65.

24. Hibbert, *Redcoats and Rebels*, 202.

25. Porter, *English Society*, 155.

26. Langford, *A Polite and Commercial People*, 720.

27. Quoted in Porter, *London*, 157.

28. Colley, *Britons*, 245–7.

29. Ibid., 248–9.

30. Langford, *A Polite and Commercial People*, 526.

31. Hoh-cheung Mui and Lorna H. Mui, *Shops and Shopkeeping in Eighteenth-Century England* (Montreal: McGill-Queen's University Press, 1989), 81.

32. Colley, *Britons*, 208.

33. Porter, *English Society*, 17.

34. Quoted in ibid., 357.

CHAPTER 2

1. Langford, *A Polite and Commercial People*, 64.

2. This number is derived from a total population of 8,700,000 in 1801 (Porter, *English Society*, 207) and Lawrence Stone's figure for title holders in *Road to Divorce: A History of the Making and Breaking of Marriage in England* (Oxford: Oxford University Press, 1995), 258: "The total number of heritable titles in 1800—that is, peers and baronets of England, Scotland, or Ireland, and those holding courtesy titles including that of 'Honourable' (many of them heirs to a title)—was 1,203." An even smaller figure is quoted by Colley in *Britons*, 154, who repeats John Cannon's claim that peers, baronets, and knights at century's end totaled only 0.0000857 percent of the population.

3. Langford, *A Polite and Commercial People*, 597.

4. Porter, *English Society*, 66.

5. Langford, *A Polite and Commercial People*, 598.

6. Porter, *English Society*, 55.

7. Ibid., 66.

8. Ibid., 58, 114, 358–9.

9. Ibid., 85.

10. Ibid., 144; Langford, *A Polite and Commercial People*, 62–3.

11. Langford, *A Polite and Commercial People*, 438, 600–601.

12. Quoted in Porter, *English Society*, 50.

13. Colley, *Britons*, 60–1.

14. Porter, *English Society*, 52, 72, 353.

15. Colley, *Britons*, 190; Porter, *English Society*, 76.

16. Lawrence Stone, *Road to Divorce*; 38.

17. Ibid., 64.

18. Gretchen Gerzina, *Black London: Life Before Emancipation* (New Brunswick, N.J.: Rutgers University Press, 1995), 19.

19. Quoted in Porter, *English Society*, 215.

20. Langford, *A Polite and Commercial People*, 486.

21. Ibid., 66. "Mrs.," by the way, did not always mean that the woman who used it was married. Lady Mary Wortley Montagu, writing in 1709 to Miss Anne Wortley, calls her correspondent "Mrs. Wortley," and in Samuel Richardson's *Pamela* (1740), both the housekeeper Mrs. Jervis and the fifteen-year-old virgin Pamela are called "Mrs." Gerzina, in *Black London*, 51, also notes the significance of Boswell's referring to Dr. Johnson's black servant as "*Mr.* Francis Barber . . . at a time when black men and women were commonly referred to by first name only."

22. This argument is made by several historians, perhaps most notably by E. P. Thompson in the essay "The Moral Economy of the Crowd," reprinted with a chapter of additional comments in his *Customs in Common*.

23. Quoted in Porter, *English Society*, 292.

24. Quoted in ibid., 294.

25. Bishop Watson and Edmund Burke, quoted in ibid., 354.

26. Quoted in ibid., 130.

27. Hannah More, "Half a Loaf Is Better Than No Bread," ll. 67–70, in Roger Lonsdale, ed., *The New Oxford Book of Eighteenth-Century Verse* (Oxford: Oxford University Press, 1987), 809–10.

28. Porter, *English Society*, 300–301.

29. *The Times*, 1795, quoted in ibid., 354–5.

30. Quoted in ibid., 86–7.

31. Ibid., 131.

32. Ibid., 119, 123–5; Langford, *A Polite and Commercial People*, 153.

33. Porter, *English Society*, 129.

34. Ibid., 212.

35. Stone, *Road to Divorce*, 99, 194–5, 232.

36. Porter, *English Society*, 128–9.

37. Ibid., 129.

38. Ibid., 131–2; Langford, *A Polite and Commercial People*, 133, 151; Porter, *London*, 149.

39. Porter, *English Society*, 131–2.

40. Porter, *London*, 149.

41. Quoted in Porter, *English Society*, 132.

42. William Sharp, 1755, quoted in ibid., 291–2.

43. Colley, *Britons*, 59; Porter, *English Society*, 226, 243; Langford, *A Polite and Commercial People*, 142–3.

44. Colley, *Britons*, 91, 97; Langford, *A Polite and Commercial People*, 489; Porter, *London*, 167.

45. Colley, *Britons*, 94–5, 240; Porter, *English Society*, 295, 297.

46. Gerzina, *Black London*, 183.

47. Ibid., 15–6.

48. Ibid., 187.

49. Ibid., 128.
50. Ibid., 178–80; Colley, *Britons*, 350.
51. Colley, *Britons*, 353.
52. Porter gives a figure of 14,000 black Londoners in *English Society* (p. 137); in his *London* (p. 132), he suggests a population of from 5,000 to 10,000. Colley, in *Britons*, lists the British slave population as 9,000 (p. 352) and the entire black population as about 20,000 (p. 355). Gerzina, in *Black London* (p. 5), estimates a black London servant population of about 15,000, based on widely varying contemporary guesses. To these must be added some number of provincial blacks and those who resided in London but were not servants.
53. Gerzina, *Black London*, 89.
54. Ibid., 64.
55. Ibid., 19.
56. Ibid., 136–7.
57. Ibid., 142–73.

CHAPTER 3

1. Stone, *Road to Divorce*, 8–9; Porter, *English Society*, 143.
2. Porter, *English Society*, 150, 266.
3. Maxime de la Falaise, *Seven Centuries of English Cooking*, ed. Arabella Boxer (New York: Barnes & Noble, 1973), 107.
4. Merlin Waterson, *The Servants' Hall* (New York: Pantheon Books, 1980), 49.
5. Porter, *English Society*, 27.
6. Langford, *A Polite and Commercial People*, 581.
7. Ibid., 503.
8. Porter, *English Society*, 273; Richard B. Schwartz, *Daily Life in Johnson's London* (Madison: University of Wisconsin Press, 1985), 175; Matthew Prior, "A Simile" (1706), in Lonsdale, *New Oxford Book of Eighteenth-Century Verse*, 48.
9. Thompson, *Customs in Common*, 367.
10. Olwen Hufton, *The Prospect Before Her: A History of Women in Western Europe 1500–1800* (New York: Alfred A. Knopf, 1996), 159.
11. Ibid., 74; Langford, *A Polite and Commercial People*, 274–5; Richard D. Altick, *The Shows of London* (Cambridge, Mass.: Belknap Press of Harvard University Press, 1978), 51–4; Porter, *English Society*, 239; Schwartz, *Daily Life in Johnson's London*, 39; Mui and Mui, *Shops and Shopkeeping*, 247; Guy Williams, *The Age of Agony: The Art of Healing, 1700–1800* (Chicago: Academy Chicago Publishers, 1996), 184–5; Eric Pawson, *Transport and Economy: The Turnpike Roads of Eighteenth Century Britain* (London: Academic Press, 1977), 191; Thompson, *Customs in Common*, 234; Colley, *Britons*, 82.
12. Hufton, *The Prospect Before Her*, 242.
13. Langford, *A Polite and Commercial People*, 111.
14. Hufton, *The Prospect Before Her*, 446.
15. Langford, *A Polite and Commercial People*, 603–4.
16. Quoted in Porter, *English Society*, 22–3.
17. Quoted in ibid., 293.
18. Thompson, *Customs in Common*, 504.

19. Mary Wollstonecraft, "A Vindication of the Rights of Woman" (1792), in Sandra M. Gilbert and Susan Gubar, eds., *The Norton Anthology of Literature by Women* (New York: W. W. Norton, 1985), 141.

20. Quoted in Langford, *A Polite and Commercial People*, 112.

21. Quoted in Porter, *English Society*, 27.

22. Colley, *Britons*, 159.

23. Quoted in Hufton, *The Prospect Before Her*, 122.

24. Ibid., 106.

25. Quoted in Porter, *English Society*, 145.

26. Hufton, *The Prospect Before Her*, 123.

27. Stone, *Road to Divorce*, 76.

28. Quoted in Porter, *English Society*, 286–7.

29. Thompson, *Customs in Common*, 502.

30. Stone, *Road to Divorce*, 65, 445.

31. Ibid., 74–6.

32. Ibid., 83.

33. Ibid., 61–3.

34. Quoted in John E. Mason, *Gentlefolk in the Making: Studies in the History of English Courtesy Literature and Related Topics from 1531 to 1774* (Philadelphia: University of Pensylvania Press, 1935), 93.

35. Quoted in ibid., 102.

36. Iona Opie and Peter Opie, *The Oxford Dictionary of Nursery Rhymes* (Oxford: Oxford University Press, 1995), 87.

37. Hufton, *The Prospect Before Her*, 108–9.

38. Quoted in Porter, *English Society*, 146.

39. David Garrick and George Colman the Elder, *The Clandestine Marriage and Two Short Plays*, ed. Noel Chevalier (Peterborough, Ontario, Canada: Broadview Press, 1995), 52, 56 (I.i. I.ii).

40. Stone, *Road to Divorce*, 97.

41. Ibid., 52.

42. Porter, *English Society*, 151.

43. Phillis Cunnington and Catherine Lucas, *Costume for Births, Marriages and Deaths* (London: Adam and Charles Black, 1972), 74–5.

44. Edward Chicken, "The Collier's Wedding" (wr. 1729? pub. 173—?), in Lonsdale, *New Oxford Book of Eighteenth-Century Verse*, 216–7.

45. *Newcastle Weekly Courant*, October 2, 1725, quoted in Thompson, *Customs in Common*, 45–6.

46. Cunnington and Lucas, *Costume for Births, Marriages and Deaths*, 64.

47. Thompson, *Customs in Common*, 484–5; Hufton, *The Prospect Before Her*, 138–9.

48. Quoted in Cunnington and Lucas, *Costume for Births, Marriages and Deaths*, 72–3.

49. Stone, *Road To Divorce*, 52–3, 56.

50. Ibid., 96–9.

51. Ibid., 107, 109–15; Cunnington and Lucas, *Costume for Births, Marriages and Deaths*, 88.

52. Stone, *Road to Divorce*, 129.

53. Ibid., 133; Cunnington and Lucas, *Costume for Births, Marriages and Deaths*, 89.

54. Quoted in Porter, *English Society*, 24.

55. Ibid., 24, 286; Stone, *Road to Divorce*, 13, 31, 166, 168–9, 203; Colley, *Britons*, 238; Hufton, *The Prospect Before Her*, 291–2.

56. Colley, *Britons*, 239.

57. Quoted in Stone, *Road to Divorce*, 211.

58. Anonymous ("Brian Bendo"), "The Dream" (1779), ll. 38, 46, in Lonsdale, *New Oxford Book of Eighteenth-Century Verse*, 652–3.

59. Hetty Wright, "Wedlock. A Satire" (wr. c. 1725, pub. 1862), ll. 15–19, 27–30, in ibid., 165.

60. Matthew Prior, "A Reasonable Affliction" (1718), ll. 7–8, in ibid., 57.

61. Quoted in Gerzina, *Black London*, 61.

62. Stone, *Road to Divorce*, 321–5.

63. Ibid., 288. On p. 336, Stone notes that the law was different in Scotland, where the guilty party was barred from remarriage as long as the former spouse was alive.

64. Ibid., 26, 280, 282.

65. Ibid., 132.

66. Ibid., 4–5, 46–7, 150, 166, 195–7.

67. Ibid., 180.

68. Ibid., 143, 153–5, 169, 202–3, 206–10.

69. Ibid., 142–3.

70. Ibid., 429.

71. Ibid., 144–7; Thompson, *Customs in Common*, 419–26, 446–52.

72. Porter, *English Society*, 261–2; Stone, *Road to Divorce*, 252, 259; Langford, *A Polite and Commercial People*, 104, 639.

73. *The Clockmaker's Outcry against the Author of . . . Tristram Shandy* (1760), quoted in Thompson, *Customs in Common*, 354.

74. Quoted in Porter, *English Society*, 25.

75. James Boswell, *The Life of Samuel Johnson* (New York: Everyman's Library, 1992), 350.

76. Thompson, *Customs in Common*, 514.

77. *Gentleman's Magazine* (1751), quoted in Stone, *Road to Divorce*, 241.

78. Stone, *Road to Divorce*, 239–40, 260–1, 430.

79. Ibid., 233.

80. Ibid., 232–3; Langford, *A Polite and Commercial People*, 79; Porter, *English Society*, 264; Schwartz, *Daily Life in Johnson's London*, 79–80.

81. Quoted in Porter, *English Society*, 265.

82. Langford, *A Polite and Commercial People*, 143–4; Porter, *London*, 183; Schwartz, *Daily Life in Johnson's London*, 77; Thompson, *Customs in Common*, 354.

83. Quoted in Porter, *London*, 171.

84. Quoted in ibid., 260.

85. Williams, *Age of Agony*, 137; Porter, *English Society*, 27, 147; Schwartz, *Daily Life in Johnson's London*, 140.

86. Williams, *Age of Agony*, 5–7; Hufton, *The Prospect Before Her*, 183; Stone, *Road to Divorce*, 62.

87. Porter, *English Society*, 100; Thompson, *Customs in Common*, 492–3, 515; Langford, *A Polite and Commercial People*, 638.

88. Stone, *Road to Divorce*, 193.

89. Randolph Trumbach, "The Birth of the Queen: Sodomy and the Emergence of Gender Equality in Modern Culture, 1660–1750," in *Hidden from History: Reclaiming the Gay & Lesbian Past*, ed. Martin Bauml Duberman, Martha Vicinus, and George Chauncey, Jr. (New York: New American Library, 1989), 135–9.

90. Ibid., 140; Patrick Pringle, *Hue and Cry: The Story of Henry and John Fielding and Their Bow Street Runners* (New York: William Morrow, n.d.), 22–3.

91. Cunnington and Lucas, *Costume for Births, Marriages and Deaths*, 13–4.

92. Williams, *Age of Agony*, 50.

93. Hufton, *The Prospect Before Her*, 197.

94. Porter, *English Society*, 145.

95. Cunnington and Lucas, *Costume for Births, Marriages and Deaths*, 19.

96. Williams, *Age of Agony*, 50–3.

97. Porter, *English Society*, 29, 267.

98. Joseph Addison, *Spectator*, no. 181, September 27, 1711.

99. Hetty Wright, "To an Infant Expiring the Second Day of Its Birth" (wr. 1728, pub. 1733), ll. 7–10, 19–20, in Lonsdale, *New Oxford Book of Eighteenth-Century Verse*, 166.

100. Porter, *English Society*, 149–50.

101. Ibid., 31, 46, 146; Langford, *A Polite and Commercial People*, 502–3, 659; Schwartz, *Daily Life in Johnson's London*, 40.

102. Quoted in Porter, *English Society*, 197.

103. Opie and Opie, *Oxford Dictionary of Nursery Rhymes*, 61–2, 78–9, 86, 88, 107, 135, 205–6, 231, 272–3.

104. Ibid., 155.

105. Ibid., 181–3.

106. Ibid., 62.

107. Sir Richard Steele, *Spectator*, no. 80, June 1, 1711; Susanna Blamire, "Stoklewath; or, the Cumbrian Village" (wr. c. 1776?, pub. 1842), in Lonsdale, *New Oxford Book of Eighteenth-Century Verse*, 646; John Winstanley, "Miss Betty's Singing Bird" (1742), in Lonsdale, *New Oxford Book of Eighteenth-Century Verse*, 135–6; Porter, *English Society*, 267–8.

108. John Gay, "Trivia: or, the Art of Walking the Streets of London" (1716), Book II, in Lonsdale, *New Oxford Book of Eighteenth-Century Verse*, 121.

109. Colley, *Britons*, 248–9; Langford, *A Polite and Commercial People*, 606–7; Stone, *Road to Divorce*, 2, 109.

CHAPTER 4

1. Langford, *A Polite and Commercial People*, 418; Porter, *English Society*, 334, 361–3; Porter, *London*, 98, 131.

2. Quoted in Porter, *London*, 94.

3. Quoted in ibid., 162.

4. Porter, *English Society*, 226.

5. Ibid., 217.

6. Schwartz, *Daily Life in Johnson's London*, 3.

7. Daniel Defoe, *A Tour Through the Whole Island of Great Britain*, ed. and abridged Pat Rogers (London: Penguin Books, 1986), 313–14.

8. Ibid., 106.

9. Schwartz, *Daily Life in Johnson's London*, 16–17.

10. Porter, in *London* (p. 42), says that deaths exceeded births until about 1780; J. H. Plumb, in *England in the Eighteenth Century* (London: Penguin Books, 1990), on p. 87, says the breakthrough was not made until the 1790s.

11. Langford, *A Polite and Commercial People*, 428.

12. Jonathan Swift, "Description of a City Shower," 1710, 11. 61–3, in Lonsdale, *New Oxford Book of Eighteenth-Century Verse*, 17.

13. Porter, *English Society*, 283; Porter, *London*, 126; Schwartz, *Daily Life in Johnson's London*, 8; Langford, *A Polite and Commercial People*, 428. The Keate quotation is from his *Sketches from Nature* (1779) and appears in Langford, 430.

14. Schwartz, *Daily Life in Johnson's London*, 12

15. Ibid., 3, 117.

16. John Gay, "Trivia: or, the Art of Walking the Streets of London" (1716), Book II, in Lonsdale, *New Oxford Book of Eighteenth-Century Verse*, 123.

17. Quoted in Porter, *London*, 94.

18. Schwartz, *Daily Life in Johnson's London*, 150.

19. Porter, *London*, 138–40.

20. Donald Cardwell, *The Norton History of Technology* (New York: W. W. Norton, 1995), 133; Schwartz, *Daily Life in Johnson's London*, 116.

21. Schwartz, *Daily Life in Johnson's London*, 114–5.

22. Ibid., 115.

23. Porter, *English Society*, 125; Porter, *London*, 148–51.

24. Porter, *London*, 157.

25. Schwartz, *Daily Life in Johnson's London*, 10.

26. Al Smith, *Dictionary of City of London Street Names* (New York: Arco Publishing, 1970), 76, 148.

27. Defoe, *Tour*, 303.

28. Altick, *Shows of London*, 93.

29. Schwartz, *Daily Life in Johnson's London*, 18; Smith, *Dictionary of London Street Names*, 158.

30. Langford, *A Polite and Commercial People*, 572; Smith, *Dictionary of London Street Names*, 94.

31. Felix Barker and Peter Jackson, *The History of London in Maps* (New York: Cross River Press, 1992), 41.

32. Defoe, *Tour*, 310.

33. Joseph Addison, *Spectator*, no. 69, May 19, 1711.

34. Defoe, *Tour*, 310.

35. Smith, *Dictionary of London Street Names*, 147.

36. Porter, *London*, 141–2.

37. David Garrick, *Bon Ton; or, High Life Above Stairs* (1775), quoted in Langford, *A Polite and Commercial People*, 601.

38. Porter, *English Society*, 141; Porter, *London*, 95, 132, 140–2; Alexander Pope, "The Alley. An Imitation of Spenser" (1727), 1. 47, in Lonsdale, *New Oxford Book of Eighteenth-Century Verse*, 88.

39. Porter, *London*, 141–2.

40. Quoted in Porter, *London*, 180–1.

41. Ibid., 142.

42. Quoted in Langford, *A Polite and Commercial People*, 422.

43. Altick, *Shows of London*, 101.

44. Quoted in Porter, *London*, 169.

45. Ibid., 99.

46. Altick, *Shows of London*, 25–6; Langford, *A Polite and Commercial People*, 574–5; T. H. Watkins, "The Greening of the Empire: Sir Joseph Banks," *National Geographic* 190, no. 5 (November 1996): 30.

47. James Stuart, *Critical Observations on the Buildings and Improvements of London* (1771), quoted in Langford, *A Polite and Commercial People*, 427.

48. Porter, *London*, 112.

49. Ibid., 106–7.

50. Ibid., 109, 134.

51. Ibid., 104–6, 178; Porter, *English Society*, 264.

52. Altick, *Shows of London*, 96–7; Schwartz, *Daily Life in Johnson's London*, 81; Porter, *London*, 141.

53. Altick, *Shows of London*, 17–9.

54. Quoted in Porter, *London*, 98–9.

55. "The Art of Politics," in Lonsdale, *New Oxford Book of Eighteenth-Century Verse*, 220.

56. E. Dower, "The New River Head, a Fragment" (1738), 1. 14, in Lonsdale, *New Oxford Book of Eighteenth-Century Verse*, 312.

57. Quoted in Porter, *London*, 184.

58. John Bancks, "A Description of London" (1738), 11. 21–24, in Lonsdale, *New Oxford Book of Eighteenth-Century Verse*, 275.

CHAPTER 5

1. Porter, *English Society*, 37.

2. John Langton, "Languages and Dialects," in *Atlas of Industrializing Britain 1780–1914*, ed. John Langton and R. J. Morris (London: Methuen, 1986), 202.

3. Langford, *A Polite and Commercial People*, 633–4.

4. Defoe, *Tour*, 230–1, 242–3.

5. Ibid., 221–2, 244–5; Porter, *London*, 134.

6. Defoe, *Tour*, 245.

7. Richard Brinsley Sheridan, *The Rivals*, ed. Alan S. Downer (Arlington Heights, Ill.: Harlan Davidson, 1953), III.iv.

8. Porter, *English Society*, 234; Langford, *A Polite and Commercial People*, 137. All further citations of hospital founding dates in this chapter come from Langford, p. 137, as well.

9. Defoe, *Tour*, 216.

10. Ibid., 255–6, 259.

11. Langford, *A Polite and Commercial People*, 94.

12. Thompson, *Customs in Common*, 365.

13. Mui and Mui, *Shops and Shopkeeping*, 70.

14. Langford, *A Polite and Commercial People*, 106.

15. Porter, *English Society*, 227, 322; Langford, *A Polite and Commercial People*, 106.

16. Quoted in Porter, *English Society*, 227.

17. Defoe, *Tour*, 193, 207, 212, 214–5.

18. Ibid., 199.

19. Porter, *English Society*, 234.

20. Ibid., 205.

21. Defoe, *Tour*, 194, 264; Schwartz, *Daily Life in Johnson's London*, 48.

22. Langford, *A Polite and Commercial People*, 418.

23. Defoe, *Tour*, 266–9.

24. Ibid., 141, 155; Langford, *A Polite and Commercial People*, 633–4; Mui and Mui, *Shops and Shopkeeping*, 163.

25. Porter, *English Society*, 331.

26. Ibid., 43; Philip Riden, "Iron and Steel," in Langton and Morris, *Atlas of Industrializing Britain*, 128.

27. E. H. Hunt, "Wages," in Langton and Morris, *Atlas of Industrializing Britain*, 62; James Dance (later Love), "Cricket. An Heroic Poem" (1744), in Lonsdale, *New Oxford Book of Eighteenth-Century Verse*, 375; Defoe, *Tour*, 145.

28. Langford, *A Polite and Commercial People*, 103–4; Porter, *English Society*, 227–9.

29. Langford, *A Polite and Commercial People*, 423.

30. Defoe, *Tour*, 163, 168–71.

31. Plumb, *England in the Eighteenth Century*, 38.

32. Defoe, *Tour*, 123–5, 165; Porter, *English Society*, 196.

33. Langford, *A Polite and Commercial People*, 418; Defoe, *Tour*, 155.

34. Defoe, *Tour*, 128–31, 139; Porter, *London*, 134.

35. Defoe, *Tour*, 129–30; Mui and Mui, *Shops and Shopkeeping*, 163.

36. Defoe, *Tour*, 141–2.

37. Porter, *English Society*, 43, 89, 200.

38. Porter, *London*, 134; Jeremy Farrell, *Socks and Stockings* (London: B. T. Batsford, 1992), 18; Defoe, *Tour*, 264.

39. Langford, *A Polite and Commercial People*, 419, 431; Mui and Mui, *Shops and Shopkeeping*, 230; Porter, *English Society*, 288.

40. Defoe, *Tour*, 263.

41. Colley, *Britons*, 16.

42. Langford, *A Polite and Commercial People*, 95, 137; Mui and Mui, *Shops and Shopkeeping*, 298–9.

43. Porter, *English Society*, 189, 191, 199, 202, 338–9; Farrell, *Socks and Stockings*, 18; Paul Jennings, *Inns, Ales, and Drinking Customs of Old England* (London: Bracken Books, 1985), 98. Cheshire had 174 people per square mile in 1801.

44. Porter, *English Society*, 43, 201.

45. Defoe, *Tour*, 50–1, 54; Farrell, *Socks and Stockings*, 18.

46. Defoe, *Tour*, 70–1, 83; Porter, *English Society*, 196, 201.

47. Defoe, *Tour*, 77–8.

48. Hunt, "Wages," in Langton and Morris, *Atlas of Industrializing Britain*, 63.

49. Defoe, *Tour*, 83–4, 88–9, 95; Langford, *A Polite and Commercial People*, 165; Porter, *English Society*, 196, 205; Porter, *London*, 134; Mui and Mui, *Shops and*

Shopkeeping, 66; P. R. Mounfield, "Leather Footwear," in Langton and Morris, *Atlas of Industrializing Britain*, 126.

50. Quoted in Porter, *English Society*, 201.

51. Mui and Mui, *Shops and Shopkeeping*, 167, 268–9. Eagleton had 2,359 pounds on hand in July 1784.

52. Defoe, *Tour*, 92–4.

53. Ibid., 100–101; Porter, *English Society*, 213.

54. Langford, *A Polite and Commercial People*, 672.

55. Porter, *English Society*, 93, 149, 197; Langford, *A Polite and Commercial People*, 672; Hunt, "Wages," in Langton and Morris, *Atlas of Industrializing Britain*, 62.

56. Schwartz, *Daily Life in Johnson's London*, 48.

57. Porter, *English Society*, 196; Defoe, *Tour*, 275; Langford, *A Polite and Commercial People*, 423.

58. Porter, *English Society*, 196; Porter, *London*, 134.

59. Helen Simpson, *The London Ritz Book of Afternoon Tea: The Art and Pleasures of Taking Tea* (New York: Arbor House, 1986); Porter, *English Society*, 247.

60. Porter, *London*, 134; Defoe, *Tour*, 262–3; Porter, *English Society*, 188, 200; Mui and Mui, *Shops and Shopkeeping*, 230.

61. Porter, *English Society*, 339.

62. Langford, *A Polite and Commercial People*, 418.

63. James Bisset, "Ramble of the Gods Through Birmingham" (1800), in Lonsdale, *New Oxford Book of Eighteenth-Century Verse*, 837; Porter, *English Society*, 226, 239.

64. Quoted in Jennings, *Inns, Ales, and Drinking Customs*, 242.

65. James Woodhouse, "The Life and Lucubrations of Crispinus Scriblerus" (wr. 1795?–1800?, pub. 1896), in Lonsdale, *New Oxford Book of Eighteenth-Century Verse*, 800.

66. Simpson, *London Ritz Book of Afternoon Tea*, 13.

67. Porter, *English Society*, 195, 323–4.

68. Ibid., 194; Langford, *A Polite and Commercial People*, 472.

69. Mrs. Delany to the duchess of Portland, 1776, quoted in Williams, *The Age of Agony*, 148.

70. Porter, *English Society*, 336.

71. Langford, *A Polite and Commercial People*, 430.

72. Defoe, *Tour*, 51.

73. Porter, *English Society*, 149, 200, 314, 336.

74. Porter, *English Society*, 239.

75. Ibid., 126.

76. Opie and Opie, *Oxford Dictionary of Nursery Rhymes*, 193.

77. Porter, *English Society*, 213; Langford, *A Polite and Commercial People*, 419, 672.

78. Langford, *A Polite and Commercial People*, 551–2, 673–4; Porter, *English Society*, 156, 180.

79. Thompson, *Customs in Common*, 364–5; Porter, *English Society*, 247.

80. Gerzina, *Black London*, 183; Schwartz, *Daily Life in Johnson's London*, 41.

81. Porter, *English Society*, 126, 226, 344.

82. Ibid., 239, 274.

83. Ibid., 127.

84. John Wolcot, "The Royal Tour, and Weymouth Amusements" (1795), in Lonsdale, *New Oxford Book of Eighteenth-Century Verse*, 746.

85. Langford, *A Polite and Commercial People*, 95; Porter, *English Society*, 226.

86. Mui and Mui, *Shops and Shopkeeping*, 89, 130, 231.

87. Langford, *A Polite and Commercial People*, 102; Williams, *Age of Agony*, 149.

88. Porter, *English Society*, 190; Farrell, *Socks and Stockings*, 18.

89. Porter, *English Society*, 35; Colley, *Britons*, 13.

90. *London Magazine*, 1766, pp. 446–7, quoted in Langford, *A Polite and Commercial People*, 476.

91. Colley, *Britons*, 114, 117; Langton, "Languages and Dialects," in Langton and Morris, *Atlas of Industrializing Britain*, 204.

92. Colley, *Britons*, 114–6, 121–2; Langford, *A Polite and Commercial People*, 327–8.

93. Porter, *English Society*, 34–5; Plumb, *England in the Eighteenth Century*, 181.

CHAPTER 6

1. Andrew Byrne, *London's Georgian Houses* (London: Georgian Press, 1986), 161, 176, 184, 194.

2. Porter, *London*, 114–5; Porter, *English Society*, 232, 247.

3. Byrne, *London's Georgian Houses*, 34–5.

4. James Cawthorn, "Of Taste. An Essay" (wr. by 1761, pub. 1771), in Lonsdale, *New Oxford Book of Eighteenth-Century Verse*, 495.

5. Susan Lasdun, *The English Park: Royal, Private & Public* (New York: Vendome Press, 1992), 110.

6. Sally Jeffery, "Architecture," in *The Cambridge Cultural History of Britain: Eighteenth Century Britain*, ed. Boris Ford (Cambridge: Cambridge University Press, 1992), 246–7.

7. Lasdun, *The English Park*, 95; Mark Girouard, *Life in the English Country House* (New Haven, Conn.: Yale University Press, 1978), 219–20.

8. Quoted in Porter, *London*, 109.

9. Porter, *English Society*, xv; Schwartz, *Daily Life in Johnson's London*, 48.

10. Porter, *English Society*, 60.

11. Byrne, *London's Georgian Houses*, 38–9.

12. Quoted in Colman and Garrick, *The Clandestine Marriage*, I.ii., p. 61; Porter, *English Society*, 220.

13. Isaac Ware, *A Complete Body of Architecture* (1756), quoted in Byrne, *London's Georgian Houses*, 160–1.

14. Ibid., 163.

15. Quoted in Porter, *English Society*, 218.

16. Ronald Hope, *A New History of British Shipping* (London: John Murray, 1990), 238–9, 242.

17. Quoted in Porter, *English Society*, 219.

18. Waterson, *The Servants' Hall*, 102–4; Hufton, *The Prospect Before Her*, 84.

19. Girouard, *Life in the English Country House*, 218–9.

20. Ibid., 202–6, 230–1.

21. Ibid., 218–20; Geoffrey Beard, "The Decorative and Useful Arts," in Ford, *Cambridge Cultural History of Britain*, 56.

22. Waterson, *The Servants' Hall*, 28–30, 76–7, 98–9.

23. Quoted in Lasdun, *The English Park*, 84.

24. Quoted in ibid., 71, 84.

25. Ibid., 88, 92, 99. Porter, *English Society*, 246, credits William Kent with the invention of the ha-ha; Langford, *A Polite and Commercial People*, p. 311, credits Charles Bridgeman.

26. Quoted in Porter, *English Society*, 60.

27. Lasdun, *The English Park*, 92–4, 98, 107–8.

28. Garrick and Colman, *The Clandestine Marriage*, II.i, II.ii., pp. 74, 81–2.

29. Quoted in Langford, *A Polite and Commercial People*, 310.

30. Watkins, "The Greening of the Empire," 38; Plumb, *England in the Eighteenth Century*, 19.

31. Cawthorn, "Of Taste," in Lonsdale, *New Oxford Book of Eighteenth-Century Verse*, 495.

32. Schwartz, *Daily Life in Johnson's London*, 106; Plumb, *England in the Eighteenth Century*, 12; Porter, *English Society*, 15, 215; Langford, *A Polite and Commercial People*, 458; John Wright, "The Poor Man's Province" (1727), in Lonsdale, *New Oxford Book of Eighteenth-Century Verse*, 197.

33. Nicholas James, "The Complaints of Poverty" (1742), in Lonsdale, *New Oxford Book of Eighteenth-Century Verse*, 343; John Hawthorn, "The Journey and Observations of a Countryman" (1779), in Lonsdale, *New Oxford Book of Eighteenth-Century Verse*, 654.

34. Jonathan Swift, "Baucis and Philemon. Imitated from the Eighth Book of Ovid" (wr. 1706, pub. 1709), ll. 93–4, in Lonsdale, *New Oxford Book of Eighteenth-Century Verse*, 12–13.

35. Quoted in Porter, *English Society*, 236.

36. Schwartz, *Daily Life in Johnson's London*, 108–9.

37. Langford, *A Polite and Commercial People*, 314, 729–39; Byrne, *London's Georgian Houses*, 38–9; Schwartz, *Daily Life in Johnson's London*, 14.

CHAPTER 7

1. Anne Buck, *Dress in Eighteenth-Century England* (New York: Holmes and Meier, 1979), 146; C. Willett Cunnington and Phillis Cunnington, *Handbook of English Costume in the Eighteenth Century* (Boston: Plays, 1972), 109–10; C. Willett Cunnington and Phillis Cunnington, *The History of Underclothes* (New York: Dover, 1992), 82–3, 177; Norah Waugh, *Corsets and Crinolines* (New York: Theatre Arts Books, 1970), 41.

2. Quoted in Waugh, *Corsets and Crinolines*, 60, 71.

3. Ibid., 47, 62; Cunnington and Cunnington, *Handbook of English Costume*, 39, 106, 114, 145–50; Aileen Ribeiro, *A Visual History of Costume: The Eighteenth Century* (London: B. T. Batsford, 1986), 13–4.

4. Joseph Addison, *The Tatler*, no. 116, January 5, 1710.

5. Quoted in Waugh, *Corsets and Crinolines*, 61, 65.

6. Ibid., 60–1; Cunnington and Cunnington, *Handbook of English Costume*, 27, 146, 148.

7. Quoted in Waugh, *Corsets and Crinolines*, 66–7.

8. Langford, *A Polite and Commercial People*, 602; Phillis Cunnington and Alan Mansfield, *English Costume for Sports and Outdoor Recreation from the Sixteenth to the Nineteenth Centuries* (New York: Barnes & Noble, 1969), 360.

9. Cunnington and Cunnington, *Handbook of English Costume*, 106–7, 109, 138, 140; Anne Buck, *Clothes and the Child: A Handbook of Children's Dress in England 1500–1900* (Carlton, Bedford, England: Ruth Bean Publishers, 1996), 108.

10. Ribeiro, *Visual History of Costume*, 13; Cunnington and Cunnington, *Handbook of English Costume*, 274.

11. Cunnington and Cunnington, *Handbook of English Costume*, 116, 118; Ribeiro, *A Visual History of Costume*, 13.

12. Cunnington and Cunnington, *Handbook of English Costume*, 121, 124, 127.

13. Ibid., 28, 142.

14. Ribeiro, *Visual History of Costume*, 15; Buck, *Dress in Eighteenth-Century England*, 144–6.

15. Waugh, *Corsets and Crinolines*, 45; Cunnington and Cunnington, *Handbook of English Costume*, 310–12; Ribeiro, *A Visual History of Costume*, 15.

16. Cunnington and Cunnington, *Handbook of English Costume*, 164–5.

17. Ibid., 166.

18. Ibid., 153–8.

19. Ibid., 135.

20. "The Female Fancy's Garland," quoted in Waugh, *Corsets and Crinolines*, 62.

21. Cunnington and Cunnington, *Handbook of English Costume*, 28; Schwartz, *Daily Life in Johnson's London*, 128.

22. Richard Corson, *Fashions in Makeup from Ancient to Modern Times* (New York: Universe Books, 1972), 277; Ribeiro, *A Visual History of Costume*, 14–5; Cunnington and Mansfield, *English Costume for Sports*, 332.

23. Schwartz, *Daily Life in Johnson's London*, 130; Cunnington and Cunnington, *Handbook of English Costume*, 384–5.

24. Buck, *Dress in Eighteenth-Century England*, 122–8.

25. Farrell, *Socks and Stockings*, 28, 35, 37, 39; Cunnington and Cunnington, *Handbook of English Costume*, 174.

26. Farrell, *Socks and Stockings*, 27

27. Cunnington and Cunnington, *Handbook of English Costume*, 175.

28. Ibid., 170–4; Gerzina, *Black London*, 82.

29. Cunnington and Cunnington, *Handbook of English Costume*, 142–3, 175–9.

30. Ibid., 144.

31. Ibid., 143.

32. Ibid., 178–9; Gerzina, *Black London*, 82.

33. Corson, *Fashions in Makeup*, 188–90, 203–4, 214, 242; Cunnington and Cunnington, *Handbook of English Costume*, 169–70. The quotations are from Tom Brown, *Letters from the Dead to the Living* (1702), in Corson, 188.

34. *The Gentleman's Magazine* (1732), quoted in Corson, *Fashions in Makeup*, 204.

35. Joseph Addison, *The Spectator*, no. 50, April 27, 1711.

36. Cunnington and Cunnington, *Handbook of English Costume*, 27–8, 168–9; Corson, *Fashions in Makeup*, 206, 260.

37. Jonathan Swift, "A Beautiful Young Nymph Going to Bed" (wr. 1731?,

pub. 1734), 11. 35–6, in Lonsdale, *New Oxford Book of Eighteenth-Century Verse*, 21; Cunnington and Cunnington, *Handbook of English Costume*, 120.

38. Corson, *Fashions in Makeup*, 190, 192.

39. *Lady's Magazine*, 1778, in ibid., 256–7.

40. Ibid., 231–3.

41. Buck, *Clothes and the Child*, 100, 116; Cunnington and Cunnington, *Handbook of English Costume*, 150–3, 160–2.

42. Schwartz, *Daily Life in Johnson's London*, 47–8.

43. Cunnington and Cunnington, *Handbook of English Costume*, 95, 255, 258; Buck, *Dress in Eighteenth-Century England*, 167.

44. Ibid., 96, 258, 260.

45. Thomas D'Urfey, "Dialogue Between Crab and Gillian" (1701), in Lonsdale, *New Oxford Book of Eighteenth-Century Verse*, 5.

46. Cunnington and Cunnington, *Handbook of English Costume*, 89–94, 241–6, 250.

47. Cunnington and Cunnington, *Handbook of English Costume*, 24; Porter, *English Society*, 151; Langford, *A Polite and Commercial People*, 477.

48. Cunnington and Mansfield, *English Costume for Sports*, 15, 17, 142, 153; Cunnington and Cunnington, *Handbook of English Costume*, 87–8, 238–9.

49. Cunnington and Cunnington, *Handbook of English Costume*, 88–9, 239.

50. Cunnington and Cunnington, *History of Underclothes*, 73–8.

51. Cunnington and Cunnington, *Handbook of English Costume*, 222.

52. Ibid. 22, 37, 47, 50, 61–3, 104, 203, 205; Diana de Marly, *Fashion for Men: An Illustrated History* (London: B. T. Batsford, 1989), 64.

53. Cunnington and Cunnington, *Handbook of English Costume*, 47, 186, 189, 208, 210.

54. de Marly, *Fashion for Men*, 59.

55. Cunnington and Cunnington, *Handbook of English Costume*, 193.

56. Ibid., 186.

57. Ibid., 104.

58. Ibid., 103.

59. Quoted in Ribeiro, *Visual History of Costume*, 14.

60. Cunnington and Cunnington, *Handbook of English Costume*, 78, 225; Buck, *Clothes and the Child*, 116.

61. Cunnington and Cunnington, *Handbook of English Costume*, 225; Cunnington and Mansfield, *English Costume for Sports*, 113.

62. Cunnington and Cunnington, *Handbook of English Costume*, 69, 214

63. Ibid., 105, 211–3; Cunnington and Mansfield, *English Costume for Sports*, 113–4.

64. Cunnington and Cunnington, *Handbook of English Costume*, 19, 211; de Marly, *Fashion for Men*, 69.

65. Cunnington and Cunnington, *Handbook of English Costume*, 103, 214.

66. Ibid., 69, 217; Ribeiro, *Visual History of Costume*, 14.

67. *Gentleman's and London Magazine*, quoted in Cunnington and Cunnington, *Handbook of English Costume*, 217.

68. Cunnington and Cunnington, *Handbook of English Costume*, 73, 75, 219–20.

69. Ibid., 66, 83, 234; Farrell, *Socks and Stockings*, 23.

70. Farrell, *Socks and Stockings*, 22–4, 28, 32–4, 39; Cunnington and Cunnington, *Handbook of English Costume*, 26, 82, 232, 234.

71. Cunnington and Cunnington, *Handbook of English Costume*, 24, 79–82, 228–9; Buck, *Dress in Eighteenth-Century England*, 131–2; de Marly, *Fashion for Men*, 61.

72. Cunnington and Cunnington, *Handbook of English Costume*, 260–1; Garrick and Colman, *The Clandestine Marriage*, 71.

73. *The Female Spectator*, 1743, quoted in Cunnington and Cunnington, *Handbook of English Costume*, 103. See also Corson, *Fashions in Makeup*, 217, 237, 241.

74. Cunnington and Cunnington, *Handbook of English Costume*, 75–6, 97, 99–101, 220–2, 261–3; Cunnington and Mansfield, *English Costume for Sports*, 115, 154, 361.

75. Langford, *A Polite and Commercial People*, 576–7; Derek Jarrett, *England in the Age of Hogarth* (New York: Viking Press, 1992), 15; de Marly, *Fashion for Men*, 71–2; Cunnington and Cunnington, *Handbook of English Costume*, 23–4; Farrell, *Socks and Stockings*, 33.

76. Samuel Richardson, *Pamela* (1740), quoted in Buck, *Clothes and the Child*, 32.

77. *The Lady's Magazine*, 1785, quoted in ibid., 32.

78. Ibid., 28, 32–3, 37.

79. Schwartz, *Daily Life in Johnson's London*, 130; Williams, *Age of Agony*, 57.

80. Buck, *Clothes and the Child*, 96, 104–5, 108; Cunnington and Cunnington, *Handbook of English Costume*, 127.

81. de Marly, *Fashion for Men*, 72.

82. Ribeiro, *Visual History of Costume*, 15; Schwartz, *Daily Life in Johnson's London*, 130; Buck, *Clothes and the Child*, 102, 108–10.

83. Buck, *Clothes and the Child*, 112–3; Ribeiro, *Visual History of Costume*, 15.

84. Cunnington and Lucas, *Costume for Births, Marriages and Deaths*, 60–3; Cunnington and Cunnington, *Handbook of English Costume*, 139–40.

85. Cunnington and Cunnington, *Handbook of English Costume*, 217–8.

86. Cunnington and Lucas, *Costume for Births, Marriages and Deaths*, 81.

87. Lou Taylor, *Mourning Dress: A Costume and Social History* (London: George Allen and Unwin, 1983), 106.

88. Ibid., 107–9.

89. Quoted in ibid., 110.

90. Cunnington and Cunnington, *Handbook of English Costume*, 218.

91. Waugh, *Corsets and Crinolines*, 41.

CHAPTER 8

1. Thompson, *Customs in Common*, 363.

2. Benjamin Franklin, "Advice to a Young Tradesman" (1748), in *American Quotations*, ed. Gorton Carruth and Eugene Ehrlich (New York: Wings Books, 1988). Franklin's sentiments were echoed by many an author in England.

3. Thompson, *Customs in Common*, 361.

4. Porter, *London*, 185.

5. Thompson, *Customs in Common*, 392.

6. Williams, *Age of Agony*, 9

7. Robert Tatersal, "The Bricklayer's Labours" (1734), 11. 9–42, in Lonsdale, *New Oxford Book of Eighteenth-Century Verse*, 278–9.

8. Langford, *A Polite and Commercial People*, 601.

9. Alexander Pope, "The Rape of the Lock," Canto I, in Lonsdale, *New Oxford Book of Eighteenth-Century Verse*, 93.

10. Quoted in Porter, *London*, 169.

11. Joseph Addison and Sir Richard Steele, *Tatler*, no. 111, December 24, 1709.

12. Lasdun, *The English Park*, 124–5.

13. Thompson, *Customs in Common*, 372.

14. Altick, *Shows of London*, 95.

15. Porter, *London*, 169.

16. Thompson, *Customs in Common*, 372.

17. Lasdun, *The English Park*, 125.

18. Altick, *Shows of London*, 124.

19. Thompson, *Customs in Common*, 373.

20. Plumb, *England in the Eighteenth Century*, 89.

21. Williams, *Age of Agony*, 91–2, 96.

22. John Gay, "Trivia: or, the Art of Walking the Streets of London," Book II (1716), in Lonsdale, *New Oxford Book of Eighteenth-Century Verse*, 123.

23. Thompson, *Customs in Common*, 51.

24. Boswell, *Life of Samuel Johnson*, 360.

25. Defoe, *Tour*, 166.

26. Porter, *English Society*, 151, 156, 275.

27. Porter, *London*, 134.

28. Porter, *English Society*, 151.

29. Thompson, *Customs in Common*, 64.

30. Ibid., 58.

31. Opie and Opie, *Oxford Dictionary of Nursery Rhymes*, 107.

32. Samuel Bamford, quoted in Porter, *English Society*, 152.

33. Colley, *Britons*, 19.

34. Porter, *English Society*, 153.

35. Defoe, *Tour*, 168, 173.

36. Altick, *Shows of London*, 102.

37. Thompson, *Customs in Common*, 202.

38. Defoe, *Tour*, 81.

39. Mui and Mui, *Shops and Shopkeeping*, 23.

40. Smith, *Dictionary of London Street Names*, 74.

41. Defoe, *Tour*, 102.

42. Ibid., 83–4.

43. Gay, "Trivia," in Lonsdale, *New Oxford Book of Eighteenth-Century Verse*, 124.

44. Defoe, *Tour*, 90.

45. Thompson, *Customs in Common*, 202.

46. Defoe, *Tour*, 51.

47. Ibid., 84.

48. Ibid., 115–6; Thompson, *Customs in Common*, 483–4.

49. Thompson, *Customs in Common*, 481.

50. Defoe, *Tour*, 51, 83–4.
51. Porter, *English Society*, 153–4.
52. Henri Misson, quoted in Porter, *English Society*, 152–3.
53. Langford, *A Polite and Commercial People*, 283–4.
54. Anonymous ("Agricola"), "The D[ave]ntry Wonder" (1757), in Lonsdale, *New Oxford Book of Eighteenth-Century Verse*, 479–80.

CHAPTER 9

1. Langford, *A Polite and Commercial People*, 180; E. H. Hunt, "Wages," in Langton and Morris, *Atlas of Industrializing Britain*, 60–2; Porter, *London*, 132.
2. Colley, *Britons*, 37; Schwartz, *Daily Life in Johnson's London*, 51; Pawson, *Transport and Economy*, 17.
3. Colley, *Britons*, 297.
4. Porter, *English Society*, 38.
5. Stephen Duck, "The Thresher's Labour" (1730), in Lonsdale, *New Oxford Book of Eighteenth-Century Verse*, 224–5.
6. Porter, *English Society*, 208–12; Cardwell, *Norton History of Technology*, 107.
7. Quoted in Porter, *English Society*, 94.
8. Langford, *A Polite and Commercial People*, 434.
9. Ibid., 432–3; Cardwell, *Norton History of Technology*, 108–9.
10. Plumb, *England in the Eighteenth Century*, 82–3; Cardwell, *Norton History of Technology*, 150.
11. Langford, *A Polite and Commercial People*, 64.
12. Stone, *Road to Divorce*, 216–7.
13. Porter, *English Society*, 85.
14. Thompson, *Customs in Common*, 369.
15. Bridget Hill, *Servants: English Domestics in the Eighteenth Century* (Oxford: Clarendon Press, 1996), 115–26; Stone, *Road to Divorce*, 62, 226–7; Langford, *A Polite and Commercial People*, 120.
16. Hill, *Servants*, 128–34.
17. Porter, *English Society*, 136.
18. Hill, *Servants*, 102–3; Stone, *Road to Divorce*, 217–8.
19. Stone, *Road to Divorce*, 217.
20. Porter, *English Society*, 49; Sir Richard Steele, *Spectator*, no. 88, June 11, 1711; Cunnington and Cunnington, *Handbook of English Costume*, 104.
21. Hill, *Servants*, 65–9.
22. Gerzina, *Black London*, 51.
23. Schwartz, *Daily Life in Johnson's London*, 48; Simpson, *London Ritz Book of Afternoon Tea*, 13.
24. Hill, *Servants*, 71–3.
25. Stone, *Road to Divorce*, 214.
26. Hill, *Servants*, 75, 89.
27. Ibid., 5, 106.
28. Ibid., 78–81.
29. Ibid., 80, 85–6; Porter, *English Society*, 90.
30. Hill, *Servants*, 33; Steele, *Spectator*, no. 88, June 11, 1711; Thompson, *Customs in Common*, 369.

31. Hill, *Servants*, 75–6, 98.

32. Ibid., 101; Porter, *English Society*, 90.

33. Hill, *Servants*, 95–7.

34. Stone, *Road to Divorce*, 218; Waterson, *Servants' Hall*, 14.

35. Hill, *Servants*, 101.

36. Ibid., 153.

37. Gerzina, *Black London*, 39; Sheridan, *The Rivals*, I.i.

38. Quoted in Hill, *Servants*, 94.

39. Hill, *Servants*, 44–6, 53, 58; Porter, *English Society*, 87.

40. Jonathan Swift, *Directions to Servants* (New York: Pantheon Books, 1964), 11–30; Gerzina, *Black London*, 37–8.

41. James Kelly, *Scottish Proverbs* (1721), quoted in Opie and Opie, *Oxford Dictionary of Nursery Rhymes*, 136.

42. Hill, *Servants*, 6, citing Patrick Colquhoun's contemporary study.

43. Ibid., 37–9.

44. Ibid., 14, 23–4.

45. Stone, *Road to Divorce*, 213; Gerzina, *Black London*, 32–3.

46. Hill, *Servants*, 11, 14, 22, 24.

47. Waterson, *Servants' Hall*, 25, 102; Farrell, *Socks and Stockings*, 38; Swift, *Directions to Servants*, 99–107.

48. John Dalton, "A Descriptive Poem, Addressed to Two Ladies, at their Return from Viewing the Mines, near Whitehaven" (1755), in Lonsdale, *New Oxford Book of Eighteenth-Century Verse*, 467.

49. Porter, *English Society*, 282, 295, 324, 326–7, 329, 335; Thompson, *Customs in Common*, 394; Cardwell, *Norton History of Technology*, 175.

50. Langford, *A Polite and Commercial People*, 502–3; Schwartz, *Daily Life in Johnson's London*, 40–1; Mary Alcock, "The Chimney Sweeper's Complaint" (wr. by 1798, pub. 1799), in Lonsdale, *New Oxford Book of Eighteenth-Century Verse*, 830–1.

51. Langford, *A Polite and Commercial People*, 338, 629; Colley, *Britons*, 73, 286; Tuchman, *The First Salute*, 134; Christopher Hibbert, *Redcoats and Rebels*, 80.

52. Colley, *Britons*, 287–8.

53. Plumb, *England in the Eighteenth Century*, 45; Porter, *English Society*, 109.

54. Sir Richard Steele, *Spectator*, no. 2, March 2, 1710–1711.

55. Tuchman, *The First Salute*, 111–2, 146–7; Porter, *English Society*, 61.

56. Porter, *English Society*, 114, 136.

57. Ibid., 190; Colley, *Britons*, 168–9, 172, 180.

58. Altick, *Shows of London*, 101.

59. Quoted in Porter, *English Society*, 19.

60. Hibbert, *Redcoats and Rebels*, 167, 183, 222–3.

61. Ibid., 176.

62. Ibid., 81–2.

63. Ibid., 83–4; Porter, *English Society*, 14; Langford, *A Polite and Commercial People*, 64.

64. Hibbert, *Redcoats and Rebels*, 84, 226; Thompson, *Customs in Common*, 479, 485; Williams, *Age of Agony*, 81–2.

65. Colley, *Britons*, 299.

66. Anonymous, "The Soldier that has Seen Service. A Sketch from Nature" (1788), ll. 1–2, in Lonsdale, *New Oxford Book of Eighteenth-Century Verse*, 751.

67. Tuchman, *The First Salute*, 9, 114, 117–20; Cunnington and Cunnington, *Handbook of English Costume*, 104.

68. Lonsdale, *New Oxford Book of Eighteenth-Century Verse*, 482.

69. Tuchman, *The First Salute*, 129; Schwartz, *Daily Life in Johnson's London*, 101.

70. Tuchman, *The First Salute*, 125, 172.

71. Ibid., 110, 117–20; Anonymous ("J. T."), "A Sea-Chaplain's Petition . . . ," in Lonsdale, *New Oxford Book of Eighteenth-Century Verse*, 482.

72. Edward Thompson, "An Humble Wish, Off Porto-Sancto, March 29, 1779" (1783), l. 9, in Lonsdale, *New Oxford Book of Eighteenth-Century Verse*, 667.

73. Mui and Mui, *Shops and Shopkeeping*, 146.

74. Ibid., 47, 56–7.

75. Ibid., 9, 16, 21.

76. Ibid., 33.

77. Ibid., 6; Thompson, *Customs in Common*, 221–2.

78. Langford, *A Polite and Commercial People*, 63.

79. Cardwell, *Norton History of Technology*, 171–2.

80. Thompson, *Customs in Common*, 364–5.

81. Ibid., 211.

82. Plumb, *England in the Eighteenth Century*, 22.

83. Porter, *London*, 140.

84. Mui and Mui, *Shops and Shopkeeping*, 36.

85. Ibid., 240; Altick, *Shows of London*, 30.

86. Porter, *London*, 147.

87. Porter, *English Society*, 78, 321.

88. Mui and Mui, *Shops and Shopkeeping*, 131, 133.

89. Langford, *A Polite and Commercial People*, 180–1; Porter, *English Society*, 85, 87, 89.

90. Thompson, *Customs in Common*, 198, from a Leeds laborer's complaint, 1795.

91. Porter, *English Society*, 197–8, 321–5, 328.

92. César de Saussure, 1727, quoted in ibid., 78.

93. Quoted in ibid., 241.

94. Porter, *English Society*, 242, 245, 248; Langford, *A Polite and Commercial People*, 107.

95. Porter, *English Society*, 246, 249.

96. Ibid., 364–5.

97. Hibbert, *Redcoats and Rebels*, 113.

98. Porter, *English Society*, 107; Langford, *A Polite and Commercial People*, 696. In addition to the 14,000, there were amateur collectors of local taxes, and the numbers of collectors continued to rise, reaching about 20,000 by 1800, according to Porter, *English Society*, 76.

99. Schwartz, *Daily Life in Johnson's London*, 160–1.

100. Langford, *A Polite and Commercial People*, 64.

101. Stone, *Road to Divorce*, 189.

102. Porter, *London*, 149.

103. Anonymous, "Between a Contractor and His Wife" (1775), ll. 108–25, 141–6, in Lonsdale, *New Oxford Book of Eighteenth-Century Verse*, 636–7.

104. Porter, *English Society*, 76, 120.

105. Ibid., 114.

106. Ibid., 300.

107. E. H. Hunt, "Wages," in Langton and Morris, *Atlas of Industrializing Britain*, 62–3, 68. The rate of pay varied widely with location; the eleven counties with the highest rates of pay ranged from 7s. 9d. to 9s. 9d. per week. Wages in the fourteen lowest-paying counties ranged from 5s. 10d. to 6s. 6d.

108. Mui and Mui, *Shops and Shopkeeping*, 112–4. All examples in this table from Mui and Mui, pp. 111–4, are taken from their excerpts of tax assessment records. Some shops were too small, and their owners too poor, to warrant assessment, and larger shopkeepers' income may not have been reported accurately. Also, Mui and Mui obviously could not reproduce every entry in the assessment records. Therefore, the figures given in my table provide a sample or range of samples of income and should not be presumed to denote an absolute maximum or minimum.

109. Porter, *English Society*, 66, 368–9. The lower figure is a c. 1700 minimum; the upper figure is c. 1800; Colquhoun gives an average of £3,000 at the end of the century.

110. Pringle, *Hue and Cry*, 42.

111. Schwartz, *Daily Life in Johnson's London*, 52; Porter, *English Society*, 62, 173, 368. In about 1801, Patrick Colquhoun thought bishops averaged £4,000 a year.

112. Waterson, *Servants' Hall*, 56.

113. Mui and Mui, *Shops and Shopkeeping*, 113–4, 129. The average income of assessed book dealers in York was £180.

114. Porter, *English Society*, 67. The brewing family in question is the Whitbreads'; the family also earned about £22,000 a year from its land holdings.

115. Schwartz, *Daily Life in Johnson's London*, 51.

116. Hill, *Servants*, 25; Waterson, *Servants' Hall*, 169.

117. Mui and Mui, *Shops and Shopkeeping*, 129. The average income of assessed cabinetmakers in York was £180.

118. Waterson, *Servants' Hall*, 56.

119. Porter, *English Society*, 92.

120. Schwartz, *Daily Life in Johnson's London*, 51.

121. Mui and Mui, *Shops and Shopkeeping*, 112–3.

122. Langford, *A Polite and Commercial People*, 64, citing Joseph Massie's contemporary estimates. Massie thought there were 11,000 clergy in this income range, which obviously does not include bishops and the like.

123. Porter, *English Society*, 68, 77, 368–9; Schwartz, *Daily Life in Johnson's London*, 26, 158. The Dissenting figure is Patrick Colquhoun's contemporary average of 2,500 family incomes.

124. Waterson, *Servants' Hall*, 26, 169. By comparison, the coachman at Lord Petre's Essex home received £21 a year in 1763 and £26 5s. a year in 1791, according to John Copeland, *Roads and Their Traffic, 1750–1850* (Newton Abbot, Devon, England: David and Charles, 1968), 145.

125. Schwartz, *Daily Life in Johnson's London*, 51.

126. Ibid., 51.

127. Mui and Mui, *Shops and Shopkeeping*, 129. The average income of York's seven confectioners and fruiterers was £119.

128. Schwartz, *Daily Life in Johnson's London*, 51–2.

129. Ibid., 51.

130. Ibid., 52; Porter, *English Society*, 76–7.

131. Mui and Mui, *Shops and Shopkeeping*, 113–4, 121, 129. The average of twenty-six assessed drapers in York was £184.

132. Langford, *A Polite and Commercial People*, 450.

133. Porter, *English Society*, 197.

134. Langford, *A Polite and Commercial People*, 659.

135. Hill, *Servants*, 87; Schwartz, *Daily Life in Johnson's London*, 51–2.

136. Mui and Mui, *Shops and Shopkeeping*, 113.

137. Porter, *London*, 149.

138. Mui and Mui, *Shops and Shopkeeping*, 112–4, 129. The average of eighteen assessed grocers in York was £200. There were also three "petty grocers" with an average income of £77.

139. Ibid., 114, 129. The average income of the seventeen assessed haberdashers in York was £149.

140. Ibid., 112.

141. Porter, *English Society*, 88.

142. Mui and Mui, *Shops and Shopkeeping*, 113–4.

143. Schwartz, *Daily Life in Johnson's London*, 51–2.

144. Defoe, *Tour*, 262.

145. Langford, *A Polite and Commercial People*, 64, citing Joseph Massie's contemporary estimate. Massie thought there were 3,000 innkeepers in this income range.

146. Mui and Mui, *Shops and Shopkeeping*, 129; Schwartz, *Daily Life in Johnson's London*, 51. All three York jewelers had an income of £150.

147. Langford, *A Polite and Commercial People*, 451.

148. Porter, *English Society*, 368–9. The figure, c. 1800, assumes that the monarch's family contains fifty members.

149. Langford, *A Polite and Commercial People*, 451, 458. These two figures include the wife's labor.

150. Porter, *English Society*, 42–3.

151. Langford, *A Polite and Commercial People*, 64, citing Joseph Massie's contemporary estimate. Massie thought there were 12,000 lawyers in this income range, which obviously excludes those who snagged political appointments like Lord Chancellor.

152. Hibbert, *Redcoats and Rebels*, 205–6.

153. Hill, *Servants*, 25, 33–4; Porter, *English Society*, 87; Schwartz, *Daily Life in Johnson's London*, 52; Waterson, *Servants' Hall*, 26; Langford, *A Polite and Commercial People*, 119. Various years and locations.

154. Waterson, *Servants' Hall*, 26.

155. Mui and Mui, *Shops and Shopkeeping*, 112.

156. Ibid., 113.

157. Langford, *A Polite and Commercial People*, 64, citing Joseph Massie's contemporary estimates. Massie thought there were 8,000 officers in this income range.

158. Tuchman, *The First Salute*, 114. The admiral in this case was Admiral Pocock; his subordinate Admiral Keppel took £25,000.

159. Langford, *A Polite and Commercial People*, 452.

160. Mui and Mui, *Shops and Shopkeeping*, 114, 129.

161. Porter, *English Society*, 14, 59, 358, 368–9; Langford, *A Polite and Commercial People*, 598; Schwartz, *Daily Life in Johnson's London*, 52. The duke of Newcastle, one of the wealthiest peers, made £32,000 in 1715.

162. John Copeland, *Roads and Their Traffic*, 153.

163. Schwartz, *Daily Life in Johnson's London*, 51; Porter, *English Society*, 217.

164. Schwartz, *Daily Life in Johnson's London*, 51.

165. Hope, *New History of British Shipping*, 215, 231–2, 247; Langford, *A Polite and Commercial People*, 64, 451. Massie thought there were 60,000 seamen making from £15 to £24.

166. Porter, *English Society*, 58–9.

167. Porter, *London*, 170.

168. Gerzina, *Black London*, 136.

169. Mui and Mui, *Shops and Shopkeeping*, 111–4; Porter, *English Society*, 70.

170. Ibid., 113–4.

171. Langford, *A Polite and Commercial People*, 64, citing Joseph Massie's contemporary estimate. Massie thought there were 18,000 soldiers in this income range.

172. Mui and Mui, *Shops and Shopkeeping*, 153. This figure represents the earnings of the framemaker's entire family.

173. Schwartz, *Daily Life in Johnson's London*, 51.

174. Porter, *English Society*, xv, 66–7, for the lower-end figure of £300, 368–9 for Colquhoun's end-of-century averages of £700 for 20,000 lesser gentry and £1,500 for 6,000 squires; Schwartz, *Daily Life in Johnson's London*, 52, gives a range of from £250 to £5,000; Langford, *A Polite and Commercial People*, 64, cites Massie, 1759, as thinking that 2,070 esquires and aristocrats made £800 or more apiece, with another 16,000 gentlemen making from £200 to £799.

175. Mui and Mui, *Shops and Shopkeeping*, 113–4.

176. Ibid., 113, 129. The average income of York's four assessed stay makers was £120.

177. Farrell, *Socks and Stockings*, 35. The pay depended on the degree of decoration or pattern in the stocking.

178. Hope, *New History of British Shipping*, 232; Williams, *Age of Agony*, 113.

179. Mui and Mui, *Shops and Shopkeeping*, 113; Porter, *English Society*, 299; Schwartz, *Daily Life in Johnson's London*, 51.

180. Defoe, *Tour*, 249; Langford, *A Polite and Commercial People*, 77; Porter, *English Society*, 368–9. The £150 figure is Patrick Colquhoun's contemporary average of 20,000 family incomes; the £600 figure is his average of the incomes of 500 educators in the universities and "chief schools."

181. Mui and Mui, *Shops and Shopkeeping*, 129. The average income of assessed tea dealers in York was £149.

182. Mui and Mui, *Shops and Shopkeeping*, 121; Schwartz, *Daily Life in Johnson's London*, 53.

183. Mui and Mui, *Shops and Shopkeeping*, 129. The average income of York's three assessed tobacconists was £110.

184. Pawson, *Transport and Economy*, 185, 188.

185. Copeland, *Roads and Their Traffic*, 40.

186. Mary Collier, "The Woman's Labour. An Epistle to Mr. Stephen Duck" (1739), in Lonsdale, *New Oxford Book of Eighteenth-Century Verse*, 325–6.

187. Pringle, *Hue and Cry*, 43.

188. Porter, *English Society*, 93, 334.

189. Ibid., 217.

190. Schwartz, *Daily Life in Johnson's London*, 51–2.

191. Mui and Mui, *Shops and Shopkeeping*, 129. There were only two assessed whip makers in York at this time.

192. Porter, *English Society*, 368–9. The figure, an average of 25,000 manufacturing families, is from Patrick Colquhoun's contemporary calculations.

193. Hill, *Servants*, 37–8; Langford, *A Polite and Commercial People*, 502–3; Plumb, *English in the Eighteenth Century*, 15–6, 88n, 158; Porter, *English Society*, 88, 135, 137; Thompson, *Customs in Common*, 109.

CHAPTER 10

1. Cunnington and Mansfield, *English Costume for Sports*, 175, 313.

2. Ibid., 301–2.

3. Sir Richard Steele, *Spectator*, September 24, 1712.

4. Cunnington and Mansfield, *English Costume for Sports*, 261, 271.

5. Ibid., 289.

6. Schwartz, *Daily Life in Johnson's London*, 64.

7. Ibid., 64; Robert W. Malcolmson, *Popular Recreations in English Society 1700–1850* (Cambridge: Cambridge University Press, 1979), 50.

8. Pringle, *Hue and Cry*, 21.

9. Lasdun, *The English Park*, 106; Porter, *English Society*, 237.

10. Alexander Pope, "Epistle to Miss Blount, on her Leaving the Town, after the Coronation" (wr. 1714, pub. 1717), ll. 25–30, in Lonsdale, *New Oxford Book of Eighteenth-Century Verse*, 99–100.

11. Cunnington and Mansfield, *English Costume for Sports*, 108.

12. Carl Chinn, *Better Betting with a Decent Feller: Bookmaking, Betting and the British Working Class, 1750–1990* (New York: Harvester Wheatsheaf, 1991), 7–8.

13. Porter, *English Society*, 237–8; Cunnington and Mansfield, *English Costume for Sports*, 136.

14. Schwartz, *Daily Life in Johnson's London*, 75; Defoe, *Tour*, 98, 686n; Langford, *A Polite and Commercial People*, 404–5.

15. Quoted in Langford, *A Polite and Commercial People*, 266.

16. Quoted in Chinn, *Better Betting*, 8.

17. Schwartz, *Daily Life in Johnson's London*, 75; Malcolmson, *Popular Recreations*, 19; Porter, *English Society*, 294.

18. Malcolmson, *Popular Recreations*, 19.

19. Quoted in Schwartz, *Daily Life in Johnson's London*, 64.

20. Porter, *English Society*, 236.

21. Cunnington and Mansfield, *English Costume for Sports*, 13; Jennings, *Inns, Ales, and Drinking Customs*, 222.

22. *The Derby Mercury*, August 16, 1745, quoted in Cunnington and Mansfield, *English Costume for Sports*, 39.

23. Porter, *London*, 175; Malcolmson, *Popular Recreations*, 72.

24. Malcolmson, *Popular Recreations*, 41–3.

25. Ibid., 34–5.

26. Ibid., 35–7. The description of camping is from 1823.

27. Porter, *London*, 177; Porter, *English Society*, 244–54; Langford, *A Polite and Commercial People*, 23, 48–9.

28. *Evangelical Magazine*, 1800, quoted in Porter, *English Society*, 308–9.

29. Langford, *A Polite and Commercial People*, 611.

30. Ibid., 309; Porter, *English Society*, 239; Garrick and Colman, *The Clandestine Marriage*, 10–11.

31. Altick, *Shows of London*, 120; Porter, *London*, 177; Porter, *English Society*, 100.

32. Schwartz, *Daily Life in Johnson's London*, 57.

33. Porter, *London*, 177–8; Gerzina, *Black London*, 14; Cardwell, *Norton History of Technology*, 169.

34. Schwartz, *Daily Life in Johnson's London*, 53.

35. Langford, *A Polite and Commercial People*, 610, 612; Sheridan, *The Rivals*, 11–13.

36. Joseph Addison, *Tatler*, no. 108, December 17, 1709.

37. Jarrett, *England in the Age of Hogarth*, 15–6.

38. Porter, *London*, 177; Porter, *English Society*, 232, 239, 243; Langford, *A Polite and Commercial People*, 315.

39. Schwartz, *Daily Life in Johnson's London*, 88.

40. Quoted in Altick, *Shows of London*, 40.

41. Ibid., 51, 53–5.

42. Ibid., 102.

43. Ibid., 101.

44. Quoted in ibid., 24.

45. Ibid., 132–3.

46. Ibid., 111, 114.

47. Schwartz, *Daily Life in Johnson's London*, 88.

48. Pringle, *Hue and Cry*, 87.

49. Porter, *London*, 178; Altick, *Shows of London*, 42–8.

50. Altick, *Shows of London*, 21, 73–4, 86, 97, 119; Opie and Opie, *Oxford Dictionary of Nursery Rhymes*, 355.

51. Jack Kelly, "Playing with Fire," *American Heritage* (July-August 1977): 81–2.

52. Altick, *Shows of London*, 60–2.

53. Quoted in Porter, *English Society*, 327.

54. Malcolmson, *Popular Recreations*, 17–8, 20–2, 31–2, 53–4; Thompson, *Customs in Common*, 54.

55. Quoted in Altick, *Shows of London*, 36.

56. George Alexander Stevens, "Bartleme Fair" (1762), II. 7–29, in Lonsdale, *New Oxford Book of Eighteenth-Century Verse*, 507–8.

57. Defoe, *Tour*, 132.

58. Quoted in Gerzina, *Black London*, 35.

59. Porter, *London*, 118.

60. Langford, *A Polite and Commercial People*, 575–6.

61. Porter, *English Society*, 106; Pringle, *Hue and Cry*, 60–1; Smith, *Dictionary of London Street Names*, 19, 34, 41–2; Mui and Mui, *Shops and Shopkeeping*, 226; Porter, *London*, 170; Altick, *Shows of London*, 19; Jennings, *Inns, Ales, and Drinking Customs*, 363.

62. Porter, *London*, 178.

63. Langford, *A Polite and Commercial People*, 242; Colley, *Britons*, 227; Schwartz, *Daily Life in Johnson's London*, 62.

64. Quoted in Porter, *English Society*, 156.

65. Colley, *Britons*, 111, 317–8; Gerzina, *Black London*, 191; Jennings, *Inns, Ales, and Drinking Customs*, 201; Langford, *A Polite and Commercial People*, 301, 356; Porter, *English Society*, 345, 349.

66. Langford, *A Polite and Commercial People*, 324, 328; Gerzina, *Black London*, 24.

67. Plumb, *English in the Eighteenth Century*, 31.

68. Cunnington and Mansfield, *English Costume for Sports*, 175.

69. Porter, *English Society*, 277.

70. Ibid., 221, 233.

71. Porter, *English Society*, 235.

72. Schwartz, *Daily Life in Johnson's London*, 29.

73. Sheridan, *The Rivals*, I.ii.

74. Quoted in Porter, *English Society*, 308.

75. Quoted in Langford, *A Polite and Commercial People*, 478.

76. William Chappell, *Old English Popular Music* (New York: Jack Brussel, 1961), 1:298–300.

77. Gerzina, *Black London*, 186–7.

78. Chappell, *Old English Popular Music*, 1:211–4.

79. Roy Palmer, *A Ballad History of England from 1588 to the Present Day* (London: B. T. Batsford, 1979), 49, 86.

80. Colley, *Britons*, 43–4, 48; Chappell, *Old English Popular Music*, 1:194–5.

81. James Thomson, "Rule, Britannia" (1740), in Lonsdale, *New Oxford Book of Eighteenth-Century Verse*, 192–3; Chappell, *Old English Popular Music*, 1:191–3.

82. Chappell, *Old English Popular Music*, 2:122–3.

83. Porter, *English Society*, 238; Schwartz, *Daily Life in Johnson's London*, 75.

84. Chinn, *Better Betting*, 14.

85. Schwartz, *Daily Life in Johnson's London*, 76.

86. Chinn, *Better Betting*, 10; Porter, *English Society*, 236.

87. Plumb, *England in the Eighteenth Century*, 13; Chinn, *Better Betting*, 14.

88. Chinn, *Better Betting*, 32.

89. Porter, *London*, 178.

90. Thomas D'Urfey, "Dialogue Between Crab and Gillian" (1701), in Lonsdale, *New Oxford Book of Eighteenth-Century Verse*, 5.

91. Langford, *A Polite and Commercial People*, 574; Chinn, *Better Betting*, 9–10; Porter, *English Society*, 238. Fox's losses of £140,000 are consistent in all three sources; however, Chinn says he achieved this monumental failure by the age of twenty-one, while Porter says it was age twenty-five. Schwartz, *Daily Life in Johnson's London*, 74, gives the relevant age as twenty-four.

92. Chinn, *Better Betting*, 19; Pringle, *Hue and Cry*, 94; Langford, *A Polite and Commercial People*, 296–7.

93. Langford, *A Polite and Commercial People*, 572–3; Chinn, *Better Betting*, 64.

94. Henry Fielding, *Joseph Andrews* (Boston: Houghton Mifflin, 1961), 123–4.

95. Quoted in Pringle, *Hue and Cry*, 21.

96. Schwartz, *Daily Life in Johnson's London*, 67–8.

97. Malcolmson, *Popular Recreations*, 47.

98. Ibid., 49–50; Schwartz, *Daily Life in Johnson's London*, 68; Smith, *Dictionary of London Street Names*, 47.

99. Quoted in Porter, *London*, 176.

100. Malcolmson, *Popular Recreations*, 45–6, 63, 66; Schwartz, *Daily Life in Johnson's London*, 67.

101. Malcolmson, *Popular Recreations*, 48–9; Schwartz, *Daily Life in Johnson's London*, 66.

102. Porter, *English Society*, 294–5.

103. Malcolmson, *Popular Recreations*, 43–4.

104. Ibid., 42–3; Schwartz, *Daily Life in Johnson's London*, 70; Porter, *English Society*, 50, 237–9.

105. Malcolmson, *Popular Recreations*, 17–9, 27–8, 34, 44; Porter, *English Society*, 236, 294–5; Schwartz, *Daily Life in Johnson's London*, 64.

106. Hugh Clout, ed., *The Times London History Atlas* (New York: Harper-Collins, 1991), 14; Langford, *A Polite and Commercial People*, 728–37; Porter, *English Society*, 236, 240, 295.

CHAPTER 11

1. Tuchman, *The First Salute*, 134.

2. Ibid., 238, 242, 251.

3. Ibid., 226, 245.

4. Ibid., p. 7; Hibbert, *Redcoats and Rebels*, 335.

5. Hope, *New History of British Shipping*, 207, 239.

6. Ibid., 207, 208, 211.

7. Ibid., 253; William Albert, *The Turnpike Road System in England 1663–1840* (Cambridge: Cambridge University Press, 1972), 7.

8. Hope, *New History of British Shipping*, 253.

9. Ibid., 211.

10. Ibid., 236.

11. Ibid., 229, 249; Plumb, *England in the Eighteenth Century*, 30.

12. Porter, *English Society*, 208; Jackson, "Sea Trade," in Langton and Morris, *Atlas of Industrializing Britain*, p. 98.

13. Hope, *New History of British Shipping*, 217, 221.

14. Ibid., 228–9, 251.

15. Albert, *Turnpike Road System*, 6–7.

16. Porter, *English Society*, 191; Michael Freeman, "Transport," in Langton and Morris, *Atlas of Industrializing Britain*, 86.

17. Pawson, *Transport and Economy*, 118, 120.

18. Porter, *English Society*, 207.

19. Langford, *A Polite and Commercial People*, 414.

20. Pawson, *Transport and Economy*, 22; Copeland, *Roads and Their Traffic*, 77. Langford, *A Polite and Commercial People* (p. 417) gives a rate of 1 ½d. on the Trent and Mersey.

21. Pawson, *Transport and Economy*, 23.

22. Schwartz, *Daily Life in Johnson's London*, 118–9.

23. Ibid., 11; Porter, *London*, 106; "The Jolly Chair-Men" (c. 1750), in Palmer, *Ballad History of England*, 58.

24. Copeland, *Roads and Their Traffic*, 12.

25. Ibid., 64–5.

26. Pawson, *Transport and Economy*, 293.

27. Ibid., 29.

28. Albert, *Turnpike Road System*, 10.

29. Porter, *English Society*, 79.

30. Copeland, *Roads and Their Traffic*, 68–9. The rates listed are for 1758. Mui and Mui, *Shops and Shopkeeping* (p. 12), and Pawson, *Transport and Economy* (p. 57), confirm the spread of hauling services to even fairly small towns.

31. Clout, *Times London History Atlas* (p. 14), gives the number as 1,100; Porter, *London*, (p. 106), gives it as 500 at mid-century; and Schwartz, *Daily Life in Johnson's London* (p. 122), gives it as 1,000.

32. Copeland, *Roads and Their Traffic*, 107.

33. Ibid., 153–4; Schwartz, *Daily Life in Johnson's London*, 121–2.

34. Schwartz, *Daily Life in Johnson's London*, 118, 122.

35. Ibid., 123; Langford, *A Polite and Commercial People*, 405.

36. Schwartz, *Daily Life in Johnson's London*, 120; Plumb, *England in the Eighteenth Century*, 147–8.

37. Copeland, *Roads and Their Traffic*, 93, 154–5; Schwartz, *Daily Life in Johnson's London*, 122; Porter, *English Society*, 193.

38. Porter, *English Society*, 45.

39. Langford, *A Polite and Commercial People*, 405–6; Palmer, *Ballad History of England*, 63–4.

40. *Harris's List of Covent Garden Ladies: Or a Man of Pleasure's Kalender for the Year 1788*, quoted in Stone, *Road to Divorce*, 110.

41. Copeland, *Roads and Their Traffic*, 133–5.

42. Ibid., 136, 142–4.

43. Langford, *A Polite and Commercial People*, 398–401, 406–7; Pawson, *Transport and Economy*, 285, 289.

44. Pawson, *Transport and Economy*, 68–9; Copeland, *Roads and Their Traffic*, 30–1; Albert, *Turnpike Road System*, 15.

45. Copeland, *Roads and Their Traffic*, 11; Plumb, *England in the Eighteenth Century*, 24.

46. Defoe, *Tour*, 144.

47. Pawson, *Transport and Economy*, 67.

48. Ibid., 293.

49. Pawson, *Transport and Economy*, 89, 91–2, 125; Copeland, *Roads and Their Traffic*, 24.

50. Pawson, *Transport and Economy*, 91, 174, 177, 193, 210; Albert, *Turnpike Road System*, 22; Langford, *A Polite and Commercial People*, 392.

51. Pawson, *Transport and Economy*, 101, 103.

52. Ibid., 84–5, 99–100, 105; Copeland, *Roads and Their Traffic*, 37; Albert, *Turnpike Road System*, 22.

53. Albert, *Turnpike Road System*, 22–3; Pawson, *Transport and Economy*, 92–3.

54. Pawson, *Transport and Economy*, 59.

55. Ibid., 204; Copeland, *Roads and Their Traffic*, 42–5.

56. Pawson, *Transport and Economy*, 85, 204; Copeland, *Roads and Their Traffic*, 44.

57. Pawson, *Transport and Economy*, 209.

58. Albert, *Turnpike Road System*, 33.

59. Pawson, *Transport and Economy*, 151, 155, 173.

60. Porter, *London*, 135; Copeland, *Roads and Their Traffic*, 85; Langford, *A Polite and Commercial People*, 404–5; Porter, *English Society*, 271, Plumb, *England in the Eighteenth Century*, 147–8.

61. Hope, *New History of British Shipping*, 213, 246–7; Hibbert, *Redcoats and Rebels*, 335.

62. Langford, *A Polite and Commercial People*, 409; Jennings, *Inns, Ales, and Drinking Customs*, 183–4; Copeland, *Roads and Their Traffic*, 109.

63. Pawson, *Transport and Economy*, 292; Cardwell, *Norton History of Technology*, 229; Copeland, *Roads and Their Traffic*, 109. According to Copeland, the first mail coach departed from Bristol.

64. Copeland, *Roads and Their Traffic*, 98; Langford, *A Polite and Commercial People*, 409; Pawson, *Transport and Economy*, 293.

65. Copeland, *Roads and Their Traffic*, 110, 114, 125–6, 129.

66. Colley, *Britons*, 41; Smith, *Dictionary of London Street Names*, 121, 131; Porter, *English Society*, 136, 234; Hibbert, *Redcoats and Rebels*, 76, 78, 117, 334.

67. Colley, *Britons*, 41, 220; Pawson, *Transport and Economy*, 33; Porter, *English Society*, 190, 234.

68. Stone, *Road to Divorce*, 186; Porter, *English Society*, 38, 137, 190, 234, 348.

69. Porter, *English Society*, 223, 235–6; Stone, *Road to Divorce*, 252.

70. Albert, *Turnpike Road System*, 14, 16, 22 (in which the date of the first true turnpike trust is given as 1706); Porter, *English Society*, 234; Pawson, *Transport and Economy*, 71, 74, 92–3, 105, 179, 206; Smith, *Dictionary of London Street Names*, 164; Hope, *New History of British Shipping*, 230, 256; Copeland, *Roads and Their Traffic*, 47, 65. Many sources give the date of the Worsley canal as 1761, the year it reached the edge of Manchester.

CHAPTER 12

1. Langford, *A Polite and Commercial People*, 569.

2. Jennings, *Inns, Ales, and Drinking Customs*, 274, 279; Porter, *English Society*, 188.

3. Porter, *English Society*, 135.

4. Langford, *A Polite and Commercial People*, 492.

5. Ibid., 569.

6. Opie and Opie, *Oxford Dictionary of Nursery Rhymes*, 49.

7. Porter, *English Society*, 188.

8. Ibid., 146, 202; Smith, *Dictionary of London Street Names*, 77.

9. Porter, *English Society*, 189; Porter, *London*, 146.

10. Porter, *English Society*, 203.

11. Defoe, "Reformation of Manners," in Lonsdale, *New Oxford Book of Eighteenth-Century Verse*, 33.

12. Porter, *English Society*, 78.

13. Ibid., 322.

14. Langford, *A Polite and Commercial People*, 372, 565; Porter, *English Society*, 206.

15. Quoted in Porter, *English Society*, 172.

16. Quoted in Porter, *London*, 134.

17. Mui and Mui, *Shops and Shopkeeping*, 161.

18. Thompson, *Customs in Common*, 323.

19. Ibid., 215–6.

20. Ibid., 193–200.

21. Quoted in ibid., 197.

22. Mui and Mui, *Shops and Shopkeeping*, 98–9.

23. John Gay, "Trivia: or, the Art of Walking the Streets of London," Book II (1716), in Lonsdale, *New Oxford Book of Eighteenth-Century Verse*, 124.

24. Mui and Mui, *Shops and Shopkeeping*, 80.

25. Ibid., 27.

26. Quoted in ibid., 237.

27. Mui and Mui, *Shops and Shopkeeping*, 245.

28. Ibid., 224.

29. Ibid., 14–5.

30. Quoted in Porter, *London*, 144–5.

31. Mui and Mui, *Shops and Shopkeeping*, 14–6.

32. Ibid., 271. This was in 1795, when shops and distributors were already quite well developed.

33. Ibid., 36, 95; Colley, *Britons*, 66.

34. Altick, *Shows of London*, 38.

35. Mui and Mui, *Shops and Shopkeeping*, 245.

36. Porter, *English Society*, 217.

37. Mui and Mui, *Shops and Shopkeeping*, 95.

38. Ibid., 200, 251.

39. Langford, *A Polite and Commercial People*, 458.

40. Mui and Mui, *Shops and Shopkeeping*, 13.

41. Langford, *A Polite and Commercial People*, 549.

42. Mui and Mui, *Shops and Shopkeeping*, 81, 112, 114, 130; Hibbert, *Redcoats and Rebels*, xviii.

43. Porter, *English Society*, 215; Thompson, *Customs in Common*, 204.

44. Gerzina, *Black London*, 58.

45. Altick, *Shows of London*, 19; Langford, *A Polite and Commercial People*, 346, 448; Thompson, *Customs in Common*, 250–51; Mui and Mui, *Shops and Shopkeeping*, 154–5, 157, 202, 212–3, 215, 233, 245–6, 265, 269; Porter, *London*, 183.

46. Thompson, *Customs in Common*, 287.

47. Defoe, *Tour*, 48; Porter, *English Society*, 60, 92; Porter, *London*, 109; Pringle, *Hue and Cry*, 93; Thompson, *Customs in Common*, 103, 147, 287.

48. Mui and Mui, *Shops and Shopkeeping*, 21–2, 153, 235, 237, 241; Porter, *English Society*, 92.

49. Altick, *Shows of London*, 47; Colley, *Britons*, 95; Mui and Mui, *Shops and Shopkeeping*, 230–3, 242; Porter, *English Society*, 234–5, 321–2; Porter, *London*, 92, 141; Thompson, *Customs in Common*, 366, 368; Waterson, *Servants' Hall*, 124, 138; Watkins, "The Greening of the Empire," 28–50.

50. Altick, *Shows of London*, 18, 27, 51, 56, 82, 88, 114, 124; Colley, *Britons*, 44; Gerzina, *Black London*, 117; Langford, *A Polite and Commercial People*, 86–7, 335, 408, 417, 572, 665; Porter, *English Society*, 163, 283, 294; Porter, *London*, 170, 174, 176; Stone, *Road to Divorce*, 102, 104; Waterson, *Servants' Hall*, 139.

CHAPTER 13

1. Stone, *Road to Divorce*, 34–5, 41.
2. Ibid., 74; Langford, *A Polite and Commercial People*, 293.
3. Stone, *Road to Divorce*, 33, 183–4.
4. Ibid., 25.
5. Ibid., 233.
6. Defoe, *Tour*, 106–7; Langford, *A Polite and Commercial People*, 443–4; Porter, *English Society*, 88, 127.
7. Porter, *English Society*, 126.
8. Pringle, *Hue and Cry*, 67.
9. Quoted in ibid., 79.
10. Quoted in ibid., 67.
11. Langford, *A Polite and Commercial People*, 302, 694; Pringle, *Hue and Cry*, 42; Porter, *English Society*, 50, 123–4; Jarrett, *England in the Age of Hogarth*, 12.
12. Pringle, *Hue and Cry*, 52.
13. Langford, *A Polite and Commercial People*, 303.
14. John Gay, *The Beggar's Opera* (i), in Lonsdale, *New Oxford Book of Eighteenth-Century Verse*, 130–1.
15. Boswell, *Life of Samuel Johnson*, 394.
16. Langford, *A Polite and Commercial People*, 64.
17. Porter, *London*, 148.
18. Stone, *Road to Divorce*, 233.
19. Schwartz, *Daily Life in Johnson's London*, 157.
20. Ibid., 137.
21. Stone, *Road to Divorce*, 31.
22. Ibid., 195–7.
23. Gerzina, *Black London*, 34.
24. Pringle, *Hue and Cry*, 53.
25. Porter, *English Society*, 134.
26. Pringle, *Hue and Cry*, 54; Stone, *Road to Divorce*, 30.
27. Pringle, *Hue and Cry*, 41; Porter, *London*, 149; Porter, *English Society*, 139–40.
28. Porter, *English Society*, 101.
29. Pringle, *Hue and Cry*, 63.
30. Ibid., 36; Jennings, *Inns, Ales, and Drinking Customs*, 128, 130.

31. Pringle, *Hue and Cry*, 43, 45–6.

32. Ibid., 44; Porter, *English Society*, 139–40.

33. Porter, *English Society*, 42.

34. Pringle, *Hue and Cry*, 36.

35. Quoted in ibid., 12.

36. Ibid., 88; Schwartz, *Daily Life in Johnson's London*, 162; Porter, *English Society*, 140.

37. Porter, *English Society*, 101, 135–6; Pringle, *Hue and Cry*, 11, 54; Stone, *Road to Divorce*, 143; Plumb, *England in the Eighteenth Century*, 26; Langford, *A Polite and Commercial People*, 391–2.

38. Porter, *English Society*, 141; Porter, *London*, 152.

39. Pringle, *Hue and Cry*, 50, 53.

40. Ibid., 96–7; Colley, *Britons*, 108.

41. Langford, *A Polite and Commercial People*, 158.

42. Ibid., 494.

43. Ibid., 496; Porter, *English Society*, 287–8.

44. Langford, *A Polite and Commercial People*, 495.

45. Pringle, *Hue and Cry*, 30–1; Porter, *English Society*, 138–9, 252; Schwartz, *Daily Life in Johnson's London*, 158.

46. Schwartz, *Daily Life in Johnson's London*, 152–3; Langford, *A Polite and Commercial People*, 159, 495–6; Thompson, *Customs in Common*, 329; Palmer, *Ballad History of England*, 67.

47. Porter, *London*, 153; Schwartz, *Daily Life in Johnson's London*, 147; Pringle, *Hue and Cry*, 49.

48. Porter, *English Society*, 18.

49. Porter, *London*, 154; Schwartz, *Daily Life in Johnson's London*, 148–9; Porter, *English Society*, 100, 186, 277; Altick, *Shows of London*, 19–20; Langford, *A Polite and Commercial People*, 156.

50. Porter, *English Society*, 17; Schwartz, *Daily Life in Johnson's London*, 150.

51. Quoted in Porter, *English Society*, 18.

52. Langford, *A Polite and Commercial People*, 41, 159–60, 300–301, 493–4; Plumb, *England in the Eighteenth Century*, 157; Porter, *English Society*, 119, 127, 278, 287; Porter, *London*, 56, 155; Pringle, *Hue and Cry*, 21; Schwartz, *Daily Life in Johnson's London*, 151–2.

CHAPTER 14

1. Quoted in Porter, *English Society*, 166.

2. Porter, *English Society*, 159.

3. Matthew Prior, "Alma: or, the Progress of the Mind," Canto II, in Lonsdale, *New Oxford Book of Eighteenth-Century Verse*, 59.

4. Porter, *English Society*, 159, 268.

5. Paul Langford, *A Polite and Commercial People*, 86–7.

6. Porter, *English Society*, 245.

7. Gerzina, *Black London*, 155.

8. Porter, *English Society*, 164; Langford, *A Polite and Commercial People*, 86; Schwartz, *Daily Life in Johnson's London*, 43.

9. Porter, *English Society*, 165.

10. Schwartz, *Daily Life in Johnson's London*, 43.

11. Porter, *English Society*, 166.

12. Ibid., 296.

13. Ibid., 298.

14. Ibid.

15. Ibid., 329.

16. Porter, *English Society*, 166, 296. On p. 166 Porter mentions a 1787 estimate of 250,000. On p. 296, he states that Manchester had 5,000 students in 1788 and, "By 1797 there were 1,086 Sunday schools across the country with 69,000 pupils, some of them adults." One assumes, therefore, that the contemporary estimate was too high. Colley, in *Britons*, (p. 226), states, "By 1800, there were 200,000 children attending Sunday schools in England and Wales."

17. Roy Porter, *London*, 167–8.

18. Quoted in Porter, *English Society*, 161.

19. Ibid., 9, 161.

20. Colley, *Britons*, 167.

21. Ibid., 164; Schwartz, *Daily Life in Johnson's London*, 52; Langford, *A Polite and Commercial People*, 86.

22. Langford, *A Polite and Commercial People*, 77; Porter, *English Society*, 151.

23. Thompson, *Customs in Common*, 388.

24. Steele, *Spectator*, no. 157, August 30, 1711.

25. Hannah More, *Strictures on Female Education* (1799), in *Selected Writings of Hannah More*, ed. Robert Hole (London: William Pickering, 1995), 172.

26. Ibid., 149.

27. Mary Wollstonecraft, *A Vindication of the Rights of Woman* (1792), in Gilbert and Gubar, *Norton Anthology of Literature by Women*, 142.

28. Sarah Fyfe Egerton, "The Emulation" (1703), ll. 19–20, 32–3, in Lonsdale, *New Oxford Book of Eighteenth-Century Verse*, 37.

29. Mary Leapor, "An Essay on Woman" (1751), ll. 29–32, in ibid., 409.

30. Porter, *English Society*, 161. Langford, in *A Polite and Commercial People* (p. 89), states that together the two universities admitted between 300 and 500 students per year from the 1720s to the 1780s.

31. Colley, *Britons*, 123.

32. Langford, *A Polite and Commercial People*, 91.

33. Porter, *English Society*, 167.

34. Waterson, *Servants' Hall*, 76–7.

CHAPTER 15

1. Porter, *English Society*, 272–3.

2. Mui and Mui, *Shops and Shopkeeping*, 9, 15, 189, 227, 245–6.

3. Defoe, *Tour*, 259.

4. Hannah Glasse, *The Art of Cooking Made Plain and Easy* (Schenectady, N.Y.: United States Historical Research Service, 1994), 10.

5. Ibid., 15.

6. Ibid., 18.

7. Ibid., 271–8.

8. Ibid., 21.

9. Ibid., 233.

10. Ibid., 330.

11. Ibid., 115.

12. Gerzina, *Black London*, 14.

13. Ibid., 14; Moses Browne, "The Shrimp" (1739), in Lonsdale, *New Oxford Book of Eighteenth-Century Verse*, 292–3; Opie and Opie, *Oxford Dictionary of Nursery Rhymes*, 411.

14. Porter, *English Society*, 216.

15. George Alexander Stevens, "Bartleme Fair" (1762), ll. 14, 21, 28, in Lonsdale, *New Oxford Book of Eighteenth-Century Verse*, 507–8; Altick, *Shows of London*, 39.

16. Schwartz, *Daily Life in Johnson's London*, 59–60.

17. Mui and Mui, *Shops and Shopkeeping*, 153–4.

18. Thompson, *Customs in Common*, 190.

19. Susanna Blamire, "Stoklewath; or, the Cumbrian Village" (wr. c. 1776?, pub. 1842), in Lonsdale, *New Oxford Book of Eighteenth-Century Verse*, 645.

20. Mui and Mui, *Shops and Shopkeeping*, 212–3. This section has excellent details about the shopping patterns of working families, including the fact that a sample family bought a little more than three to twelve pounds of cheese per month. This figure, of course, does not include any cheese that might have been made at home.

21. Samuel Bamford, quoted in Porter, *English Society*, 153.

22. Edward Chicken, "The Collier's Wedding" (wr. 1729?, pub. 1732——?), in Lonsdale, *New Oxford Book of Eighteenth-Century Verse*, 216.

23. Jonathan Swift, quoted in Plumb, *England in the Eighteenth Century*, 180.

24. Thompson, *Customs in Common*, 321.

25. Quoted in ibid., 258n.

26. Schwartz, *Daily Life in Johnson's London*, 98.

27. Defoe, *Tour*, 222.

28. Samuel Ogden, quoted in Porter, *English Society*, 20.

29. Moritz, quoted in Porter, *English Society*, 273.

30. Richardson Pack, "An Epistle from a Half-Pay Officer" (wr. 1714, pub. 1719), l. 31, in Lonsdale, *New Oxford Book of Eighteenth-Century Verse*, 111.

31. James Cawthorn, "Of Taste. An Essay" (wr. by 1761, pub. 1771), in Lonsdale, *New Oxford Book of Eighteenth-Century Verse*, 494.

32. Robert Campbell, *The London Tradesman* (1747), quoted in de la Falaise, *Seven Centuries of English Cooking*, 105.

33. Williams, *Age of Agony*, 94.

34. Schwartz, *Daily Life in Johnson's London*, 153.

35. Ibid., 104, 124.

36. Jennings, *Inns, Ales, and Drinking Customs*, 177.

37. Quoted in Porter, *London*, 165.

38. Schwartz, *Daily Life in Johnson's London*, 104.

39. Porter, *London*, 171.

40. Catherine Clive, *The Rehearsal or, Bayes in Petticoats*, II.i.168–71, in Garrick and Colman, *The Clandestine Marriage*, 208.

41. Moritz, quoted in Schwartz, *Daily Life in Johnson's London*, 102.

42. Simpson, *London Ritz Book of Afternoon Tea*, 13.

43. John Clayton, *Friendly Advice to the Poor* (1755), quoted in Thompson, *Customs in Common*, 386.

44. Colley, *Britons*, 69.

45. Mui and Mui, *Shops and Shopkeeping*, 218–9.

46. Ibid., 13, 250; Colley, *Britons*, 69.

47. Mui and Mui, *Shops and Shopkeeping*, 254.

48. Schwartz, *Daily Life in Johnson's London*, 74.

49. Pringle, *Hue and Cry*, 45.

50. de la Falaise, *Seven Centuries of English Cooking*, 104.

51. Porter, *English Society*, 59, 76, 139.

52. Jennings, *Inns, Ales, and Drinking Customs*, 135.

53. Henry Fielding, *Enquiry into the Causes of the late Increase of Robbers* (1751), quoted in Pringle, *Hue and Cry*, 93.

54. Fielding, *Enquiry*, quoted in Schwartz, *Daily Life in Johnson's London*, 73.

55. Quoted in Porter, *London*, 181.

56. Pringle, *Hue and Cry*, 93.

57. Ibid., 59–63.

58. Jennings, *Inns, Ales, and Drinking Customs*, 129–30.

59. Pringle, *Hue and Cry*, 70.

60. Jennings, *Inns, Ales, and Drinking Customs*, 118.

61. Boswell, *Life of Samuel Johnson*, 545, 655–6.

62. Chappell, *Old English Popular Music*, 2: 180.

63. Quoted in Porter, *English Society*, 217.

64. Schwartz, *Daily Life in Johnson's London*, 161.

65. Ibid., 74.

66. Jennings, *Inns, Ales, and Drinking Customs*, 100–101. Jennings claims the inventor of porter was a brewer named Harwood and gives the date of its introduction as 1750; R. B. Weir, in "Distilling," in Langton and Morris, *Atlas of Industrializing Britain*, 120, states that porter was introduced in 1722 and that it gradually replaced ale as the preferred drink of Londoners.

67. Boswell, *Life of Johnson*, 655–6.

68. Schwartz, *Daily Life in Johnson's London*, 73. He gives a figure of 1,178,856 barrels for "the principal brewers" in 1786.

69. Ibid., 73–4.

70. Altick, *Shows of London*, 97.

71. *London Magazine*, 1775, 271–3, quoted in Langford, *A Polite and Commercial People*, 601.

72. Jennings, *Inns, Ales, and Drinking Customs*, 130.

73. Cunnington and Cunnington, *Handbook of English Costume*, 103.

CHAPTER 16

1. Porter, *English Society*, 309.

2. Ashley Montagu, *The Anatomy of Swearing* (New York: Macmillan, 1967), 213–4; Addison, *Spectator*, no. 371, May 6, 1712; Langford, *A Polite and Commercial People*, 499; Porter, *English Society*, 293, 295.

3. Sir Francis Grant, Lord Cullen, *A Discourse Concerning the Execution of the LAWS Made Against Prophaneness, &c.*, quoted in Montagu, *Anatomy of Swearing*, 201.

4. Williams, *Age of Agony*, 95; Stone, *Road to Divorce*, 215; Montagu, *Anatomy of Swearing*, 208–10; Porter, *English Society*, 9.

5. Porter, *English Society*, 307; Cunnington and Cunnington, *Handbook of English Costume*, 25–6.

6. Montagu, *Anatomy of Swearing*, 205, 215–7, John Winstanley, "Miss Betty's Singing Bird" (1742), ll. 13–24, in Lonsdale, *New Oxford Book of Eighteenth-Century Verse*, 135.

7. Montagu, *Anatomy of Swearing*, 304, 312.

8. Ibid., 204–5, 245, 317–8; Thompson, *Customs in Common*, 67.

9. Montagu, *Anatomy of Swearing*, 204–5, 215–21; Sheridan, *The Rivals*, I.i.

10. Montagu, *Anatomy of Swearing*, 282, 297.

11. Ibid., 215–7, 204–6; Clive, *The Reharsal*, II.i, in Garrick and Colman, *The Clandestine Marriage*, 213; Sheridan, *The Rivals*, I.i., II.i, II.ii, V.ii.

12. Sheridan, *The Rivals*, I.i.; Montagu, *Anatomy of Swearing*, 217.

13. Altick, *Shows of London*, 19–20.

14. Quoted in Porter, *English Society*, 9.

15. Pringle, *Hue and Cry*, 23; Porter, *London*, 173.

16. Casanova, quoted in Porter, *English Society*, 259; Gerzina, *Black London*, 97; Williams, *Age of Agony*, 95; Schwartz, *Daily Life in Johnson's London*, 171.

17. V. G. Kiernan, *The Duel in European History: Honour and the Reign of Aristocracy* (Oxford: Oxford University Press, 1988), 104, 121.

18. Ibid., 113–4.

19. Ibid., 134.

20. Gerzina, *Black London*, 67.

21. Langford, *A Polite and Commercial People*, 588; Porter, *English Society*, 9; Kiernan, *The Duel in European History*, 125.

22. Kiernan, *The Duel in European History*, 101; Langford, *A Polite and Commercial People*, 588.

23. Langford, *A Polite and Commercial People*, 589; Kiernan, *The Duel in European History*, 118.

24. Langford, *A Polite and Commercial People*, 578; Porter, *English Society*, 280.

25. Kiernan, *The Duel in European History*, 142, 144, 148.

26. Ibid., 144–5, 147.

27. Ibid., 138–40.

28. Ibid., 136, 144, 147.

29. Ibid., 146–8.

30. Ibid., 102, 105, 147; Langford, *A Polite and Commercial People*, 590.

31. Steele, *Tatler*, no. 25, June 7, 1709.

32. Quoted in Thompson, *Customs in Common*, 91.

33. Ibid., 66.

34. 1 Geo. I, Stat. 2, Chap. 5.

35. Thompson, *Customs in Common*, 80–2.

36. Ibid., 326–8.

37. Ibid., 310–11.

38. Hannah More, "The Riot; or, Half a Loaf is Better than No Bread. In a

Dialogue Between Jack Anvil and Tom Hod" (1795), in Lonsdale, *New Oxford Book of Eighteenth-Century Verse*, 809–10.

39. Andrew Charlesworth, "Labour Protest, 1780–1850," in Langton and Morris, *Atlas of Industrializing Britain*, 186.

40. Langford, *A Polite and Commercial People*, 215; Jennings, *Inns, Ales, and Drinking Customs*, 125; Pringle, *Hue and Cry*, 62–3, 66, 83–5; Thompson, *Customs in Common*, 75–6, 310.

41. *Ipswich Journal*, August 26, 1749, reprinting an account from a London paper, quoted in Malcolmson, *Popular Recreations*, 51.

42. Thompson, *Customs in Common*, 471–3, 475–7, 484–5, 492–3.

43. Ibid., 333.

44. Langford, *A Polite and Commercial People*, 380; Porter, *London*, 158; Schwartz, *Daily Life in Johnson's London*, 26.

45. Porter, *London*, 56, 158.

46. Quoted in Porter, *English Society*, 73.

47. Ibid., 165.

48. Schwartz, *Daily Life in Johnson's London*, 105; Mason, Gentlefolk in the Making, 267; Langford, *A Polite and Commercial People*, 587.

49. Mason, *Gentlefolk in the Making*, 97, 102, 206, 270–1, 275.

50. Thomas Fuller, M.D., *Introductio ad Sapientiam* (1731), quoted in ibid., 94.

51. Porter, *English Society*, 16.

52. Ibid., 464–5.

53. Quoted in Hibbert, *Redcoats and Rebels*, 77–8.

54. Randolph Trumbach, "The Birth of the Queen," in Duberman, Vicinus, and Chauncey, *Hidden from History*, 134–5.

55. Daniel Defoe, *The Great Law of Subordination Considered; or the Insolence and Insufferable Behaviour of SERVANTS in England duly enquired into* (1724), quoted in Thompson, *Customs in Common*, 352.

56. John Gay, "Trivia: or, the Art of Walking the Streets of London" (1716), quoted in Mason, *Gentlefolk in the Making*, 268; Langford, *A Polite and Commercial People*, 425.

57. Mason, *Gentlefolk in the Making*, 97, 267, 279–80. The quotation is from William Pitt, earl of Chatham, in advice addressed to his nephew, Thomas Pitt, later Lord Camelford.

58. Hill, *Servants*, 89; Hope, *New History of British Shipping*, 231; Langford, *A Polite and Commercial People*, 44, 737; Montagu, *Anatomy of Swearing*, 213–4; Porter, *London*, 140; Pringle, *Hue and Cry*, 72–4.

CHAPTER 17

1. Schwartz, *Daily Life in Johnson's London*, 52, 126.

2. Joseph Addison, *Spectator*, no. 21, March 24, 1711.

3. Langford, *A Polite and Commercial People*, 89, 639; Porter, *English Society*, 77, 150; Schwartz, *Daily Life in Johnson's London*, 133–4, 137.

4. Colley, *Britons*, 123; Porter, *English Society*, 162.

5. Porter, *English Society*, 75.

6. Schwartz, *Daily Life in Johnson's London*, 132–3; Langford, *A Polite and Commercial People*, 78.

7. Williams, *Age of Agony*, 102.

8. Ibid., 102–4, 106–12, 115–7, 212; Schwartz, *Daily Life in Johnson's London*, 134–5.

9. George Crabbe, "The Village," Book I, ll. 284–7 (1783), in Lonsdale, *New Oxford Book of Eighteenth-Century Verse*, 675.

10. Williams, *Age of Agony*, 180.

11. Ibid., 176.

12. Ibid., 191–2; Altick, *Shows of London*, 83.

13. Williams, *Age of Agony*, 101; Schwartz, *Daily Life in Johnson's London*, 142.

14. Schwartz, *Daily Life in Johnson's London*, 75.

15. Williams, *Age of Agony*, 99–100.

16. Ibid., 93–4.

17. Langford, *A Polite and Commercial People*, 138–9.

18. Williams, *Age of Agony*, 95–7.

19. Langford, *A Polite and Commercial People*, 134–6; Schwartz, *Daily Life in Johnson's London*, 142; Porter, *English Society*, 285.

20. Porter, *English Society*, 284.

21. Ibid., 132, 157, 195, 335; Langford, *A Polite and Commercial People*, 141.

22. Williams, *Age of Agony*, 81–2, 101.

23. Schwartz, *Daily Life in Johnson's London*, 101, 128; Williams, *Age of Agony*, 200; Porter, *English Society*, 17, 220.

24. Schwartz, *Daily Life in Johnson's London*, 152–3.

25. Langford, *A Polite and Commercial People*, 543; Porter, *English Society*, 117–8.

26. Sir Richard Steele, *Tatler*, no. 1, April 12, 1709.

27. Porter, *English Society*, 272; Schwartz, *Daily Life in Johnson's London*, 130–1.

28. Schwartz, *Daily Life in Johnson's London*, 14, 15, 100; Gerzina, *Black London*, 26.

29. Quoted in Porter, *English Society*, 283.

30. William Shenstone, "The School-Mistress. A Poem. In Imitation of Spenser's Style" (1737), ll. 75–81, in Lonsdale, *New Oxford Book of Eighteenth-Century Verse*, 307.

31. Porter, *English Society*, 273.

32. Schwartz, *Daily Life in Johnson's London*, 105.

33. Simpson, *London Ritz Book of Afternoon Tea*, 13.

34. Williams, *Age of Agony*, 41–5.

35. Ibid., 34–5, 39–42, 177; Langford, *A Polite and Commercial People*, 111.

36. Williams, *Age of Agony*, 45.

37. Schwartz, *Daily Life in Johnson's London*, 142–3.

38. Ibid., 40; Williams, *Age of Agony*, 51, 57–8, 61–5; Altick, *Shows of London*, 52.

39. Schwartz, *Daily Life in Johnson's London*, 137; Williams, *Age of Agony*, 179.

40. Porter, *English Society*, 16–7.

41. Gerzina, *Black London*, 15; Corson, *Fashions in Makeup*, 288; Schwartz, *Daily Life in Johnson's London*, 131.

42. Schwartz, *Daily Life in Johnson's London*, 127.

43. Williams, *Age of Agony*, 132–5.

44. Ibid., 72–8; Schwartz, *Daily Life in Johnson's London*, 126–7.

45. Langford, *A Polite and Commercial People*, 630; Williams, *Age of Agony*, 216; Hibbert, *Redcoats and Rebels*, 61; Tuchman, *The First Salute*, 129.

46. Williams, *Age of Agony*, 63.

47. Opie and Opie, *Oxford Dictionary of Nursery Rhymes*, 49; Altick, *Shows of London*, 73–4; George Galloway, "Gavin Wilson (Boot, Leg and Arm Maker)" (1795), in Lonsdale, *New Oxford Book of Eighteenth-Century Verse*, 805.

48. Langford, *A Polite and Commercial People*, 107.

49. Ibid., 102.

50. Williams, *Age of Agony*, 146–7.

51. Ibid., 147.

52. Anonymous, "The Diseases of Bath. A Satire" (1737), in Lonsdale, *New Oxford Book of Eighteenth-Century Verse*, 301–2.

53. Sir Richard Steele, *Tatler*, no. 21, May 28, 1709, and no. 107, December 15, 1709; Joseph Addison, *Tatler*, no. 224, September 14, 1710; Williams, *Age of Agony*, 184–5; Mui and Mui, *Shops and Shopkeeping*, 228–31.

54. Langford, *A Polite and Commercial People*, 487; Schwartz, *Daily Life in Johnson's London*, 137.

55. Williams, *Age of Agony*, 179.

56. Porter, *English Society*, 277.

57. Schwartz, *Daily Life in Johnson's London*, 173.

58. Lady Mary Wortley Montagu, "A Receipt to Cure the Vapours" (wr. 1730?, pub. 1748), in Lonsdale, *New Oxford Book of Eighteenth-Century Verse*, 146.

59. Porter, *English Society*, 275–6; Schwartz, *Daily Life in Johnson's London*, 137.

60. Porter, *English Society*, 152.

61. Plumb, *England in the Eighteenth Century*, 96.

62. Schwartz, *Daily Life in Johnson's London*, 136.

63. Ibid., 135; Porter, *English Society*, 276.

64. Quoted in Porter, *English Society*, 20.

65. Jarrett, *England in the Age of Hogarth*, 186; Porter, *English Society*, 275.

66. Williams, *Age of Agony*, 152, 154.

67. Altick, *Shows of London*, 44–5.

68. Ibid., 88.

69. Williams, *Age of Agony*, 158–61.

70. Altick, *Shows of London*, 45; Williams, *Age of Agony*, 165.

71. Stone, *Road to Divorce*, 168–9.

72. Porter, *English Society*, 146.

73. Thompson, *Customs in Common*, 45.

74. Cunnington and Lucas, *Costume for Births, Marriages and Deaths*, 159, 162–3; Farrell, *Socks and Stockings*, 37.

75. Cunnington and Lucas, *Costume for Births, Marriages and Deaths*, 162, 192–3, 254, 290–1.

76. Ibid., 194, 196; Thomas Parnell, "A Night-Piece on Death" (1721), ll. 71–6, in Lonsdale, *New Oxford Book of Eighteenth-Century Verse*, 118.

77. Schwartz, *Daily Life in Johnson's London*, 144.

78. Ibid., 17; Plumb, *England in the Eighteenth Century*, 12.

79. Porter, *English Society*, 140; Smith, *Dictionary of London Street Names*, 83; Schwartz, *Daily Life in Johnson's London*, 145.

80. Porter, *English Society*, 257.

81. Williams, *Age of Agony*, 13, 24, 45, 74–8, 87; Porter, *English Society*, 273, 284; Porter, *London*, 167; Langford, *A Polite and Commercial People*, 136–7, 139, 639, 729–36; Schwartz, *Daily Life in Johnson's London*, 131; Tuchman, *The First Salute*, 129. Different sources sometimes give different dates for hospital foundings, sometimes listing the date of charter, sometimes the date construction was begun, and sometimes the date construction was completed.

CHAPTER 18

1. Langford, *A Polite and Commercial People*, 454.
2. Ibid., 452–3.
3. Porter, *English Society*, 358.
4. Ibid., 59.
5. In Scotland, however, the Kirk's governing body, the General Assembly, remained active and was a prominent political body. See Langford, *A Polite and Commercial People*, 325.
6. Stone, *Road to Divorce*, 74.
7. Porter, *English Society*, 172.
8. Thomas Holcroft, "Gaffer Gray," 1794, ll. 18–21, in ibid., 684.
9. Porter, *English Society*, 175; Porter, *London*, 124, 166.
10. Porter, *English Society*, 299.
11. Quoted in ibid., 169.
12. Daniel Defoe, "Reformation of Manners," in Lonsdale, *New Oxford Book of Eighteenth-Century Verse*, 33–4.
13. Porter, *English Society*, 169.
14. Quoted in ibid., 279.
15. Simpson, *London Ritz Book of Afternoon Tea*, 13.
16. Porter, *English Society*, 174, 280.
17. Langford, *A Polite and Commercial People*, 499.
18. Quoted in Porter, *London*, 158.
19. Porter, *English Society*, 179.
20. Langford, *A Polite and Commercial People*, 551–2.
21. Jarrett, *England in the Age of Hogarth*, 182; Porter, *English Society*, 177.
22. Plumb, *England in the Eighteenth Century*, 94.
23. A good description of the workings of classes and bands can be found in ibid., 93.
24. Porter, *English Society*, 91.
25. Ibid., 177.
26. Quoted in Porter, *English Society*, 178.
27. Quoted in ibid., 49.
28. Evan Lloyd, "The Methodist," in Lonsdale, *The New Oxford Book of Eighteenth-Century Verse*, 541–2.
29. Langford, *A Polite and Commercial People*, 265–6.
30. Ibid., 256.
31. Porter, *London*, 166.
32. Porter, *English Society*, 179.
33. Ibid., 183.
34. Ibid., 181.

35. Porter, *London*, 132. In his *English Society*, Porter gives the total number of Jews as 10,000 (p. 182); in *London* he gives the number of London Jews as about 20,000.

36. Edmund Burke, quoted in Tuchman, *The First Salute*, 102.

37. Francis Place, quoted in Porter, *English Society*, 269.

38. Colley, *Britons*, 41–2.

39. Jennings, *Inns, Ales, and Drinking Customs*, 118.

40. Altick, *Shows of London*, 86.

CHAPTER 19

1. William H. Brock, *The Norton History of Chemistry* (New York: W. W. Norton, 1993), 136.

2. James Thomson, "To the Memory of Sir Isaac Newton" (1727), in Lonsdale, *New Oxford Book of Eighteenth-Century Verse*, 190.

3. Plumb, *England in the Eighteenth Century*, 104.

4. Brock, *Norton History of Chemistry*, 109.

5. Ibid., 99.

6. Ibid., 101.

7. Ibid., 104–5, 113–4.

8. Ibid., 104.

9. Plumb, *England in the Eighteenth Century*, 103.

10. Brock, *Norton History of Chemistry*, 108.

11. Ibid., 107–8.

12. Ibid., 109–10.

13. Ibid., 83–4.

14. Quoted in Brock, *Norton History of Chemistry*, 111–2.

15. Ibid., 120–1.

16. Ibid., 115–20.

17. Cardwell, *Norton History of Technology*, 146–7, 189–90; Kenneth Warren, "Chemicals," in Langton and Morris, *Atlas of Industrializing Britain*, 114, 118.

18. Cardwell, *Norton History of Technology*, 157–8.

19. John North, *The Norton History of Astronomy and Cosmology* (New York: W. W. Norton, 1995), 381.

20. Ibid., 411, 403.

21. Ibid., 400.

22. Ibid., 382, 385, 399–400.

23. Ibid., 445.

24. Ibid., 447.

25. Ibid., 396–7.

26. Ibid., 407.

27. Watkins, "The Greening of the Empire," 45–7.

28. Peter J. Bowler, *The Norton History of the Environmental Sciences* (New York: W. W. Norton, 1993), 149.

29. Ibid., 177–9.

30. Ibid., 169.

31. Moses Browne, "The Shrimp" (1739), in Lonsdale, *New Oxford Book of Eighteenth-Century Verse*, 292.

32. Bowler, *Norton History of the Environmental Sciences*, 147.

33. Watkins, "The Greening of the Empire," 42.

34. Bowler, *Norton History of the Environmental Sciences*, 106–7.

35. Ibid., 132–6.

36. Paul Laxton, "Wind and Water Power," in Langton and Morris, *Atlas of Industrializing Britain*, 69–71.

37. Philip Riden, "Iron and Steel," in Langton and Morris, *Atlas of Industrializing Britain*, 128.

38. Cardwell, *Norton History of Technology*, 118–20.

39. Ibid., 122–3.

40. Ibid., 130.

41. Ibid., 164.

42. Ibid., 129.

43. Ibid., 140.

44. Porter, *English Society*, 196.

45. Cardwell, *Norton History of Technology*, 166–7, 208–9.

46. Nick von Tunzelmann, "Coal and Steam Power," in Langton and Morris, *Atlas of Industrializing Britain*, 78.

47. John Dalton, "A Descriptive Poem, Addressed to Two Ladies, at Their Return from Viewing the Mines, near Whitehaven" (1755), in Lonsdale, *New Oxford Book of Eighteenth-Century Verse*, 468.

48. Cardwell, *Norton History of Technology*, 142, 144.

49. John Dyer, "The Fleece," Book III (1757), in Lonsdale, *New Oxford Book of Eighteenth-Century Verse*, 173.

50. Porter, *English Society*, 313.

51. Cardwell, *Norton History of Technology*, 141.

52. Altick, *Shows of London*, 86.

53. Ibid., 73–4.

54. Porter, *English Society*, 272.

55. Cardwell, *Norton History of Technology*, 175. Invented c. 1790, it was first used in textile mills.

56. Ibid., 138.

57. Dean Tucker, quoted in Porter, *English Society*, 272.

58. Langford, *A Polite and Commercial People*, 279–80.

59. Quoted in Porter, *English Society*, 277.

60. Altick, *Shows of London*, 26.

61. North, *Norton History of Astronomy*, 378.

62. Bowler, *Norton History of the Environmental Sciences*, 149.

63. Langford, *A Polite and Commercial People*, 662–3.

64. Porter, *English Society*, 353; Brock, *Norton History of Chemistry*, 148–9.

65. Porter, *London*, 150.

66. Cardwell, *Norton History of Technology*, 151; Langford, *A Polite and Commercial People*, 660–2.

67. Quoted in Altick, *Shows of London*, 76.

Glossary

Abigail. A housemaid.

Bills of Mortality. 109 parishes in metropolitan London or the weekly death statistics from those parishes.

Blue stocking. Member of a specific circle of intellectual women led by Elizabeth Carter, Elizabeth Montagu, and others; any noticeably well-educated woman.

Charlie. A London watchman.

Churching. The symbolic return of a woman to society after childbirth, in which prayers and blessings are offered for her in church.

Cit. A townsman or trader.

Closed robe. A dress which does not part below the waistline to reveal the petticoat.

Closet. A small personal office in a private home, not a place for storing clothing.

Cottager. One who lives in a cottage, often a rural laborer.

Cuckold. A man whose wife is committing adultery.

Curate. A poorly-paid assistant to a parish priest.

Dissenter. A Protestant, but not a member of the Church of England: for example, a Quaker, a Methodist, or a Baptist.

Dowry. A gift of money given by a bride's father to the groom.

Enclosure. The conversion of common land, farmed or grazed by the inhabitants of an entire village, into separate, fenced fields owned by individuals.

False rump. A cork shape worn behind to make the back of a dress puff out.

Fifteen, The. The Jacobite invasion of Britain in 1715.

Footpad. A thief who steals on foot rather than mounted on a horse; a mugger.

Fop. An outlandishly dressed, often somewhat effeminate man.

Forty-Five, The. The Jacobite invasion of Britain in 1745.

Franking. Sending free of charge.

Freeholder. One who owns his or her land outright, rather than renting it.

Gentry. People deriving most or all of their income from landholdings; gentlemen and their families.

Gothic. A style of architecture imitating medieval architecture; a fiction genre, usually a romance or horror story set in the Middle Ages.

Hoop. A framework below a skirt to make it puff out and away from a woman's legs.

Huguenot. French Protestant.

Jacobite. A supporter of returning the exiled Stuart family to the English throne.

JP. Justice of the Peace; a magistrate.

Living. A clergyman's post or benefice.

Macaroni. Specifically, a member of the Macaroni Club. Generally, a person with exaggerated, ultra-fashionable taste in clothing.

Morris dancers. Men dancing in groups, smacking sticks together, and wearing bells on their ankles. Morris groups frequently included special characters, like the "hobby horse," a man wearing a fake horse around his waist, or the "fool," a jester.

MP. Member of Parliament

Neoclassical. A style of architecture that recreates and reinterprets Greek architectural elements.

Nonconformist. Dissenter; Dissenting.

Old Bailey. London's Central Criminal Court.

Open robe. A dress whose skirt parts in the middle from the waist to reveal an underskirt or petticoat.

Ormolu. Gilded bronze.

Palladian. A style of architecture based on the writings of Andrea Palladio, who in turn imitated the work of the Roman architect Vitruvius.

Peer. Person holding a rank above baronet.

Pluralist. A clergyman holding more than one living.

Pound. The basic unit of English currency, equal to twenty shillings and indicated by the symbol "£."

Prorogue. Dismiss, as Parliament.

Skimmerton. A noisy procession designed to shame a local offender into compliance with "normal" behavior. Also "skimmington."

Stays. A corset.

Tithes. The taxes paid to a clergyman by his parishioners, forming the principal part of his income.

Ton. High fashion.

Bibliography

Albert, William. *The Turnpike Road System in England 1663–1840*. Cambridge: Cambridge University Press, 1972.

Allen, Robert J., ed. *Addison and Steele: Selections from the Tatler and the Spectator*. 2d ed. Fort Worth: Holt, Rinehart and Winston, 1970.

Altick, Richard D. *The Shows of London*. Cambridge, Mass.: Belknap Press of Harvard University Press, 1978.

Barker, Felix, and Peter Jackson. *The History of London in Maps*. New York: Cross River Press, 1992.

Boswell, James. *The Life of Samuel Johnson*. 1791. Reprint. New York: Everyman's Library, 1992.

Bowler, Peter J. *The Norton History of the Environmental Sciences*. New York: W. W. Norton, 1993.

Brock, William H. *The Norton History of Chemistry*. New York: W. W. Norton, 1993.

Buck, Anne. *Clothes and the Child: A Handbook of Children's Dress in England 1500–1900*. Carlton, Bedford, England: Ruth Bean Publishers, 1996.

———. *Dress in Eighteenth-Century England*. New York: Holmes and Meier, 1979.

Byrne, Andrew. *London's Georgian Houses*. London: Georgian Press, 1986.

Cardwell, Donald. *The Norton History of Technology*. 1994. Reprint. New York: W. W. Norton, 1995.

Chappell, William. *Old English Popular Music*. 1893. Reprint. New York: Jack Brussel, 1961.

Chinn, Carl. *Better Betting with a Decent Feller: Bookmaking, Betting and the British Working Class, 1750–1990*. New York: Harvester Wheatsheaf, 1991.

Clout, Hugh, ed. *The Times London History Atlas*. New York: HarperCollins, 1991.

Colley, Linda. *Britons: Forging the Nation 1707–1837*. New Haven Conn.: Yale University Press, 1992.

Copeland, John. *Roads and Their Traffic 1750–1850*. Newton Abbot, Devon, England: David and Charles, 1968.

Corson, Richard. *Fashions in Makeup from Ancient to Modern Times*. New York: Universe Books, 1972.

Cunnington, C. Willett, and Phillis Cunnington. *Handbook of English Costume in the Eighteenth Century*. Boston: Plays, 1972.

———. *The History of Underclothes*. 1951. Reprint. New York: Dover, 1992.

Cunnington, Phillis, and Catherine Lucas. *Costume for Births, Marriages and Deaths*. London: Adam and Charles Black, 1972.

Cunnington, Phillis, and Alan Mansfield. *English Costume for Sports and Outdoor Recreation from the Sixteenth to the Nineteenth Centuries*. New York: Barnes & Noble, 1969.

Defoe, Daniel. *A Tour Through the Whole Island of Great Britain*. 1724–1726. Reprint. Edited and abridged by Pat Rogers. London: Penguin Books, 1986.

de la Falaise, Maxime. *Seven Centuries of English Cooking*. Edited by Arabella Boxer. New York: Barnes & Noble, 1973.

de Marly, Diana. *Fashion for Men: An Illustrated History*. 1985. Reprint. London: B. T. Batsford, 1989.

Farrell, Jeremy. *Socks and Stockings*. London: B. T. Batsford, 1992.

Fielding, Henry. *Joseph Andrews*. 1742. Reprint. Boston: Houghton Mifflin, 1961.

Ford, Boris, ed. *The Cambridge Cultural History of Britain: Eighteenth-Century Britain*. 1991. Reprint. Cambridge: Cambridge University Press, 1992.

Garrick, David, and George Colman the Elder. *The Clandestine Marriage and Two Short Plays*. Edited by Noel Chevalier. Peterborough, Ontario, Canada: Broadview Press, 1995.

Gerzina, Gretchen. *Black London: Life Before Emancipation*. New Brunswick, N.J.: Rutgers University Press, 1995.

Gilbert, Sandra M., and Susan Gubar, eds. *The Norton Anthology of Literature by Women*. New York: W. W. Norton, 1985.

Girouard, Mark. *Life in the English Country House*. New Haven, Conn.: Yale University Press, 1978.

Glasse, Hannah. *The Art of Cookery Made Plain and Easy*. 1796. Reprint. Schenectady, N.Y.: United States Historical Research Service, 1994.

Hayes, John. *London: A Pictorial History*. New York: Arco Publishing, 1969.

Hibbert, Christopher. *Redcoats and Rebels: The American Revolution Through British Eyes*. New York: Avon, 1990.

Hill, Bridget. *Servants: English Domestics in the Eighteenth Century*. Oxford: Clarendon Press, 1996.

Holland, Barbara. "Bang! Bang! You're Dead." *Smithsonian* 28, no. 7 (October 1997): 122–33.

Hope, Ronald. *A New History of British Shipping*. London: John Murray, 1990.

Hufton, Olwen. *The Prospect Before Her: A History of Women in Western Europe 1500–1800*. New York: Alfred A. Knopf, 1996.

Jarrett, Derek. *England in the Age of Hogarth*. 1974. Reprint. New York: Viking Press, 1992.

Jennings, Paul. *Inns, Ales, and Drinking Customs of Old England*. London: Bracken Books, 1985.

Kelly, Jack. "Playing with Fire." *American Heritage,* July–August 1997, 81–82.

Kiernan, V. G. *The Duel in European History: Honour and the Reign of Aristocracy*. Oxford: Oxford University Press, 1988.

Langford, Paul. *A Polite and Commercial People: England 1727–1783*. 1989. Reprint. Oxford: Oxford University Press, 1992.

Langton, John, and R. J. Morris, eds. *Atlas of Industrializing Britain 1780–1914*. London: Methuen, 1986.

Lasdun, Susan. *The English Park: Royal, Private & Public*. New York: Vendome Press, 1992.

Lonsdale, Roger, ed. *The New Oxford Book of Eighteenth-Century Verse*. 1984. Reprint. Oxford: Oxford University Press, 1987.

Malcolmson, Robert W. *Popular Recreations in English Society 1700–1850*. 1973. Reprint. Cambridge: Cambridge University Press, 1979.

Mason, John E. *Gentlefolk in the Making: Studies in the History of English Courtesy Literature and Related Topics from 1531 to 1774*. Philadelphia: University of Pennsylvania Press, 1935.

Montagu, Ashley. *The Anatomy of Swearing*. New York: Macmillan, 1967.

More, Hannah. *Selected Writings of Hannah More*. Edited by Robert Hole. London: William Pickering, 1996.

Mui, Hoh-cheung, and Lorna H. Mui. *Shops and Shopkeeping in Eighteenth-Century England*. Montreal: McGill-Queen's University Press, 1989.

North, John. *The Norton History of Astronomy and Cosmology*. 1994. Reprint. New York: W. W. Norton, 1995.

Olsen, Kirstin. *Chronology of Women's History*. Westport, Conn.: Greenwood Press, 1994.

Opie, Iona, and Peter Opie. *The Oxford Dictionary of Nursery Rhymes*. 1951. Reprint. Oxford: Oxford University Press, 1995.

Palmer, Roy. *A Ballad History of England from 1588 to the Present Day*. London: B. T. Batsford, 1979.

Pawson, Eric. *Transport and Economy: The Turnpike Roads of Eighteenth Century Britain*. London: Academic Press, 1977.

Plumb, J. H. *England in the Eighteenth Century*. 1950. Reprint. London: Penguin Books, 1990.

Porter, Roy. *English Society in the Eighteenth Century*. 1982. Reprint. New York: Penguin Books, 1990.

———. *London: A Social History*. Cambridge, Mass.: Harvard University Press, 1995.

Pringle, Patrick. *Hue and Cry: The Story of Henry and John Fielding and Their Bow Street Runners*. New York: William Morrow, n. d.

Ribeiro, Aileen. *A Visual History of Costume: The Eighteenth Century*. 1983. Reprint. London: B. T. Batsford, 1986.

Robertson, William H. *An Illustrated History of Contraception*. Carnforth, Lancashire, England: Parthenon Publishing, 1990.

Schwartz, Richard B. *Daily Life in Johnson's London*. 1983. Reprint. Madison: University of Wisconsin Press, 1985.

Sheridan, Richard Brinsley. *The Rivals*. Edited by Alan S. Downer. Arlington Heights, Ill.: Harlan Davidson, 1953.

———. *The School for Scandal*. New York: Dover, 1991.

Simpson, Helen. *The London Ritz Book of Afternoon Tea: The Art and Pleasures of Taking Tea*. New York: Arbor House, 1986.

Smith, Al. *Dictionary of City of London Street Names*. New York: Arco Publishing, 1970.

Stone, Lawrence. *Road to Divorce. A History of the Making and Breaking of Marriage in England*. 1990. Reprint. Oxford: Oxford University Press, 1995.

Swift, Jonathan. *Directions to Servants*. 1745. Reprint. New York: Pantheon Books, 1964.

Taylor, Lou. *Mourning Dress: A Costume and Social History*. London: George Allen and Unwin, 1983.

Thompson, E. P. *Customs in Common: Studies in Traditional Popular Culture*. New York: New Press, 1993.

Trumbach, Randolph. "The Birth of the Queen: Sodomy and the Emergence of Gender Equality in Modern Culture, 1660–1750." In *Hidden from History: Reclaiming the Gay & Lesbian Past*, edited by Martin Bauml Duberman, Martha Vicinus, and George Chauncey, Jr. New York: New American Library, 1989.

Tuchman, Barbara. *The First Salute: A View of the American Revolution*. New York: Alfred A. Knopf, 1988.

Waterson, Merlin. *The Servants' Hall*. New York: Pantheon Books, 1980.

Watkins, T. H. "The Greening of the Empire: Sir Joseph Banks." *National Geographic* 190, no. 5 (November 1996): 28–50.

Waugh, Norah. *Corsets and Crinolines*. 1954. Reprint. New York: Theatre Arts Books, 1970.

Williams, Guy. *The Age of Agony: The Art of Healing, 1700–1800*. 1975. Reprint. Chicago: Academy Chicago Publishers, 1996.

Index

About the Author

KIRSTIN OLSEN is the author of several books including *Chronology of Women's History* (Greenwood, 1994).

Edwards Brothers Malloy
Thorofare, NJ USA
September 17, 2013